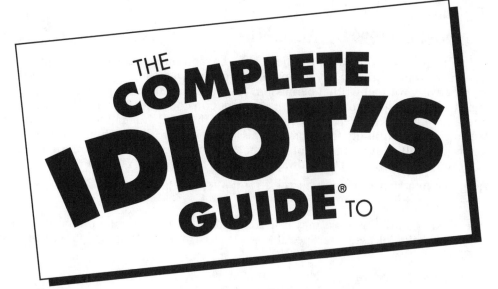

THE **COMPLETE IDIOT'S GUIDE**® TO

Meditation

by Joan Budilovsky and Eve Adamson

alpha books

A Division of Macmillan General Reference
A Simon & Schuster Macmillan Company
1633 Broadway, New York, NY 10019-6785

For Bud

Copyright © 1999 by Amaranth

Macmillan Publishing books may be purchased for business or sales promotional use. For information please write: Special Markets Department, Macmillan Publishing USA, 1633 Broadway, New York, NY 10019.

International Standard Book Number: 0-02862907-8
Library of Congress Catalog Card Number: 97-80976

01   8   7   6

Interpretation of the printing code: the rightmost number of the first series of numbers is the year of the book's printing; the rightmost number of the second series of numbers is the number of the book's printing. For example, a printing code of 99-1 shows that the first printing occurred in 1999.

Printed in the United States of America

Alpha Development Team

Publisher
Kathy Nebenhaus

Editorial Director
Gary M. Krebs

Managing Editor
Bob Shuman

Marketing Brand Manager
Felice Primeau

Editor
Jessica Faust

Development Editors
Phil Kitchel
Amy Zavatto

Assistant Editor
Georgette Blau

Production Team

Book Producer
Lee Ann Chearney, Amaranth

Production Editor
Christy Wagner

Copy Editor
Cliff Shubs

Cover Designer
Mike Freeland

Photo Editor
Richard H. Fox

Cartoonist
Deanna Reeves

Illustrator
Wendy Frost

Photographer
Ann Censotti

Book Designers
Scott Cook and Amy Adams of DesignLab

Indexer
Chris Barrick

Layout/Proofreading
Juli Cook
Laura Knox
Terri Edwards
Donna Martin

Contents at a Glance

Contents

Foreword

I found this book to be full of information, humor, and wisdom. It is an excellent resource and guide—and definitely not for idiots! An idiot is silly, ignorant, and unschooled, according to my dictionary, and this gem would never be noticed or read by one. The material presented here is put together in a way that makes it simple to understand and useful to beginners or accomplished meditators. If you are interested in living and have the inspiration, then here is the information.

Do not be frightened by the word *meditation*. It has been a part of the process of self-transformation for thousands of years. To quote from one Hindu Mahatma, "Action, wisdom, devotion, and meditation are the keys to self-transformation." They are all combined here for you to take advantage of.

Meditation can give you the benefits of not living constantly with a sense of time and urgency. You will be able to get in touch with your sense of the eternal. And as a benefit, if you never know what time it is, you avoid aging. That's a wonderful side effect among many that studies have shown are good for the state of health of meditators.

You will be more aware of your authentic nature, have more energy and freedom, and find yourself happier and more loving. These things happen not because you meditate upon these desires and thoughts, but as the side effects of what this guidebook will teach you about meditation. The authors present the information in a style I enjoyed reading. Their childlike sense of humor is woven through the vast and informative contents, making it easy and joyful, at times, to read.

Carl Jung said analysis is like having surgery without anesthesia. Well, my sense is that meditation and analysis can give you the same result, but meditation is a painless way to self-exploration and discovery. It also costs less and can be done on your schedule.

People often discuss concentration as the key factor that meditation focuses on and teaches. I feel that the word *concentration* can be misleading because meditation doesn't limit one but creates a greater awareness of life and creation. So read, meditate, and enhance your awareness of your life and become more mindful of the life around you.

Meditation for me is also a connection to our Creator's wisdom. Prayer and meditation are forms of the same thing and that is why the names and labels we place on our actions can be confusing to some. When we meditate and use it as a ladder to reach a level of creativity, we are becoming cocreators and are becoming aware of the wisdom of the source of creation.

My final word of advice is to tell you to read this book, learn from it, and meditate. I guarantee that the revelation that ensues will lead to your transformation. Now don't be an idiot and ignore my advice.

—Bernie Siegel, M.D.

Bernard S. Siegel, M.D., a New Haven surgeon, is the author of the best-selling *Love, Medicine and Miracles*, *Prescriptions for Living*, and other books.

Introduction

Where are you right now? "Sitting here reading this book," you might answer, rolling your eyes. Of course you are! But that's not what we mean.

We mean, where is your mind right now? As you skim the pages of this book, are you thinking about where you have to go next, or where you've just been? Are you mentally reviewing your endless "to-do" list, or planning how many errands you can squeeze in on the way home from the bookstore, or thinking about how much work you can get done before the end of the day? Or maybe you aren't really anywhere because stress has closed down the brain train, and you feel a little bit like you're stuck on a broken-down subway, getting nowhere fast.

And, while we're at it, how does your body feel right now? Are you relaxed, fidgeting, bored, tired, tensed up? How does your body feel, right now, in this moment? Is your physical self sending your mental self a subtly, or not-so-subtly, opinionated message? If your body could talk to you just this minute, what would it be saying? "Slow down and listen to me," perhaps? "Pay attention!"

Stress is an insidious force most of us are subject to on a daily basis. Along with it come mindlessness, unhappiness, dissatisfaction, physical discomfort (and even, sometimes, illness), and "settling" for a life less than we once imagined. But you can do more than merely get through the day. You don't have to compromise your dreams. You can be the best possible you, and you can live the life you always wanted to live. How? By getting back in touch with who you are, what you want, and where you are going. By paying attention to your mind-body.

Meditation in its many manifestations is the key. It's too easy to spend your life on hold, waiting to be done with this task or this job or this stage of your life. Meditation can teach you to live in the now, to know yourself—body, mind, and soul—better, and to find the life you need. It can dissolve the stress and the insecurities that hold you back, clearing the path for a journey in which each step is the destination. Meditation teaches you to be alive *right now* because this is your life. With a little retraining and a few simple techniques, you can harness the awesome power of your own mind-body. Meditate and get back in touch with you. Learn to wake up. Learn to *live*. Don't miss another moment.

How to Use This Book

This book is divided into seven parts, each designed to help you make meditation a part of your daily life—indeed, a part of *you*. As you read this book, you'll find that meditation is not just about your mind or just about your body; it's about your *mind-body*. And you'll discover (no doubt to your amazement!) that meditation not only relaxes and centers you, but it also gives you a confidence and renewed energy that will enhance your productivity and help you make the most of each and every moment. Meditation *boosts* energy!

Part 1, "Feeling Great? Meditate!" tells you what meditation is and why you'll benefit from it. Meditation is not only a great stress reducer, but it's also mind-body fitness and healing power, too. People around the globe and throughout history, from the Buddha to The Beatles, have benefited from a regular practice of meditation. You can, too! You'll start by performing a mind-body scan meditation to see what your mind and body are telling you today.

Part 2, "Let's Get Spiritual: The Path to Bliss," talks about the ways in which meditation will lead you to a consideration of life's bigger questions—from ethics and morality to whether there's a universal consciousness. But do you need to be spiritual to meditate? Absolutely not. What meditation does do, however, is help you discover who you are, and in that effort, to contemplate the nature of your inner self, your soul. How many of us make that a priority? We'll also show you how prayer, from religious ritual to simple positive affirmations, has tangible health benefits; medical studies show that prayer enhances healing and well-being. Find out how to make meditative prayer a part of your daily life—even if you're not religious!

Part 3, "Let's Get Physical: The Path to Optimal Health," tells you what's happening in your brain during meditation. Meditation boosts mind power! We'll show you what neurophysiologists are saying about *your* brain on meditation. You'll also learn about the many energy systems various cultures have used to describe the human life force, as well as the three bodies (physical, astral, and causal), and the five sheaths of existence. We'll show you how to use the chakras—psychospiritual energy centers in the body—to channel and release the life force energy through meditation. Also, find out about auras and natural medicine techniques, such as Reiki, acupuncture, biofeedback, and therapeutic touch. Lastly, you'll discover the relationship between meditation, sleep, and dreaming.

Part 4, "Prepare Your Self for Meditation," introduces the concept of mindfulness and teaches you how to use mindfulness meditation techniques to combat stress. We'll tell you how to set up a meditation space at home, both indoors and outdoors, and give you advice on how to choose the best meditation class (if a group effort is more your style). Tips and strategies for beginning your daily meditation practice are included, with a whole chapter on breathing techniques and exercises that'll show you why breathing is essential to meditation.

Part 5, "Ready, Set, OM!" gives you seated meditation positions—from easy pose to Lotus, as well as chair meditations. A chapter on walking meditations takes you from country to city to sacred walks, such as labyrinth walking. Movement meditations include an introduction to yoga, T'ai Chi, and QiGong. Learn how to use yoga's ultimate relaxation pose, shavasana, as a wonderful mind-body meditation to combat insomnia or just to destress yourself after a hard day at home, school, or the office. Also, find out how to use mantras, words spoken during meditation, to enhance your meditation practice—seated, walking, or moving!

Part 6, "More Ways to Meditate," gives you even more alternatives. Mandalas, beautiful circular art forms, are wonderful subjects for meditation; find out how to create your own personal mandala, too. Use guided imagery and creative visualization techniques. Discover how sports, automatic writing, and automatic drawing can help you reach a meditative state of peak performance called "flow." Learn how to adapt the world's great traditions, from Christianity to yoga to the Kabbalah to Native American wisdom to Buddhist Sutras to create your own profound meditative exercises.

Part 7, "Meditation for Your Life," gives you invaluable information on how to use meditation to benefit your health and well-being, including how to address medical problems and conditions from back pain to heart disease and more. Find out what the best foods are to enhance meditation and how diet impacts your mind-body's health. Learn special meditative techniques for women (from fertility to pregnancy to breast-feeding to menopause), men, children, and seniors, too. Find out how to research the world's sacred places and what's involved in making a trip overseas to your "Om Away from Om." Lastly, consider whether, through meditation, humankind brings a collective consciousness to the Earth. We are the world! Join in and heal the Earth through meditation.

Meditation Wisdom

Throughout this book, we'll be adding four types of extra information in boxes, to help you attain enlightenment:

From A to Om

These boxes will give you definitions for meditation-related terms. Considering their meaning can be a great subject for your meditation sessions!

Mindful Minute

These boxes are full of fun anecdotes and trivia about meditation that'll enhance your understanding of the many forms and types of meditation practiced by people across the globe and throughout history.

Relax

These cautionary boxes contain information about how to avoid potential problems and overcome misconceptions about meditating.

Bliss Byte

These special boxes will offer you tips and advice for living your meditation.

Acknowledgments

Thank you to our parents: Joan's, who through ways both quiet and genteel raised her to accept yet question everything, and by doing this, led her toward a meditative path; and Eve's, who keep trying to call meditation "prayer," but who make a valiant effort to relate to the universalist point of view.

Thank you to Joan's brother, John, fondly known as "Bud," for his courageous and fun-loving spirit. Bud passed away in the conclusion of writing this book, but not before bringing into this world, with his dear wife, Luli, their beautiful daughter Josephine. May Josephine continue her incredible journey with Bud's courageous, fun-loving spirit in peace and love.

Thank you to Joan's sister Jane, whose children's, Richard's and Rebecca's, laughter and youthful insights help to keep her grounded. Thank you to Kathie Huddleston (Yoyoga webmaster) who is constantly offering the helpful reminder, "Yoga, Joan, yoga..." Thank you to Chuck Reiter, who is constantly offering the additional helpful reminder, "Breathe, Joan, breathe." Thank you to Rudi Martin, for encouraging Joan and reminding her of the love in "Michigan, Joan, Michigan." Thank you also to Joan's many friends and students and teachers who keep her on time and on track.

Thanks to Eve's two kiddos, Angus and Emmett, whose boisterous boy-child spirits continue to make meditation a necessity. Special thanks to Angus, for offering the helpful reminder, "Mommy, close your eyes and say that 'OM' thing!" and for trying it himself in all his two-year-old wisdom.

Thank you to Lee Ann Chearney at Amaranth for her continual positive encouragement and editorial expertise, to Katie Lahiff, for her sensitive and thorough tech review, and to the staff at Alpha Books: Lloyd Short, Kathy Nebenhaus, Gary Krebs, Bob Shuman, Christy Wagner, Felice Primeau, Deanna Reeves, Georgette Blau, Jessica Faust, Phil Kitchel, Amy Zavatto, Cliff Shubs, Mike Freeland, Richard H. Fox, Scott Cook, and Amy Adams. Thanks, as always, to our talented illustrator Wendy Frost and wonderful photographer Ann Censotti. Also thanks to photographer Saeid Lahouti. We continue to skip gratefully along the orange-and-blue-book road with you.

And thank you to everyone who has ever aggravated, irritated, ignored, or pushed us to the brink of reason. Because of you, we have become better meditators, breathers, truth-seekers, and practitioners of patience.

Through our meditations, we send out love, blessings, and joyful energy to all of you.

Special Thanks from the Publisher to the Technical Editor

The Complete Idiot's Guide® to Meditation was reviewed by an expert who not only checked the accuracy of what you'll learn in this book but also provided valuable insight to help ensure that this book tells you everything you need to know about meditation and its effects on the mind, body, and soul. Our special thanks are extended to Kathleen Lahiff, also known as Swami Nadananda, Mahaswami.

Swami Nadananda, Mahaswami has been a lifelong student of spiritual, mystical, and religious practices of all traditions. She is a disciple of Goswami Kriyananda, who carries the flame of the lineage of Babaji and Paramahamsa Yogananda. Goswami Kriyananda, founder of the Temple of Kriya in Chicago, ordained her into swamihood in 1994 and elevated her to Mahaswami in 1997. Swami Nadananda, Mahaswami remains affiliated with the Temple of Kriya where she leads music meditations, teaches in the Seminary and Hatha Yoga teacher training programs, and performs ordinations.

A professional musician and music instructor, Swami Nadananda, Mahaswami has been especially drawn to the musical aspects of the various spiritual traditions: mantra, chants, prayers set to music, the effects of sound on the spiritual-psycho-physical being. She has directed and performed on several recordings of mantra and spiritual songs and currently has in production a recording of prayers, chants, and mantra from around the world.

Part 1
Feeling Great? Meditate!

Meditation is power. Sure, it may not look like much, just sitting there on the floor or in a chair, not doing anything and—seemingly—not getting anything done. But in reality, you are getting much done and much accomplished when you meditate. In this first section, we'll introduce you to the power of meditation: mind power, fitness power, stress busting power, and the power that comes from learning to love and accept who you are right now.

Like physical exercise for the body, meditation is mental exercise for the mind and spirit. Creating a buffer zone between you and the stresses of life, meditation is an oasis of tranquility. For thousands of years, people all over the world have enjoyed the power of meditation. You can enjoy the power of meditation, too, as it changes you, making you healthier, calmer, more immune to stress, and filled to the brim with joy.

Chapter 1

Flexing Your Mind Muscle

In This Chapter

➤ What's so great about meditation?

➤ How do you stop thinking? (And why would you want to?)

➤ How meditation can be considered a workout

➤ The healing power of meditation

➤ Meditation and your self-image

➤ Living mindfully

Ommm...Ommm...Ommm... Oh, hello! Don't mind us, we were just finishing up our daily workout. "Workout?" you might ask, incredulously. "But you were just sitting there on the floor with your eyes closed!" You bet it was a workout, and not an easy one, either, but well worth the effort! You'd be surprised how difficult "just sitting" in meditation can actually be.

Meditation puts you in tune with the universe. *Om* is a Sanskrit word meant to give voice to the sound of the universe's vibration. It is often used in meditation to help center and clear the mind so the mind-body can become more conscious. Om is thought to be the basis of all sounds—and of all manifest creation!

"But what kind of a complete idiot works out by sitting down and chanting to get in tune with the universe? That's not going to tone your muscles!" you may protest. Actually, we think we're pretty smart to take advantage of the amazing power of meditation—the ultimate workout for the mind-body, the "mind-muscle," and the whole self.

You see, fitness, health, self-concept, well-being, confidence, happiness, and contentment all originate in the mind-body, that "whole you" that is more than just your body or just your mind. But your whole self won't, and can't, feel truly balanced or effective if your workout only works out the body half of the mind-body. Enter meditation, the key to mental maintenance, mind-body integration, and ultimately, personal joy.

The mind-body *is* the whole self. The term carries with it the connotation that mind and body are inextricably linked, and what affects, benefits, changes, or hurts one does the same for the other.

What Is Meditation?

But what is meditation, anyway? That depends largely on who your teacher is and on what tradition you base your practice. Many cultures consider meditation an integral part of life, but what form that meditation takes varies widely. In this book, we'll try to give you a broad base of meditation knowledge. Who you are, what you believe, how you think, and what your interests are will all influence the type of meditation that will work best for you.

"Meditation" often means something different to different cultures or traditions who practice it. For example, many people consider prayer and meditation to be the same—regardless of what religion their prayers are made in the context of! As you read this book, you'll come to a definition of meditation that works best for your own interests and inclinations. Some of the schools of thought we'll talk about are listed below.

➤ Breath meditation

➤ Mantra or sound meditation

➤ Mandala/visual meditation

➤ Movement meditation, including T'ai Chi, QiGong, and Hatha Yoga

➤ Classic Zen Buddhist meditation

➤ Classic yoga meditation

➤ Meditation from other cultures, including Chinese, Native American, and Jewish meditation

➤ New Agemeditation

➤ Prayer

➤ Mindfulness meditation

➤ Medical meditation, as used in stress-reduction clinics and for other medical problems

➤ Guided imagery

➤ Creative visualization

➤ Creativity meditation, or art as meditation (writing, drawing, sculpting, etc.)

We're sure you'll find at least one, and probably several, type of meditation that will appeal to you and that you'll love to incorporate into your daily life.

To Think, or Not to Think?

As different as meditation traditions and systems may be, most have a few things in common. One of those things is learning how *not* to think—how to slow down. All meditation techniques use a focusing of attention to one-pointedness so that the thoughts are no longer scattered and undirected.

Now, slowing down your thoughts, almost "nonthinking," is a tricky notion. It doesn't mean nonconsciousness. In fact, concentrated thought (letting go of the thousand details that pass nonstop through our frenzied brains) is a key to super-consciousness. No one will deny that thinking is helpful, even necessary for survival, but our over-developed human brain really took that "thinking" ball and ran with it. These days, we've become so adept at thought that we can think up just about anything, from the theory of relativity to the recipe for chocolate génoise. The problem is that even when we want to relax for awhile, we just keep on thinking. And our thoughts are seemingly random, instead of focused and steady. Meditations use verbal tools, such as mantras, and visual tools, such as mandalas, to help boost concentration and focus thoughts.

Relax

"Difficulty" in the Western mind often implies the need to grunt and groan and force yourself to do something—thereby bringing a lot of emotional energy to bear on whatever the difficult thing is—the exact opposite of what you want to do in a meditation practice. We want you to turn to meditation as an enjoyable experience!

Bliss Byte

It isn't easy to stop thinking, but focusing on a sound or visual image can help to keep superfluous thoughts away. Repeat a mantra, which is a word or series of words chosen for their vibrational centering qualities (see Chapter 19, "Mantras: Sacred Formulas to Live By"). Or gaze at a candle flame or a mandala, which is a symmetrical, usually circular, design meant to center the mind by drawing the eyes toward a visual center (see Chapter 20, "Mandalas: The Circle of Life").

If you've ever been plagued with insomnia, lying wide awake in bed at 4:00 A.M., wondering what you'll wear for the meeting tomorrow or if you remembered to pay the electric bill or whether your daughter's new boyfriend has a criminal record, you understand the value of being able to turn off the thought faucet. Your thoughts can actually clutter pure consciousness and your awareness of your own mind. Learning when thinking is helpful and knowing when to give it a rest builds your mind power, just like lifting weights and then resting for a day builds your muscles—the actual increase in muscle fiber happens during those days of rest, when your body repairs itself.

The same thing applies to meditation. Your brain works hard at thinking all day long. Give it a little break each day, and it will grow stronger, more effective, more efficient, and more aware.

Bliss Byte

Meditation can make you feel better when you aren't at your best, but if you are feeling depressed, angry, or negative, physical exercise is sometimes a better quick-fix. Meditation is best practiced when you are feeling positive. Otherwise, start with a brisk walk, run, aerobics class, or yoga workout. Remember our saying: "Feeling down? Move around. Feeling great? Meditate!" However, a meditation practice begun and sustained through good times will come to one's aid when times are rough.

Variations on meditation take the slowing down of your thoughts and the quieting of your mind further. Once you've mastered clearing your mind, you can then introduce concepts, thoughts, problems, or needs into your meditation. Answers to problems may suddenly become clear. Changes you would like to make may become manifest if you periodically visualize them as already having occurred. Thoughts, answers, insights, and meaning may offer themselves to you in an environment where, at last, they can be heard because they are no longer drowned out by your brain trying to remember that last item on the grocery list or that client's first name.

To Have It All, Let It All Go

Another benefit to meditation is the way it can adjust your thinking. When you live for a little while each day in a space filled with nothing but pure, uncluttered awareness, you begin to see things in perspective. The little things that were ruling your life suddenly look little—what those rich neighbors think of your not-so-upscale used car, or whether the boss noticed that run in your pantyhose during your big meeting. The important things—whatever they are for you (love? happiness? *nirvana*?)—regain a significance they may have lost in the clutter of everyday living.

How does meditation accomplish this reprioritizing? By teaching your mind to let go of attachments. Nothing is really ours as we pass through this world. We find people to love, but not to own. And as far as "stuff" is concerned, well…it's all just stuff, right? Meditation can help to make this more clear. Of course, everyone's priorities are

From A to Om

Nirvana is the Buddhist term for the state of absolute bliss attained upon recognition that the self is an illusion and nonexistent.

different, and meditation too, is a highly personal and individualized experience. But in general, it will help you see that letting go of the concept of ownership, greed, and desire for the material aspects of life will actually result in ultimate happiness. You'll suddenly feel as if you "have" it all.

Bliss Byte

Even though many schools of meditation suggest that the material world is an illusion, that doesn't mean you'll have to sell your house, give away the bulk of your wardrobe, and hand your money over to anyone. In fact, material comfort can actually reduce stress, making meditation even more effective. The trick is not to be too attached to anything that could be lost at any moment.

Meditation Is a Great Stressbuster

It isn't easy to get through the day without hearing something about stress in the modern world. Television shows, magazine articles, and books tell us that we are a stressed-out society. They tell us what causes our stress, they tell us why stress is bad, and they give us all kinds of suggestions about what we should be doing to relieve our stress. In fact, the barrage of stress-talk out there is pretty darned stressful!

But it's true that we are a stressed-out society. Stress helps to define the character of the modern world, and it can even be helpful when you need to get a job done fast or when you need to handle an emergency. In fact, stress is incredibly beneficial in times of crisis. The problem is, long-term stress is dangerous and damaging to your health.

The stress/illness link is a hard one to pinpoint because stress causes such a wide variety of symptoms and has different manifestations in different people, but stress is most directly associated with the *adrenal glands*. These glands secrete hormones in reaction to situations or conditions, whether physical or psychological, that cause tension or strain to the body and/or the mind.

One of the best known of these hormones is *adrenaline*, which heightens our senses and reflexes, preparing us for action to handle the stress. Another is *cortisol*, a hormone that has been shown in many studies to be elevated in times of stress and decreased by relaxation activities like meditation and massage. Some of the physical symptoms of stress caused by the secretion of stress hormones are:

➤ Elevated blood pressure

➤ Muscle contraction

➤ The movement of blood toward the muscles and nervous system and away from the digestive organs

➤ Fluid retention in the kidneys

➤ Increased levels of chemicals responsible for coagulating blood

➤ The break-down of certain proteins to form glucose, which acts as an anti-inflammatory

From A to Om

Adrenal glands, located at the top of each kidney, produce special hormones in response to stress, such as **adrenaline** (also called epinephrine) and corticosteroids, including **cortisol** (also called hydrocortisone). These hormones prepare the body to react to a crisis, causing changes such as deepening breathing, speeding up heart rate, raising blood pressure, flooding muscles with oxygenated blood, and preparation for anti-inflammatory and healing action.

These conditions are useful in emergencies. For example, muscles prepare for defensive or offensive action. Fluid is retained in the kidneys and the blood becomes ready to coagulate quickly in case of bleeding. The body readies itself to fight inflammation and infection. But bodies aren't meant to function under these conditions for long periods of time. Eventually, your body will break down.

Of course, stress is inevitable in our culture and the best way to handle it is to avoid what stress you can, but also to prepare your mind and body to handle the necessary stress. A healthy diet will help and so will exercise. But in this particular world at this particular time, most of us don't have to face wild animals, hunting and digging for our own food, and the physical drama of a nomadic existence. Our stresses are mainly mental. How many times a day do you clench your fists, your face, or your mind and think, "What am I going to do about *this*?"

That's why meditation is so crucial for handling stress, right now, today, in your life. Needless to say, any practice that puts your life in perspective, makes your priorities clear, and stems the incessant chatter in your brain will relieve stress. But meditation relieves stress in other ways, too. Meditation has measurable physical effects, and the relaxed state it induces in the body seems to affect the body's health directly.

Many studies have demonstrated the beneficial effects of meditation (some studies included other stress-relief techniques and/or lifestyle changes like yoga practice), which include:

➤ Fewer doctor visits

➤ Lower cholesterol levels

➤ Lower blood pressure levels

➤ Less heart disease

➤ Reversal of arteriosclerosis (hardened arteries)

➤ Reduced angina (chest pain)

➤ Lower levels of stress hormones in the blood

➤ Altered brain wave patterns reflective of a calmer state

➤ Fewer accidents and less absenteeism at work

➤ Less depression

➤ Increased confidence, awareness, and general health

And that's just the beginning! Believe it or not, meditation can actually increase your fitness level.

Meditation Promotes Mind-Body Fitness

We can hardly talk about mental fitness without bringing physical fitness into the conversation. Really, fitness applies to your whole self, physical and mental, so anything that helps one aspect will help the other.

For example, meditation helps you have a calmer, more tranquil mind that can better handle stress. It also reduces stress in your body, so your body is able to maintain a healthy state more effectively. A healthy body feels good, and feeling good makes you feel even better about yourself and your life. When you feel good, you want to maintain

Mindful Minute

Anyone who maintains an aquarium knows that caring for the fish involves paying attention to what's called **fish stress**. Small details, such as water, tank size, and temperature, all contribute to the health of the fish. If even one thing is off too much, or everything *is* off a little, the fish are said to be "stressed" and will die. People should take care of themselves the same way.

From A to Om

Angina is chest pain or discomfort due to some degree of obstruction in the coronary arteries and may be caused by any condition in which the heart has to work harder, such as physical or emotional stress, strain, or exertion.

From A to Om

Hatha Yoga is a form of yoga that emphasizes physical postures or positions, called **asanas**, for increased health and awareness. For more on yoga, see *The Complete Idiot's Guide to Yoga* (Alpha Books, 1998), by the authors of this book.

the feeling. When you feel good about yourself, you want to take care of yourself. Exercise is one of the best ways to take care of yourself and can help to increase and maintain that feeling of health and well-being. Exercise has also been shown to improve the mental state, from a general mood lift to lessening the symptoms of severe depression. A positive mental state is ideal for meditation, and meditation can make the most of a positive mental state. See how it's all connected?

Mind-body fitness is the ultimate fitness goal, and the only true complete approach. Meditation, then, should be as integral to your fitness program as your daily run in the park, your weightlifting sessions, or your *Hatha Yoga* class.

Meditation Is Healing Power

But meditation is more than stress relief, fitness ally, and preventive medicine. Meditation can help when injury or illness is already in the picture. Studies have shown how meditation and similar relaxation techniques can reverse certain aspects of heart disease. Meditation is also used with sometimes-dramatic effectiveness in pain clinics, helping patients to deal with pain more effectively, and in some cases, to reduce or eliminate pain.

Mindful Minute

The words **meditation**, **medicine**, and **medication** all share the same Latin root, *medicus*, meaning "to cure," and originally, "to measure." Jon Kabat-Zinn, Ph.D., the founder and director of the Stress Reduction Clinic at the University of Massachusetts Medical Center, once explained (in an interview with Bill Moyers) that both medicine and meditation have to do with measure. Both work to restore "right inward measure, when everything is balanced and physiologically homeostatic."

Meditation comes in many forms, and some forms may be more effective than others for particular health problems, but the overall benefits are undeniable. The mind is a powerful ally in healing the body, and meditation keeps the mind primed.

It also keeps the mind-body balanced. It's easy to become imbalanced when life gets busy—we neglect our health maintenance routines, become increasingly stressed, and suddenly lose perspective. Have you ever exploded over something clearly not worth a major episode, such as a misplaced pen or a coffee spill? Maybe a headache puts you out of commission for the rest of the day because it becomes the proverbial straw that broke the camel's back. "Forget it!" you might cry, throwing up your hands. "I'm going home to bed!" Stress throws us out of balance because it alters our body systems away from their normal operating conditions, or *homeostasis*.

To compensate, we often take medications, which may further imbalance our homeostasis (although in some cases, of course, medication can help to restore an imbalance). For some conditions, including general stress and many chronic health problems, meditation is a better and more effective way to restore homeostasis than aspirin, antacids, or caffeine pills. Meditation "reminds" your body of how it is supposed to be by clearing out the distractions and stressors lingering in your busy brain. Meditation can help the body to get back on track and reclaim its healing power. And when you finally start to heal, you'll start feeling really, really good.

From A to Om

Homeostasis means balance, whether of the internal systems of the body or entire ecosystems. It refers to a condition in which all systems are working together effectively to maintain a balanced, healthy, operational environment.

Love Thy Mind, Love Thy Body, Love Thyself

One of meditation's most important benefits may be the effect it has on your self-concept. Sure, you like yourself. You're okay. But you probably have a long list of your own glaring imperfections, even if most or all of them are things no one would notice but you. Most people are fairly self-critical, and self-examination is good. You can learn from your mistakes if you study yourself and use what you observe to continually evolve. But self-flagellation isn't good. If you can't give yourself a break, why should anyone else?

Meditation takes away all that petty, nit-picky self-loathing. Depending on your philosophy, meditation helps you to love yourself by showing you who you really are inside, by teaching you that you are simply one individual expression of nature, or by empowering you to know and control your own mind-body (and not become so attached to your concept of it).

Moving toward any of these ideas will help you learn to love your mind, love your body, and meet your mind-body (perhaps for the first time). Most important, meditation can teach you to love yourself—your whole self.

So, even if you've always thought meditation sounded a little weird, you are probably willing to admit the benefits sound compelling. What have you got to lose? Twenty minutes? Chances are, it will eventually become the best 20 minutes of your day.

Mindful Minute

Personal happiness may be one of the most important factors in determining health. One study conducted by psychiatrist George Vaillant followed 200 Harvard graduates for 30 years, correlating annual health surveys with psychological tests. Those who were "extremely satisfied with their lives" experienced one-tenth the rate of serious illness and death compared to those in the "thoroughly dissatisfied" group, even when alcohol and tobacco use, obesity, and ancestral longevity were factored out. "Be happy" may indeed be an important prescription for health.

Living Your Meditation

Maybe you've decided you can probably squeeze 20 minutes of meditation into your schedule. But guess what? Those 20 minutes are only a start. No, we're not going to suggest you quit your job and spend your entire day sitting in the lotus position chanting "Om." What we will suggest is that even when you aren't sitting in meditation, you can be *living* your meditation.

Living your meditation doesn't mean being zoned out or out of touch with reality. On the contrary, it means going through your days sharply focused, centered, and living in the now. Your daily meditation sessions will help to clear, calm, and focus your mind. The result? The rest of your life will become clearer, calmer, and more focused.

Practicing mindfulness throughout your day is the key to prolonging and making the most of the effects of your meditation sessions. Mindfulness is like proactive meditation, and it can dramatically improve your life.

Many people go through their lives on automatic pilot. They are so absorbed in routines and obligations that they never really notice where they are, how they feel, what they are doing. Especially during times of stress, it is difficult to notice what's going on. How well do you actually remember your wedding, the birth of your child, or that speech you gave? You may have been too nervous, in too much pain, or too distracted with the details to actually experience your experience.

Mindfulness changes all that. Mindfulness means going through life awake and aware. To live mindfully simply means to pay attention—to your body, to your mind, to your surroundings, to the people in your life, to the tasks you undertake, to the beauty of the world, to every detail of existence—not to control it, shape it, force it, or be worried by it. Simply to experience it. To live mindfully means to *live*, with a capital "L."

Bliss Byte

For the incredibly stressed, it may seem impossible to stop the mind from racing. One way to start is with a daily 10-minute mindfulness walk. The only rule: Notice. How does your body, your breathing, and the air feel? Notice the sights, sounds, and smells around you. If your mind strays, guide it back to your immediate surroundings. Live completely in the "now" for 10 minutes. Eventually, you'll be able to extend mindfulness to other areas of your life.

Of course, living mindfully isn't easy. If it were, we'd all be doing it! It's a lot easier to drive your car on cruise control than to operate a stick shift. It's easier to take the elevator than to climb the stairs. And it's easier to cruise through life without noticing. But not noticing has a physical, mental, emotional, and spiritual price.

The Price of Mindless Living

Maybe you used to live mindlessly, and then something went wrong. Pain, accidents, illness, and personal tragedy have a way of jolting us awake. Whether we are suddenly plagued with a migraine headache, the flu, arthritis, or frequent accidents, we may feel betrayed. "Hey, what's this? Why has my body betrayed me?"

We certainly won't pretend to explain the source or cause of pain, illness, and accidents. If they occur, one way to deal with them is to consider them a wake-up call to your mind-body. *Hello in there? You are important. You deserve the very best in life. You are the very best of life! Wake up! Learn. Listen, listen, listen.* As Swedish statesman and former secretary general of the UN (1953–1961) Dag Hammarskjöld once wrote, "The more faithfully you listen to the voice within you, the better you will hear what is sounding outside."

Don't resort to clobbering yourself or retreating to a state of self-pity. Use this valuable wake-up call to ask yourself *"What is this experience saying to me? How can I best take care of my mind-body? What do I need to change?"*

Even small symptoms may be sending you a message. Are you tired all the time? Do you get colds a lot? Do you often feel so stressed you want to scream, even though you aren't sure why? Or maybe you know why you are stressed, but you don't have the time or the energy to do anything about it. After all, you can't tell off your demanding boss, you aren't about to trade in your three kids, you don't have time or money for marriage counseling, you'll always be out of shape because you hate to exercise, and it's all you can do to get through the end of the day with a clean kitchen and an almost-balanced check book. Right?

Relax

Some doctors estimate that 50 to 80 percent of physical illness is stress related. The result of long-term stress varies between individuals, but may include chronic indigestion, headaches, back pain, lowered immunity, fatigue, ulcers, atherosclerosis, and even the onset of rheumatoid arthritis.

Mindful Minute

According to the yoga sutras, concentration precedes meditation on the path to enlightenment. Most meditation techniques are actually concentration techniques. Concentration is the process of continually bringing the attention back to focus on whatever the object of focus is—and meditation occurs when one becomes absorbed in this process.

We're happy to tell you you're wrong. We're not going to advocate that you go and tell off your boss, but we do know that you don't have to live with negative stress. You don't have to miss out on your life. You can regain control and attain serenity of mind. You can wake up, and you can certainly enjoy yourself again. All it takes is a little mental maintenance to unlock a happier, healthier, calmer, better you. And meditation is the key.

The Least You Need to Know

➤ Meditation is fitness for the whole self, toning the mind and relaxing the body.

➤ Thinking can clutter awareness. Meditation teaches the temporary suspension of thought by showing us how to become absorbed in one-pointed focus.

➤ Long-term stress is dangerous to your health, and medical studies prove meditation relieves emotional and physical stress.

➤ Meditation can help in healing and in managing pain, from the chronic pain of arthritis to minor discomforts.

➤ Meditation can improve your self-image.

➤ Living mindfully all day long can help you make the most of your life.

Chapter 2

Meditation Power: Beyond Words

In This Chapter

➤ Isn't meditation just for yogis and Buddhists?

➤ Meditation around the world

➤ A self-awareness quiz

➤ Finding teachers everywhere

➤ Enlightenment is for you!

It isn't easy to describe the power of meditation. Although we can describe to you some of the techniques people use to meditate, we can't describe exactly what will happen to you. Why not? Because what happens to us when we meditate is different than what will happen to you, or your sister, or a Zen master, or your next door neighbor, or an Indian swami, or a Catholic priest. Meditation is a highly individual experience and truly beyond words.

That doesn't mean we don't have a lot to say on the subject, however! While we may not be able to define what enlightenment means for you exactly, we can certainly fill you in on some of the most powerful effects of meditation. These potent effects have been well-known to many cultures for many centuries and can change your life, too. You need more mind power, you say? The key is as old as humankind.

Who Meditates?

Maybe you're still having a hard time with the idea of you—plain-old regular everyday you—meditating. Isn't it something for monks and martial arts masters? You can imagine Bruce Lee meditating, perhaps, or Chuck Norris, or even Richard Gere. And you can certainly imagine a monastery full of chanting Buddhist monks, can't you?

But *you*? In your blue jeans and T-shirt and Nike shoes? You in your bathrobe or your business suit? Hey, whatever makes you comfortable!

Anyone can meditate and meditate well. It doesn't matter what your religion is or where you live. It doesn't matter what your job or health or wardrobe or family is like. It doesn't even matter if you have an interest in full *enlightenment*, *samadhi*, or *nirvana*—or whether you've aspired to reach that first glimpse of enlightenment, *satori*. All that matters is a personal commitment to improve your mind, and by extension, your life.

And believe us, you won't be among the first to give it a try. Not by a long shot.

From Buddha to The Beatles

Who was the first to meditate? Some might answer, "The *Buddha*," as he lived in the sixth century B.C., founded Buddhism, and attained enlightenment while meditating under a Bodhi tree, or so the legend has it. But *the* Buddha, whose real name was *Siddhattha Gotama*, wasn't actually the *first* Buddha. Buddhas (literally, "enlightened ones") existed before him. And he didn't invent meditation. Buddhas, ascetics, monks, and ordinary folk alike were meditating long before Siddhattha Gotama came along. He learned how to meditate from fellow truth-seekers during his travels—as they struggled together against the grain of the practices of the day. Even then, the meditative path usually was the road less taken.

After the Buddha attained enlightenment, he traveled widely, teaching what he had discovered about the meaning of life and helping others to reach enlightenment too. He had many followers, and those followers had followers, and those followers had followers. And so, Buddhism spread.

Sometime around A.D. 475, one of those who followed the Buddha's teachings and who was also a teacher traveled to China. His name was Bodhidharma, and his teachings became widely accepted in China, mingling with *Taoism*, which was (and is) the prevalent Chinese philosophy/religion. The result was known as *Ch'an Buddhism*. Sometime around A.D. 1200, Ch'an Buddhism reached Japan and became known as *Zen Buddhism*. Buddhism comes in many forms, but Zen Buddhism is probably the most well known in the West. Zen Buddhism's aim is to achieve enlightenment through meditation. (Other forms of Buddhism advocate reaching enlightenment in other ways, such as service to humankind or the study of sacred texts.) *Tibetan Buddhism* has also gained many students and followers in the West recently.

Zen Buddhism quickly spread all over the world, to Korea, Tibet, Vietnam, and eventually to the West. Today, many Americans call themselves Zen Buddhists, and certain Zen terms such as satori, nirvana (both words describe enlightened states), and even *koan*, are familiar to many Westerners.

But many Americans also call themselves yogis. India, though the homeland of Buddhism, has contributed its own traditions to the American scene. The Beatles and the Beach Boys in the 1960s were two popular proponents of meditation based on yogic principles, devoted to the Maharishi Mahesh Yogi, who teaches his own variation on the ancient yoga meditation techniques. Today, popular workout gurus like Jane Fonda and Kathy Smith have yoga videos on the market, and books on techniques for improving awareness and mind-body interaction are flying off the shelves.

As the twenty-first century approaches, people are searching for meaning in their lives, as well as a way to deal with the onslaught of stress in the modern world. Meditation is an answer for many. CEOs do it, teenagers do it, yoga teachers and physics teachers and English teachers do it. Chefs, mail carriers, artists, athletes, homemakers, publishers, actors, dog walkers, and film makers do it.
Let's do it! Let's meditate.

From A to Om

Taoism is both a religion and a philosophy in China that advocates following the Tao, or the way of nature (although the word "Tao" is translated in many different ways, including "Way of the Cosmos," "Way of Heaven," "Way," "One," or "Path"). Simplicity, unity of all things, and becoming one with the Tao are all concepts of Taoism.

From A to Om

A **koan** is short question, riddle, or verbal illustration meant to demonstrate a Zen realization. Because words are contrary to Zen realizations, however, koans don't make sense on the surface. *What is the sound of one hand clapping?* The point is to pop your mind into a different, enlightened way of seeing. Koans *do* have correct answers, obvious to the enlightened. Supposedly, a Zen master can tell if your answer is enlightened or if you've been told. You can't cheat!

Bringing the Mind Home

We don't like to tell you that you "should" do anything, so we'll just say that if you choose to meditate and if you stick with it, you'll notice real and unmistakable changes in your life. How long has it been since you looked inward rather than outward? "Who are you?" is a much different question than "What do you do?" You see, there's a difference between meditation and thinking.

Thinking, for most of us, usually involves the external. *Where is my appointment this afternoon? What will I wear to the seminar? I can't forget to buy milk on the way home! That new office manager is pretty cute. I wonder why my car engine is making that strange noise. And what on earth did the dog do to the kitchen?* Sound familiar?

For many people, the noise in the head is a continuous clamor of worries, wonders, wishes, wheres, whys, whats, whens, whos, and hows. The world is a busy and distracting place, and there it is, all around us. It isn't easy to ignore.

Bliss Byte

During your meditation practice, rather than trying to tune out that annoying clamor in your head, try simply observing it. Look at the thoughts that come and go. Don't judge them. Don't let them engage you. Just look at them as if they belong to someone else or as if they are balloons floating by on a breezy day. There goes a red one. There goes a green one. Here comes a blue one, and there it goes.

But what about your inner life? How much time do you spend dwelling inside yourself? It's quiet in there. It's peaceful. The outside world doesn't hold much influence down there, and guess who's down there, waiting? Someone you might like to know a little better. Someone wonderful and miraculous and joyful at the core. You.

Nothing about meditation should ever worry you. However long it takes to meditate well is good, because everyone's different—whether that means seeing improvement in a week, a month, or in a blue moon! Meditating is like going home after a long and hectic vacation. You open the door to that old, familiar house. You kick off your shoes, sink into your favorite chair, close your eyes, and know you're home at last. Ommmm. Sweet Om.

Around the World in 90 Oms: Meditation in Different Cultures

Using the mind well takes practice. Why should we assume we can automatically make the best use of our minds? We don't assume that about our bodies. Nobody can wake up in the morning and do five back-flips without ever having learned or practiced gymnastics.

Many Eastern cultures have long recognized that the mind requires similar practice to perform well. We Westerners sometimes take the mind for granted, then don't understand when it suddenly fails us (*Where on earth did you put those car keys?*). But some traditional Western cultures have used forms of meditation for centuries, too. Let's take a little trip around the world and see how the world meditates.

The Zen of Self-Cultivation

For Zen Buddhists, meditation, or *zazen*, is the way to reach enlightenment. After all, that's how the Buddha did it!

According to Zen Buddhism, practiced now all over the world, 10 fetters exist that keep us from true freedom and enlightenment. They include:

™The illusion of ego

➤ Skepticism

➤ Attachment to ritual

➤ The delusion of the senses

➤ Ill will

➤ Materialism

➤ Desire for an immaterial life

➤ Arrogance

➤ Restlessness

➤ Ignorance of the true nature of reality

To be free of these 10 fetters leads to enlightenment. On the more positive side, Buddhism also speaks of 10 perfections. These perfections are qualities of an enlightened person and are goals for the enlightened-to-be:

➤ Generosity

➤ Morality

➤ Renunciation

➤ Wisdom

From A to Om

Zazen is the Japanese word for the Zen Buddhist technique of meditation.

➤ Energy

➤ Patience

➤ Truthfulness

➤ Resolution

➤ Lovingkindness

➤ A calm mind

Zen Buddhism is hard to discuss because its philosophy puts little stock in words, and Zen Buddhists claim that Zen cannot be understood intellectually. Zen can only be experienced, never described. But the method can be taught—and the method is zazen. Zazen can involve a number of techniques, including breath observation or the contemplation of a riddle, or koan (a statement or question that appears irrational but makes sense to someone who is enlightened). To solve a koan properly, you must enter a different state of mind. And so the emphasis is placed on the person answering the question, not on the question or its answer.

Yoga Union

Meanwhile, back in India, meditation was and is alive and well in another form: yoga. As Buddhism was catching on in China, Japan, and elsewhere, Buddhism's country of origin has stayed true to its 5,000-year-old yoga traditions. Actually, Indian systems of health, spirituality, and healing take several interrelated forms, including *Ayurveda*, that each include meditation as an important component.

From A to Om

Ayurveda, from the Sanskrit roots *ayus*, meaning "life," and *veda*, meaning "knowledge or science," is an ancient system of health with the purpose of maximizing human potential and defying sickness and aging through specific healing techniques, including the prescription of certain foods, herbs, exercises, massages, and meditations.

Westerners used to think of yoga as a form of stretching exercise that included pretzel-like poses and impossible contortions. Today, yoga is a popular form of mind-body fitness and classes are available in most cities. Yet, yoga in America still tends to emphasize the physical. More precisely, most yoga in America focuses on the physical body. But yoga has a lot more to it than physical fitness.

Actually, yoga has several different paths. For example, *Karma Yoga* is the yoga of action. *Bhakti Yoga* is the yoga of devotion and love of God. *Jnana Yoga* is the yoga of knowledge and emphasizes the intellect. *Raja Yoga*, considered the most comprehensive and "highest" form of yoga, has many components, but its primary purpose is to control the thought process by transforming physical and mental energy into spiritual energy. Raja Yoga's main practice for accomplishing this is, you guessed it, meditation! Hatha Yoga is part of Raja Yoga because it helps the practitioner to gain control over the body through specific postures, breathing exercises, and relaxation techniques. Body control is a first step toward mind control.

Bliss Byte

Yoga, from the Sanskrit root *yuj*, meaning "to yoke" or "join together," is a 5,000-year-old method of mind-body health with a goal of enlightenment. It has many paths, or methods:

➤ **Karma Yoga**, which emphasizes action and service to others

➤ **Bhakti Yoga**, which emphasizes love of God

➤ **Jnana Yoga**, which emphasizes intellectual striving

➤ **Hatha Yoga**, which emphasizes balance through physical and mental exercises

➤ **Raja Yoga**, sometimes called the "King of Yogas," which emphasizes techniques for controlling both mind and body—including exercises, breathing and relaxation techniques, and meditation

For our purposes, we'll emphasize Raja Yoga because Raja Yoga emphasizes meditation. Raja Yoga was first described in writing by an Indian sage, Patanjali, in his book of aphorisms called the *Yoga Sutras*. Patanjali lived thousands of years ago, and his *Yoga Sutras* described an eightfold path for mind-body mastery. This path includes rules for living, exercises, breathing techniques, concentration techniques, meditation, and finally, enlightenment (for more detailed descriptions of the components of the eightfold path, see Chapters 4, "Living the Good Life," and 5, "The Soul Has Many Mansions").

From A to Om

Patanjali was probably born between 200 B.C. and A.D. 400. He is the author of the *Yoga Sutras*, a collection of succinct aphorisms in Sanskrit that have largely defined the modern practice of yoga.

Raja Yoga and Zen Buddhism have a lot in common. They both rely on meditation techniques designed to free the mind from the illusion of the self to result in a union with the universal consciousness. But other traditions are remarkably similar, too. Whether you consider it simply a pure, blissful state of existence, a connection to the universe, or call it "God," "meditation," or "prayer," people all over the world have been trying to get in touch with their higher selves or a higher power for centuries.

Christian and Hebrew Traditions

Although meditation is mentioned occasionally in the Bible, the Christian and Hebrew traditions tend to emphasize the word "prayer" instead. Prayer and meditation have a lot in common, however, and are even considered synonymous by many practitioners. Both have varying techniques, some using the repetition of a sound (such as "Yahweh," which is a name for God, "love," or "Amen"), some using a mental image (such as a candle flame or a Hebrew letter), and some focusing on divine love and whatever that means to the meditator. Meditation can certainly involve reflection on a religious concept, although it isn't a religion itself. It is a method.

Prayer can be considered a form of meditation and was both practiced and taught by prophets of the Old and New Testaments of the Bible. Both Hebrew and Christian techniques of meditation are practiced today and have much in common with Eastern meditation techniques. Although some people claim that the philosophies are worlds apart (for example, that Western traditions are God-centered while Eastern traditions are self-centered—a vast and false over-simplification), the fact is, what you meditate *on* is a personal matter and not reflective of meditation itself. Meditation can enhance the practice of any religion, or lack thereof. It clarifies and quiets the mind so that whatever you believe in, whatever force moves you, and whatever answers you require can come shining through.

Indigenous Cultures and Meditation

Of course, meditation isn't reserved for the major world religions and the more populous cultures. Many indigenous cultures use meditation as an integral part of their existence. Many Native American cultures have a tradition of vision quests in which the quester spends several days alone in nature, fasting and meditating, waiting for a transforming vision and/or encounter with nature. (Organized vision quests have recently become popular, allowing for anyone to go on a quest—this time, with a leader and group of fellow questers instead of alone for a solitary experience.) *Shamans* and medicine men of many cultures use meditation and also dream interpretation for healing and spiritual guidance. Nature and meditation are tied together in many cultures because nature is thought to guide us, answer our questions, and heal us if we listen and watch for signs. What better way to quiet the mind and tune in to the signs than through meditation?

From A to Om

Shamans are intermediaries between the natural and supernatural worlds and are also often healers, such as medicine men or women. A shaman is generally a person of importance in indigenous cultures.

Meditation in a Twenty-First Century World

Ancient as it may be, meditation is timeless, and at the same time, remarkably timely. Life in the twenty-first century is sure to be filled with many of the stresses of twentieth century life, and then some. Society is changing in response to these stresses, which range from the personal to the international (overpopulation, environmental destruction, terrorism, the list goes on). But the world continues to search for meaning and a more spiritual existence. Relieving stress for physical functioning is not enough. People in the twenty-first century will insist on more. They are already insisting on more.

Meditation is an important step in the evolution of humankind. As the mind of the individual improves, the society as a whole improves. Meditation has benefits beyond the personal. It will prepare you to face life in the twenty-first century by rivaling technology's techniques for dealing with stress. For example, computers are designed to make our lives easier and they do. But they often bring a whole array of new stresses with them—from the physical strain of hours spent sitting in front of the monitor to the dizzying range of choices that come with an instant-gratification mentality that challenges our focus of concentration.

Meditation may help you to shift your priorities, to keep the important things in sight. Materialism may begin to seem crude and unfulfilling. Achieving quality time with your thoughts may become a lot more important than mindlessly surfing the Internet. You may begin to look deep inside *yourself* for resources, answers, and serenity. And you may very well find them.

Relax

Don't be too eager to conquer the advanced stages of meditation. Before you can present questions or problems to your inner self in search of answers, you need to learn how to control the "mind noise" that's so distracting to clear thinking. Learning to slow down the thought process is difficult and takes time. Be patient!

Are You Self-Aware? A Meditation Self-Awareness Quiz

Of course most of you are probably just beginning your meditation journey, and "self" awareness may only be a hazy notion or seem a low priority in getting through your day. How self-aware are you? Take our quiz to find out, then read on to see how meditation can help you at your particular stage in the journey of the self. Be honest! Circle the letter of the answer that best describes you.

1. When you look in the mirror for the first time each day, what is the first thing you usually notice?
    A. My hair—ugh! Good thing no one sees me but the people who really love me a lot!
    B. All those little pores on my nose. There must be some product to get rid of those...
    C. My expression. It's a good indicator of my mood!
    D. I don't habitually look in a mirror.

2. If you had to spend an entire day alone, how would you feel about the prospect?
    A. That would be horrible! What would I do? Whom would I talk to?
    B. It would be okay if I could have a TV and lots of books and magazines, or maybe get some work done.
    C. It might be interesting to spend some time thinking over different areas of my life.
    D. I'd love it! Relaxing, rejuvenating, and what else can I say—I'm great company!

3. Close your eyes and envision your ideal self. How is that self different from the you of the present moment?
    A. Better body, nicer face, and really great hair.
    B. More successful and richer.
    C. Happier and more content.
    D. We're one and the same!

4. How would you describe your health habits?
    A. I love certain foods that I probably should give up, but can't. I really hate to exercise. I often feel guilty about my lack of commitment to good health habits.
    B. Pretty good. I eat right and exercise because I want to look really great.
    C. I try to take care of my body, and I find I'm usually in a better mood if I eat well and exercise.
    D. I keep both my mind and body in shape because it helps me to maximize my physical and mental potential.

5. How would you describe your health itself?
    A. I don't have any major health problems. I don't pay much attention to my health unless I come down with something.
    B. Very good. I take all precautions to avoid getting sick. Sick people can't be productive! If I do get sick, I try to ignore it.

C. I keep up with the latest health research and try to practice preventive health care for my overall health. If I get sick, I consider all the different healing alternatives to find the most effective course for me.

D. I may be healthy or I may have certain health problems, but I continually monitor my health—physical, mental, and emotional—and listen to what my mind-body needs. I strongly believe the mind can be a significant influence in healing the body.

6. What do you think is the difference between the "real you" and the "you" everyone sees each day?

A. The real me is much less accomplished, talented, and in-control than the "me" everyone knows or thinks they know. Sometimes I feel like a fraud.

B. The real me is actually an idealized version of myself—smarter, better looking, more in-control, more successful. I'm working hard to become the real me through whatever methods seem workable. This me you see is just temporary.

C. The real me is the outside me, but with more vulnerabilities and fewer material concerns.

D. The real me is a more complex and subtle version of the me everyone else sees. In essence, though, we are the same. I feel like all sides of myself are consistent.

7. What is the most significant way you've changed in the past five years?

A. I'm a few pounds heavier with a few more gray hairs, but basically the same. My life just keeps chugging along.

B. I'm aging fast! I hate to see my younger self fading away, but I'm fighting it at every turn.

C. I'm older and wiser. I've learned a lot about life in the past five years.

D. I've become much more aware of who I am and where my life is heading. I'm closer to goals I've set for myself and I'm happier and more at peace.

8. What do you hope will be the most significant difference about yourself in five years from now?

A. I hope I don't gain too much more weight! I also hope I'll be making more money, though I doubt I will be.

B. I've got big plans. I'll be in better shape, I'll be more organized, I'll have more money, and my life will be close to perfect.

     C. I hope I'm in a more secure position, both externally and internally. I imagine I'll be more mature and, I hope, less stressed about daily life.

     D. I hope I will be living in a state of enlightenment.

9. How would you characterize your spiritual life?

     A. I go to my place of worship on the significant holidays, most years, like a person is supposed to. Otherwise, I don't think about spiritual matters too often.

     B. Who has time for a spiritual life? There are things to do, people to see, places to go, contacts and money to make!

     C. I may or may not go to a place of worship, but I think about spiritual matters fairly frequently, and I am interested in exploring the possibilities of a more spiritual existence.

     D. My daily life equals my spiritual life. Almost everything I do, I do with my spiritual goals in mind.

10. Who are you?

     A. You mean you want to see some I.D.?

     B. Here's my resume.

     C. I am a human being striving to live a good and happy life.

     D. I am the creation of and the manifestation of universal consciousness.

How did you do? Tally up your answers and see how many of each letter you chose. Then, read the section under the letter you chose most often. If you chose several letters about equally often, read both sections. Lots of us have a little of several types within us.

➤ **If you chose mostly As:** You aren't too fond of self-analysis. You constantly doubt yourself, criticize yourself, and may assume that others share your opinions about yourself. Choosing mostly As says nothing about your *actual* self-worth, only your self-perception. Whether you have been overly criticized in the past or simply feel unable to get control over your personal habits, you aren't particularly content. You function in society just fine most of the time, but your life could be so much richer and fuller if you could learn to nurture yourself and treat yourself with a little more lovingkindness.

Movement meditation is an ideal pursuit for you. Begin to look inward without a judgmental eye. Simply look. Who are you? No, don't start judging. Just look. *Who are you?* Gradually, you'll begin to recognize within yourself the miraculous and uniquely individual human being you are. Take a mindful walk in the fresh air or begin a regular yoga practice. Combine movement with meditation and observe the changes within *and* without you. It's a wonderful world—and you're a part of it!

➤ **If you chose mostly Bs:** You're a go-getter. The problem is you may tend to chase things that won't actually bring you happiness. You are, deep down, discontent with who you are, but you have a very detailed plan about how to change all that. Rather than accepting yourself, you've constructed an idea of another, new-and-improved you. Whether you think more money, better looks, a more in-shape body, a more prestigious job, or the perfect relationship is the answer to re-inventing yourself, chances are your plans are generally based on external concerns. If you ask people who have these things, however, most of them will tell you that the money, the looks, the job, the soulmate are great, but not the answer to true happiness. For that, you have to look inside.

Because you are so action-oriented, meditation will probably be challenging for you. How can you just sit still like that when you've got so much to do? Meditation can benefit you by peeling away the layers of your material existence, then the layers of your desires, to see what's underneath. Afraid you'll find nothing at all? Don't worry. There's something there—a precious jewel, untouched by any mistakes you've made or wrongs that have been done to you. That jewel is worth more than all the material wealth in the world. You just have to search for it with the same energy and vigor with which you attempt to reshape your external self.

➤ **If you chose mostly Cs:** Most people who pick up this book are probably a lot like you. You live your life, doing what you need to do, but more and more often, you find yourself wondering about what else there is out there for you. You aren't looking for material wealth so much. You're looking for spiritual wealth. You know there's a lot more to you than you're putting into play. You suspect you could be happier, calmer, more alive. On the other hand, you don't want to be thought of as weird or "out there." You've got responsibilities and the necessary worldly concerns.

Meditation doesn't have to be "out there" at all. In fact, meditation is the opposite of "out there." It's all about "in here." Meditation is quiet self-reflection. It hushes up that frantic inner voice that, granted, propels you through your day, helping you to get everything done. But you can do without it for 20 minutes or so each day. You don't need it while meditating, and meditating will help you shut that voice off. Then you can listen for what the universe, or God, or your inner self has been trying to tell you all along. Wonderful secrets lie in there, waiting to whisper themselves to you. All you have to do is listen, and you are ready to listen. You've been watching the signs, and you're just not sure if you should trust them or follow them. Follow this one. We'll show you how.

➤ **If you chose mostly Ds:** What are you doing reading this book? You can't fool us! You're already meditating, aren't you! Or you've been praying or practicing some form of self-actualized living. You're in touch with who you are, you cherish and love yourself, and you feel like you know your place in the universal scheme of things. You're also in touch with a higher power, whether you believe that power is outside you, within you, or both. You are making the most of your life, and you are truly alive. But go ahead and read this book, anyway. Why not? There's always more to learn on the soul's magnificent journey.

Please Pass the Karma

Karma is the law of cause and effect, and even though the term is from a Sanskrit word, the concept certainly isn't limited to those in India. Karma is simply a name for the age-old concept, "what goes around comes around." It can also be viewed as a sort of universal balancing act. The universe wants to stay in balance, and everything you do, say, or even think has an immediate effect on the universe. In some way or another, those effects will be balanced. According to Eastern thought, karma has to do with proclivities, habits, and desires from the past, including past lives. *Everything* is karmic—everything we are today is a manifestation of past patterns, and everything we do is shaping our future.

From A to Om

Karma is a Sanskrit word referring to the law of cause and effect, or universal balance. Everything you do, say, or think has an immediate effect on the universe that will reverberate back to you in some way.

That doesn't mean that bad people will always be punished or good people will always get their reward. Karma isn't payback or some universal system of revenge. It simply means that "for every action, there is an equal and opposite reaction," to quote a centuries-old rule of science from Newton's Laws of Motion (for more on this, see the section on T'ai Chi in Chapter 17, "Movement Meditation: Get Your Groove").

But you can control how karma affects you. When you become more self-aware, you'll begin to notice that what you say, do, and think hold significance. You have an effect on the world around you, and once you notice it, you can learn to control it. Do you want to be peaceful? Think and act peacefully. Do you want love? Think and act with lovingkindness. Is it excitement and adventure you're seeking? Think and act with exuberance, joy, and enthusiasm.

But becoming self-aware and staying in constant touch with your affect on the world around you doesn't happen overnight. Meditation can get you in touch, sharpen your awareness, and help you to use karma in a way that will enhance your life and lead you to enlightenment, whatever that means for you.

Your Teachers Are Everywhere

If you're feeling a little overwhelmed, don't worry. No one charts their life journey on their own. You can learn a lot about meditation and self-awareness from books, but you also learn, little by little, step by step, from teachers. That doesn't mean you have to take a class in meditation, yoga, Buddhism, religion, or anything else (although classes can be very helpful, if you're the type who enjoys them). It doesn't mean you have to have a personal guru. Your teachers are everywhere you look. Parents, siblings, and friends teach us about love, compassion, and service (even if they teach us by demonstrating what we shouldn't do!). Mentors, strangers, thieves, and good Samaritans alike teach us life lessons we can carry with us to help us grow.

Of course, you are your own best teacher. You decide which lessons to take to heart and which ones to blow back into the sky like dandelion fluff. And the best way to get in touch with your inner teacher is to take a course in you. Spend some time each day in meditation and learn what you have to tell yourself.

Desperately Seeking Samadhi

Mindful Minute

A **guru** is a personal spiritual advisor who assists in the attainment of enlightenment. The Sanskrit word literally means "dispeller of darkness." The guru/disciple bond is stronger than that of a teacher and student and lasts until the disciple is enlightened or the disciple breaks the link. The guru actively propels the disciple toward enlightenment, but acts primarily on the "inner planes."

We don't mean to make meditation sound like a panacea, and it certainly isn't an easy process. Especially at first, meditation can be frustrating, and it may seem like your efforts are yielding nothing at all. The more you want your life to change, the more you need some sort of enlightenment, the harder it can be to exercise the patience, will, and self-discipline it takes to reap the harvest of a consistent meditation practice.

Bliss Byte

Try this concentration exercise: Look at your right thumb. Move it around. Try to sense what the thumb is feeling. Is the joint loose? Does it hurt? Where? How does it move? Now bring it to stillness. With each breath, relax your thumb a little more. Imagine going deeper, relaxing the veins and bones. Now bring your focus into one single hair on your thumb and begin again. If you feel tense and can't seem to focus on the hair, pull back to the thumb.

To some extent, we're all desperately seeking samadhi, or some degree of internal peace, happiness, and fulfillment. Who wouldn't want a life of pure bliss, without inner turmoil, without stress, without misery? Life can be tough, and getting through it well is tougher still. But meditation is a way to begin, gently and quietly. Meditation nurtures the soul back to health, opens an inner dialogue, and rocks you into serenity. To find that quiet space deep inside yourself where only truth exists is to find a little island of bliss in a sometimes difficult and unpredictable world. We're here to help you find that island. Think of us as your travel agents! You deserve that daily vacation. Are you packed?

The Least You Need to Know

➤ Anyone can meditate, no matter their beliefs.

➤ For centuries, meditation has existed in different forms and in different cultures all over the world.

➤ Although ancient as humankind, meditation is perfectly suited to enhance twenty-first century life.

➤ "Self" awareness is an evolutionary process. Start today!

Chapter 3

Your Personal Mind-Body Scan

In This Chapter

➤ Learning how to pay attention

➤ Reasons why concentration can be difficult

➤ What it means to live life mindfully

➤ Signs that stress is getting the best of you

➤ How to do a mind-body scan

How are you? "Fine," you may respond automatically. Isn't that what you're supposed to say? Isn't that what we all say whenever someone asks that over-used and under-meant question? But we'd like to ask it again, and this time, we'd like you to answer with something different. Try to make it something that seems to you a little more accurate. Ready?

How are you?

Your answer: _____.

Okay, that's better, but we're still not quite sure you've answered the whole question. Once again?

How are you?

Your answer: _____.

No, how *are* you?

Your answer: _____.

No, really, *how are you?*

Your answer: _____.

Chances are, by this time, after "Your answer:" you've written something to the effect of, "Enough already!" But we aren't trying to irritate you. We're trying to get you to think about the question. Of course, the question can be answered on many levels, since "you" can mean many things. For example, how is your health? (Do you have a cold? Feeling great?) How is your mood? (Rotten? Joyful?) How is your appearance? (Are you having a good hair day or a bad hair day?) But when we ask the question, what we really mean is, *how is your mind-body?*

"How is my mind-body?" you might laugh. "What the heck is that supposed to mean?" We're glad you asked! It isn't an easy question, but there are ways to find the answer. They just take a little attention. And paying attention is what this chapter is all about.

Learning to Pay Attention

Maybe you think you pay attention all the time. You succeed in life. You keep your house clean. You talk to your partner, your kids, your parents, your siblings, or whomever needs to bend your ear. You pay your bills. You drive to work without getting in an accident. You're great at your job. And you couldn't do all that without paying attention, right?

Paying attention to the most crucial external aspects of your life is important for proper functioning. Most of us learn to cultivate this kind of attention from childhood. ("You'll learn to tie your shoes if you pay attention!" "You can get this math problem if you pay attention!")

Bliss Byte

If you tend to be a daydreamer, you may have been told back in school that you weren't paying attention. Actually, daydreaming is a way to pay close attention—just not to things in your external environment. Indulge in a good daydream today. Set aside 10 minutes, unplug the phone, find a quiet room, get comfortable, close your eyes, and visualize anything you like—your hopes, dreams, favorite place, whatever makes you feel happy.

What you probably haven't been taught since childhood is to pay attention to yourself. And we don't mean brushing your teeth, showering, and putting on deodorant. We mean paying attention to your mind-body and everything that affects it. We're talking about all those things you do without thinking, all those things you feel without noticing, and all those things you live through without really living through them. Here are a few examples. When was the last time you really paid attention to:

➤ The taste, smell, and texture of every bite of an entire meal? How about that ice cream cone you had yesterday?

➤ The way all the muscles in your body feel during a workout?

➤ All the manifestations of nature when you take your morning walk?

➤ The aroma, color, and feel of a flower?

➤ The way a child moves at play?

➤ The sounds of each of the different instruments in a symphony performance?

➤ The exact shape of your living room?

➤ The way the sky looks just before you get into your car and the way it feels to drive down the highway?

➤ The exact feel of your body when you first wake up in the morning, when you are busy going about your day, and as you begin to wind down in the evening?

Mindfulness comes from paying attention to each nuance and detail of your experience that comes to your awareness through each of your senses.

Paying attention to things like these is "meditation while living." It can also be called *mindfulness*. But make no mistake—it isn't easy. It's much easier to drive to the grocery store, get the things on your list, drive home, put the food away, and get on with your life than it is to really *live* your trip to the grocery store.

From A to Om

Mindfulness is a form of meditation originally developed in the Buddhist traditions of Asia but practiced today by many, from meditators in monasteries to physicians in stress-reduction clinics. Mindfulness can be defined as awareness of each moment as it occurs.

Do we detect a smile? Do you think it's silly—or even a waste of time—to really *live* a trip to the grocery store? We would argue that it's neither silly nor a waste of time to really live *any* moment of your life, no matter how seemingly mundane. Paying attention to everything you do, feel, say, think, and experience is an amazing way to live. It is eye-opening. Sure, living on automatic might sometimes make things more efficient. Life is easier when you don't have to process everything around you (and of course, you couldn't process *everything*). Yet, in our rush for more efficient and productive lives, we've cut out something very important: the life part. That's what mindfulness is all about.

Maybe you think that attention to your inner life and perceptions is too self-indulgent. You've got enough to do! But you know what? A little self-indulgence isn't necessarily a bad thing. In fact, paying attention to your own experience of life can make you happier, more productive, more efficient, and more able to give to others. So when you think about it, mindfulness is the ultimate gift to those you love and care for.

Bliss Byte

A massage nurtures the connection between your body and mind and is a great counterpart to meditation. When you receive a massage, you may become more acutely aware of places in your body that, without a massage, you wouldn't have noticed. Hello, lower back...ouch! Or how about that overly sensitive calf muscle? Massage helps release minor tensions before they develop, easing the body to ease the mind.

"Don't Give Me a Koan I Can't Solve!"

Some of you are probably thinking that you can't imagine practicing mindfulness on a daily basis, but you aren't sure why. The idea just doesn't appeal to you. It isn't because you think it's too self-indulgent, exactly. It isn't even because you don't think you have the time. What is it? We'll take a guess.

Think of something in your past that you weren't particularly good at. Maybe it was math, gym class, spelling, or keeping your room clean. Now think about why you have unpleasant memories about that subject. Did a teacher become frustrated because you couldn't understand the concept of long division? Did your classmates choose you last for their dodge-ball teams? Did you feel publicly humiliated in a spelling bee when you repeatedly failed to remember "*i* before *e*, except after *c*"? Did you cringe every time your mother screamed, "I thought I told you to clean that room yesterday! No dessert for you tonight!" And it was chocolate cake!

Bliss Byte

We've already talked about koans, those short riddles meant to jog your mind into a higher plane. Here's one for you to ponder in a future meditation session from *Zen Flesh, Zen Bones,* a collection of Zen and Pre-Zen writings compiled by Paul Reps. (Don't worry—it isn't supposed to make sense to the rational mind.):

When the question is common
The answer is also common.
When the question is sand in a bowl of boiled rice
The answer is a stick in the soft mud.

Whatever your past imperfections, one thing is clear: It isn't any fun to keep trying at something you aren't good at. If you and your sister both started tennis lessons at the same time and she was a little prodigy and you whacked the ball out of bounds every single time you hit it, you probably weren't motivated to continue your lessons. (Unless you were exceptionally strong-willed—and we're sure many of you were!)

Maybe, on the other hand, you were great at English or art or games that didn't involve being smacked with a big red ball. And maybe you could have been better at your more difficult subjects if you would've practiced more often. But practice isn't as rewarding when you believe you lack skill.

The same goes for meditation. For some people, meditation, even daily mindfulness, is easy. Some people tend to be more introspective or observant of minutiae than others, and for them, meditation is a joy. But for others, meditation doesn't come naturally. In fact, it's darned difficult! So why bother?

If you are someone who would much rather play dodge ball than sit quietly noticing your inner life for 20 minutes every day, you may be reluctant even to try meditation. Why try something at which you'll certainly fail? Why waste time trying to solve a koan if you know enlightenment isn't imminent?

Because meditation, unlike many other pursuits, isn't goal-oriented. Therefore, you can't fail. Sure, we talk about "enlightenment" being the ultimate goal, and that's a more traditional approach. But it doesn't have to be *your* approach. Sitting quietly for one minute watching your mind race without letting it involve you can be a very successful meditation session. Noticing the details of how your dinner tastes can be a successful meditation session. You can't fail. Or, let's say, you can't fail *as long as you try*. The only way to fail at meditation is not to try it at all.

Don't think of meditation like a sport, a school subject, or even a skill. It is a journey, and it's your own, individual journey. No one else's experience can dictate whether your experience is successful. Your meditation techniques can evolve, but you can't fail. You can only grow.

Meditation Is About Your Body, Too

Another misconception about meditation is that it's all about your mind. We've already talked about your mind-body, which means the whole you, mind and body inextricably intertwined. The implication of the idea of having a mind-body is that mind and body affect each other. That means your mind can have a direct effect on your body, and an increasing number of studies are supporting this hypothesis. We believe it—we've seen it happen!

What can your mind do for your body? Meditation techniques are frequently employed in pain clinics, such as the Stress Reduction Clinic at the University of Massachusetts Medical Center, to help patients manage severe and/or chronic pain. Meditation techniques can also help lessen or even alleviate the pain of childbirth.

Meditation can help you perform better in your favorite sport. At the University of Rochester, psychologist Robert Ader has pioneered the field of *psychoneuroimmunology* (PNI), which studies the ways in which thoughts, emotions, the brain, the nervous system, and the immune system are all linked together. Mind-body medicine is becoming an important field of research and study. It isn't on the fringe anymore. And that means your body can begin to benefit today from the power of your mind.

Mindful Minute

Research studies demonstrate the link between stress levels and the immune system. In a 1991 study published in the *New England Journal of Medicine*, a correlation between stress levels and susceptibility to the common cold was found. Another study showed adverse affects on the immune system in subjects who experienced 77 hours of noise and sleep deprivation, and also in people whose spouses had recently died. Yet another study showed decreased immune function during final exams in medical students.

Of course, meditation can't do everything. It can't, on its own, cure disease, and lack of it can't cause disease, as some would have you believe. The mind-body connection isn't so obvious and simplistic as thinking, "Cancer be gone," and having it disappear. Thinking, "I hate my life" won't cause cancer, either. Complex interactions take place inside every human being that science and medicine are just beginning to understand. Don't fall prey to those who oversimplify the connection or try to make one rule fit all (especially if they're trying to get you to buy something!).

The mind can also influence the body in ways other than those related to pain and illness. Athletic performance, job performance, creativity, and the ability to manage stress are all realms ruled by the mind and performed by the body. Meditation can help you to be at your best in everything your body does.

Recognizing Symptoms of Distress

You know the symptoms of a cold or the flu. You might have personal experience with the symptoms of arthritis, migraine headaches, a sprained ankle, or any number of physical ailments. But how well do you know the symptoms of mind-body distress? These symptoms are clever. They disguise themselves as a host of other ailments and so are difficult to pin down. But you can make some good guesses. Examine the following list and check all the symptoms you have experienced at least once in the last two weeks or that you usually experience once or more per week:

❏ Headache

❏ Joint pain and/or inflammation

❏ Depression—"the blues"

❏ Nervousness or anxiety

❏ Restlessness

❏ Excessive worrying

❏ Binge eating or loss of appetite

❏ Muscle stiffness

❏ Dizziness

❏ Unexplained weight gain or loss

❏ Skipped heartbeats or racing pulse

❏ Loss of desire to be around people

Relax

Guilt doesn't heal! Although stress and long-term negativity can certainly affect your health, don't shoulder the burden of thinking illness is caused by not being positive enough. Studies show a positive attitude can promote recovery, however, so it's never too late to become an optimist! Use your mind to your advantage without letting someone's ideas about mind-body medicine discourage or frighten you.

Relax

Any symptom of physical or mental discomfort or distress may be a signal of an underlying condition your physician can easily diagnose and treat. Illness and emotional distress often go hand in hand. Communication with your doctor is very important. Discuss any symptoms you have, even ones that may not seem important or overwhelming, with your doctor. Talk to your doctor about stress-reducing techniques, such as meditation.

❐ High blood pressure

❐ Low blood pressure

❐ Unexplained fear

❐ Irritability

❐ Difficulty concentrating

❐ Tremors or shakiness

❐ Unexplained crying

❐ Sweating

❐ Nausea

❐ Constipation

❐ Nervous stomach

❐ Vomiting

❐ Loss of sex drive

❐ Panic attack

❐ Pain in any part of the body that can't be attributed to an injury or illness

❐ Fatigue when you've had enough sleep

❐ Insomnia

❐ Forgetfulness

❐ Lack of motivation that compromises your ability to accomplish important work

If you checked even one or two of the above list, and especially if you checked more than five, you are probably suffering from the effects of too much stress and not enough mindfulness. All of the above symptoms can certainly have physical causes, such as the onset of a physical illness. Yet, all are often "nonsymptoms" that physicians can't explain and that are never attributed to any actual, known condition. What are sufferers of such symptoms to do?

We aren't physicians and would certainly advise you see one to rule out a medical problem for any physical or emotional condition that's causing you discomfort. After that, though, if you still can't find an answer (or receive an answer to the tune of, "It's nothing to worry about," "It's probably stress-related," or "Well, we don't know what it is, but you can take these drugs…"), we would like to suggest you tune in to your mind-body and pay a little more attention to what's going on inside. Perhaps you'll want to consider finding a new doctor who is more open to treating the "whole" person and who will take the time to discuss holistic alternatives with you. Tell your doctor that you are interested in the medical mind-body connection and that this emphasis is important to you in determining your care and treatment.

Talk to your doctor about incorporating the stress-reducing benefits of meditation into his or her treatment plan for your health and well-being. Meditation can complement treatment for both minor and major conditions and illnesses (see more about this in Chapter 26, "Rx: Meditation"). And when you're already feeling good, it can enhance a feeling of wellness and keep those daily aches and pains under control. Ask your primary care physician about meditation at your next office visit. Remember that meditation alone can't replace necessary medical treatment from a licensed health care professional. Before you try to meditate your pain away, see your doctor!

Do Your Own Mind-Body Scan

Mindfulness isn't easy and most people can't simply start paying attention out of the blue. It's harder than you might think! You're driving down the highway, and you start to notice how the steering wheel feels, how the road looks as you drive over it, the sky's particular shade of blue…did you turn off the coffee pot? Oh, you can't forget to buy stamps. And look—you're almost out of gas. Do you have enough cash or will you have to stop at the ATM machine? Of course, the bank is still open, so you could do the drive-thru, and it's right next to the grocery store, and you do need milk— whoops. So much for paying attention!

If this sounds like you, don't despair. You can't be expected to jump right in, just like that. You didn't start your education in college. You started in preschool or kindergarten. Think of the mind-body scan as Meditation Kindergarten.

For example, wise yogis tell us that the purpose of yoga exercises or postures is to help the body become stronger and more flexible so that it can sit peacefully and motionless for longer periods of time in silent contemplation and meditation. In fact, in yoga philosophy, which includes a series of steps toward enlightenment, exercises or postures are to be learned and practiced before meditation. According to yogic thought, the body must be controlled before the mind can be. If you aren't in good physical condition, and you've ever tried to sit cross-legged on the floor for more than a minute or two, you'll understand why body control comes first!

The mind-body scan is simply a technique for noticing how you feel, in minute detail. It also involves some relaxation and breathing techniques, which help you to keep your focus. There are various ways to do a mind-body scan, of course, but a few rules apply. The mind-body scan is performed lying down, making it more comfortable than sitting meditation, especially for those who aren't in the greatest physical shape.

It also involves focusing on each part of your body, from bottom to top, noticing how it feels, observing any pain or discomfort, and also anything that feels particularly comfortable or good—but without becoming emotionally involved with the feeling. As you scan, you can also visualize that your scan is picking up any impurities or negative thoughts and jettisoning them as purified joy with every exhalation of your breath. When you reach the top of your head, you can feel cleansed!

You can do the mind-body scan on your own, in whatever way you like, but keep in mind it should go slowly and take at least 10 minutes, preferably 30 minutes or more, if you have the time. But just in case you like a little more structure, we'll guide you through a mind-body scan. You can read the following text and remember it approximately; you can have someone read it to you (slowly!) as you try it; or you can tape yourself reading it so you can play the tape whenever you like. Feel free to edit the following in ways that make it more appealing to you or more appropriate for your particular situation, whatever that may be.

Bliss Byte

Here is a simple exercise to help you relax and help the world relax too. As you inhale, imagine you are inhaling pure love. As you exhale, imagine you are exhaling pure peace. Inhale love, exhale peace. Stay with this for awhile, taking long, even breaths. A fun and even more productive variation: Try doing this with a group of friends. This simple technique may help prevent road rage, world rage—and your rage.

First, lie on your back on a comfortable but firm surface, such as on a blanket or mat on the floor. A bed will work, too, although it doesn't offer quite the ideal degree of support. Relax, take a deep breath, and exhale slowly. If your mind starts to wander during the body scan, gently bring it back to the place you were when you wandered away, and continue. Ready? Let's go!

Close your eyes and begin to breathe deeply. Listen to your breath. Feel it going in and out. Relax. Imagine that with every inhalation, you are bringing positive energy into your body, and with every exhalation, you are releasing discomfort and stress. Feel where your body is touching the floor and where it doesn't touch the floor. Imagine your body is very, very heavy and is sinking into the floor. Relax. Breathe.

Now bring your attention to the toes of your left foot. Can you feel them without moving them? If not, move them a little. There they are! Move up to your left ankle. Feel it. Rotate it a little if you can't feel it. Then, slowly, very slowly scan your left leg, moving up over the shin and calf, and around the knee. Is your knee bent or locked? Bring your attention up to your thigh and into your hipbone. How do your hips feel? Are they centered on the floor? Are the joints comfortable or achy? How are your buttocks centered? Is your lower back swayed, or pressing into the floor? Keep breathing, positive in, discomfort out. You may soon be feeling all of the negative energy dissipating, releasing, disappearing.

Now bring your attention to the toes of your right foot. Can you feel them without moving them? If not, move them a little. Move up to your right ankle. Rotate it a little if you can't feel it. Next feel your shin, your calf muscle, and your knee. Is your knee slightly bent or locked?

Now feel your thigh muscle and then your hipbone. Are your hips more relaxed than when you noticed them a moment ago? Keep breathing. Positive in, negative released.

Now bring your attention to your lower back, around to your abdomen, into your upper chest and upper back. How do your shoulder blades feel against the floor? Are your shoulders drawn up or relaxed? How is your spine touching the floor? Move to the base of your neck. Can you feel it? Move up your neck to the base of the skull. How does it feel at the place where your neck and skull attach? Now move your attention around your skull. Feel your ears, your scalp, and the roots of your hair. Move over your forehead, your eyes, your nose, your cheeks, and your mouth. Is your jaw tight or relaxed? Can you feel your teeth? What is your tongue doing? Feel the inside of your mouth, your lips, your chin, and your throat. Now move back up your face to your forehead, then back to the crown of your head. Keep breathing, positive in, negative out. Imagine the last of the negative energy disappearing with one long exhale. Take your time with the exhale and as you let the breath out, make a "sss" sound.

Last, lie quietly for a few more minutes. Try to spread your attention over your entire body. How do you feel? Where is your mind? Are you focused in the now and the physical sensation of lying on the floor, or is your mind still trying to wander off? Whatever your mind is doing, don't let it disturb or engage you. Simply notice. Now, slowly open your eyes. What do you see? Sit up. How do you feel? Stand up. Here you are! Hello! Now you can proceed with your day.

If you fell asleep and missed it all, that's okay. The point isn't to fall asleep, of course, but you probably needed the cat nap. You'll get it next time.

Bliss Byte

Every once in a while, do a shoulder scan while driving your car. Notice where your shoulders are riding. Nice and low, or up around your ears? Take a deep breath and as you exhale, lower your shoulders and feel the stretch in your neck, freeing circulation to your head. You'll also be able to turn your head more easily to see your side mirrors, revealing all the crazed shoulders-up drivers around you.

Creating Balance and Harmony

Living mindfully and keeping your attention on your experience and the way it feels to go through life does more than help to sharpen your mind and enhance your health. It also adjusts your life in little, almost magical ways. When you pay attention, your mind-body pounces on the opportunity to bring itself into balance—it's finally got your attention! You may begin to have improved health habits, you might obsess about the little things less often, and you may find yourself spending long hours contemplating a beautiful sunset or a well-written book, or engaging in one of those really great conversations that change your thinking about the world or result in a new friend.

How can mindfulness do all that? Let's look at an example. When you're carefully focused on the taste and experience of everything you eat, suddenly junky, tasteless, overly sweet, salty, or chemical-laden food won't be as satisfying. Fresh, pure, healthy food, on the other hand, will taste better than you can imagine. Or, if a junk-food indulgence is what you crave, it will be so satisfying that you won't have to eat that entire box of snack cakes. One or two will be supremely enough.

Or consider exercise, which may begin to feel like a pleasure rather than a burden or a chore. When you notice how your body responds to physical activity, you can appreciate the effects and the sensations more intensely and exercise will have much more of a positive pay-off.

If you truly pay attention, you'll be a much better listener. People who talk to you will notice that you are actually hearing what they say. The result is often that they'll say things they really want you to hear, and you'll be able to answer them more meaningfully. That's how great friendships are born (or reborn)!

Mindfulness can change your life in so many ways, you'll just have to try it and experience the transformation yourself. Start with the mind-body scan, then continue on with the other techniques in this book. Now that's living!

The Least You Need to Know

➤ Paying attention isn't easy. You have to learn the basics first, and eventually you'll be a master.

➤ Meditation helps your body as well as your mind—both in terms of health and in terms of general physical functioning.

➤ The mind-body scan is a good way to begin learning how to pay attention and live mindfully.

➤ Mindful living puts more balance and harmony into your life.

Part 2
Let's Get Spiritual: The Path to Bliss

Meditation is much more than a great way to manage stress. It can also become an important part of your spiritual journey. Since humankind first looked inward and contemplated the question, "Who am I and what am I doing here on Earth?" meditation has been helping to clear the way so that the answers can become apparent.

No, you don't have to be spiritually minded to enjoy the benefits of meditation, but for those interested in humankind's spiritual quest throughout the ages and for those embarking on their own quest for truth, meaning, and happiness in this life, meditation, and its cousin, prayer, are useful and invaluable tools.

Studies have demonstrated that meditation and prayer can heal the body, nurture the spirit, and put us into contact with a higher force, whether from without or from within ourselves (or both). Studies also suggest that meditation and/or prayer directed toward the healing of another may actually have an effect, even if the person who is the subject of the healing thoughts doesn't know he or she is being prayed for! Now that's meditation power.

Chapter 4

Living the Good Life

In This Chapter

➤ Can you meditate if you're not really religious?

➤ Ethics, meditation, and your personal belief system

➤ Dharma, plus yamas and niyamas

➤ How looking inward helps you to see more clearly

Are you living the good life? Some days you probably feel like you are and other days like you definitely are not. But have you ever taken the time to sit down and decide what "the good life" means for *you*?

When we say "good life," we don't mean that you should have plenty of wine, women (or men), and song to fill your days (though for some people, that's just dandy). We don't mean you should have enough money to buy whatever you want. We don't even mean that you should be a "good" person by strictly following a set of beliefs that an authority figure—such as your parents, the company you work for, your church, a club or other organization, or even "the media"—puts before you.

What we mean is, do you have a personal vision for yourself and your life? Do you have opinions or beliefs about "right" and "wrong," and do you act with conviction according to those opinions or beliefs? Do you feel good about who you are and the way you live your life?

Bliss Byte

Tape record a list of qualities about yourself that you really like or of qualities you would like to have. You can state them as affirmations:

"I am a good listener."

"I am free of pain."

"I am kind, giving, loving, intelligent."

Every once in awhile, play back the recording and listen. Really listen! Discover the power of the spoken word. Words are energy on many levels of meaning, not the least of which is the energy of sound vibration flying through the air.

Of course, we all have plans, hopes, and dreams, but how far do we go to make them come true? How far are we *able* to go? Maybe you always wanted to be a great writer, but you don't even have time to write to your mother. Maybe you love to cook, but most nights, it's frozen dinners and a can of diet soda because you've got so much work to do. Maybe you long to save the world, but you can't seem to muster the energy to rinse out those soda cans, so you guiltily throw them away and hope the Earth doesn't mind too much.

Not accomplishing your dreams and being the person you want to be isn't just a matter of not having the time, the energy, or even the moral fortitude. Living any life other than the one you want—and know is right—is often the result of a lack of focus, self-discipline, vision, planning out short-term and long-term goals, and, sometimes, self-esteem.

Yes, you guessed it—meditation can help you with all that. So can some of the meditation-related philosophies from different cultures for which meditation is important. But first, let's clear up some misconceptions about meditation before we determine what the "good life" means to you and how you can start living it.

"Do I Have to Be Spiritual to Meditate?"

Most of us have a general idea of how we'd like our lives to go, but far fewer have a plan for achieving personal satisfaction. An even smaller subset of those include some form of spirituality in their life plans and philosophies, whether that means practicing a particular religion, or whether it means simply looking for meaning in the ether, in your own heart, or in your personal efforts to help your fellow human beings.

But a so-called "spiritual life" isn't for everyone, and it isn't in everyone's plans. That's fine. You are who you are, and you have your own journey. Meditation can be a boon to your life, nevertheless, because you don't have to be spiritual to meditate. You don't have to be religious, you don't have to believe in a higher power, you don't even have to believe the sun will come up tomorrow. Meditation isn't about what you believe. It's about the "now."

In meditation, you live in the now and embrace the present moment. You feel it, experience it, live it. Maybe you will eventually end up pondering questions about your life or thinking about a religious concept, but that's highly individual. So, if you are turned off by the idea of meditation because you think it's not grounded in reality or that it's too philosophical or too ethereal, fear not.

Meditation is the awareness of the flow of reality in space and time. Unlike philosophy, which strives to achieve an order to reality through mental reasoning alone, meditation looks for a deep acceptance, a knowing that comes from the mind-body. And ethereal? What's more practical than a process that helps you to think better and more clearly, be healthier, and thrive in life?

Relax

Some people aren't interested in meditation because they think it's too spiritual, but others avoid it because they think it is opposed to their beliefs or somehow against their religion. Meditation is simply a method for clearing the mind and relaxing. The religions and philosophical systems that use it (and there are many!) are interesting to study in conjunction with meditation, but they aren't themselves meditation. Meditation fits into any belief system.

What often happens when someone begins to meditate, however, is that some of the "big" questions begin to materialize. What is the meaning of "good" and "evil"? What is "right" and what is "wrong"? What does it mean to be virtuous, and what are the "right" priorities? (We put all these terms in quotation marks because we don't believe they have strict definitions that are exactly the same for everyone in every culture.)

That's not to say any of these questions will *ever* occur to you before, during, or after meditation. But they might. If you are so inclined, why not consider them? Numerous recent studies demonstrate that people involved with a belief system or who practice a religion are generally happier, less depressed, healthier, and longer-lived. A little spirituality, in whatever form suits you, might make you a happier, healthier person.

But once again, we'll say that if you are diametrically opposed to things spiritual and aren't interested in anything that can't be proven using the scientific method, don't reject meditation. Plenty of scientific studies have demonstrated its benefits. Read Chapter 7, "Neurophysiology: This Is Your Brain on Meditation," to find out more about the science and physiology of meditation.

Common Misconceptions About Meditation

Thinking meditation is too New Agey or hocus-pocus isn't the only misconception floating around out there about meditation. Even though you've already read a few chapters, you, too, may still harbor some misconceptions. Test yourself! Mark each of the following statements either true or false, according to what you think is true. (If you've been paying attention to the first three chapters of this book, you'll probably get most of them correct!)

True	False	
❏	❏	You have to sit like a yogi to meditate.
❏	❏	You have to chant some weird foreign word to meditate.
❏	❏	You already have to be an expert at concentrating to meditate.
❏	❏	You have to take a class to learn how to meditate.
❏	❏	Only Buddhists or Hindus meditate.
❏	❏	You need to have a special environment to meditate successfully. (How about a mountaintop in the Himalayas?)
❏	❏	Meditation is contrary to certain religions.
❏	❏	Meditation is a 1970s thing. Nobody does it anymore.
❏	❏	You have to be at peace to meditate.
❏	❏	You have to know what you are doing to try it.
❏	❏	You will get weird and spaced out if you meditate.
❏	❏	You have to know what a chakra is (and believe in them, besides) to meditate.
❏	❏	You will smile at your obnoxious neighbor if you meditate. (Okay, this one might be true!)

Mindful Minute

Chakras are psycho-physical-spiritual centers of energy that exist between the base of your spinal column and the crown of your head, according to yogic thought. Chakras are often described as the centers where the astral (or subtle) body and the physical body converge, where mass is converted to energy and vice versa. **Mantras**, words chanted during meditation, resonate within the body and the chakras. The chanted words evoke and release specific energies.

Did you mark them all false? Good for you! Because every one of the above statements is a common misconception about meditation. You don't have to sit in some uncomfortable or impossible position. Some meditation techniques can be performed while lying down (though most involve sitting so you will not fall asleep and can remain fully conscious). You can chant a mantra while meditating, but it doesn't have to be a foreign word. It can be any word that means something to you.

You don't have to be an expert at concentrating to start a regular practice of meditation. Actually, meditation is a concentration builder! So the people who have a hard time concentrating should be first in line to learn! While you can pay to learn certain meditation techniques, you certainly don't have to take a class. There are many ways to learn to meditate, and the most important way is to practice, practice, practice. And practice doesn't cost a thing!

You already know that while many Buddhists and Hindus meditate, so do many Christians, Jews, Muslims, Native Americans, and even atheists! That's because meditation fits with any religion or lack of religion. You can meditate anywhere—from a Zen garden to your living room to a busy airport terminal. Meditation won't "space you out," and there aren't any prerequisites regarding either inner peace or knowledge of Eastern religious concepts.

As far as meditation being a 1970s thing, sure, it did become popular in the West in the 1970s, but it's much bigger now. It's taken more seriously, practiced more widely, and embraced with greater acceptance than ever before as a technique for enhancing mental acumen, physical health, and general well-being. And one reason you'll end up smiling at your neighbor is because you'll feel so great.

Bliss Byte

When you first sit to meditate, you'll probably notice your thoughts jumping around from here to there. You might begin to feel anxious, thinking you can't possibly do it correctly. Or, you may become bored. Really bored! Don't worry. You aren't doing anything wrong. This is part of the whole point, to witness your mind at work and your consciousness as it frets, changes, and gets bored. Just keep observing. Don't judge. And, most of all, don't give up, get up, or give in. Keep at it. Meditation takes practice, time, and cultivates patience.

What's Your Idea of the Good Life? A Self Quiz

But what about that "good life" business we were talking about? Oh yes—your life plan! That vision of yourself you try to work toward in your spare time. Let's talk about that.

Living your dream, accomplishing your goals, and being happy don't usually just happen. The good life takes some work, direction, commitment, and discipline. Yes, more than you can accomplish in your spare time. To live the good life, you really have to start *living the good life*! But before you can start working on your personal ethics and goals and putting your ideals into practice, though, you have to know what they are.

So what about your personal answers to the "big" questions? Have you thought about them recently? Take our mini ethics quiz to determine your ethical profile and the mode of meditation that might best agree with you. Bear with us—these are big questions with no right or wrong answers. Just go with the answers that seem most right to you. Don't worry about them.

1. In your opinion, which answer best describes a "good" person?

    A. Someone who follows the guidelines of his or her chosen religion, obeys the law, and tries not to do harm to others.

    B. Someone who thinks for him- or herself and considers every situation, following his or her conscience, despite what any laws or rules have to say about a situation.

    C. The concept of "good" is illogical, but humans use it to describe some one who acts in a way that will best benefit the species as a whole.

    D. Someone who puts others before him- or herself.

    E. A goody two-shoes? Someone you wouldn't want to invite to your party? Oh, I know! Someone who follows the Boy Scout and Girl Scout creeds even though they're all grown up?

2. What do you think about the concept of evil?

    A. It is the opposing force to good in the world—also, a force inherent in some people who break the law and harm others.

    B. Evil is going against what you know is right.

    C. There is no such thing. Evil is simply an easy way for people to describe things that could hurt them or that are destructive to their survival or happiness.

    D. Evil is living solely for yourself.

    E. Evil is just a word for the kind of fun most people are afraid to have!

3. In your opinion, what powers the universe?

    A. God.

    B. No one knows for sure, but it must be something since all cultures have tried to describe it and so many claim to have experiences of the divine.

    C. Entropy.

    D. Love.

    E. I dunno, a diesel engine?

4. Finish the following sentence: Morality is _____:

    A. Actively living by a set of rules meant to encourage a better life.

    B. Being true to yourself.

    C. Strictly a human-derived concept developed due to our overly evolved brains.

    D. Helping and giving to our fellow humans.

    E. "Morality" sounds too much like "more reality." Who needs that?

5. What one word from the following list would best describe you?

   A. Agreeable.

   B. Intelligent.

   C. Realistic.

   D. Giving.

   E. No one word could come close to describing me!

6. The meaning of life can be discovered through:

   A. The guidance of others, whether spiritual leaders, personal advisors, counselors, or the teachings of historical figures.

   B. Something that must be determined on one's own through introspection and contemplation.

   C. Personal investigation of and interest in the world, its physical laws, and its great biological, geological, and/or chemical diversity.

   D. Selfless service to others.

   E. Oh, c'mon. Eat, drink, and be merry, for tomorrow we may die. Life's a beach. What more meaning do you need?

Now, count up how many of each letter you chose:

➤ **If you chose mostly As:** You are a rules person. You like order, regularity, and you probably have a very neat desk. Although you're far from mindless, you like to have a set of beliefs on which to hang your ethical hat. Rather than have to confront each new life question head-on, you prefer to have a framework already in place so you can easily apply it to any situation. Once you've found a leader, a system, or a philosophy you agree with, you trust it to work for you in life. You will probably enjoy a method of meditation that fits into your personal belief system and has set rules to describe the techniques.

➤ **If you chose mostly Bs:** You are a thinker. You may or may not have certain religious beliefs, but if you do, we'll bet you've examined them in excruciating detail to make sure they agree with what your inner voice tells you is right and wrong. You figure it all out for yourself. For you, answers are not "one size fits all." You probably never get to vote in primary elections because you're a registered independent. You'll probably try out lots of types of meditation to determine which one works best for you. Try them all! But certainly try them. You value your mind, and your own will above all else, and meditation will hone that sharp intellect until it's truly formidable.

➤ **If you chose mostly Cs:** You think like a scientist. You don't like to put much stock into things you can't prove or that others before you haven't already proved. You also have the pioneering spirit of the scientist and you value a realistic, practical approach. Just the facts, ma'am! But don't think for a minute that you shouldn't try meditation. Valid and respected scientific studies have documented and continue to document the beneficial health effects of meditation. The human brain is a spectacular piece of equipment by any standards, and meditation is simply mind-body maintenance. Read up on the research. Investigate. Then, when you've found enough convincing data, give it a try. You won't be disappointed.

➤ **If you chose mostly Ds:** You are one of those jewels put on earth to help others. Even though you probably feel selfish sometimes, your modus operandi is service to humankind. Although they may not always show it, many admire you and don't know how you can give so much of your energy to others. It isn't easy! A life of service, whether as a teacher, a health practitioner or healer, a counselor, a spiritual leader, a volunteer, or even a parent can be exhausting and depleting. Meditation can be the one part of your day you give back to yourself so that you can keep on giving. Consider it more important than getting the oil changed in your car. Without it, you might well break down. And then, where would the world be?

➤ **If you chose mostly Es:** You don't like to get too serious too often, so we don't blame you if you don't get too engaged in this quiz. You laugh a lot at (and with) life, and you're probably a skeptic at heart. But even someone who's skeptical of belief systems (or all systems) can benefit from meditation. You'll likely revel in the inner bliss meditation could reveal for you. The world may not give you everything you want. People, institutions, and philosophies may continue to disappoint you. But everything you really want is right there inside you if you are willing to dive in and dig it out. C'mon—it'll be fun!

Bliss Byte

Another benefit of meditation is that it can help to resolve sleep problems. When you can voluntarily quiet the mind, you can get to sleep more easily, and the quality of your sleep will probably improve, too. Use the mind-body scan technique from Chapter 3, "Your Personal Mind-Body Scan," to help you relax into sleep. According to the Dalai Lama, sleepers can practice "dream yoga" by trying to achieve the clear light of sleep. This is a very advanced meditation skill that involves going one step beyond lucid dreaming (the conscious awareness that you are dreaming) to reach the conscious awareness of sleep itself. For more on sleep, read *The Complete Idiot's Guide to Getting a Good Night's Sleep* (Alpha Books, 1998).

Ethics for Everyone

Spending time determining your own ethics is far from a waste of time. Knowing what you believe is an important step toward knowing who you are and getting what you want and need in life. But each person's ethics are bound to be different—when it comes right down to it, your ethics are your own personal business (unless, of course, they result in your hurting others—then they become everyone's business).

But meditation, while not having anything to do with ethics itself, can help you in the complex process of defining your own belief system. Because it helps you to still that mental noise that is usually present, it can teach you to focus more deeply on yourself and what you believe, if that's where you choose to turn your focus.

Ethics certainly aren't reserved for Eastern philosophers or the religious world. To the ancient Greek philosopher Aristotle, ethics was a science and not by any stretch of the imagination a matter of opinion. In our modern culture, plenty of secular figures express their ethics and even serve as ethical models. Steven Spielberg, for example, makes movies such as *Schindler's List*, *Amistad*, and *Saving Private Ryan*, which express what it means to confront good and evil in a modern world. His movies explore what happens when ordinary people are placed in extraordinary circumstances where what they believe in is challenged. We watch the characters grapple with where and how to place their trust and loyalty.

Contemporary literary figures such as John Grisham continually address and investigate such issues as justice (*The Rainmaker*) and racism (*The Chamber*). The late physicist Carl Sagan, too, frequently addressed ethical issues, from abortion to the nature of religion itself and humankind's place in the universe.

The regular practice of meditation helps you to gain a quiet centering from which to contemplate what is important to you and why it's important. As you grow more confident in your "self" awareness, you'll be better able to deal with the complex decisions and issues that arise every day in our fast-paced, ever changing world. Instead of reacting, you'll be acting proactively, with a centered, deeply considered belief system that's come from within your self.

> **Mindful Minute**
>
> The word **meditation** comes from the Indian Sanskrit word *medha*, which can be translated as "doing the wisdom." It can also be traced to the Latin root *meditari*, which means "to muse or ponder."

Taking Refuge in the Dharma

Whatever you think about ethics (the subject or what your own ethics may be), one way to understand how the concept fits into meditation is to look at ethics from the perspective of another culture's philosophy. In yogic thought, ethics aren't a list of rules you're supposed to follow or even a philosophy. Instead, *yogis* believe in something called the *dharma*.

From A to Om

A **yogi** is someone who practices yoga—anyone...and that means you, too! (That is, if you practice yoga.)

Dharma, according to yogic thought, is variously translated, but you could call it the universal tendency or movement toward the good. The world is moved by it, the universe is fueled by it, and people can choose to live in it (sort of like stepping into a river), or choose to ignore it. If you choose to live in it, certain ways of thinking and certain actions will clearly be right or good, and others won't. But when you're standing there on the bank, how do you know if you want to step in or not? What, according to dharma, is right thinking, right action, and right speech? And if you do decide to live in the dharma, how do you know you'll know what's right?

Here are some of the meanings associated with the concept of dharma:

➤ Dharma comes from the root *dhri* meaning "to hold" or "to retain," leading to an understanding of dharma as "that which upholds and sustains."

➤ Ethically, dharma also signifies "righteous" or "virtue" according to yoga scholar Georg Feuerstein.

➤ Dharma can also refer to "form" or "quality" in a technical sense.

For Westerners, the whole concept of dharma can sound a little nebulous. We like our clear-cut, no-nonsense Ten Commandments, United States Constitution, that posted sign at the swimming pool that says "Children under 12 must be accompanied by adults." No doubt about the meaning of that one! But philosophically speaking, if you live in the dharma, you'll know what's right and what's wrong. But living in the dharma isn't easy. It takes effort (sort of like walking in a river). And those who have lived there in the past have given future dharma-seekers some rules to help make it a little easier.

From A to Om

Dharma is that which upholds and sustains. It is sometimes translated into English as "duty" or "ethics," but it exists apart from humans, as opposed to a moral code that humans devised.

You don't need to be a yogi to make the concept of dharma your own. You can take the guidelines for living and apply them to your own life without embracing any other religion or even philosophy. Read on to see what wise yogis recommend to make life easier, happier, and more fulfilling.

Rules for Living

Some of us love rules because they help us with how to reign in our behavior. Some of us hate them because we're free spirits and think we can make rules for ourselves. But there's no denying that rules can make life easier, as long as they are rules that make sense and promote a better existence. If one follows the order of the universe, life is harmonious. If not, chaos reigns—in the bigger picture, as well as the personal.

Rules do something else besides nudge us toward the dharma. They help us learn discipline. Now, maybe you're one of those few incredibly self-disciplined people who have no trouble eating right, exercising, and doing unto others as you would have them do unto you. But most of you probably have trouble, at least once in a while, maintaining discipline. But to get the most out of your meditation sessions, a little discipline helps a lot. And if you're living in a way that feels good and is in harmony with your ethics, the dharma—or whatever you think governs what's right and good— clearing your mind will be even easier.

In yogic thought, something exists called the *Eightfold Path*. It is a list of steps toward enlighten-ment, or pure consciousness. Following the Eightfold Path, step by step, is one way to work toward greater happiness in your life and in your soul. Meditation is step number seven! According to yogic thought, six other steps should be mas-tered first before meditation can be practiced well.

We aren't suggesting you work through the Eightfold Path in order. But knowing all the steps can offer you an interesting perspective and possible structure for your journey toward a better you. So why not take a look?

From A to Om

The **Eightfold Path** is a system of standards and guidelines for living (and eventually, for attaining enlightenment) recorded by the Indian sage Patanjali in his written text, the *Yoga Sutras*.

Yoga's Yamas

The first two steps of the Eightfold Path consist of two sublists. The first list is the *yamas*, or things that are helpful to avoid. The second list is *niyamas*, or things that are helpful to do. (The rest of the Eightfold Path will be described in the next chapter.) You can view these lists as guidelines for more successful living.

➤ **Do No Harm.** The first yama (*ahimsa*) is about nonviolence. Avoiding violence in your actions, your words, and even your thoughts is the point of this yama. That includes controlling your temper and not physically harming people, but it can also include avoiding negative thoughts about others and even about yourself. Not eating meat is a component of this yama for many yogis because to eat meat is to be complicit in the killing of an animal.

➤ **Tell No Lies.** The second yama (*satya*) is about truthfulness. It involves more than avoiding the big lies, like not reporting that extra little $300,000 of income you made last year. It also means being truthful about the little things like not telling a secret you promised not to tell or telling your boss you can't come into work because you've got the flu, when really you just feel like sleeping in and watching the soaps all day. Truthfulness builds character and personal integrity.

➤ **No More Stealing.** The third yama (*asteya*) is about refusing to steal, whether that means a candy bar, a million dollars in jewelry, or somebody else's great idea.

➤ **Cool It, Casanova.** The fourth yama (*brahmacharya*) is about chastity. No, we don't mean love is forbidden! Far from it. But this yama is about holding the opposite sex in high esteem and only joining physically with your partner when you can do so virtuously, in a committed and loving relationship of mutual respect. It also means rejecting casual sexual relationships and sex *solely* for the physical pleasure.

➤ **Don't Be Greedy.** The fifth yama (*aparigraha*) is about rejecting a materialistic way of thinking and living. It's about simplicity and learning to live only on what you need. Greed can manifest itself in other ways, too: monopolizing conversations, jealousy of the possessions of others, and dissatisfaction with your place in the world. (We don't mean you can't aim high in life, but we do mean that you can cultivate satisfaction with the unchangeable aspects.)

Yoga's Niyamas

The next list consists of things to do, rather than things not to do. Focus your attention on the following five qualities, and you'll be feeling great about yourself in no time!

➤ **Purity.** The first niyama (*shauca*) is about maintaining a study of the sacred texts of different religions, to inspire and teach you. And of course, it can be a productive component of a meditation practice.

➤ **Contentment.** The second niyama (*santosha*) is about finding happiness with what you have and with who you are. As we said before, that doesn't mean you can't improve yourself or attempt to get a better job, become healthier, or find more productive relationships. It does mean re-evaluating the obstacles in your path as opportunities and taking full responsibility for your own life.

➤ **Discipline.** The third niyama (*tapas*) is about discipline. Doing anything on a daily basis to improve your health (such as eating good food and exercising, even brushing your teeth!) is disciplined. So is practicing yoga or going to aerobics class, controlling your temper, getting your daily chores completed, or finishing that assignment at work before the deadline. Discipline isn't easy, but the more you cultivate it, the easier all the other yamas and niyamas, not to mention meditation, will become.

➤ **Self-Study.** The fourth niyama (*svadhyaya*) is about paying attention to who you are, what you do, how you feel and think, and what you believe. Don't just notice what you do, though. Think about it. Why do you always snap at your mother when she mentions your weight? Why do you always get a little blue when it rains? Do you act according to your beliefs? If not, are they really your beliefs, or do you have others you hadn't realized? Self-study can also involve the study of the sacred texts of different religions, to inspire and teach you. And of course, it can be a productive component of a meditation practice.

From A to Om

Niyamas are five yoga observances or personal disciplines: **shauca** means purity, or inner and outer cleanliness; **santosha** means contentment; **tapas** means self-discipline; **svadhyaya** means self-study; and **ishvara-pranidhana** means devotion.

➤ **Devotion.** The fifth niyama (*ishvara-pranidhana*) is about focusing on the divine, whatever that means to you. It doesn't mean you have to be religious or even believe in any sort of God, although that can certainly be one meaning. It can also mean simply letting go of your ego and the focus on yourself and looking outward to the highest ideal. It can also be as simple as your devotion to life itself!

Simple, right? Well, no, adhering to all the yamas and niyamas all the time isn't easy. But it will help you to control your behavior, your thinking, and your actions. And when you've got control over those, learning to meditate is a breeze!

Balancing Opposites: The Yin and the Yang of It

As we all struggle to find our own way in the world, through whatever methods work for us, we may also notice something else that can, once again, be best described by turning to the philosophy of another culture. This "something else" is, essentially, that our bodies, our minds, and our environments are in constant flux to find balance. If you've ever felt imbalanced by stress, physical exertion, mental effort, anger, or even love, you know what we mean.

In China (although many other cultures have since embraced the idea) exists the idea that the body is a microcosm of the world, and the

Mindful Minute

Yin and **yang** are two interconnected forces inherent in all things, and they describe the balance inherent in nature (it's we humans who get out of balance!). According to astrology, the Sun signs Taurus, Cancer, Virgo, Scorpio, Capricorn, and Pisces have yin energy, while Aries, Gemini, Leo, Libra, Sagittarius, and Aquarius have yang energy.

world is a microcosm of the universe. Therefore, qualities we ascribe to nature can also be ascribed to the body. One of the basic laws of this system is that everything in nature is balanced. Two interdependent forces exist, called *yin* and *yang*. These terms can be used to describe anything. For example, female, moon, and the body are yin; male, sun, and the mind are yang. Also, in everything that is primarily yin, there is also a bit of yang, and vice versa. The yin-yang symbol demonstrates this balance.

The yin-yang symbol illustrates the harmonious balance of opposites.

Because our mind-bodies and our environment are continuously balancing themselves, we may sometimes feel out of control. After that killer test where you wowed your teacher with your superior intellectual insights, your mind is suddenly incapable of remembering where you put your keys. When you get *too* yin, yang steps in. When you get *too* yang, yin steps in.

Of course, sometimes nature needs a little help, and Chinese medicine, for example, is based around balancing yin and yang (among other components of the mind-body) through herbal preparations and other medicines. To help you get your yin and yang in balance…you guessed it! Meditation can make you feel more balanced, no matter what terms you want to assign to the imbalance. It'll put some yang in your yin, some yin in your yang, and a spring in your step to boot! Yin and yang can also be thought of in terms of the Western medical concept of homeostasis—the body's constant re-balancing process to achieve harmony in relation to its environment.

Going Inward to Turn the Gaze Outward

Maybe all this Eastern philosophy is a little weird to you, and you aren't too excited about pursuing it, or maybe you think it's just your style and you'd like to read more. The point of introducing it all (admittedly in a very simplified form) is twofold:

1. We want to let you in on some other ways of thinking because the more you stretch your mind, the more flexible it will be.

2. We want to help you find ways to simplify, clarify, and control your thought process that will work in conjunction with your meditation practice.

3. We want to impress upon you the importance of looking inward.

Looking inward, really seeing inward, does so much more than reveal who you are, though that's certainly more than enough of a reason to practice it. It will also help you see the world in a whole new way, with new clarity, perspective, and joy. Looking at the world through the mirror of your own consciousness will reveal a reality you never knew existed—a world more beautiful and blissful than before.

Mindful Minute

Chinese medicine is a complex subject with many aspects, including the balance of yin and yang in the body. The branches of traditional Chinese medicine (also called TCM) are meditation, astrology and geomancy (divination through geography, lines, or figures), martial arts, diet, massage, acupuncture, moxibustion (burning herbs on the surface of the skin to stimulate healing), and herbal medicine.

The Least You Need to Know

➤ You don't have to be spiritual or religious to practice meditation successfully.

➤ Determining your own ethics or moral code can help you to gain control over your behavior and thoughts, facilitating the meditation process.

➤ Other cultures have different ways of looking at morality, good and evil, and right and wrong. Examining these various systems can help to open your mind to new ways of thinking.

➤ Learning to look inward will teach you how better to look outward.

The Soul Has Many Mansions

In This Chapter

➤ Meditation and your spiritual journey

➤ Teresa of Avila on the contemplative life

➤ More about yoga's Eightfold Path

➤ How many steps did the Buddha require?

➤ Making your own path

To start this chapter, we'd like to share a quote from Teresa of Avila, a sixteenth century nun and mystic, from her book *The Interior Castle*, which detailed the steps necessary for leading the contemplative or monastic life:

> *It is a shame and unfortunate that through our own fault we don't understand ourselves or know who we are. Wouldn't it show great ignorance, my daughters, if someone when asked who he was didn't know, and didn't know his father or mother or from what country he came? Well now, if this would be so extremely stupid, we are incomparably more so when we do not strive to know who we are, but limit ourselves to considering only roughly these bodies. Because we have heard and because faith tells us so, we know we have souls. But we seldom consider the precious things that can be found in this soul, or who dwells within it, or its high value. Consequently, little effort is made to preserve its beauty. All our attention is taken up with the plainness of the diamond's setting or the outer wall of the castle; that is, with these bodies of ours.*

Although most of you probably aren't considering entering a monastery anytime soon, you *can* live a contemplative life. We know you've got stuff to do. We all do. You've got places to go, people to see, money to earn, bills to pay, social ladders to climb, glass ceilings to shatter. We know what modern life is like. Still, the contemplative life is possible.

The challenge is to see life for what it is: a series of details. If the first thing on your priority list is to get ahead in your job and the 251st thing is to get to know yourself better, you'll have a lot harder time with those first 250 items on your list. Put "get better acquainted with myself" first, and everything else will make more sense.

How do you do that? We've been giving you some strategies, but let's go further. We'd like to introduce you to yourself, with the help of a few pretty hefty historical figures who long ago developed what you might call "systems of self-acquaintance."

Saint Teresa of Avila (1515–1582) was a Carmelite nun and Christian mystic from Spain who founded the religious order of the Discalced (also called Barefoot, literally "unshod"—the nuns often went without shoes or wore simple rope sandals) Carmelite nuns, who enforced strict observance of the original, severe Carmelite rules at the convent. (St. Teresa also wrote her *own* rule.) Teresa of Avila's writings, all published posthumously, are still read today. They include a spiritual autobiography, *The Way of Perfection*, which consisted of advice to her nuns; *The Interior Castle*, a description of the progressive steps involved in the contemplative life; and *The Foundations*, the story of the founding of the Discalced Carmelites. Teresa of Avila was canonized to sainthood by the Catholic Church in 1622; she was proclaimed a Doctor of the Church (the first woman to receive this honor) in 1970. Her feast day is October 15.

According to Teresa of Avila, the soul is like a magnificent castle filled with many mansions. If you spend all your time in one room, or just walking around the exterior of your castle admiring its walls (in other words, your external self), you're missing out on adventure, delight, and joy beyond description.

According to Patanjali, author of the *Yoga Sutras*, meditation is one of the latter steps in an eight-step journey toward enlightenment. The Buddha, too, advocated eight steps leading to enlightenment. Teresa of Avila, Patanjali, and the Buddha may be worlds apart in the details of their spiritual journeys, but their goals are essentially the same: total dissolution of the self and union with something higher.

But let's start with a brief discussion of you.

Putting Ethics to Work in the Mind-Body

How are you supposed to put your newfound (or old-and-familiar) ethical framework to work? How do you start looking inward and applying it to your outward behavior? And do you behave according to your beliefs? Do you tell yourself that stealing is wrong and then turn around and take credit for someone else's idea for that big new project at work? Do you proclaim that honesty is the best policy and then tell your kids the park is closed today because you really don't feel like going? Do you advocate nonviolence and then work out at the gym until you pull, tear, and strain every muscle in your body (violence to yourself counts!)?

In other words, are you internally and externally consistent?

Most of us aren't completely consistent. We're human. If you feel like your internal and external selves haven't even met, you can certainly move in the direction of a more unified you. One clue that you need a little more unification is if you try to meditate but feel you have no direction or clear purpose. Maybe you're afraid to completely clear your mind and quiet your thoughts. What if you don't like what you find? Maybe you're unsure about how meditation fits into the rest of your life, your beliefs, and your spiritual journey.

Mindful Minute

The book of Psalms in the Bible's Old Testament mentions the word "meditation" several times. A few examples (Revised Standard Version): "My mouth shall speak wisdom; the meditation of my heart shall be understanding" (Psalm 49:3); "Oh, how I love thy law! It is my meditation all the day" (Psalm 119:97); "I have more understanding than all my teachers, for thy testimonies are my meditation" (Psalm 119:99).

Why not take a look at history and those who have devoted their lives to the pursuit in question for answers and guidance? Let's get some advice from some of the great truth-seekers.

St. Teresa of Avila's House of Meditation

Many great thinkers, philosophers, and mystics throughout history, associated with every religion imaginable, have put together methods for spiritual progress. St. Teresa of Avila is one of them. Teresa of Avila supposedly received many visions of the afterlife and the other spiritual realms, and struggled her entire life with both physical pain and suffering (she was chronically ill) and spiritual suffering, as she attempted to find a path to ultimate spiritual union with her God. Nonetheless, she is said to have been a jolly, clever, charismatic, and eloquent person who was both extremely disciplined and surprisingly fun.

Much of her writing involves methods of prayer and contemplation, and she often speaks of dissolving attachments to earthly things, mastering the passions, and transcending desire (concepts familiar to both Western and Eastern philosophical traditions). In her famous work, *The Interior Castle*, she lists seven mansions, or steps, toward spiritual union (or, in Catholic-speak, spiritual marriage). Although much of what she says involves medieval concepts such as intentional suffering, self-defilement, spiritual guilt, and penance (people were pretty tough on themselves back then!), many of her revelations are still relevant for the truth-seeker in today's kinder, gentler spiritual climate.

Below, we'll list her mansions for you, but we'll give you updated descriptions (ours, not St. Teresa's, though based on hers) of what they are and how to use them—a sort of twenty-first century Interior Castle! No self-defilement required, and you're even allowed to wear shoes!

Relax

If you constantly condemn yourself for what you didn't, couldn't, and shouldn't have done or said, try this exercise: Look in a mirror. Don't judge, just look. Now, notice where your eyes are. Well, look at that! They're on the front of your face, not the back of your head. So stop looking backward. Look forward and embrace the present moment. You can't do anything about the past, but you can make "right now" great!

➤ **The Mansion of Humility.** In this first mansion, the search for truth begins with a sort of ego confrontation. In this mansion, you ask your soul, "Who do you think you are, anyway?" If the answer involves the external (I'm a doctor, a parent, a teacher, rich, poor, pretty, too fat, a slob, a perfectionist, the owner of a really cool car, etc.), then you've got some illusions to dissolve. Take away everything that has to do with the outside world and look at what's left. Keep looking until you see something. Don't worry. You're in there somewhere!

➤ **The Mansion of Meditation.** Actually, Teresa called this the "mansion of the practice of prayer," but she frequently used prayer and meditation interchangeably. To her, prayer was that same sort of inner-looking and slowing of the thought process often described as meditation. In this mansion, the truth-seeker (that's you!) begins to do the work of quiet sitting, observation, and looking inward, as well as outward communion with others on the same path. This stage is tough. You'll confront lots of inner resistance (boredom, restlessness, even a rebelliousness against the required discipline of sitting). You'll also start to discover that you won't be able to do anything very well unless you get to know yourself better—that awkward "the more you know, the less you know" stage! You might even wish you'd never embarked on this difficult journey. But persevere—riches are forthcoming!

➤ **The Mansion of the Exemplary Life.** This is the mansion where you practice "walking your talk" (or "walking your thought"?). Once you've confronted your inner self and your beliefs, how can you manifest that inner you? This stage can be frustrating, too. It's one thing to have a spiritual revelation about truth, but quite another to act on it. According to Teresa of Avila, complete renunciation of the self is necessary to make it through this stage. Otherwise, you'll just burn out. (No, she didn't exactly say "burn out," but that's what she meant.) Whether acting according to your beliefs means simply deciding to stop fudging the truth, leading a simpler material life, or actually changing the course of your life to champion an important cause, such as health care or education, this mansion will help you to evolve. How? By transforming the outer you to be more consistent with the inner you.

➤ **The Mansion of Spiritual Consolation.** This is where the bliss begins to set in. Once you've reached this step, you'll start to attain little moments of pure joy. They won't last long. They won't be the sumptuous dinner that is enlightenment, but they'll be like little enlightenment hors d'oeuvres. The Buddhist term for this brief bliss byte is *satori*. As you move toward self-actualization and true knowledge of the inner you, you will finally be getting some payoff. But keep working—according to St. Teresa, you're not there yet!

➤ **The Mansion of Incipient Union.** This stage, according to Teresa of Avila, is beyond description. In this mansion, thought is no longer possible and has been transcended. St. Teresa compares this stage to a butterfly who has broken free from its cocoon and, no longer a lowly worm, is able to fly. Yet, the butterfly can't find any place satisfactory to land. It searches for the divine because it is no longer "of" the earth. Attachments, desires, and material possessions are nothing to the butterfly, and seekers at this stage may despair at having to deal with mundane details necessary for life. They are so close to pure consciousness! Teresa emphasizes, though, that as tempting as it may be to revel in that butterfly state, continuing to do good works and serve humankind is crucial. Even if you aren't "of" the world, you still must and should be "in" the world.

➤ **The Mansion of Favors and Afflictions.** This stage is one step away from spiritual union with the divine, and it's tough. At this stage, according to Teresa, the seeker has distinguished him- or herself fairly obviously as having accomplished an amazing spiritual feat. But good and bad come with distinguishing oneself. Some might think that anyone this spiritual must be a little bit wacko. Others might praise and even worship the seeker of truth, and it isn't easy to ignore worship. The danger is in taking the credit or the glory because then the external self becomes re-engaged and all that work is for nothing. This mansion has lots of delights, too, however. Being this close to pure bliss is like standing in the lobby during a concert. You can hear the beautiful music, but it's a little muffled, and you can't actually see. Yet, you are nonetheless stricken with the beauty of the sound.

➤ **The Mansion of Spiritual Union.** Teresa actually calls this stage the "Mansion of Spiritual Marriage," but we like "Union" better. At this stage, at long last, the seeker becomes one with God (or the universe, nature, Great Spirit, love—whatever works for you). The butterfly is dead, and happy to be so because now it is fully absorbed into a greater, more blissful, perfect existence.

Whew! Okay, we admit that's all a little heavy—but she was a medieval mystic, after all. Some, or all, or possibly none of these "mansions" may appeal to you as worthy of exploration. But if they do, well, there they are for your contemplation!

Bliss Byte

Some historical figures who were spiritual leaders also sometimes tended toward extremes, whether of self-mortification or other manifestations of religious fervor. More often, however, spiritual leaders in all religions advocate moderation. The Buddha advised his disciples to avoid both extreme sensual indulgence and extreme self-mortification. According to the Buddha, sensual indulgence is low, coarse, vulgar, ignoble, and unprofitable, retarding spiritual progress, while self-mortification is painful, ignoble, unprofitable, and weakening to the intellect. Instead, the Buddha advocated the Middle Way, which he said opens the eyes and bestows understanding, which leads to peace of mind, to the higher wisdom, and to full enlightenment.

The Struggle Toward Bliss

If you take nothing else from Teresa of Avila's mansions of the soul, take this: The journey toward spiritual fulfillment isn't easy. It's a struggle. Meditation, your primary vehicle on your journey, is difficult, too. You get bored. You get restless. Your mind races. Your mind wanders. You get an excruciating itch on your lower back. Your posterior keeps falling asleep, then that tingling sensation down your right leg… arghhhh!

But your journey will also be fraught with joys, little moments of bliss, and revelation after revelation about yourself and your place in the world. And then one day, nirvana!

Meditation Is Only One Stop from Nirvana!

Of course, Christian mystics don't have a premium on steps to enlightenment. Remember Patanjali's Eightfold Path? We introduced the first two steps, the abstentions, or yamas, and observances, or niyamas, in the last chapter. The other six steps complete the Eightfold Path, which is designed to lead those who follow it to eventual enlightenment, or to a state of pure consciousness and complete union with nature, the universe, God, Great Spirit, or once again, whatever holds ultimate meaning for you.

The Eightfold Path is meant to be practiced in order. Meditation is actually number seven, just before enlightenment! According to Patanjali, the behavior, the body, the breath, the senses, and the concentration must first be mastered before meditation can be practiced successfully. Of course, that doesn't mean you have to master each level before you can give meditation a try. The Eightfold Path might not be the exact path for you. But if you do like the idea of going by the (yoga) book, check out the rest of the Eightfold Path.

You can also think of the steps of the Eightfold Path as limbs spreading from a growing tree. Each step, or limb, is practiced with the others and becomes part of an organic whole. As you progress along the Eightfold Path, your understanding of each element of the path deepens and flourishes. You are the tree of life! *You* are the path.

Work Out: Control Your Body (Asana)

The third step (after step one, the yamas, and step two, the niyamas—see the previous chapter) of the Eightfold Path involves body control, or the practice of *asana*. Asana are the postures of yoga that most people think of when they think of yoga. Learning the postures of yoga helps to control the body so that it remains both steady and comfortable. It isn't easy to meditate well (let alone attain enlightenment!) if you aren't comfortable in your body. If you are flexible, strong, and feeling great, your body is less likely to "get in the way" during the special time you've reserved for meditation.

Learning the yoga poses can be a lifelong endeavor. The poses range from simple to extremely challenging, and although people of any fitness level can practice yoga, the advanced poses take remarkable strength, flexibility, balance, and control. Opportunities to learn yoga abound. Look for classes in your area, rent one of the many yoga videos, or read a good yoga book.

Yoga poses can actually be a sort of meditation on their own, too. If your mind becomes calm and centered, focused on nothing but the feel of the poses, then you're practicing a variety of moving meditation. A few sitting yoga poses are particularly helpful to the practice of meditation, as well. See Part 5, "Ready, Set, OM!" for more on seated, walking, and movement meditation.

Mindful Minute

Patanjali was probably born between 200 B.C. and A.D. 400. He is the author of the *Yoga Sutras*, a collection of aphorisms in Sanskrit that have largely defined the modern practice of yoga. Although no one knows exactly who Patanjali was, some call him the Adhisesa, or the first servant of God who, being close to God, was privy to divine insight. Patanjali culled the sections from the Vedas (those ancient Hindu spiritual texts) having to do with the mind and relevant to yoga, then organized them into short, essential, universal aphorisms meant to be more accessible than the vast text of the Vedas.

From A to Om

In the yoga sutras, **asana** refers to the pose of sitting, keeping the body still, for meditation. All the other poses are part of other systems, Hatha Yoga, mainly.

Sitting with the spine upright and aligned helps to increase alertness. Photo by Saeid Lahouti.

Come Up for Air: Breath Control (Pranayama)

The journey of meditation begins breathing exercises are excellent meditation preparation. Breathing does more than give you something to focus on. According to yoga philosophy, it infuses your body with the very force of life. In Sanskrit, breath control is known as *pranayama. Prana* is a word for the life force that flows in, through, and around all living things, and even animates the Earth itself and the entire universe. It is pure energy, and the only way to fill yourself with it is to breathe—and breathe well.

From A to Om

Prana is a form of energy in the universe that animates all physical matter, including the human body, and is taken into the body through the breath. **Pranayama** is the practice of breathing exercises designed to help you master control of the breath and to help infuse your body with prana.

Pranayama practice works to change the mind; the breath also relates directly to the mind. Our state of mind is linked to the quality of the prana within. As the mind changes, so does the quality of the prana; we influence the flow of prana by influencing the breath. These are all linked together: mind, prana, breath. Pranayama exercises are designed to aid you in increasing the prana within you and to allow the prana to flow properly and freely; working with the breath and mind allow you to achieve this. Just breathing in doesn't mean you're inhaling prana. You need to use both the breath and your mind to effect a positive change in your body; then, and only then, does prana enter to nourish and restore you.

How hard can it be to breathe? Most people tend to breathe with rather shallow breaths, but breathing techniques teach you how to breathe more deeply, from the abdomen up, to take fullest advantage of both oxygen and prana. In Western medicine, certain medical problems are attributed to having insufficient oxygen in the bloodstream, something that deep breathing can address. Some Western holistic health practitioners maintain that deep breathing can be an important preventive health practice. In Eastern medicine, disease is sometimes believed to be caused by too little prana inside the body. Again, deep breathing can correct that imbalance.

And like the yoga postures, deep breathing itself can be a meditative practice. Many basic descriptions of how to meditate advocate simply paying attention to the breath, hearing and feeling it as it moves in and out of the body. Through attention to the breath, the mind becomes focused and the chaos of mental activity can rest.

Try this deep breathing exercise as a way to center yourself before or during meditation. Breathe comfortably; no part of the breath(ing) should be forced or strained.

➤ Place your hands on your abdomen.

➤ As you inhale, expand your abdomen and feel your hands push outward.

➤ As you exhale, relax your abdomen down.

This abdominal breathing helps to strengthen the diaphragm muscle at the base of your lungs, an important muscle in our respiration.

When you breathe deeply, you can feel your breath moving in and out. Concentrate and you can feel your lower back expand on inhalation, too.

Empty to Be Full: Detachment (Pratyahara)

The next branch of the Eightfold Path is detachment, or *pratyahara*. This step involves losing your senses. No, we don't mean going crazy! We mean learning to shut off your sense impressions—just temporarily, of course.

We have senses for good reason. They help us survive, enjoy life, and stay both safe and healthy. Who wouldn't want to be able to smell a rose garden, see a brilliant sunset over the ocean, taste a freshly picked apple, or feel a cool spring breeze? But sometimes the senses can be distracting and may even become a source of obsessive behavior. It's one thing to savor every bite of a piece of delicious chocolate cake. It's another to be so obsessed with chocolate (or red wine or bacon or taco chips or whatever) that you binge on it every day.

From A to Om

Pratyahara is the practice of withdrawing the senses and focusing inward.

Senses can also distract us from meditation, and learning to suppress them is an important skill for successful meditation. Just imagine trying to meditate in a room filled with the aroma of baking bread or the sound of blaring music, or in a place that is uncomfortably cold. It isn't easy to focus inward, but it's even harder if your external environment continually engages your senses.

Meditation is therefore best practiced in an environment with few sensual distractions. But even in a quiet room alone, the senses can still be a distraction. An itch here, a sore knee there, a pang of hunger, the sound of a dog barking down the street. Therefore, practicing withdrawing the senses can help with meditation. It isn't easy, but when the external world fades away, you'll be able to look inside yourself without distraction. Besides, your senses need an occasional rest, just like the rest of you!

Bliss Byte

If withdrawing all your senses at once seems overwhelming, try one sense at a time! Try this exercise with a trusted partner. One person is blindfolded, the other person leads the blindfolded person around a garden, pausing at various places so the blindfolded person can explore minus sight and via the other senses. Have you ever caressed and truly felt the incredible silkiness of a white pine? Smelled the pungent aroma of a marigold? Touched a willow leaf to your cheek?

Don't Panic, Focus: Concentration (Dharana)

Most of us know what it's like to be unable to concentrate, especially when we're tired, hungry, or under a lot of stress. The next step, or limb, in the Eightfold Path involves the practice of concentration. Concentration isn't just something that randomly happens. It takes practice, and the more you learn how to cultivate it, the better at it you will become. Some meditation techniques involve concentrating on one thing: an object like a candle flame or a *mandala*, a sound like the sound of your breath or a mantra, or even a single thought. The point is to concentrate until you have dissolved all boundaries between yourself and the object of your concentration, and can then see that you and the object and indeed, all of existence, are one.

From A to Om

Dharana is the technique of orienting the mind toward a single point in order to cultivate concentration.

But long before you reach such a stage, you can still get a lot better at concentrating than you are today. Just keep practicing at it. Impossible as it seems the first time you try, you'll steadily improve with persistence. The ability to concentrate will not only make your meditation more productive, but will help you in many other aspects of your life.

If you're looking for something to use as a point of concentration, try any of the following (each involves engaging one of the senses primarily). Sit

From A to Om

A **mandala** is a beautiful, usually circular geometric design that draws the eye to its center and can be used as a point of focus in meditation.

a comfortable distance away from the object so that you are not straining to see, hear, or smell it, or become overwhelmed by its close presence. To immerse the self fully in the object brings one to a sense of appreciation of the beauty that exists within as well as without.

Objects to look at:

➤ A candle flame or burning end of an incense stick

➤ A favorite small figurine

➤ A drawn or painted symbol, such as a circle or square

➤ A flower

➤ A clear container of water

Sounds:

➤ The sound of your own breath

➤ The sound of your own voice repeating a mantra

➤ Soothing music

➤ The sound of the ocean or the wind in the trees

➤ A bell, chime, or gong

Aromas:

➤ Burning incense

➤ Essential oil in a warmer

➤ A home-cooked meal or a fresh-baked pie

➤ An aromatic flower or herb

➤ A wood-burning fire in a wood stove, fireplace, or campfire

Ideas:

➤ Love

➤ Nature

➤ God

➤ Peace

➤ Who are you?

Feeling Great? Meditate: Meditation (Dhyana)

From A to Om

Dhyana is the Sanskrit word for meditation, and refers to the process of quieting the mind to free it from preconceptions, illusions, and attachments.

The penultimate leg of the Eightfold Path is the actual practice of meditation. With the ability to control your body and your breath, as well as your senses and concentration, meditation will be easier and more productive. At this stage of the game, the goal of meditation is to move beyond the ability to concentrate. You are on the verge of realizing your ultimate union with the world around you. You are part of nature, part of the natural scheme, part of God or Great Spirit or love or divinity. When everything else falls away—physical and mental distractions, attachment to material things, even sensual awareness, pure being—samadhi is what's left.

Last Stop, Nirvana: Pure Consciousness (Samadhi)

And then you're there! Pure consciousness, samadhi, nirvana, absolute bliss—to Patanjali and to many thinkers and meditators before and after him, this is the final and ultimate goal of meditation. Can you really attain it? Of course—many have before you.

That doesn't mean you will experience it yet, however. That's fine. But who knows…the more you meditate, the more you contemplate, the more you study yourself, the more you learn to control your behavior, your body, your breath, your senses, and your concentration, the more you might find yourself being drawn to the idea of pure consciousness. It's your call and your journey, but as you travel, it never hurts to keep an open mind. Sometimes that other fork in the road looks a little more interesting than the one you'd planned to take.

How will you know when you've reached enlightenment? We offer this ancient Chinese proverb: "Before I was enlightened, I saw a tree. After I was enlightened, I saw a tree." Start looking!

From A to Om

Samadhi is the Sanskrit term for the state in meditation when perfect bliss and union with all things is achieved. Consciousness alone shines forth!

Buddha Says, Get It Right!

Patanjali wasn't the only great thinker with an Eightfold Path. The Buddha advocated one, too, but his steps are a little different. According to the Buddha, suffering can be eliminated by adopting the Middle Way of self-conquest, which means avoiding extremes and working to eliminate selfish desire, which is the root of all suffering in the world. To do this, the Buddha suggests eight steps:

➤ **Right Understanding.** This step involves seeing life as impermanent and full of suffering, understanding the nature of existence and of the moral law, and understanding the cycle of *reincarnation*, or birth, death, and rebirth that continues until the seeker has attained enlightenment.

Mindful Minute

Suffering, according to yogic and Buddhist thought, is that idea that we're unhappy because we don't have something or, if we do have it, we're afraid we're going to lose it. There is no security or permanence in life, as we know it. **Dukha** (suffering) is sometimes translated as "dissatisfaction." It can also be understood as incompleteness. Only enlightenment brings freedom from these human states.

Bliss Byte

Reincarnation is the belief that the soul evolves in different incarnations and physical bodies or guises. Each life is uniquely individual. We are not just the same person born over and over again, but really a progression, as the Dalai Lama says, like beads on a string, separate. As Teresa of Avila would say, from moth to butterfly. Once enlightenment is achieved, the soul is released from the cycle of rebirth.

➤ **Right Thought.** This step requires that the mind be kept free from sensual desire, cruelty, and negative thinking. Also, the mind should be ready to disregard anything that hinders its progress toward enlightenment, a single-mindedness toward liberation.

➤ **Right Speech.** This step means not lying, gossiping, or speaking harshly of anyone. Behind this step lies the philosophy that thought and action are inseparable. What you speak, you will eventually live. Also, right speech shouldn't be too loud or passionate and shouldn't arouse the emotions of others. It should be calm, straightforward, sincere, unprejudiced, kind, and wise.

➤ **Right Action.** This step has five substeps: 1. No killing, but instead practicing love and nonviolence; 2. No stealing, but instead being generous; 3. Practicing self-control and not abusing the senses; 4. Speaking sincerely and honestly; and 5. Not drinking alcohol or taking intoxicating drugs, but instead being restrained and mindful.

➤ **Right Livelihood or Vocation.** This step means that the seeker should only pursue an occupation that is just, nonviolent, and not misleading to others. Traditionally for Buddhists, the following jobs are considered "wrong living": arms dealing, slave trading, flesh trading (whether prostitution or selling meat for food), selling intoxicating drinks, and selling poison. This would include soldiers (arms dealing), fishermen and hunters (flesh trading), and anything to do with financial greed. It isn't the making of money that's frowned upon but the motivation. If it is a selfish, all-consuming action for its own sake, there's the rub. Instead, the seeker should look for ways to serve humankind.

➤ **Right Effort.** This step means working toward a better self by attempting to keep wise thoughts, words, and deeds in the forefront of the mind, while attempting to banish unhealthy or unwise thoughts, words, and deeds.

➤ **Right Mindfulness.** This step means keeping constantly alert to and aware of the state of the body, the emotions, the mind, and the intellect. Mindfulness is thought to keep the seeker from being led astray by untruth. It is a sort of "living meditation," in which the intellect (what Buddhists believe is merely the sixth sense) is kept active in order to make the seeker more in-tune with the true nature of reality.

➤ **Right Concentration.** This last stage is similar to Patanjali's final step. Its goal is to be able to concentrate so wholly and completely on a single object that all desire is overcome and true knowledge of the object is attained. This is accomplished via meditation, in which one sits quietly, patiently pushing all thoughts aside. With practice, right concentration can be attained and the five hindrances—sensuality, ill will, lethargy, restlessness and worry, and skeptical doubt—can be overcome. Eventually, the seeker will find the way to pure consciousness, or nirvana.

The Greatest Journey Begins with a Single Step

Yet, don't let the lofty sound of "pure consciousness" deter you. We know, we keep repeating it—but we aren't trying to be intimidating or discouraging. As we've said, "enlightenment" needn't be your ultimate goal in meditation. Maybe you just want a good, easy stress-management technique you can squeeze into your morning or after-work routine without having to attend a class or put on workout clothes. Great! In fact, goals of any kind should be put aside in meditation practice. Your path will come clear the more you meditate.

We're just giving you options, a little history, and the fruits of some of the great meditators to ponder, consider, discard if you like, adapt as you like, or tuck away in a corner of your mind-body for later.

Mindful Minute

According to Buddhist thought, meditation is being fully aware in the current moment. It is not sitting a certain way, holding the hands a certain way, or breathing a certain way. These are simply techniques to help us become more aware of the true nature of our selves.

No matter what your reasons for, or method of, meditation, taking that first step and making the commitment to begin a meditation practice is making a commitment to your physical health, your mental health, and your emotional well-being. It is taking care of yourself. It is akin to uttering a resounding "Yes!" to life, to living, to truly being alive. It is a decision to wake up. Good morning! It's going to be a beautiful day.

The Least You Need to Know

➤ Lots of historical figures have developed systems for spiritual development.

➤ Saint Teresa of Avila wrote of the concept of different "mansions" of the soul that need to be explored to reach eventual union with God: humility, practice of prayer, the exemplary life, spiritual consolation, incipient union, favors and afflictions, and the mansion of spiritual union or marriage.

➤ Patanjali delineated eight steps that lead to enlightenment: certain abstentions, observances, exercises, breath control, control of the senses, concentration, meditation, and finally, pure consciousness.

➤ The Buddha also suggested eight steps to enlightenment: Right Understanding, Right Thought, Right Speech, Right Action, Right Livelihood, Right Effort, Right Mindfulness, and Right Concentration.

➤ You don't have to follow anyone else's spiritual method, but you can use the ideas of others to help craft your own journey of self-discovery through meditation.

Say a Little Prayer

Let's talk about prayer. The word "prayer" has a lot of connotations for a lot of people. Prayer can be as individual and unique as each human being.

Just as the word "meditation" may have negative connotations to people of certain religious beliefs, the word "prayer" may have negative connotations to people who aren't affiliated with any religion or who have rejected religion for a variety of reasons. Still others use the words "prayer" and "meditation" interchangeably. But if you want to get really technical, there is sometimes a difference between meditation and prayer. Meditation is an inward looking, listening, observing, and/or being present in the moment. Prayer is directed outward, toward something (or someone), whether that means talking or simply perceiving.

But then there's meditative prayer! There are several definitions of prayer and meditation; some make them indistinguishable, some make them one and the same. You'll need to explore the relationship between prayer and meditation that feels comfortable to you.

Bliss Byte

One simple way to combine prayer and meditation is to meditate using, as a mantra, the word "God." (If "God" doesn't work for you, try "love" or "peace.") Repeat it slowly, focusing on the sound of the word. Imagine that the air you breathe in and out, and which carries the sound waves of your mantra, are filled with divine spirit.

But perceiving what? The answers to that one are as varied as the people reading this book. Up to this point, we've used a lot of different words to express the idea of a higher power—God, nature, the universe, universal consciousness, Great Spirit, Goddess, love—all attempting to describe something we can't ever fully describe.

But why describe that higher power? It's more interesting, certainly more productive, to commune with it, speak to it, and experience it. Even if you don't know what it is, even if you can't quite agree with any particular theology or organized religion or creed, even if you aren't convinced anything is actually "up there" or "out there," why not try speaking to it? Heck, if the scientists feel space exploration is a legitimate endeavor, you can certainly send out a prayer up there and see what happens.

If you do have faith in a higher being or consciousness, refining and regulating your communication, communion, or conversations may work wonders in your life. Prayer can serve as a source of great inner strength, confidence, and faith.

Bliss Byte

Some people can relate better to the idea of a Goddess than a God. Goddess can be variously interpreted, as Mother Earth; as one of the great goddesses of mythology such as Athena, Artemis, or Persephone; or as the feminine principle in the universe. Try this goddess prayer/meditation: Sit quietly, close your eyes, and imagine the universe as the mother of the world. Imagine her taking you in her arms and rocking you. Feel her pure love, unaffected by anything you have ever done or said or become. Let her rock you in this love and feel the peace of complete acceptance. Let yourself be a child, complete and fully taken care of and loved.

You Gotta Have Faith

How can you have a conversation if you're the only one talking? Ah, but you aren't! That's the wonderful part. If you talk to the universe, the universe will talk back to you. (Just so we remain completely unaffiliated with a particular belief system, we'll use the term "universe" for the purposes of this chapter. Substitute any word you like—God, Goddess, Nature, Great Spirit—in your own mind if that helps.)

No, you won't hear a booming baritone voice reverberating from the backlit clouds. Sure, if the universe could afford his fee, it might hire James Earl Jones to speak for it, but the universe doesn't deal in fees. It speaks in more subtle ways, and to get the message, you have to pay attention.

And to pay attention, you have to have faith. If you are one of the many out there who attended church or synagogue as a child and no longer make a habit of it, you probably remember hearing a lot about faith. "If only you had faith…" You'd be successful, loved, happy, well adjusted, and everything would go your way. Uh-huh. Right? Hmmm…

Well, faith isn't a meal ticket. You can't wish your problems away simply because you have "faith" they'll disappear. On the other hand, strongly believing does influence the vibrations of the universe (or, so we strongly believe!). So perhaps having faith that things will work out, that you can find happiness, and so forth, can help to effect the change.

We need, though, to distinguish between faith and simply having a positive attitude. Faith is more than wearing rose-colored glasses. And it's not the same thing as hope. Faith is an abiding inner certainty. As your practice of meditation deepens and grows, so should an inner sense of belief that will lead you to have faith in what you "know." Even if that faith means going against the grain or embracing something that isn't readily apparent.

Whether your faith is rooted in religious traditions, or whether it comes from somewhere else, meditation is a great way to explore and strengthen your own personal belief system. Faith doesn't have to be about religion, but it is a part of every person's spiritual growth on the path to self-actualization. When "having faith" and "knowing" begin to seem like two sides of the same coin, you're getting close to a yoga definition of enlightenment. You don't have to be convinced of what you already know! Following the mystical path is all about knowledge based on experience. What others must take on faith, the mystic "knows."

Many religions have mystical subgroups. Kabbalah and Hasidism are two branches of the Jewish religion that emphasize Judaism's mystical aspects. Sufis and dervishes are mystical branches of Islam. Christian mystics from the Middle Ages, such as St. John of the Cross, St. Teresa of Avila, and Dame Julian of Norwich, are still well known today for their insightful writing. Many different branches of *mysticism* share similar meditation techniques, often indistinguishable from eastern techniques such as Zen or yoga meditation. Rather than externally directed prayer, mystical meditation tends to be a more internalized listening, stilling of the mind, and obliteration of the senses in an attempt to directly perceive divinity or receive guidance.

What Do You Mean by Faith?

But what is faith, exactly? *Webster's New World Dictionary* lists several definitions:

1. *Unquestioning belief, specif. in God, religion, etc.*

   We aren't too keen on that one, just because we don't like the "unquestioning" part. Questioning is good, healthy, and so human.

2. *A particular religion.*

   Sure, you can be of the Jewish faith, the Islamic faith, the Christian faith, or of any number of faiths out there. But still, that's not the one we're looking for. Onward.

3. *Complete trust or confidence.*

   That's the one!

From A to Om

Mysticism is the belief in direct experience of God, universal consciousness, or intuitive truth. James H. Austin, M.D., author of *Zen and the Brain*, defines mysticism as "the ongoing practice of reestablishing, by the deepest insights, one's direct relationship with the ultimate, universal reality principle."

Faith is a conviction that rests upon the foundation of our own personal moral and ethical belief systems. If you're feeling depressed or that life is overwhelming, meditation can be a great way to go to the heart of what you believe and to build a solid sense of knowing, and of self-esteem, that will help you move toward happiness and well being. We do build our faith. As personal conviction grows in meditation, so too does the strength to sustain a faith that really *will* become equivalent with "knowing" or "enlightenment."

Bliss Byte

Looking for a new way to express your faith? Why not try a pilgrimage? Visit a place you wouldn't normally visit that holds spiritual significance for you (see Chapter 27, "Om Away from Om: Spiritual Travel," for a list of sacred places around the world). The birth- or death-place of a spiritual leader, perhaps; an ancient place of worship; even just a beautiful place in nature that you think reflects some higher power's creation, manifestation, or action. Once you are there, spend quiet time meditating, soaking up the essence of the place. Use all your senses. Then, send out a prayer of thanks for the experience.

And That Higher Power Thing?

Some of you may suspect we are avoiding the issue of religious faith. Well, sort of. We don't want to focus on one particular religion, and the particulars of our own religious beliefs aren't relevant here. But we will say that if you have faith in a certain creed, a God with certain characteristics, a philosophy of reality, or simply in a conscious higher power that bestows meaning to life, you are probably more content, happy, and confident than someone who believes life is meaningless. You are also less likely to suffer from or even die from a variety of illnesses, according to several medical studies. But more on that later in Chapter 26, "Rx: Meditation."

Take this opportunity to think about what you do believe. Since many polls have revealed that approximately 90 percent of Americans pray, chances are you (or the person next to you) believe prayer does *something*. We like to think that we are all encircled by and radiating a guiding universal force and energy, that we can communicate with it, that it *is us*, and that it can help us in our lives. Prayer is a method of communicating with it, and can work in concert with meditation for a fuller, more spiritual experience. Think of prayer and meditation as the right and left foot. Coordinate them, and you can go anywhere!

Mindful Minute

Do you believe in angels? If you do, you aren't alone. According to one poll, 72 percent of all Americans, 76 percent of all teenagers, and 78 percent of all women believe in angels. Some people talk to their guardian angel. Others say that a distinct and unmistakable voice tells them when trouble is happening, such as when a child is in danger. Many of these people never believed in angels until they had an experience with them.

We're All Connected

But prayer doesn't absolutely have to focus on a higher power. We can also focus on each other. As we said before, prayer reaches outward, while meditation reaches inward. You can reach outward toward a higher power, and you can reach outward toward your fellow humans, even to the Earth itself. Prayer has a mystical power to it, no matter what religion it is based in, and studies have shown that prayer, whether religious or nonreligious (in the form of directed healing thoughts), may actually have a measurable effect.

From A to Om

Sentient beings are human beings or any kind of beings who share the characteristic of consciousness and the ability to perceive.

All *sentient* beings on the Earth have something in common: We are all sentient beings on the Earth! We are all connected to each other and to some force that animates us, whether that means we were created by it or are suffused with it at this moment, or both. Why not use this interconnectedness to heal each other and heal the world?

According to those who teach and practice Transcendental Meditation, or TM, large groups of people meditating can actually influence world events by altering the vibrations of the universe. TM was introduced to the West by the Maharishi Mahesh Yogi, who came to the United States in 1955 after graduating from Allahabad University with a degree in physics, studying for 13 years with Swami Brahmananda Saraswati (a world-famous teacher) and spending two years in the Himalayas in silence (talk about a long meditation session!). In the 1960s, the Maharishi had many celebrities as students, including The Beatles and the Beach Boys. Today, TM is the most studied form of meditation. Over 4,000 pages in over 100 scientific journals have appeared describing scientific studies on the effects of TM.

Herman Melville Knew It!

If you're one of the many people out there who was assigned to read *Moby Dick* in school and never quite finished it (or never quite started it!), you might not have gotten to the chapter called "The Monkey-Rope." In that chapter, Ishmael and Queequeg (two of the primary characters) are tied together with a long rope. Ishmael stands on the deck of the whaling ship and Queequeg stands far below on the back of the whale, stripping off the whale blubber. Queequeg's job is hazardous, and he runs the risk of slipping or being tossed into the sea. And if Queequeg goes, Ishmael goes with him.

How like Ishmael and Queequeg we all are! Ishmael goes on to consider this—how every human is intricately and even perilously connected to so many others. In today's age of communications, we are even more connected than ever before. Imagine how reliant you are on your telephone, your fax machine, your computer. Think how crucial your coworkers are to the performance of your job; how important are those who provide you with the means to buy food, clothing, shelter, who have organized systems that allow us to heat and cool our houses, have running water, or electricity. Not to mention the emotional importance of your personal relationships!

We're also connected by our mutual sense of obligation to each other, support of each other, and need for each other. We find life partners so we can have someone for physical and emotional support. We need friends to talk to and spend time with. We need parents to protect us in childhood, and then, they sometimes need us to protect them as they age. Even without any sort of ineffable mutual "energy," and even beyond our *collective unconscious*, we would be hard pressed to completely escape the mutual influences and ties of society. Sure, some have done it. But not many. Complete solitude seems to go against human nature.

The collective unconscious is a concept developed by Carl Jung, one of Sigmund Freud's earliest colleagues and the founder of the school of analytical psychology. (For more on Freud and Jung, see Chapter 9, "Are You the Dreamer, or the Dream?") According to Jung, everyone has a personal unconscious containing the results of the individual's life experiences and also a collective unconscious, which contains experiences of the entire human race. The collective unconscious contains archetypes or basic ideas common to all people throughout time, and these archetypes can affect our behavior as intuition. It can also be viewed as an unconscious connection between all people of all times.

Healing Thoughts for All Sentient Beings

You can pray for enlightenment. You can pray for insight. You can even pray that you'll win the lottery. But perhaps one of the most productive ways to pray (especially if prayers really do affect what happens in the world) is to pray for each other. In her famous book on her after-death experience, *Embraced by the Light*, Betty Eadie claimed to have been told that the most potent and most easily heard prayers coming from Earth toward heaven were prayers by mothers for their children. Sincere yearning to help someone and thoughts or prayers directed toward that person may very well help. Hard to prove? Sure, but scientists are giving it their best shot.

Mindful Minute

Some common archetypes of human experience are: the Anima and Animus (female and male spirits, respectively), the Wise Old Man, the Earth Mother, Darkness, and the Trickster.

One perspective several research studies use is the idea of *distance intentionality*. This simply means that someone prays or mentally tries to affect something or someone from a distance. Praying that your mother's health will improve is an example, if you are not actually with her when you pray. The concept is neither new nor uniquely Western. Many ancient cultures and indigenous peoples believed that, for example, a sorcerer or witch doctor could cure someone or, conversely, hex, harm, or even kill someone from afar. Prayer is a version of this same idea, whether it seeks as its source of power some divine power or some inner power (or the inner divine power!).

From A to Om

Distance intentionality is a concept that refers to directing an intention toward something at a distance. Prayer is one example.

Distance intentionality defies the concept that disease—or any physical condition, for that matter—is somehow isolated within the body. Rather, it suggests that some force, energy, or flow encompasses all of us, allowing the energies of some to influence the healing of others. Imagine we are all in a river. If you ripple the water with your hand, someone else will feel the waves downstream. Whether distance intentionality is tapping into the collective unconscious, the power of a divine force, or some universal energy, we don't claim to know. But if it works, prayer can have a very real effect. So what are you waiting for?

The next time you are meditating, after you have relaxed and calmed your mind (see Part 4, "Prepare Your Self for Meditation," on how to get started), imagine someone—just one person—who seems to need guidance, love, or some sort of help. Very slowly, inhale until you can't inhale anymore. Hold the breath for a few seconds and imagine suffusing it with love, positive energy, joy, and clarity. Then close your eyes, visualize the person (or animal), and very slowly exhale. Imagine the love and positive energy flowing via your breath straight into the heart of the person who needs it, filling and surrounding him or her. Repeat this several times.

Bliss Byte

Who knows what changes the world would experience if everyone sent out daily healing prayers? However, don't let that substitute as a way to help people in more physical ways, too. Brighten your day and someone else's life by volunteering at a soup kitchen, tutoring in an adult literacy program, giving clothes to a shelter, working on a hotline for runaway teens, helping to find homes for abandoned animals, or working to heal the Earth.

Form Your Own Prayer Group

If one prayer is good, a lot of prayers are great! Meditation and prayer are usually solitary pursuits, but a prayer group can be a great way not only to meet with people of similar beliefs but also to boost your prayer power.

If you belong to a church, synagogue, or other similar organization, or if you are taking a yoga or meditation class, you can probably find other people who would be interested in starting a prayer group. (See Part 4 for more information on meditation groups and classes.) Groups of between three and 12 people are easiest to manage at first, although prayer chains can be much more widespread (in a prayer chain, prayer concerns are passed around via phone calls or other modes of communication to a network of people). Meet with your prayer group weekly, monthly, or however often fits your schedule. Begin meetings by raising concerns, such as someone or a community who needs help, or a world problem that needs solving. Then, pray together.

Another interesting facet of a prayer group can be discussions of prayer itself, prayer techniques, prayer and meditation, prayer-related philosophical discussions, etc. The group members can read different works on the subject and discuss them, even try different techniques together. Refining your prayer and meditation skills in the company of your friends can be fun and spiritually (not to mention socially) rewarding.

Spirituality and Healing

We've been talking about how prayer may actually affect what happens in the world. Such a concept may be difficult for the scientifically minded, but anecdotal evidence has supported the idea since, well…the beginning of prayer! The sacred texts of the world's many religions and cultures are full of examples, of course, but what about more concrete evidence? It's out there, too.

A lot of scientists and researchers have an answer for this evidence: the *placebo effect*, which refers to the idea that if someone believes something will work, it will work, or at least, convince the person it has worked to such an extent that he or she believes symptoms or a condition itself has disappeared.

We'd like to suggest another perspective. What is the placebo effect, really? It's evidence for the power of the mind. If you *believe* prayer or meditation will help to relieve your pain, and it does, of course it is *in your mind.* That's great! Your mind is helping to relieve your pain. What's worth discrediting in that scenario? It's a simple, logical example of the connection between mind and body.

From A to Om

The **placebo effect** refers to the idea that if someone believes something will work, it will work. Traditionally used to discount certain scientific studies as invalid (if someone knows, for instance, that the pill they are taking is supposed to cure headaches, their headaches will be more likely to be cured), we would argue that the placebo effect is evidence to support the importance of the mind in healing.

And whether or not your mind is funneling that power from some higher source or just making use of its remarkable and often untapped inner powers? Well, though the issue may be more than a matter of semantics, if you are in pain, it might matter less to you *why* prayer works than *that* it works. God, the mind, saints, life energy, angels, faith itself— whatever the healer, the healing is unmistakable.

Former Surgeon General C. Everett Koop, after being criticized for mixing medicine and religion in his practice, has been quoted as saying, "I have found there are very few atheists among the parents of dying children." Koop has also predicted that spirituality will become an increasingly important part of modern health care. He said, "Doctors…if they're smart, use whatever the patient has to help that patient's healing." And, according to a recent article in the *Tampa Tribune*, dozens of studies on prayer and healing are cropping up, some funded by the government; up to one-fourth of the nation's 125 medical schools now offer courses that address spirituality; and the Templeton Foundation recently awarded "faith and medicine" grants to Johns Hopkins School of Medicine and four other schools to support teaching on health care and spirituality.

Medical Studies Show Prayer Works

If a few scientists out there didn't at least wonder about prayer and healing, they wouldn't be conducting studies on the subject. Yet, they are, and some of those studies have proved quite surprising. Though some studies are more scientifically rigorous than others, many of them have shown that prayer by subjects, and also prayer *for* subjects by other people, *even when the subjects didn't know they were being prayed for,* does seem to have an effect on health and recovery from illness.

In 1988, Randolph Byrd, a cardiologist at the San Francisco General Medicine Center Hospital, conducted the first major (and subsequently quite famous) study of the effects of prayer. Over a period of 10 months, Protestants and Catholics were randomly assigned one of 393 patients in the coronary care unit. They were instructed to pray for these people, whom they didn't know, on a daily basis. The results showed that those patients who were being prayed for had fewer complications and life-threatening events, less congestive heart failure, fewer cardiopulmonary arrests, and fewer pneumonia cases than those in the control group. In addition, no one who was prayed for needed breathing machines, while 12 in the control group did.

The study and others like it have since been criticized for having certain faults, but many other studies have adhered to strict scientific standards. According to Larry Dossey, M.D., a former internist, cofounder of the Santa Fe Institute of Medicine and Prayer, and author, one problem with these studies is the effect of what he calls "extraneous prayer." In other words, if someone is in a crisis, you can't strictly monitor who is praying for that person because people typically pray in a crisis.

Several studies cited by Larry Dossey in his writings have attempted to circumvent this problem. A Salem, Oregon, organization called Spindrift and various scientists working out of the mainstream or studying parapsychology have studied the effects of prayer on plants, bacteria, and germinating seeds because these are simpler organisms than humans and can be more easily controlled. The results? Test tubes filled with bacteria that were prayed for showed a reduction in the growth of bacteria compared to the test tubes that weren't prayed for. Plants sprayed with a saltwater solution then prayed for grew and thrived better than plants sprayed and not prayed for. Crazy? Perhaps. But curious and intriguing, as well.

Bliss Byte

What do you have faith in? What do you trust? Make a list. It might include such things as family, the Earth, love, human nature, God, or friendship. Make your list as specific as possible: "My friendship with my sister," "My love for my children," "The power of nature to guide me." Carry your list with you in your wallet or purse. When you're feeling sad or spiritually lost, pull it out and read it over and over until you feel better.

Of course, much work remains to be done on the subject. But, as Dr. Dossey also suggests, why wait until research proves without a doubt that prayer works? Prayer isn't like some experimental drug you aren't allowed to use until the FDA approves it. It's free, it can't hurt you, and it doesn't have any negative side effects. So use it to your heart's content. It may make your heart more content—and healthier, too!

Battling Depression

Obvious physical conditions like heart disease aren't the only conditions that respond to prayer. Studies have also shown that prayer can have a transformative effect on people suffering from clinical depression. Depression can be the result of a chemical imbalance, but it is often triggered by a life event. Common symptoms of depression are a lack of sleep or getting too much sleep, general fatigue, loss of interest in daily activities, lack of appetite, and loss of concentration. Prayer helps bring a sense of focused thought back to the depressed person and encourages a sense of connection to others.

Depression can sometimes be a prelude to a spiritual breakthrough. St. John of the Cross, a medieval mystic, referred to the "dark night of the soul," which was, in essence, a severe depression just before spiritual bliss. According to a survey on contemporary religious experience, periods of depression are common precursors to religious experiences. In his best-selling book, *Care of the Soul*, Thomas Moore writes about the "gift" of depression. By facing the underlying source of a bout with depression, Moore asserts, feelings of sadness can help us to grow and evolve as we work through the things that trouble us. Prayer can be a gentle way to refocus the mind-body into a more positive state.

If you are suffering from depression, try the following prayer exercise, which we like to call the Gratitude Walk:

Relax

According to a recent study, one in four women and one in 10 men suffer from depression. Treatment is often very successful, ideally a combination of counseling and medication to correct chemical imbalances. If you've been seeking help from a higher power, remember: That higher power gave humans the ability to develop medications and therapies to help themselves. Many people claim their lives have been saved by medical treatment for depression.

Put on your walking shoes. Step outside, preferably during the middle of the day when the sun is out. Start walking, briskly, even if you don't feel like it. As you walk, listen to your breathing. Is it becoming faster, deeper, more shallow? Now, look around. As you walk, what are you passing? The same sights you always see as you drive down your street? Look again. What can you notice about the houses, the storefronts, the cars, the streets you pass that you might not have noticed before? Look for details and list them: the seven ceramic ducks on the neighbor's front lawn, the not-so-clever bumper sticker on that mini-van, the different shades of grass on each lawn, the pitch and volume of that little poodle's bark, the color of the sky. Breathe the air, feel it on your face, inhale it, exhale it.

Now, don't just observe: Look for what you find pleasing, beautiful, funny. That goofy-looking cat. That bright, beautiful maple tree just starting to turn orange. That huge pile of snow-white cloud. Those kids playing kick-the-can. The smell of a bakery. That neat little window box of rose-colored geraniums. Can you feel what the season is by the way the air feels and smells?

If you can't quite make the leap to gratitude for all the beauty around you, that's okay. Just keep looking (and listening and feeling) for things that please you. Keep your walk brisk and lively, and keep walking for at least 20 minutes, preferably 30 or more.

Do it again tomorrow. And the next day. And every day. If you can't make yourself do anything else all day, at least do this. It's raining? Bring an umbrella. It's snowing? Wear a warm coat. But get out there, move, and soak in the good stuff. (See Chapter 16, "Walking Meditation: Peace Is Every Step," for more on walking meditation.)

Remembering How to Pray

Mindful Minute

As Larry Dossey, M.D. (a former internist and the cofounder of the Santa Fe Institute of Medicine and Prayer), once said, "One of the oldest men on Earth lives in Iraq; he's at least 120 years old and drinks and smokes all the time. And history is full of very spiritual people who were sick all the time. In the Bible, Job was described as perfect and look what happened to him. The Buddha died of food poisoning." Although a staunch believer in the power of prayer, Dossey emphasizes that faith and healing are not directly correlated. If you get sick, it doesn't mean you weren't praying well enough. But if you do pray, you may be able to improve your situation.

If the last time you prayed your age only had one digit and you were kneeling next to your bed with a watchful parent at your side, you may have forgotten some of the basics. Praying might feel uncomfortable at first and more awkward than simple meditation, especially if you haven't given much thought to your spiritual life lately.

It isn't easy to jump right into a prayerful state with both knees. You need to warm up before you exercise, right? A prayer warm-up doesn't hurt, either. To help you get into the right frame of mind, we'll instruct you in prayer preparation. Then we'll guide you through some prayer exercises, too, in case you aren't quite ready to wing it, or if you are looking for some new strategies.

Get Ready: Prayer Preparation I

Before you begin to pray, prepare your mind. Sit comfortably in a hard-backed chair in a quiet room where you won't be disturbed for at least 15 minutes. (For more on chair meditations, see Chapter 15, "Seated Meditation: Finding Center.") Keep your back straight. Close your eyes, or, if this makes concentrating more difficult, leave them slightly open and focus on an object that you can bring your attention to if your mind begins to wander.

Now, notice your breathing. Don't change it. Simply notice it. Direct all your attention to the feel of your breath moving in and out of your nostrils. Keep your attention here for a bit. Next, shift your attention to your feet. Feel the way your shoes feel on your feet or the way your feet feel against the floor. Don't move them. Just feel. Next, feel how your body is touching the floor or chair. Notice all the places it is touching. Are there places you know it is touching but that you can't feel? Keep trying to feel it.

Last, feel the air on your skin. Feel it on your face, your hair, your arms and hands, anywhere your skin is exposed. Does the air feel cool? Warm? Is it moving or still? Is it humid or dry? Feel the way you are placed in the air. Feel how it makes way for your presence, and how it moves in and out of you. Feel how integrated you are with the air.

Bring your attention back to your breathing for another minute or two. This exercise is designed to be profoundly relaxing.

Get Set: Prayer Prep II

Now that your body is relaxed, you can begin to orient your mind in a prayerful direction. Sit quietly with your back straight, either in a chair or cross-legged on the floor, in a room where you won't be disturbed.

Think of one thing for which you are grateful. There are probably many, but focus on just one, such as your good health, a child, a pet, a favorite tree in your backyard, a friend. Now, think about that thing. What does it look like? How does it feel? Imagine all the details of your object of gratitude. Don't concentrate on your gratitude, but on the actual qualities of the thing. Spend about five minutes on this.

Now, do a quick body scan. How do you feel? Has the focus on something that is such a positive force in your life relaxed you further? Oriented your mind toward the positive? Put you in a state of thanks? Good!

Go! Prayer Exercise I

If you haven't prayed for a while, you may feel most comfortable and familiar praying just before you go to sleep. Tonight, before you lie down to sleep, sit up with your back straight, close your eyes, and one by one, give thanks for each one of your senses.

➤ **Thank you for the gift of sight.** Today, I saw beautiful things. (Think of one.) Today, I saw things that taught me something I didn't know. (Think of one.) Today, I saw things that made me grateful to be alive. (Think of one.)

➤ **Thank you for the gift of hearing.** Today, I heard something beautiful. (What was it?) Today, I heard something that taught me something I didn't know. (What was it?) Today, I heard something that made me grateful to be alive. (What was it?)

Mindful Minute

Impairment of the senses can be its own kind of gift and challenge. Indeed, many people don't believe they are "impaired" at all. For example, in the Deaf community, deafness is accepted as a personal detail no different than someone's height, weight, or eye color. The Deaf communicate in American Sign Language (ASL), the third most spoken language in the United States today.

➤ **Thank you for the gift of smell.** Today I smelled something wonderful. (What was it? Food? A flower? A lovely perfume? The aroma of someone you love?) It made me glad to be alive.

➤ **Thank you for the gift of taste.** Today, I tasted something delicious, and it made me happy. (What was it?)

➤ **Thank you for the gift of touch.** Today, I touched something beautiful. (What was it?) Today, I touched something that I had never touched before. (What was it?) Today, I touched something that made me glad to be alive. (What was it?)

If you find at the end of your day that you *didn't* smell or taste or touch anything new or life-affirming, make an attempt to use each of your senses in a positive way tomorrow. Then, tomorrow night, and every night thereafter, you'll be able to fill in the blanks of this exercise. Chances are, you'll also enjoy your days more.

Prayer Exercise II

Here's another prayer exercise to try at night. On an evening when the sky is clear, go outside to a peaceful place or sit at a window in a room with the lights out. Look at the stars. Scan the sky for a while, then find one star that somehow appeals to you or attracts you in some way. You don't have to know why. Just follow your instinct.

Now, focus on the star. Think about what it is. Think about how you and that burning star are billions…trillions?…of miles apart, yet somehow, connected. Keep your eyes focused on the star. Feel its energy, and send your energy toward it. Watch it sparkle. Imagine what it looks like from a closer distance. Imagine how big it might be. Consider how different your distant perspective is.

Why you are able to see this star, your star? Is the universe sending you a message? Listen as you gaze at the star. Answers may come to you. They may not. But consider how beautiful something can be from so far away. What does that mean for you? Give it 10 minutes or so. Then close your eyes and, keeping the picture and the meaning of your star inside you, continue with the rest of your evening.

Prayer Exercise III

Place two chairs together in a quiet room. Sit in one. Now, visualize someone you love who is not physically with you. A meaningful religious figure is a good choice (your guardian angel, a saint, Jesus, Buddha, etc.), but it could also be someone who has passed away. Imagine how that figure looks sitting across from you. Imagine the details of the face, the clothes, the hands, the feet.

Now, simply, talk to that person. What do you want to tell them? Pour out your heart, ask questions you've wondered about, or simply tell the person about your day.

Bliss Byte

Light a candle and gaze into the flame. Imagine the flame is the universal source of divinity, love, inspiration, or creativity. As you gaze at it, feel those qualities in you awakening and recognizing their universal counterpart. Spend some time allowing your inner divinity, love, inspiration, or creativity to fully awaken. Allow the flame to spark a flow of warm, positive energy inside you; use that spark to feed the fire of the flame you are meditating upon.

Banishing Doubt and Calming Fears

Whatever your techniques, whatever your beliefs, whatever your spiritual journey, prayer could work for you. For some, it is more comfortable and natural than meditation. For others, it is a lovely complement to meditation. For still others, it is uncharted territory. But tapping into a higher power, whether God, nature, the higher realms of your own mind, or the collective unconscious, could transform your life.

No matter how you feel most of the time, during prayer you may find relief from your doubts and fears about your life, your abilities, even the meaning of life itself. Prayer is comfort food for the soul, and you don't have to go hungry.

Relax

Even when you think you know what would be best for someone else, your agenda may be quite different from theirs, or you might not see a complete picture of a situation. Sometimes you may not even know what is best for yourself! When in doubt about what to pray for, a good way to pray is to ask that the person you are praying for receive what he or she needs most at this time. You can pray in this way for yourself, too.

The Least You Need to Know

➤ Prayer can complement meditation as an important vehicle in your spiritual journey.

➤ You don't have to believe in a specific religion or a specific higher power to pray. You need only an outward-directed focus rather than an inward-directed focus.

➤ Prayer may affect actual events, such as the health and well-being of those prayed for.

➤ Praying may positively affect your own health.

➤ Meditation techniques can prepare you for prayer.

➤ Prayer techniques can structure or vary your prayer.

➤ Prayer is comfort food for the soul.

Part 3

Let's Get Physical: The Path to Optimal Health

Meditation has lots of wonderful side effects. Even though it isn't exercise in the traditional sense, it nonetheless benefits the body in many of the same ways in which physical exercise does. Brain scans of people meditating reveal better blood flow, better connections between different areas of the brain, and physiological changes that indicate profound states of relaxation and stress reduction.

With a few simple techniques such as the mind-body scan, anyone can enhance their concentration, ease muscle tension, and actually reduce stress hormone levels. We'll show you how! Meditation also helps life-force energy to flow unimpeded through the body, maximizing physical, mental, and spiritual health. Used in conjunction with certain types of bodywork therapies and with dreamwork, meditation can have an even more profound effect on your physical body and your brain.

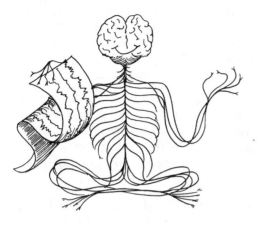

Chapter 7

Neurophysiology: This Is Your Brain on Meditation

In This Chapter

➤ Meditation and your brain waves

➤ How meditation promotes mental efficiency

➤ Concentration, focus, and relaxation

It might be tempting, at this point, to think that all this meditation business is happening in your mind. Well, sure it is, but not only in your mind. Things are happening in that meditating brain of yours—interesting things. Sure, studies have demonstrated meditation's relaxing effect, and everyone knows stress-management techniques are valuable allies to good health. In fact, a National Institutes of Health panel recently found strong evidence that relaxation and behavioral techniques such as biofeedback are effective in reducing chronic pain and insomnia.

For this chapter, we'd like to get physical and show you what's going on in your brain during meditation. Studies have proven that meditation does have a physical effect on your brain and body.

Meditation Makes Your Brain Stronger

Your brain isn't a muscle, so how can it get stronger? Although it isn't an actual muscle, it has similarities to a muscle. When you exercise your muscles, especially with weight-bearing exercises like weight lifting, push-ups, sit-ups, and running or jogging, you cause tiny tears in the muscle fibers. When these tears heal, they bulk up the fibers to be even stronger than before. That's why the rest period between exercise sessions is important. It is during rest that your muscles strengthen.

Your brain doesn't have muscle fibers, but it does have *neurons*, or nerve cells, not to mention *neurotransmitters*, the chemicals that deliver messages back and forth between neurons. Everyone is born with billions of neurons (approximately 12 billion in your brain alone), and although they can't be regenerated, research suggests we can strengthen the connections they make with each other. We can also slow their inevitable loss.

From A to Om

Neurons are nerve cells, and **neurotransmitters** are the chemicals produced in nerve cells that travel from one nerve cell to another, delivering marching orders from the brain to the rest of the body.

Mindful Minute

Even during sleep, the mind is active. In fact, there's as much activity going on as when we're awake. But the body is "paralyzed" from acting on the brain's messages during dreams; this is called **atonia**, our muscles relax. So, even sleep can't be considered a "rest" from brain activity.

Some neurons are bound to be damaged due to aging. Injuries (such as a severe bump on the head) or illness that cuts off oxygen to the brain (a stroke, for example) may cause the loss of many more neurons. Sometimes neurons can repair themselves, and sometimes they can't.

But evidence suggests that we can keep our neurons more active by our own efforts. One way is to use them. Keeping your brain active into old age can be an effective way to combat senility. Another way to keep your neurons in tip-top shape? Treat them like muscles. Every day, for just a little while, give them a meditation workout.

Ever wonder what a neuron looks like? Neurons look a little like spiders. Each neuron has a cell body, and extending from that body are "legs," or branches, called *dendrites*. Also extending from the cell body is a single long fiber called an *axon*, and at its tip are more little extensions, like tiny roots. Dendrites receive messages from the body and carry them to the center of the nerve cell. The messages are then carried away by the axon and sent on to the next neuron. Although neurons don't actually touch each other, messages "jump" from neuron to neuron, almost instantaneously in a kind of chain reaction, via an electrochemical process that utilizes chemicals called *neurotransmitters*.

Neurophysiology: The Brain, the Body, and Meditation

The effect of meditation on the brain and the body is the subject of much research. A number of rigorous scientific studies on the subject have appeared in scientific journals on psychology, psychiatry, psychobiology, alternative medicine, and neuroscience (the study of the brain). For example, studies have demonstrated that during Transcendental Meditation (TM), blood flow to the brain increases. Neurophysiology, or the study of brain physiology, can offer an interesting perspective to the concept of mind-body medicine.

Are the changes in the brain and body experienced during meditation due solely to its relaxing effect on the body? Certainly that is part of it. But studies on the effects of meditation have been compared with studies on the effects of resting, and the results aren't exactly the same. Resters tend to have slowed arousal responses, while meditators didn't, for example. That means that resting can dull your senses, making you slower to react to a stimulus such as a threat. Meditation, on the other hand, seems to awaken the senses, making you more easily roused by a stimulus such as a threat. Meditation doesn't "space you out," nor does it slow your reactions, as a nap certainly would. Instead, it seems to fine-tune your attention. People who are meditating, then, are not falling asleep—even if they appear to be!

There are several problems with physiological studies of meditation. Anyone being studied is likely to be more tense and self-conscious than normal, so the difference between "before" and "after" states measured in meditators might be exaggerated under the conditions of a study. Also, because the brain is so powerful, if a meditator knows what a researcher is looking for (or even suspects, not having been told), the meditator may be able, subconsciously, to influence the body to produce the desired effect. For example, if you suspect a researcher wants to discover that meditation lowers your blood pressure or oxygen consumption, your body may oblige by lowering your blood pressure or oxygen consumption, even if you aren't trying, consciously, to cause that change. For rebellious types, the effect might be the opposite. "So those researchers think they'll find that meditation relaxes me? I'll show them!" And tension sets in!

Mindful Minute

Researchers have discovered that meditation shares many of the physiological qualities of Stage I nonREM sleep. This is the stage where you begin to become drowsy. However, they agree that sleep and meditation are two separate phenomena. Different studies show that people who meditate regularly have more efficient REM sleep, the sleep stage during which dreams occur, making your sleep more restful and rejuvenating.

Another problem is that meditative experiences are largely subjective. You can measure all the bodily processes that you like, but no instrument, no matter how fine-tuned and precise, can measure the full spectrum of an enlightenment experience.

Kensho: Seeing the Essence

Is there any way, then, to objectively prove an enlightenment experience? As an example, consider *kensho*. Also called insight-wisdom, kensho is like a pre-enlightenment experience. It is a moment of profound wisdom or insight where truth and the essence of all things are suddenly clear. An example is suddenly discovering the answer to a koan. Kensho is temporary and short-lived, one of those "ah-HA!" experiences. Does it register in the brain?

From A to Om

Kensho, also called insight-wisdom, is a sudden-understanding experience of seeing into the essence of things. It is considered a step toward true enlightenment.

Mindful Minute

Meditation can give you control over bodily functions you never knew you could control, including your temperature. Dr. Herbert Benson, M.D., of Harvard University, visited a Tibetan monastery in northern India and filmed a group of Tibetan monks meditating. The temperature in the meditation room was 40°F and the monks were wrapped in sheets that had been dipped in ice-cold water. Reportedly, the monks generated such heat while meditating that steam quickly began to rise off their bodies, and the sheets were completely dry in 40 minutes.

For one thing, you never know when kensho will occur, so it isn't easy to be ready to "measure" it. But those who have experienced it can talk about it, and there do seem to be some patterns. Kensho seems to happen more frequently:

➤ In the early morning hours (in fact, the Buddha was said to have attained enlightenment upon seeing the first morning star)

➤ When in an unfamiliar surrounding

➤ In the spring, specifically May and June

Morning and spring are both awakening phases of cycles, and unfamiliar surroundings may force chemical reactions in the brain that wouldn't normally occur. But the neurophysiology of kensho is still mostly theoretical. We don't yet have the means or the information to pin down the elusive experience of enlightenment, but that doesn't mean we can't continue to study the subject. Considering the positive changes meditation invokes in the body, scientists will certainly keep trying!

Riding the Brain Waves

Brain waves are caused by electrical activity in the brain, and they can be measured by a test called an electroencephalogram (EEG). This test involves recording the brain waves via electrodes placed on the scalp, or even sometimes on the brain itself, as during surgery.

The brain doesn't produce a lot of electricity—maybe enough to light a 25-watt bulb. But the brain waves are nevertheless revealing. They can come from different parts of the brain and occur at different frequencies. Delta waves are the slowest, cycling $1/2$ to 2 cycles per second. Alpha waves cycle about eight to 12 times per second. Theta waves cycle at four to seven times per second. Beta rhythms cycle 14 to 30 times per second, and gamma waves cycle 30 to 50 times per second.

Each type of brain wave can be attributed to certain types of mental states (although not always reliably). Studying the brain waves during meditation, then, can give us some clues about what's going on during different phases of meditation. Here are some generalizations:

➤ Alpha waves are generally associated with relaxed, attentive states. When you think, mostly nonvisually (such as thinking about a concept rather than daydreaming), your alpha waves may tend to increase. Alpha waves usually slow when you fall asleep or when you engage in complex thought. Alpha waves are often dominant in the first stages of meditation when you attempt to concentrate on the sound of a mantra, the feel of your breath, or an object (you're looking at it, which is visual of course, but that's different from visualizing in your mind). However, alpha waves have been detected in people reporting a wide range of mental states, from happy relaxation to attentiveness to internal reflection.

➤ Delta waves are the slow waves that are characteristic of very deep sleep.

➤ Theta waves aren't usually present in normal waking states, but they begin to replace alpha waves as consciousness gives way to sleep. Theta waves may also appear during daydreams and during activity that requires mental effort when the subject is relaxed. Theta waves don't always appear consistently, though, so they are hard to categorize.

➤ Beta waves may appear when people are feeling the effects of stress, whether in a negative way (such as anxiety) or a positive way (such as excitement). They may also be present during states of alertness or concentration, or even when subjects are feeling very happy and content. Typically, beta waves increase when we are paying close attention to something, but the increase doesn't last (maybe because it's hard to pay close attention to something for a long time). After an hour or two, alpha and theta waves take over again. Beta waves sometimes occur in the deepest, most advanced stages of meditation.

➤ Gamma waves are the fastest waves and can be found in many parts of the brain. They are difficult to attribute to any particular state, but one study showed an increase in gamma waves when subjects were asked to respond quickly to clicking sounds.

> **Mindful Minute**
>
> Many studies have measured the brain waves of experienced and inexperienced meditators alike. One study showed that during walking meditation, about half the recorded brain waves of Zen monks were alpha waves, while only 20 percent of the brain waves in inexperienced meditators were alpha waves. A control group of nonmeditators exhibited no alpha waves during walking. This study could be evidence for a state of increased attentiveness in daily life bestowed by practicing meditation.

Something else interesting that happens to brain waves during meditation is that they tend to synchronize. Several studies on Transcendental Meditation have demonstrated that brain waves tend to synchronize their peaks and valleys. In normal states of awareness, brain waves appear randomly, with each peak and valley occurring seemingly independently of the others. What does it mean, then, that brain waves tend to organize themselves during meditation? Scientists aren't sure, but intuition suggests some sort of enhanced centering, tranquility, and an inner sense of order.

A Tibetan Monk's Brain on Meditation

Aside from your brain waves, what does your brain actually look like during meditation? Does it change? Apparently. A study sponsored by the Institute for the Scientific Study of Meditation (ISSM) used a brain imaging technology called SPECT imaging (single photon emission computed tomography) to take pictures of the brains of Tibetan Buddhist meditators who were seasoned practitioners of meditation. The images show which areas of the brain are more active by showing where blood flow increases.

Images were taken of the Tibetan Buddhist's brains during meditation and when not meditating. The images taken during meditation clearly showed two things:

➤ The front of the brain, which is the area typically involved in concentration, is more active during meditation. Because meditation requires focused attention and concentration on something, whether the breath, a visual point, or a sound, increased activity in the frontal lobe makes sense.

➤ The parietal lobe shows decreased activity. This area typically governs our sense of where we are in space and time. For example, you know you are sitting in a chair in your living room reading this book or perhaps standing in a bookstore flipping through the pages. You know what day it is, what year, what city you are in, what state, what country, what planet, etc. Meditators sometimes describe the feeling that their orientation in space and time becomes suspended during meditation. Decreased activity in the parietal lobe would correspond with this sensation.

What does this mean for you? Even if you aren't an experienced Tibetan Buddhist meditator (we're guessing you probably aren't, though we could be wrong!), does your brain show similar changes during meditation? More research has to be done before that question can be answered accurately, but chances are that although the changes in a novice meditator are probably less dramatic, they are also probably similar.

Drawing the Dot: Finding Your Third Eye

Put your index finger on the bridge of your nose, right between your eyes. Now draw a straight line upward about an inch or so. That's the spot!

What spot? Why, your *urna*, of course. That's what the Buddhists call it. Yogis call it your *ajna chakra* or your *sun chakra*. Native Americans use it to call forth visions and signs. In plain ol' English, it's sometimes called your *third eye*. Third eye? Yep! Squint if you will in the mirror but you won't see an actual eye there.

However, according to many cultures and philosophies, something very real is there. This point on your forehead is an energy center of unclouded perception, the area Buddhists associate with *kensho* or insight-wisdom, the area yogis associate with entrance into and knowledge of the astral and subtle bodies (see Chapter 10, "Is Any Body Home?").

To some it is the area associated with psychic abilities. It is also a great center of focus for meditation. Close your eyes and imagine focusing on the spot you just found with your finger. Try to "look" there with your closed eyes. You'll probably see blackness at first, then possibly swirling colors, shapes, maybe even a kaleidoscope effect. Pretty, and relaxing, too! If you keep at it, the color show may eventually fade away in favor of a truly relaxed state and quite possibly, truly remarkable perception. It is important not to strain the muscles of the eyes when looking inward to the ajna chakra. Allow your gaze to be soft and relaxed.

But is anything "scientific" going on in the area of your third eye? Nothing has definitely been proven. But who knows? If humans have been perceiving the existence of something in that spot for so long, perhaps something is going on up there. Perhaps our brains are evolving into an even higher state of awareness, and perhaps our third eyes have something to do with it. Only time will tell.

> **From A to Om**
>
> The **urna** is the so-called "third eye," the area of the forehead between and about an inch or two above the eyes within your head, thought to be an energy source and the source of unclouded perception. In Sanskrit, the spot is called the **ajna chakra**. In yoga, it is also sometimes called the **sun chakra**.

> **Relax**
>
> According to some, wearing metal on the body (such as metal jewelry) affects the body's energy field. You might want to consider removing all metal jewelry while meditating. Also, try and have the energies around you be as natural as possible. For example, sit on a cotton or wool rug instead of a polyester one.

Blending Ritual: Religious and Scientific

Whether your tendencies and preferences fall on the religious or the scientific side of the spectrum, you can still find a meditation principle, practice, and ritual that makes sense for you. If you tend to be more scientific in your approach, focus on the brain-boosting benefits of meditation, the research, and the way it can improve your health. If spirituality is your mode, approach meditation from a more transcendent standpoint. Maybe prayer is your favorite mode, or perhaps you like the idea of giving yoga or Buddhist methods a try.

Something else to consider is stretching your focus to encompass, at least to a small degree, the aspects of meditation that go against your natural inclination. You can't grow, whether intellectually or spiritually, if you never challenge yourself.

Bliss Byte

The idea of balance is an important aspect of most meditation traditions. In Chinese, the yin/yang symbol represents balance. In Hatha Yoga (the yoga emphasizing the practice of physical postures), *Ha* is male and *tha* is female. Hatha Yoga also includes postures requiring balance of the body. When meditating, consider the idea of balance. If your mind is overwhelmed with mundane details, clearing it can put your mind-body (your life!) back into balance.

For the empirically minded, pick a culture that interests you—say, India, Japan, or Tibet. Study that culture. Get some books at the library or look around on the Internet for information about the history and culture, the cuisine, the clothing, the philosophy, the politics, etc. Take about a month to learn everything you can. Try cooking food from your chosen culture, learning a few words of the language, maybe even meeting someone from there (ask around). As part of your cultural study, examine in detail that culture's meditation techniques and try them every day for your "culture month." Imagine you are from that culture. Are you a Tibetan monk? A yogi? A Zen Buddhist? Approach your meditation practice as if it were just part of your daily routine. What a great way to expand your horizons and knowledge of the world!

For those of you with spiritual tendencies, meditation may be a joy. However, it may also be tempting to desire instant enlightenment, and when this doesn't occur, you may become frustrated by the very mundane and boring process of getting "good" at meditation. Try a systematic, scientific approach to your meditation practice, even if it goes against your nature. Meditate at a specific time each day, for a set length of time. Rather than letting your mind get caught up in dreams of enlightenment and spiritual awakening (which actually is a fairly common hindrance to the real business of meditation), be pragmatic and disciplined in your approach. Focus on your breathing or whatever your choice of focus is, and dutifully bring your mind back to your focus—and nothing else!—for your allotted time. You'll contend with boredom. You'll contend with tedium. You'll contend with the very real *fact* of just sitting. Why aren't you a Buddha yet? Because you aren't ready yet. Let meditation teach you its lessons.

Also for the spiritually minded, try the "cultural immersion" approach suggested above. It's a great way to expand your horizons, your knowledge of the world, and your sense of enlightenment and spirituality as a truly international (universal!) phenomenon.

Meditation and Neurotransmitters: Getting the Message Across

But back to the science. Another compelling aspect of meditation and neurophysiology is that the activity of neurotransmitters, those chemical messengers shooting back and forth between nerve cells, can actually change nerve cell metabolism and even the structure of the cell membranes. Specifically, neurotransmitter release can make nerve cells more easily excitable or more resistant to stimulation.

If processes in the brain can change the brain, and if meditation creates processes in the brain, then meditation can change your brain. Not dramatically, of course. You may find yourself tapping into a wellspring of psychic intuition you never realized you had. Meditation does indeed make you more sensitive to subtler and subtler vibrations.

For example, meditators' quickened reaction times may be due to the brain learning to make the most efficient use of its speedier neurotransmitters, such as *acetylcholine*. It appears meditation can actually make your mind work more efficiently!

Building Concentration

Meditation also has a measurable effect on your ability to concentrate. According to researchers, concentration can, to an extent, be cultivated. As we saw in the section on brain waves, beta waves are often dominant during periods of intense concentration, but don't last for more than an hour or two. After that, concentration levels seem to drop no matter what the subjects do, and alpha and theta waves kick in, signaling that intense concentration is at an end.

Mindful Minute

Neurotransmitters can be divided into stimulators and suppressors. Chemicals in the first group stimulate the area they target, whether muscles or feelings of hunger. These include acetylcholine, dopamine, epinephrine, norepinephrine, and phenylethylamine. The second group consists of chemicals that inhibit the area they trigger, from dulling pain to inducing sleep. These include dynorphin, endorphins, gamma-aminobutyric acid, glycine, and serotonin.

If something interests you, you'll be more likely to concentrate on it, of course. If something is boring, boring, boring, you'll have a much harder time concentrating. In fact, most meditation techniques are concentration techniques. That's why meditation is such a great way to cultivate concentration. It can get boring, and there's your opportunity to practice! Just like anything else, the ability to concentrate does improve with practice, and daily meditation is the perfect venue.

We heard a story about a meditation student who complained to the teacher that just focusing on the breath was boring. The teacher (a Zen master, we're sure!) plunged the student's head into an icy-cold river and held it down. The student struggled for a while until the teacher let him up and said, "Now, tell me how boring the breath is!" American religious thinker, Thomas Merton, wrote this about boredom (we're paraphrasing…): "If you find something to be boring, keep doing it more and more until you get so bored that eventually it becomes interesting!"

Perhaps the abilities of experienced meditators intimidate you. You could never concentrate that well, for that long! You probably couldn't perform as a circus acrobat or understand an esoteric physics theorem, either—certainly not without training and practice! People can accomplish amazing feats with directed practice. You can, too.

Bliss Byte

Another effective way to learn how to improve your concentration is **biofeedback**. Biofeedback is a technique through which you learn to control various internal processes, such as brain waves or blood pressure, by seeing them displayed on a monitor. Subjects who suffered from chronic anxiety were taught to control and increase their alpha waves (the brain waves associated with relaxed attention, as in the first stages of meditation). They reported a subsequent sense of well-being, compared to subjects who were unsuccessful at the technique and whose anxiety remained unchanged.

Can You Focus?

Of course, we can tell you to practice, practice, practice, but it isn't always easy. Staying focused on your point of concentration is tough, but trying to meditate without a point of focus is almost impossible, especially for beginners.

Although some meditation techniques advise meditating with your eyes closed (and for some, this is easier), meditating with your eyes slightly open has a few advantages:

➤ It allows you to have a visual point of focus. Having something to look at helps to keep your eyes from darting around, which may inhibit your concentration.

➤ It may make you less likely to fall asleep.

➤ Even if your point of focus is a mantra or your breath, having a visual point on which to fix your eyes (without letting it engage your attention) can help you to keep your attention singularly focused. Otherwise, your eyes may distract you by "trying" to see something via your imagination.

➤ Opening your eyes only partially keeps external distractions to a minimum, while still keeping you grounded.

Bliss Byte

Some good visual points of focus, whether your primary focus for meditation or not, are:

➤ A steady candle flame (no draft!) or other light source

➤ A mandala

➤ A star in the sky

➤ A flower

➤ Any small object (a beautiful figurine or a plain old pencil eraser)

➤ A spot on the wall

The Mind-Body Scan Revisited: YOU Control Your Body

We can quote research studies at you until we're blue in the face, but it won't mean anything to you unless you experience it yourself. So, experience it for yourself! Remember the mind-body scan in Chapter 3? Let's try it again, but this time, rather than passively observing how your body feels, you'll be a little more proactive.

First, lie on your back on a comfortable but firm surface, such as on a blanket or mat on the floor. A bed will work, too, although it doesn't offer quite the ideal degree of support. Place a small pillow under your head to support your neck and a blanket roll under your knees to help alleviate any lower back pain you might be experiencing. Relax, take a deep breath, and exhale slowly. If your mind starts to wander during the body scan, gently bring it back to the place you were when you wandered away, and continue.

Close your eyes and begin to breathe deeply. Listen to your breath. Feel it going in and out. Relax. Imagine that with every inhalation you are bringing positive energy into your body, and with every exhalation, negativity is released. Now, consciously breathe more deeply. Let each slow exhalation fill your body from the base of your abdomen, slowly, slowly, all the way up to the top of your chest. Don't raise your shoulders. Expand your abdomen like a balloon as you fill it with air. Then, very slowly, making a "SSS" sound, let the air out. Let out all of it, until you absolutely can't exhale another puff. Do it a few more times and really notice how different conscious deep breathing feels.

Now feel where your body is touching the floor and where it doesn't touch the floor. Imagine your body is very, very heavy and is sinking down into the floor. Relax. Breathe. Focus on your shoulders. Visualize them actually sinking and melting into the floor. Now do the same to your upper back, then your lower back. Notice if your lower back is swayed and really concentrate on allowing it to relax and melt downward. Imagine your arms and legs becoming heavier and heavier, merging with the floor. Now your neck and head are sinking down. Every muscle is melting down, down, relaxing into the earth.

Now bring your attention to the toes of your left foot. Slowly squeeze them, as if you were picking up a pencil with them. Squeeze tighter, tighter, tighter…then relax them as completely as you can. Now move up to your left ankle. Rotate it a little, then flex it, tensing the muscles around it and in your left calf. Hold the flex for a few seconds, then relax completely. Next, bring your attention to your left knee. Contract your left thigh muscle, raising the knee and the upper leg slightly off the floor. Hold the contraction for a few seconds, then let your leg fall back to the floor, relaxed. Do the same for your left hip, squeezing your left buttocks muscle, then relaxing your entire left leg into the floor. Does it feel more relaxed than before? It should.

Now, repeat the entire process with the right leg. Keep breathing.

Bring your attention to your lower back and around to your abdomen. Contract your lower abdominal muscles and both buttocks muscles as tightly as you can. Hold, hold, hold…relax. Let your entire lower torso sink even more deeply into the floor. Now, tense your upper abdominal muscles while squeezing your shoulder blades together as tightly as you can. Hold for a few seconds, then release your entire upper torso deeply into the floor. Let your spine melt into the earth.

Now move up your neck to the base of the skull. Lift your head slightly off the floor as you tense your neck muscles and scrunch up your face as tightly as you can. Squeeze those face muscles! Squeeze! Now relax your entire head and neck.

Lastly, lie quietly for a few more minutes. Spread your attention over your entire body. How do you feel? Where is your mind? Are you focused in the now and the physical sensation of lying on the floor or is your mind still trying to wander off? Scan quickly over your body a few times, searching out remaining areas of tension. You are on a search and discover mission! Whenever you detect an area of tension (a shoulder, your neck, your lower back), once again tense the muscles in that area as tightly as you can for several seconds, then release. Keep it up until the tension releases with your muscle release.

Whatever your mind is doing, don't let it disturb or engage you. Keep it focused on your relaxation process. When you've banished all your tension, lie still for five to 10 minutes. Imagine your body is completely merged with the ground, in perfect union with Mother Earth. Then, gradually allow your awareness of your muscles to return. Slowly move each body part a little, then sit, then stand. You should feel very relaxed, both physically and mentally. And you did it all on your own!

Bliss Byte

Try breathing into your arms. It may sound strange, but your skin breathes, too. Imagine helping your skin to release what it doesn't need. Visualize inhaling deeply through your upper arms and exhaling slowly through your lower arms. Repeat for a few deep breaths. Since your skin covers your entire body, you can do this exercise with any area of your body. Really get into that skin!

Meditation: The Ultimate Natural High

After the mind-body scan revisited, you may feel great. Or, you may still be snoozing, but that's okay. The more you practice, the better you'll get at staying awake. But if you think that felt great, just imagine how 20 minutes of daily meditation will make you feel. Once relaxation is under your control, you can master concentration. After that, you can master the expansion of your awareness.

Stress, anxiety, even insecurity are often treated with drugs and in this day and age, although excellent drugs have been developed to treat chemical imbalances, nothing beats the natural high attained through diligent meditation. From pain relief to union with the universe, meditation has a natural high for everyone.

The Least You Need to Know

➤ Meditation strengthens your mental processes in ways that can be both objectively measured and subjectively experienced.

➤ Your brain waves and brain blood flow change in response to meditation.

➤ Meditation seems to encourage the neurotransmitters that improve reaction time.

➤ Science and spirituality need not exist in separate camps. Meditation can encompass both views.

➤ Meditation builds concentration, focus, and control over the body's relaxation mechanisms.

Energy Central

What *animates* you? What makes the "machine/computer" of your mind-body move, act, react, interact? What possesses you to think, respond, dream, listen, contemplate, ruminate, meditate? What spark pops you into *being*?

Different cultures have different answers to these questions, but the answers are largely similar. We each seem to have a unique energy that manifests itself in us. But is the energy *really* unique? Is your energy the same as your friend's energy? You might say no, but perhaps your energy only *seems* different. Perhaps your energy moves in and out of you, in and out of all of humanity, around and through the whole world, even the universe. Perhaps that animating energy is what ties us all together.

Prana, Chi, the Force: Whatever You Call It, Get with It!

According to yogic and Buddhist thought, as well as many other schools of thinking such as traditional Chinese medicine (TCM), the universe and all its inhabitants are joined by a life-force energy. This energy runs through meridians in the body, is

From A to Om

Prana, c'hi, chi, qi, and ki are all names for life-force energy that animates the body and the universe, and which, when unblocked and properly directed, can help the body to heal itself.

Mindful Minute

The National Institutes of Health (NIH) Office of Alternative Medicine allocated $700,000 of its 1998 budget for acupuncture research. According to the NIH, "The objective of Acupuncture Clinical Trial Pilot Grants is to increase the quality of clinical research evaluating the efficacy of acupuncture for the treatment or prevention of disease and accompanying symptoms."

inhaled with each breath, pools and stagnates, flows and releases, like an intricate universal river system. Yogis call it *prana*. The Chinese call it *c'hi* or *chi*. The Japanese call it *ki*. In fact, too many cultures to name have names for it. If you've seen the movie *Star Wars*, you surely remember The Force. Same thing!

Is this life-force energy real? When we look around us, we don't see energy waves and flows in the air. We can't measure it. Certain scientific instruments can measure electrical fields on the body, and a few studies have measured electrical changes over the areas of the body called *pressure points* through which chi can be manipulated. The concept would seem to be merely theory. Yet, many have made compelling arguments for its existence:

➤ Many of the world's cultures—today and throughout history—have come up with the concept of life-force energy.

➤ Acupuncture, an ancient Chinese technique that works on the principle of life-force energy and manipulating it by inserting needles into pressure points, works so well to treat chronic pain that many insurance companies are covering treatment.

➤ Energy-based bodywork treatments designed to enhance healing and well-being are immensely popular and have a large body of anecdotal evidence to support their effectiveness. In many of these treatments, the subject is never actually touched by the practitioner. Only his or her energy is manipulated by the movement of hands just above the body.

➤ Most people can feel their own energy levels. Sometimes they are high, sometimes they are low.

And is life-force energy something you can use? You bet! Many ancient systems have formulated methods for unblocking chi, filling the body with prana, and suffusing your whole being with life-force energy. Yoga, massage, bodywork, Chinese medicine, homeopathy, and meditation are some of the main methods for getting in tune with your life-force energy and using it to your best advantage. (For more about massage, read *The Complete Idiot's Guide to Massage*, Alpha Books, 1998, written by the authors of this book.) Start thinking in terms of how to best facilitate your life force, and pretty soon that light saber will fly right into your hand when you need it most! (Well, maybe not—but you'll probably feel like it could!)

Life's Animating Quality

This life-force energy isn't just in your body. It emanates from you, flows in and out of you, and animates every sentient being and, according to some, every object—trees, rocks, mountains, clouds, buildings, cars, and even the Earth itself. Learning to use and enhance your life-force energy can do more than improve your health and well-being. It can also connect you to the Earth, your fellow humans, and nature. It *does* join you to all those things, and makes you part of them, and them part of you. Breathe it in, unblock it, move with it, and recognize it in yourself and in the world around you. Meditate on it, and with it, and in it.

From A to Om

Pressure points are points along the energy channels in the body where energy tends to pool or get blocked. Pressing, massaging, or otherwise manipulating these points can help to rejuvenate energy flows through the body, facilitating the body's ability to balance and heal itself.

Are You Blocked? Another Self Quiz

Of course, meditating on, with, and in your life-force energy is easier said than done, especially if you are blocked. Blockages can create paralysis or result in physical or emotional problems. Not many people are completely unblocked in every way. Are you blocked? Take our quiz to determine if you are and in what way. (Note: We aren't using any particular established theory of energy blocks, but instead are using the term more loosely to refer to blocks that could both cause or be caused by physical or emotional states.)

Answer each question yes, no, or not sure/maybe sometimes...

1. Do you suffer from allergies? _____

2. Do you find it difficult to express yourself in writing? _____

3. Do you feel as if you remember little about your childhood? _____

4. Do you experience pain at least once a week (for example, headaches, backaches, or joint pain)? _____

5. Do you suffer from depression or sometimes feel a noticeable lack of emotion? _____

6. Do you feel like you don't have an outlet through which to express yourself creatively? _____

7. Do you feel uncomfortable with casual touching, such as a hug from a friend or a pat on the back? _____

8. Would you describe quantitative thinking as more "comfortable" than creative thinking? _____

9. Do you suffer from chronic muscle tension? _____

10. Do you feel more negative than positive emotions about any family member? _____

11. Did you enjoy creative tasks as a child but felt obligated to give them up as an adult? _____

12. Do you have high blood pressure? _____

13. Do you feel like you could have been a great *something* (artist, musician, parent, philosopher, humanitarian) but instead chose a path that involved less commitment or was "safer"? _____

14. Do you suffer from insomnia? _____

15. Are you addicted to nicotine, alcohol, caffeine, or drugs? _____

16. Has it been more than a month since you experienced a feeling you would describe as "inspiration"? _____

17. If you were given a professional massage for a gift, would you avoid getting the massage because it would be too uncomfortable, embarrassing, or intimidating? _____

18. Are you chronically tired even when you've had enough sleep? _____

19. Have you tried repeatedly to keep a journal to record your thoughts and feelings, and are you always unable to keep it up for more than a few weeks? _____

20. Do you seem to get colds more often than other people you know do? _____

21. Would you describe yourself as uncreative? _____

22. Are there people in your life you haven't forgiven? _____

23. Do you think you are untalented? _____

24. Do you have a general feeling of unhealthiness or unwellness, even if you can't describe any particular symptoms? _____

25. Do you feel guilty about spending time doing something creative that isn't related to your job, your household duties, or what you see as your other obligations? _____

26. Do you dislike who you are? _____

27. Do you eat a lot of processed foods? _____

28. Do you sometimes feel inexplicably angry? _____

29. Do you feel like you are more your mind than your body? _____

30. Do you have any phobias (irrational fears)? _____

Give yourself two points for every yes answer and one point for every not sure/maybe sometimes answer.

➤ **If your score was between 31 and 60:** You're experiencing some major blocks, and whether they are based in physical or emotional problems, they are almost certainly causing some health problems for you, even if minor ones. If you remain blocked, these physical problems may worsen, may disappear and reappear as more serious problems, and/or may expand into your emotional realm. They may already be affecting your emotional life, personal relationships, and self-esteem. Try improving your diet and exercise habits, receiving periodic massage or other bodywork, and consulting a physician or qualified holistic health practitioner for advice on your physical symptoms. Also consider seeking a counselor or receiving some type of bodywork that manipulates energy. Moving meditation may be just the ticket for shaking those blocks loose. Sitting or prone meditation, particularly in the form of the mind-body scan, can help you to get back in touch with your body to determine where any physical blockages are. But when you are feeling at your worst, exercise or practice moving meditation rather than sitting and dwelling.

➤ **If your score was between 10 and 29:** You have some blocks, like most people do. Some of them may be serious and causing you some physical and/or emotional problems. But you can deal with these blocks, and you can get rid of them. Meditation can be a great way for you to get back in touch with your inner self. Remembering who you are and learning to trust your instincts can help you to become unblocked; meditation is a great technique to facilitate this. It can also clue you in to other worthy avenues to pursue, such as bodywork, counseling, or medical treatment.

➤ **If your score was between 0 and 9:** Compared to most, you are relatively unblocked. You are in touch with your inner feelings, you take care of your body, and your energy is flowing freely. You still may have an issue or two in your emotional life, or a physical problem or two that, while not life-threatening, affects your health. Meditation may be easy for you, and you can benefit from it immensely. You have fewer barriers than most in your path, so meditate whenever you can. Sitting meditation, moving meditation, creative visualization, mindfulness meditation—try it all! Become an expert. You may just attain enlightenment!

Relax

Energy blocks are complex. Blocks due to physical causes can create emotional problems, blocks due to emotional problems can cause physical problems, and any number of factors can influence many aspects of the mind-body simultaneously. Rather than trying to diagnose your energy blocks yourself, see a qualified health care practitioner who is knowledgeable about energy therapy.

Meditation for the Body Chakra

According to yogic theory, the body contains seven primary energy centers called *chakras*. These centers of energy roughly correspond to the spine and nervous system centers in anatomy. They are beyond definition, though they are psycho-spiritual centers through which life-force energy travels. The *Saturn chakra* is located at the base of your spine, and in it lies a powerful but often dormant energy source. Yoga philosophy calls this source of energy *kundalini energy*, and compares it to a snake lying coiled and sleeping inside every person. Awakening this energy causes it to rise up through the chakras. When it reaches the top chakra, located at the crown of the skull, you may be able to realize and grasp your full potential and become enlightened about the unity of all things.

Meditating on the chakras.

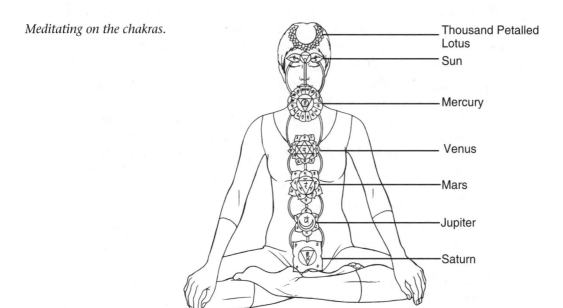

Chakras are psycho-spiritual energy centers in the body. The seven major chakras are:

➤ The Saturn, or Muladhara, chakra at the base of the spine (source of dormant energy)

➤ The Jupiter, or Swadhishthana, chakra behind the lower abdomen (source of creative energy and passion)

➤ The Mars, or Manipura, chakra behind the navel (source of action energy and of the digestive fire)

➤ The Venus, or Anahata, chakra behind the heart (source of compassionate energy and emotion)

➤ The Mercury, or Vishuddha, chakra in the throat (source of communication energy)

➤ The Sun, or Ajna, chakra on the forehead at the site of the urna, or third eye (source of intuitive energy, unclouded perception, and intuition)

➤ The Thousand Petalled Lotus, or Sahasrara chakra, at the crown of the head (source of enlightenment energy and self-realization)

Each (and every) chakra can become blocked, and certain exercises, such as yoga postures, can help to open them. Meditation, too, can help to open them. If you're feeling blocked (or even if you would just like to enhance your energy in a certain area), try one or two or all of our chakra meditations.

Saturn Chakra: Coiled Energy

The Saturn chakra lies at the base of your spine, where kundalini energy waits to be awakened. While sitting comfortably, close your eyes and focus your attention on the base of your spine. Sense the Earth beneath you. Feel the connection between your Saturn chakra and the ground below. Feel the Earth's energy powering your Saturn chakra and merging with your kundalini energy. Imagine this energy flowing slowly up your spine and out each of your limbs. Imagine it flowing upward out of the crown of your head. Imagine the energy pulsing and flashing, flushing and suffusing you with crackling, spectacular power. Now, allow the energy to dissipate slowly, falling back, leaving you energized but calm. Bring the energy back down into your Saturn chakra, ready to be activated when you need it. Feel again your connection with the earth's energy. Breathe.

Mindful Minute

Kundalini is often compared to a sleeping snake that, when awakened, is said to travel up through the chakras to the crown of the head. Once there, it can effect spiritual changes, such as enlightenment, and even, according to some, physical changes in the body, such as the ability to control previously involuntary bodily functions. It is the energy of self-actualization.

The Saturn chakra connects you with the Earth beneath you.

Jupiter Chakra: Creation Energy

The Jupiter chakra is associated with creative energy and passion.

Your Jupiter chakra is located in your lower abdomen. It is the seat of your creative energy. Sitting comfortably, close your eyes and focus your attention on your Jupiter chakra. Imagine your life-force energy concentrating in your lower abdomen. Imagine it intensifying, looking for an outlet. The energy builds, then transforms into pure creativity. Imagine this creativity mobilizing and flowing through your body, into your brain. Imagine it filling and activating your brain, preparing you to use it for whatever purpose you require. You become pure creativity. You can do anything. Breathe and imagine that creative energy stilling, holding, waiting for instructions. Open your eyes. Now go create something!

Mars Chakra: Action Energy

Your Mars chakra is located behind your navel. It is the seat of action energy. Sitting comfortably, close your eyes and focus your attention on your Mars chakra. Breathe deeply, and with each breath, imagine that energy is flowing from the air around you and from the Earth below you into your Mars chakra, where the energy accumulates. Imagine it stirring and swirling and sparking. Consciously release this energy into the rest of your body. Feel it flowing down your legs and into your feet. Feel it flooding your chest and streaming down your arms. Feel your hands and fingers tingling. Imagine it flowing into your head and awakening your brain. Imagine your hair standing on end, energy streaming out of your scalp. Feel the energy straightening your spine, activating your muscles, and awakening your mind. Now, open your eyes slowly and feel how energized you are. The rest of your day should be a breeze!

The Mars chakra is the seat of action energy.

Venus Chakra: Heart Energy

The Venus chakra is associated with compassionate energy.

Your Venus chakra is located behind your heart. It is the seat of compassionate energy. Sitting comfortably, close your eyes and focus your attention on your Venus chakra.

Breathe, and with each breath, imagine pure love streaming from your heart into the world. With your first 10 breaths, send compassion and love into the room where you are meditating. With the next 10 breaths, imagine the compassionate energy flooding out the doors to fill your entire house or apartment. With the next 10 breaths, imagine the love energy overflowing your house or apartment, spilling out the windows and doors and encompassing your neighborhood. The next 10 breaths flood your town or city with compassionate energy. The next 10 breaths fill your state. With the next 10 breaths, compassionate energy flows over the entire country. Then, the continent. With the last 10 breaths, embrace the entire planet in love. You can even extend out beyond the Earth to the other planets, galaxies, and realms of existence. Feel how strong and far-reaching your energy can be. Before you know it, compassionate energy will start bouncing back to you.

Mercury Chakra: Communication Energy

The Mercury chakra is associated with communication.

Your Mercury chakra is located in your throat. It is the seat of communication. Sitting comfortably, close your eyes and focus your attention on your Mercury chakra. Breathe and imagine your throat opening. Consider how you tend to communicate, then imagine that when your Mercury chakra is open, you can communicate effortlessly, speaking to others in a way that perfectly expresses your thoughts. Imagine the power of communication flowing from the universe, God, or whatever source makes sense to you, into your Mercury chakra, and then back out of you. Contemplate the way Ghandi, the Buddha, Moses, Mohammed, and other gifted spiritual leaders were able to communicate with divine and inspirational simplicity. You, too, have the ability to communicate at much deeper levels.

Sun Chakra: The Third Eye

The Sun chakra, or third eye, is the seat of perceptive energy and unclouded thinking.

Your Sun chakra, or third eye, is located on your forehead, between and just above your eyes. It is the seat of perceptive energy and unclouded thinking. Try this one outside on a sunny day, if possible. Sitting comfortably (try a blanket, quilt, or mat on the grass), close your eyes and tilt your face toward the sun. Focus your attention on your Sun chakra and imagine yourself communicating with the sun. Feel its rays flowing directly into your Sun chakra. Imagine your Sun chakra opening and instead of being blinded by the sun, imagine you can suddenly see everything with a clarity you've never experienced before. With your eyes still closed, imagine looking around you and seeing your house, your yard, or whatever your surroundings are, in an entirely new light—the light of the enlightened sun and the light of unclouded perception. How do things look? Sharper, more beautiful, radiating energy? How would you see the people in your life when looking at them through your Sun chakra? Now, open your eyes slowly. Do things look different than before? You may actually be seeing more clearly.

Thousand Petalled Lotus: Enlightenment

The Thousand Petalled Lotus is the chakra located at the crown of your head. It is the seat of enlightenment energy. Sitting comfortably, close your eyes and focus your attention on your Thousand Petalled Lotus. Imagine it opening slowly, like the petals of a flower just beginning to bloom. Quietly repeat to yourself the words "All is one." Say them slowly, hearing the way they sound, contemplating what they mean. Say it again and again until you feel as if your Thousand Petalled Lotus is opening in full and magnificent bloom. Ommmm.

The Thousand Petalled Lotus is the chakra of bliss, the enlightenment energy.

Oops, Your Aura Is Showing!

With all this energy flowing around and through you, wouldn't you think you might be able to see it? Actually, according to some, you can. Anyone can. All you have to do is develop your auric sight.

Although their existence is controversial, many believe that auras are the visual result of the vibrations that surround every material object. People have them, objects have them, plants, animals, trees, even articles of clothing, kitchen utensils, and bodies of water. Scientists will tell you that everything is made up of atoms, molecules, electrons, etc., and that these subcomponents of existence are by no means solid or still. They are filled with space and they move. So it makes sense that we are vibrating creatures, down to the atomic level.

We also emit electromagnetic energy. We emit heat. And some of that energy is emitted as ultraviolet light. According to auric theory, the part of our energy emitted as ultraviolet light is the part related to our consciousness, emotions, intentions, and spirituality. Auras, especially around the head, can reveal someone's basic character, mood at the moment, level of spiritual attainment, and even whether or not they are telling the truth.

The color of an aura is indicative of a person's basic mental, emotional, and spiritual state. Bright, clear colors mean a person is well intentioned, has a good nature, and is spiritually advanced. Dark, muddy, or cloudy colors denote bad intentions, materialistic natures, dark or depressed thoughts, pain, or anger. Auras can also contain little shoots and bursts of color within them. For example, bursts of purple are indicative of spiritual thoughts.

Chakras Have Colors, Too

Every chakra is associated with a color, and many claim that with practice, you can actually see a person's chakra glowing with that color. For example, the Sun chakra (or third eye) in the middle of the forehead appears a deep indigo. The more colorful and glowing the color, the more spiritual the person.

Each chakra is associated with the following color (although be aware that different people may associate the chakras with different colors than we do, and different colors mean different things to different people). Feel free to add these colors to your chakra meditations.

Thousand Petalled Lotus	Violet
Sun chakra	Indigo
Mercury chakra	Blue
Venus chakra	Green
Mars chakra	Yellow
Jupiter chakra	Orange
Saturn chakra	Red

A Special Way of Seeing

Learning to see an aura isn't difficult, but it becomes even easier with practice. Experienced auric-seers barely have to concentrate to see someone's aura, and the colors and subcolors are obvious and clear. Like to give it a try? We'll teach you how to see your own aura. Then, you can also apply the same technique to look at someone else's aura.

Here's how it works:

➤ Stand about four or five feet from a large mirror. The wall or surface behind you should be white or off-white (any solid, unmarked light color will do, but white is easiest). Lighting should be adequate but not too bright, and the surface behind you should be evenly lit without bright spots or shadows.

➤ Fix your eyes on the reflection of your Sun chakra, that point between and about one or two inches up from your eyes (the third eye).

Relax

If you're having trouble seeing auras, try squinting slightly. Squinting makes it easier for some people to master the technique.

➤ Gaze at that point for one full minute without moving your eyes away. You can blink, but don't look anywhere else. Then, still without moving your eyes away from that point, survey the area around your head via your peripheral vision. It might be hard to see at first, and you might be tempted to look directly at it, but don't. It works best if you keep your eyes fixed to your third eye. Eventually, you should see a sort of halo or illuminated area around your head. That is your aura. Notice the color or colors you see.

➤ The first time you try this exercise, you may only be able to keep it up for a couple of minutes, but if you gradually increase your time to 10 or 15 minutes per day, you'll get better and better. You'll be able to see auras everywhere.

But what do the aura colors mean? Maybe your aura was a beautiful sky blue, a pale turquoise, or a sunny yellow. Different sources interpret colors in different ways, and so to some extent, only you can interpret the color of your aura and what it means (even though many people out there will be happy to interpret your aura for you, for a fee, of course). There are a few basic characteristics that many people agree belong to different colors, however. We'll give you some generalizations, but your instinct about why your particular aura is blue, orange, or yellow at the particular moment is probably the most accurate.

Aura Color	Qualities
Blue	Calm, relaxed, tranquil, maternal, attentive, and caring
Brown	Unspiritual, unsettled, anxious, nervous, distracted
Gray	Depressed, pessimistic, negative, repressed anger
Green	Intelligent, straightforward, natural healer, quick thinker, close to nature, a doer
Orange	Creative, inspiring, compassionate, powerful, able to inspire and/or manipulate people
Pink	Protected, dominated by pure and radiant love
Purple/violet	Spiritual, intuitive, psychic abilities, dedicated to leading humanity toward the next step in higher consciousness
Red	Physical, materialistic, passionate, easily excited, emphasis on the body, intense emotion
Sulfur-colored	Discomfort, pain, irritation, festering anger
Turquoise	Full of energy, natural leader, organized
White	Innocence, purity, spirituality, or serious illness, altered state due to artificial substances
Yellow	Joyful, playful, blissful; when gold, rare spiritual development, highly evolved

Some aura theorists believe that all young children and infants can clearly see auras, but they lose this natural ability as they age. Another theory is that in past ages, more people could see auras and that in paintings, halos around saints and religious figures, such as Jesus and the Buddha, were actually auras perceived by the artists. Aura theorists often advise that anyone claiming to be a spiritual leader should have a bright golden-yellow aura. If they don't, they shouldn't be trusted as spiritual guides. Legend has it that both Jesus and the Buddha had large golden auras around their heads, and expansive pink auras around their entire bodies, suggesting spiritual perfection.

During the 1940s, a Russian photographer developed a photographic technique through which energy fields could actually be documented. Kurlian's images of both objects and people were stunning, and proof to many that auras do exist and that energy-based healing therapies are actually based on something real and measurable. One image of a leaf cut in half revealed an energy field that still surrounded the entire leaf. People who have experienced amputation often experience pain in the amputated area, and stories abound of bodyworkers who manipulated the energy over where the missing limb would have been and are able to elicit positive results in their patients.

Aura Meditation Exercise

Although auras tend to have a primary color reflecting someone's basic nature, they also change according to mood, health, and other factors. Some people believe you can actually alter the color of your aura through concentration. Aura meditation is a great way to adjust your aura to a healthful and productive state. It also offers a great point of focus for your concentration.

Try the following aura meditation exercise after you've spent a few weeks practicing how to find your own aura and feel comfortable doing so. It should take 20 to 30 minutes:

➤ Sit down comfortably about four or five feet in front of a mirror so that you are backed by a light-colored background. You can use a chair or you can sit on the floor.

➤ Find your third eye (as instructed above) and fix your gaze upon it. Breathe normally but listen to your breath. Concentrate all your energy on that one spot on your forehead for one full minute.

➤ After a minute is up (don't look at a watch—don't move those eyes—but you can count off 60 seconds to yourself as you concentrate), find your aura by using your peripheral vision. Notice its color.

➤ Now think about blue. Blue is the color of relaxation and balance. Imagine your entire body relaxing. Imagine a brilliant blue color washing over your entire being, dissolving muscle tension and all your worries, washing them away in sapphire waves of blue. Keep your eyes fixed on your third eye, but think blue, blue, blue. Try to adjust your aura to become bluer, brighter, and clearer. Stay with blue for at least five minutes.

➤ Now, think about green. Imagine that your body is now so relaxed that it is ready and able to heal itself. Imagine that all things amiss in your system, from a stuffy nose to a scrape on your knee, allergies, high blood pressure, arthritis, or whatever, are open and ready for healing. Green is the color of natural healing abilities. Visualize a beautiful, grassy green color flowing over your body. Breathe it in and out. Notice how green feels as it moves through you, knitting, repairing, unblocking, flushing, and calming your system into a more healthful state. Try to adjust your aura to become greener, brighter, and clearer. Stay with green for at least five minutes.

➤ Now, think about yellow. Yellow is the color of pure joy. Imagine your body immersed in a brilliant column of sunny yellow light. This light dissolves all your sorrows, all your attachments, everything that causes you to feel sadness or suffering. Imagine yellow flowing through you, filling you with joy, bliss, and a playful spirit. Now imagine the yellow column of light is shot through with showers of sparkling, gleaming gold. Imagine your higher self emerging, merging with the universe in a transcendent yet warmly familiar unity. Feel as if you are finally at home. Let the smile show on your face. Feel the bliss. Is your aura shimmering?

➤ Bask in gold for a while, then briefly recall the feel of yellow, green, and blue. Breathe deeply for another minute or two, then close your eyes. You'll see the imprint of your aura for a couple of seconds. Bid it farewell, open your eyes, and move on with your day, at peace.

Bliss Byte

As you look at other people's auras, you might notice that many people have small auras. People who become caught up in worldly endeavors and materialism, ignoring their spiritual sides, supposedly have shrunken auras. In contrast, meditation is thought to expand the aura.

Natural Medicine Goes with the Flow

It's great to learn how to direct your own energy, but maybe you have a true gift for healing and could help heal the energy of others. Many are doing just that, practicing different forms of healing and bodywork to help re-align and replenish life-force energy in others, as well as teaching others to replenish and manage their own energy. Techniques abound, but here are a few of the most popular.

Reiki

Pronounced *ray-kee*, *Reiki* is a type of bodywork that emphasizes the manipulation of life-force energy through the chakras. The Reiki practitioner places his or her hands on the receiver over the chakras, working along the front and the back of the body. Each touch is held for several minutes, allowing universal life-force energy to flow through the practitioner into the receiver (the energy comes from the universe, not from the Reiki practitioner, who serves as a channel, not as an energy source).

The theory is that chakras are special places on the body where energy can enter, and placing hands over them allows them to open and receive energy. The more energy in the body, the better it can heal, align, and balance itself.

There are several levels of Reiki accomplishment, culminating in the title of Reiki Master. Training involves a process that unblocks the practitioner's own chakras so they can serve as ideal energy channelers.

Although you can't learn Reiki from a book alone, try the following Reiki meditation. The area you are holding is your point of concentration. Remember those chakras? Work through each one, holding your hands over the area for about three minutes each. As you hold your hands over your chakras, imagine tapping life-force energy from the universe and feel it flowing into your chakras, suffusing your body and soul with vitality:

1. Sit or stand comfortably with your back straight. Place the fingers of both hands along your eyebrows with your little fingers resting on the bridge of your nose. Your palms should be cupping your cheeks. Press very gently with your fingers around the eyes. Hold.

2. Place your palms on either side of your head so your fingers barely touch across the crown of your head. Hold.

3. Reach around to the back of your head and, fingers barely touching, cradle the back of your skull. Hold.

4. Next, place your right hand gently on your throat and your left hand across the top of your sternum so that the fingers of your left hand rest beneath the wrist of your right hand. Hold.

5. Now place your palms on your lower chest near the bottom ribs. Hold.

6. Place your palms over your stomach so your fingers touch over your navel. Hold.

7. Place your palms over your lower abdomen with your fingers pointing diagonally downward and touching just over your pubic bone. Hold.

Joan performs step eight in this self-Reiki meditation.

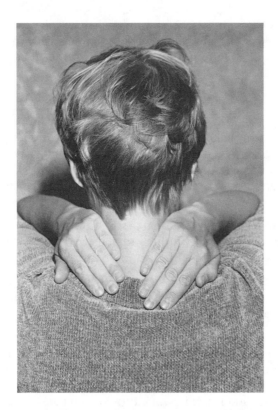

8. Place your hands over your shoulders behind you and press your palms against your upper back, fingers pointed down. Hold.

9. Bend your left arm behind you and rest your hand over your right shoulder blade. Hold. Repeat on the other side. Hold.

10. Place both hands around your lower ribcage on your back, just above your waist. Hold.

11. Place both hands over the tops of your hip bones on your back, just above your buttocks. Hold.

12. Now, bring your hands back to the front and cup your right hand in your left hand. Breathe in and out naturally for another three minutes, feeling the life-force energy moving through your body, flushing away negativity and replacing it with healing and joy.

Acupuncture

Acupuncture is a centuries-old technique that originated in China. Hair-thin needles are inserted into pressure points for pain relief and healing. The theory goes that by stimulating pressure points, acupuncture releases blocked areas and equalizes life-force energy, allowing the body to solve its own pain and heal itself. Some people meditate during their acupuncture treatments to facilitate the process.

Many insurance companies in the United States now cover acupuncture treatments, and although many mainstream physicians admit they don't know why it works, they also admit that it *does* work. Before receiving treatment, make sure you find an acupuncturist who is properly trained and licensed.

Biofeedback

Biofeedback is a type of therapy that teaches individuals to gain control over the parts of the nervous system that regulate bodily functions such as skin temperature, heart rate, brain waves, and blood flow. By watching or listening to representations of bodily functions via a monitor, individuals learn how different states "feel" and gradually can learn to alter those feelings, thereby altering the function itself.

Although biofeedback techniques can be used to teach people to control a wide range of body functions, some of the most common are breathing, heart rate, muscle tension, skin temperature, electrodermal activity (subtle changes in sweat activity), pulse, and brain wave activity (see Chapter 7, "Neurophysiology: This Is Your Brain on Meditation"). Biofeedback can be a great partner for meditation. The techniques it teaches promote body control and mental focus, both of which make meditation more effective.

Bliss Byte

Proponents of energy therapies often quote physicist Albert Einstein because his theories (to drastically simplify them) postulate that all objects are surrounded by electromagnetic fields of energy about to become matter. His famous equation, $E=mc^2$, theorizes that energy and matter can each be transformed into the other, back and forth. Einstein once said, "Up to the twentieth century, reality was everything humans could touch, smell, see, and hear. Since the initial publication of the chart of the electromagnetic spectrum, humans have learned that what they can touch, smell, see, and hear is less than one-millionth of reality."

Therapeutic Touch

Therapeutic Touch (TT) is a controversial technique in which patients are treated by practitioners who never touch them. The theory behind TT is similar to the theory behind Reiki: life-force energy can become imbalanced, and the TT therapist acts as a channel for life-force energy to flow into the receiver. However, in TT, the practitioner's hands usually stay about four to six inches above the skin of the receiver, touching only the body's energy field. Some practitioners even incorporate guided visualizations, transforming the session into a sort of mind-body meditation.

The Least You Need to Know

➤ We are all surrounded by, suffused with, and animated by life-force energy that also permeates and fuels the universe.

➤ Chakras are energy centers in the body, each governing certain types of energy and serving as portals for energy to enter and exit the body, and to be transformed.

➤ The electromagnetic field around all objects and living things is called an aura. You can learn to see auras, and their colors can reveal a person's inner nature, mood, and intentions.

➤ Many healing therapies use the concept of life-force energy, including Reiki, acupuncture, biofeedback, and Therapeutic Touch.

Are You the Dreamer, or the Dream?

Who are you in your dreams? If you're like most people, sometimes you are *you*, and sometimes you are watching yourself do things, and sometimes you are someone else altogether. You may have places you visit over and over again in your dream landscape that don't exist in real life; perhaps you know people in your dreams who don't exist in real life. But wait—when it comes to dreams, what is real life and what is dream life? Can we be sure which is which? And what does any of it have to do with meditation?

What Is Real?

For centuries, philosophers have been playing with the question of reality. What is the "self"? What does it mean to exist, to be real? As the seventeenth century philosopher/mathematician Rene Descartes once said: "I think, therefore I am." Is the act of thinking what makes reality? You've probably heard the old conundrum: "If a tree falls in a forest and no one hears it, does it make a sound?" Technically, we know the answer. Sound waves are emitted, so it does make a sound. Whether the sound is heard or not is irrelevant. But that isn't the point of this particular koan. The point is, if someone isn't there to observe an event, is it real? The question urges us to meditate upon the very nature of reality.

Each of us exists in our own minds, and many have argued, therefore, that objectivity doesn't exist. We can only be subjective because we can never remove ourselves from our personal perspective. Any attempt to be objective is merely an artificial construct.

Mindful Minute

The scientific method is a method of inquiry into the question "how" rather than the question "why" (the realm of philosophy). The scientific method involves forming a hypothesis, then setting out to prove or disprove it using objectivity, reproducible results, inductive reasoning (from specific examples to general theories), and/or deductive reasoning (from general theories to specific results). Experiments are performed and a conclusion is drawn.

Of course, one of the goals of meditation is to lose subjectivity. Eastern philosophers, especially, advocate losing the self and attachments to the world, which are all products of subjective thinking, through the process of meditation. Not an easy task. Some might argue that such a task is impossible and that any sense of the loss of self during meditation is just an illusion. Eastern philosophers would counter that instead, the self *itself* is the illusion, and that any sense of self, or even of worldly reality, is the artificial construct.

Of course, at this point in our human evolution, we can't prove either hypothesis—that self or lack of self is the true reality. Such issues are difficult (if not impossible) to study using scientific method, and scientific study may not even be the way to find an answer.

But what about when we dream? Dreams and sleep have been studied extensively. Have we come to any conclusions that are more concrete when it comes to the dream realm? We know a few things. For example, brain waves exhibited during dream sleep are almost indistinguishable from brain waves exhibited when awake. That's why dream sleep (or *REM sleep*) is often called *paradoxical sleep*. Yet dream sleep obviously isn't the same as being awake. Falling asleep is, in a sense, losing the self, or at least, the conscious self. Conscious control takes a break, allowing the *unconscious mind* to take over. Dream sleep is like being awake with the unconscious mind behind the wheel. The unconscious mind consists of the thoughts, feelings, desires, and impulses of which the individual is unaware but that influence behavior.

The unconscious mind is a vast, unexplored territory. Who knows how subjective, objective, or even "real" the unconscious is? Many philosophers/psychologists have speculated—Plato and St. Augustine, Freud and Jung, to name a few prominent thinkers—but the workings of the unconscious mind can't be measured. The best we can do is try to remember our dreams, those leftover symbols, landmarks, and glimpses of the topography of the unconscious mind.

So, dare we turn Descartes' idea on its head and say, "I dream, therefore I am not?" Or, "I dream, therefore, for a short while, I am not?" Our dream lives may be as close as we can get to peering over the edge of reality and seeing what else is out there, for only in sleep is our conscious mind no longer able to exercise its subjectivity.

Separating the Dreamer from the Dream

So let's explore that dream world a little further. Let's say you have a dream that you're a bird flying in the sky, looking down on the Earth. Are you quite sure, after you awake, that you dreamed you were a bird? Could you, perhaps, be a bird dreaming you are a person? The Chinese philosopher Chuang-tzu once dreamed he was a butterfly who was very happy with himself. When he awoke, he, too, wondered whether he was a man dreaming he was a butterfly, or a butterfly dreaming he was a man. (Remember Teresa of Avila's butterfly from Chapter 5, "The Soul Has Many Mansions"?)

You'll probably agree that in both cases (yours and Chuang-tzu's), the first scenario is probably the "real" one. But then, why did you dream you were a bird, or a cow, or someone of the opposite gender, or even someone a lot like you but not exactly the same?

Theories abound. Perhaps you're working out emotional dilemmas by acting out different realities in your dreams. Maybe your brain is simply sifting through the huge amount of sensory stimuli you accumulate each day to keep the important stuff and discard the unimportant stuff, like some ethereal secretary cleaning out your mental file cabinet. Or maybe all that neuron firing is totally random.

Whatever your personal opinion, your dreams can be a tool to help you know yourself better. They can also be a tool for your meditation sessions, just as meditation sessions can be a tool for dream work. Together, dreams and meditation can be the

From A to Om

Paradoxical sleep is another name for the stage of sleep usually referred to as **REM (rapid eye movement) sleep**, where dreams occur. During this stage of sleep, brain waves resemble brain waves when the individual is awake, yet muscles are completely relaxed, producing a paralyzing effect (so we don't get up and act out those dreams...). This lack of muscle tone is called atonia.

Mindful Minute

Rene Descartes (1596–1650) was a French philosopher and mathematician who is sometimes called the father of modern philosophy. Descartes attempted to apply rational, inductive reasoning to philosophy using principles inherent in science and math. He once said, "In our search for the direct road to truth, we should busy ourselves with no object about which we cannot attain a certitude equal to that of the demonstration of arithmetic and geometry."

key to unlocking the secrets of your unconscious, and unlocking that least-known part of yourself can lead to greater self-knowledge.

Dreams have traditionally been of great inspiration to artists. Salvador Dali, William Blake, Henri Rousseau, and Jasper Johns all used dream imagery in their paintings. George Frederic Handel reportedly heard the ending of his famous work, *The Messiah*, in a dream. Ingmar Bergman, a renowned Swedish director, frequently used his own dream imagery in his films. Orson Welles used his own dream imagery in his film *The Trial*. Mary Shelley created the Frankenstein monster from a nightmare. Edgar Allen Poe, Robert Louis Stevenson, William Burroughs, Jack Kerouac, Franz Kafka, and Charlotte Brontë all used dreams for inspiration and imagery in their writing.

Freud: The Royal Road to the Unconscious

Mindful Minute

Sigmund Freud (1856–1939) was an Austrian physician, neurologist, and the founder of psychoanalysis, a technique of talk therapy for investigating unconscious mental processes and treating psychological disorders and illnesses.

Sigmund Freud's book *The Interpretation of Dreams* is arguably the most important and influential text on dream interpretation. Freudian theories on dream interpretation as a key to the unconscious mind are widespread and have influenced Western culture to an immeasurable extent. Freud called dreams the "royal road to the unconscious." He saw them as important keys to unraveling the unconscious aspects of the human psyche. He believed dreams contained symbols that represented inner conflicts, repressed emotions, and often angry, violent, or "inappropriate" sexual thoughts. In fact, Freud has been widely criticized for asserting that human nature is not essentially good at its core, but essentially driven by base instincts.

Because of societal structure, however, base instinct is often inappropriate. We can't walk around grabbing food whenever we want it, dropping to the floor to sleep whenever we are tired, lashing out and hurting people whenever we are angry or threatened, or ravishing anyone who catches our fancy. Instead, according to Freudian theory, we repress these desires into our unconscious, along with memories of our past experiences (particularly from childhood), things we do that we wish we hadn't done, and things that were done to us that angered, scared, or hurt us.

In our dreams, the window to the unconscious cracks open, and we get little peeks of what we've pushed down there, manifested as symbols and stories our psyche weaves out of all the bits and pieces, wishes, and fears. Interpreting our dreams, ideally with the help of a trained therapist, can explain many of our otherwise inexplicable problems in life: phobias (fears, such as of heights or enclosed spaces), depression, self-destructive feelings, obsessions, fantasies, or problems with relationships and self-esteem.

Freud also once said that we don't have dreams so they can be interpreted, and that dreams were merely "guardians of sleep," keeping internal conflicts from awakening us. But perhaps they can also be used to solve problems and to understand ourselves better.

Jung: Universal Archetypes

Carl Jung was a colleague of Freud's who later went his own way, broadening upon Freud's theories. Jung interpreted mental and emotional disturbances as attempts by an individual to find personal and spiritual wholeness. He believed in the unconscious, but divided it into two types, personal and collective. In the collective unconscious, Jung theorized, lie the archetypes shared by all humankind. These archetypes represent societal or human beliefs and morals, and are represented in ancient mythology, fairytales, and other universal stories.

To Jung as well as Freud, dreams are keys to the unconscious. But for Jung, dreams from the collective unconscious represent our basic human beliefs. When we face dilemmas in life, these archetypes tend to arise with greater frequency, helping us along our road to personal fulfillment.

Mindful Minute

Carl Jung (1875–1961) was a Swiss psychiatrist who founded the analytical school of psychology. Jung coined many common psychological terms used today, such as "complexes" (as in "inferiority complex") and the notion of extroverts and introverts. He believed dreams were attempts to work toward wholeness by integrating the different levels of the unconscious.

Jung believed that each of us is seeking wholeness and that integrating our personal unconscious and our collective unconscious was the way to achieve this wholeness. Because both the personal and collective unconscious can be represented in our dreams, interpreting those dreams, even if just for ourselves, can be a way to begin this integration. To Jung, life was a journey of growth and self-examination was the vehicle.

The Dalai Lama: Finding the Clear Light of Sleep

In Tibetan philosophy, sleep is like a mini death, a sort of practice for death. The period of time between death and rebirth when the soul is in a sort of transition (known as the *bardo*) is comparable to the period of time between deep sleep and dream sleep, called the Clear Light of Sleep. Ideally, although asleep, the soul is conscious, yet this kind of consciousness is marked by complete clarity of mind, inner peace, and understanding. While some Westerners consider sleep as an unconscious time, according to certain types of Buddhism, sleep is ideally a super-conscious, super-aware period.

Mindful Minute

The Dalai Lama is believed by Tibetan Buddhists to be a reincarnation of the Buddha. When the Dalai Lama dies, his soul is thought to enter a new life, who, after being identified by traditional tests, will become the next Dalai Lama. The current and fourteenth Dalai Lama, Tenzin Gyatso, was forced into exile in India on March 16, 1959 by the Communist Chinese government occupying Tibet. In 1989 he received the Nobel Peace Price for leading nonviolent opposition to Chinese rule of Tibet.

Maybe that doesn't sound too restful. How can you relax if you are super-conscious? Actually, this state is also the ideal meditation state, and many religions and philosophies that advocate meditation believe that meditation is more restorative than sleep. In fact, many seasoned meditators are said to require minimal sleep because they derive such profound rest from a deep meditative state.

About dreams and meditation, the Dalai Lama once said, "Tibetan Buddhism considers sleep to be a form of nourishment, like food, that restores and refreshes the body. Another type of nourishment is *samadhi*, or meditative concentration. If one becomes advanced enough in the practice of meditative concentration, then this itself sustains or nourishes the body."

As you can see, the lines between sleeping, dreaming, and meditating sometimes blur. The goals are similar, the results similar, and the brain wave patterns similar. The philosophies on these subjects vary widely but also have their similarities. Dreaming, meditating, and self-study corresponding with both are all roads to greater self-knowledge and, ideally, greater bliss.

Meditation, Sleep, and Consciousness

But let's get back to science for a bit. Many people have compared the sleep cycle to the meditation process, and the similarities are striking. Meditation seems to be like a fusion of unconscious and conscious states. Brain waves look like the meditator is asleep (and admittedly, sometimes meditators do fall asleep). But even in studies where the meditator had to press a button to signal each progressively deeper stage of meditation and was able to do so successfully, brain wave patterns still were similar to those of sleep.

Understanding the Sleep Cycles

To best compare the states of sleep and meditation, it will help to have a little background on the sleep cycle. Although sleep cycles vary in different people, most of us go through several sleep cycles of between 90 and 110 minutes every night.

The sleep cycle consists of four stages plus dream sleep. In stage 1, the sleeper becomes increasingly drowsy and drifts into sleep. Brain wave activity changes from random, fast waves to regular *alpha waves* as drowsiness sets in. Then, when we fall asleep, even slower *theta waves* dominate.

In stage 2, sleep becomes deeper, though the sleeper is still fairly easy to awaken. EEGs during stage 2 reveal regular waves with occasional bursts of energy, indicating brain activity is still sporadic. In stage 3, brain waves become slower and more even while body temperature and heart rate slow down. During stage 3, the sleeper is difficult to awaken and brain waves are dominated by large, slow *delta waves*. In stage 4, the deepest level, brain wave patterns are also dominated by delta waves. This deepest level of sleep usually begins about an hour after the commencement of stage 1.

After reaching stage 4, the stages reverse. When the sleeper reaches stage 1 again (or sometimes stage 2), he or she enters REM sleep. REM stands for rapid eye movement (so called because the eyes move visibly during REM sleep), and it is dream sleep. During REM sleep, brain waves resemble waking brain waves, becoming faster, more active, and more random. Blood pressure, heart rate, and breath rate all increase as well. Muscles, however, become temporarily paralyzed. This paralysis keeps us from physically acting out our dreams (so the theory goes), and when this mechanism malfunctions, sleepwalking may result.

After REM sleep, the sleeper usually awakens, even if very briefly or not fully. Then the cycle starts again. The time each stage lasts varies in individuals and also throughout the night. In the first few cycles, REM sleep is comparatively brief, but takes up a larger portion of the cycle toward morning. Naps taken in the morning, or an hour or two after awakening from a night's sleep, are often primarily REM sleep. Afternoon naps contain less REM sleep, and then the whole process begins again in the evening.

Meditation, too, is thought to occur in four cycles of progressively deeper concentration. Meditators don't dream, however (unless they fall asleep).

From A to Om

Alpha waves are brain waves that cycle up and down on an EEG about eight to 12 times per second and usually correspond with a drowsy state or, in meditation, a very relaxed yet alert state. Slower **theta waves** cycle between three to seven times per second and usually correspond with light sleep or deep meditation. The slowest **delta waves** cycle between $\frac{1}{2}$ to two times per second, and usually correspond with deep sleep.

Relax

Never practice meditation while driving! Falling asleep is common during meditation, so you certainly don't want that to happen as you speed down the interstate. The only kind of meditation to practice during driving is mindfulness meditation, during which you become acutely aware of what you are doing. Everyone should drive mindfully!

Instead, they seem to be able to remain in a state that is not sleep, yet not really waking, either, at least according to EEG readings. One study showed experienced Zen meditators exhibiting a mixture of alpha and theta waves, the characteristic brain wave patterns of light sleep.

Fusing the Sleeping and Waking Consciousness

In other words, meditation is essentially a fusion of sleeping and waking consciousness. What does all this have to do with dreaming? If dreaming is the key to unlocking our unconscious minds, and meditating is a way to sleep while staying awake, meditation may also be able to reveal our unconscious minds while conscious.

Meditation can also be an arena in which we can consider our dreams, open our minds to their meaning, and perhaps gain new insights about ourselves.

Bliss Byte

What you eat affects your mood, energy level, and feeling of "lightness" or "heaviness." It can also affect the quality of your sleep. Try not eating for at least three or four hours before going to sleep. Don't drink any caffeinated beverages after dinnertime. Avoid alcoholic beverages (you might get to sleep faster, but your quality of sleep will be impaired). Your internal energies can then be more clearly focused on subconscious exploration.

From A to Om

The **hypnogogic state** is the transitional state between waking and sleeping when the mind is particularly open to suggestions or images from the unconscious, and the individual may have strange visual, aural, or tactile "experiences" or hallucinations. The **hypnopompic state** is the equivalent transitional state between sleeping and waking.

Hypnogogic and Hypnopompic Experiences

Have you ever thought you heard someone call your name just as you were falling asleep? What about hearing music playing or a phone ringing? Do you remember a fragment of someone standing in the doorway, of a chair next to your bed starting to move, or even seeing brightly colored shapes? You've had a hypnogogic experience. The *hypnogogic state* is the transitional state between waking and sleeping; it has the quality of a hallucinatory fragment. The *hypnopompic state* is a similar experience, but occurs in the transition between sleeping and waking.

During hypnogogic and hypnopompic states, you are conscious or feel you are, yet your unconscious mind has a strong hold on you. You are in the borderlands of your mind and may be able to apprehend images or ideas from your unconscious that you wouldn't normally have access to.

The meditative state, again, is ideally similar to these transitional states. Tuning into hypnogogic and hypnopompic experiences, remembering them, and making an effort to consider them may help you retain their feeling and perhaps find it again during meditation.

In fact, the whole point of attempting to remember altered states of consciousness such as these or your dreams when applied to meditation is to tune your mind in to its other realms. It's a little like trying yoga when you've never done any physical activity beyond walking, sitting, and lying down. It stretches your mind in ways it isn't accustomed to stretching. By becoming more flexible, your mind becomes stronger, meditation becomes easier, your mind becomes clearer, you tune in to even more experiences, and voilà! You know yourself.

Do You Remember Your Dreams?

Although most people remember their dreams, a few people typically don't, and some even claim they don't dream. Even though people who sleep experience REM sleep, no one has definitively proven that they always dream during REM sleep. This period is considered dream sleep because in research studies, most of the time when people are awakened during REM sleep, they can vividly describe a dream.

Mindful Minute

For more on dreams and keeping a dream journal, read *The Complete Idiot's Guide to Interpreting Your Dreams* (Alpha Books, 1998).

But not always. Sometimes, people can even describe fragments and impressions that seem dreamlike when awakened from nonREM sleep (although these are not dreams).

If you're like most people, however, you do remember your dreams some of the time. Would you like to remember them more often? Like anything else, remembering your dreams is just a matter of...you guessed it! Practice. People who study dreams suggest that keeping a dream journal next to your bed is one of the best ways to train yourself to remember your dreams. Dreams are always freshest right after awakening since awakening typically occurs just after REM sleep.

To begin using a dream journal:

➤ Find or buy a blank notebook. On the first page, write the following statement (or a different statement about your purpose that you create):

My dream journal contains clues to myself. By recording my dreams each day, I am making a commitment to know myself better. By meditating on the contents of this dream journal, I am moving toward self-actualization.

➤ Keep the dream journal and a pen next to your bed so that you can quickly jot down the impressions you remember from your dream whenever you awaken. (Dream memories usually fade very quickly, so write them down immediately, even if you are still drowsy.)

➤ Every morning for two weeks, try to piece together the night's dreams immediately upon awakening and without opening your eyes. Recall the imagery, the sequence, the characters, the setting. Then, open your eyes and immediately write down everything you can remember. After you've written it down, give your dream a title. The title may be revealing to you later.

➤ Can't quite find the words to describe your dream or a part of it? Draw a picture.

➤ Whenever possible during these first two weeks, take a nap one to two hours after you wake up in the morning. REM sleep is most prevalent at this time of the day. Don't forget to keep your dream journal by your side. (Most of us can't afford to nap at this time, of course, but if you have the kind of schedule that allows it, give it a try.)

➤ Each night before you go to bed, or whenever you're about to take a nap, spend five to 10 minutes meditating by relaxing and repeating the mantra: "I will dream, I will remember." Or, if you are facing a particular decision, ask yourself what you should decide and leave your mind open to answers. Don't try to answer your own question consciously. Just let the question hang there as you fall asleep.

➤ After two weeks, go back and read your dream journal, then write freely about any patterns, symbols, or meanings you perceive. You should be in the habit of recording your dreams by now. Keep it up!

➤ Keep dreaming, keep recording, and keep meditating!

Dreamwork Meditations

Once you are used to recording your dreams, you'll find you remember them more often and their meanings come to you more easily. Sure, sometimes it helps to have a professional psychoanalyst interpret your dreams, but you may be able to discover their meanings on your own. Who knows you better than you? Only you were there throughout your entire history—every moment, every experience, and every perception. You are best equipped to imagine what your dreams say about you.

Bliss Byte

If you find it difficult to grab a pen and write legibly when you first awaken, try tape-recording your dreams instead. Keep a tape recorder by your bed and whenever you awaken from a dream, gab to your heart's content about all the details you can remember. You can transcribe your dreams later, at your convenience, or simply keep a library of dream tapes for your listening pleasure. Label tapes with dates and the titles you give your dreams.

But if you do want to work with your dreams, try the following suggestions for dream-work meditations. Before any dreamwork meditation session, relax, sit comfortably with your back straight, and begin by focusing on your breathing.

➤ Consider an image, place, or person you've seen in more than one dream. Imagine all the details. How does the image, person, or place look? Fill in the things you can't remember by letting your imagination produce the details. For example, if you have recurring dreams about a house, picture the house in your mind. What color is it? What are the details of the architecture? Imagine each of the rooms. What is the furniture like? Are there people at home? Who owns the house? Why are you there or not there? Keep digging by asking yourself as many questions as you can about your chosen image, place, or person. If thoughts occur to you about the meaning of the dream or what it represents, great! If they don't, don't press it. Just keep filling in the dream with your imagination and see where it takes you. When your unconscious is ready to reveal the meaning, it will reveal the meaning.

➤ Think of a good dream you had. Go through the sequence of your dream in your mind, re-living the order of events. Does the chronology make sense to you in any way? Now consider the characters of the dream, if any. Are they people you know, strangers, or a combination? Are you in the dream as you or are you watching yourself in the dream? Now imagine the setting. Where did the dream take place? Did the setting change? Why do you think the dream was set where it was set? Now, consider why the dream was good. Did it give you a secure, comfortable feeling? Was it about love, success, or happiness? What elements gave it its "goodness"? What does the dream say about you?

➤ Think of a disturbing dream you had. Break it down into all its elements. What bothered you about it? Was it the way you were in the dream or the way someone else was? Was it scary, sad, or tragic? Now imagine what the dream could represent. Are you nervous about something that is going to happen? Are you feeling like one of your relationships isn't right? If the dream was about death or destruction, these things usually symbolize change rather than something necessarily negative. Are you anticipating, dreading, or even wishing for a major change in your life? How could you interpret the dream in a positive way, as instructing you about how you feel and what you should do?

Bliss Byte

Boo! Do you have scary dreams? Although nightmares are more common in children, adults have them sometimes, too, especially during stressful times. Learning how to dream lucidly—that is, to realize you are dreaming during your dream—is an effective way to take control of your scary dreams and turn them into empowering dreams during which you face your fears and challenges. Note: If your nightmares don't let up or are very disturbing and are affecting your waking life, explore them with the help of a licensed therapist or mental health professional.

Using Your Dreams to Empower Meditation

As you seek to know yourself better through meditation, your dreams can be a powerful tool. Use them in your meditation as if they are secret passwords allowing you access to ever-new, hidden levels of yourself. You say you keep dreaming about a friendly dog? A waterfall? A dark castle? An attractive stranger who holds you in his or her arms? Clues! What do they mean? There's your meditation. Focus on the clue. Examine it. Dissect it. Name it. Describe it. Look at it from all sides. Apply it to yourself, to your loved ones, to your dilemmas. Where does it fit? Which lock does it open? Eventually you'll find the answer.

Or maybe you won't. Plenty of people will argue that some dreams are just dreams, that they are random images or are discarded, insignificant experiences your brain is simply processing before tucking away. But trust your intuition. Some dreams just "feel" meaningful or seem like they hold answers for you. Focus on those dreams.

Getting to Know Your Shadow Self

The "you" in your dreams changes, but chances are, that "you" is frequently different from the "you" you usually know. Think of the "dream you" as your shadow self, someone deep inside you who, although buried, can influence the behavior and thoughts of the "outer you." Get to know this shadow self.

How? By studying what your shadow self does, where it goes, who it is. When re-reading your dream journal, pay attention to the character of "you." Think about this character's motivations, actions, and feelings. In any particular dream, what makes this character feel good or bad, guilty or blissful? Where does the character tend to be? Who does the character tend to be with? What do you think about this character? Do you feel like this person is you or someone completely different, even though the character is obviously "you" in the dream? Write down your thoughts and read them again later. Meditate on them. Meditate on your shadow self, and try to discover more about it. If you work together with your shadow self and not at odds with each other, you—the integrated you—can eventually emerge.

Sometimes your shadow self can be the "dark" side of the person you present to the world, those parts of you that you find hard to acknowledge or accept. Meditation can be a way to come to terms with parts of yourself that make you feel uncomfortable. In Jungian psychological terms, the "shadow" can be half of the yin and yang balance of two archetypal behaviors. For example, the Western hero in the white hat and the villain in the black hat. Both are a part of us.

Lucid Dreaming

Wouldn't it be fun if, while you were dreaming, you could *know* you were dreaming? Maybe this has actually happened to you before. For some, lucid dreaming, the conscious awareness that you are dreaming, is a lifelong goal. According to one survey, about 58 percent of people have had at least one lucid dream, but only about 20 percent have them frequently. But dreaming lucidly is a skill that can be developed and refined. Lucid dreaming can then be harnessed as a further way to direct the mind. It is itself a sort of meditation wherein the mind has powers it doesn't have while awake.

Bliss Byte

To enlist technology in the service of lucid dreaming, look into one of several lucid dream machines designed to help invoke lucid dreams. The sleeper wears a mask that contains lights, hooked to a small computer. The machine can sense when the sleeper enters dream sleep and signals the dreamer with flashing lights inside the mask, subtle sounds, or both, designed to signal the dreamer that he or she is dreaming. These machines are available in many catalogues and some progressive bookstores and boutiques that carry unique items and meditation supplies. And of course, you can purchase them on the Internet!

Lucid dreams have been proven to exist. Subjects hooked up to an EEG were instructed to move their eyes in a specific pattern using right-left motions when they became aware during their dreams that they were dreaming. (The eye movement was the only movement they could make since other muscles are in temporary paralysis during REM sleep.) In several studies, while the EEG revealed that subjects were indeed sound asleep and dreaming, the subjects did give the appropriate signal and, when awakened, described remembering to give the signal in their dreams. Women are more likely to dream lucidly than men (but men are frequently successful, too).

Lucid dreaming can allow you to confront and conquer fears (a common scenario for lucid dreams), enjoy supernatural abilities or situations you could never actually experience, and even explore symbolic representations of yourself and your life challenges. What a great opportunity for fun and personal growth! Why not give it a try? To help yourself dream lucidly, or simply to dream with more clarity and to remember your dreams better, try the following tips:

➤ Meditate! People who meditate are more likely to dream lucidly.

➤ Pick a symbol from your memory that represents something significant to you but is easy to visualize—a star, a statue, or an ordinary object, for example. Decide this will be your lucidity object, and when you see it in your dream, you'll know you are dreaming.

➤ When you awaken in the middle of the night from a dream, keep imagining the dream to get yourself back into it again. Tell yourself that when you return, you'll know you are dreaming.

➤ Before you go to sleep, tell yourself you will be on the lookout for things that couldn't happen in reality. When you recognize these absurdities in your dream (e.g., elements of your childhood home and current home in one place, or something impossible occurring, such as a flying dog or an English-speaking elephant), you may realize you are dreaming.

➤ Slow down the pace of your waking life.

➤ Spend some quiet, reflective time before going to sleep. Turn off the TV!

➤ Practice falling asleep more slowly, gradually lengthening breaths and the time between waking and sleeping.

➤ Try to increase your awareness upon first awakening. See if you can become conscious of your very first waking breath.

➤ Avoid using alarm clocks. If you have to, you have to, but they aren't the kindest way to awaken.

➤ Get enough sleep! You may need more or less than other people in your family, but get as much as you need (few people in our society today get enough sleep).

Mindful Minute

According to one study, people who meditate are more likely to experience lucid dreams than people who don't meditate. Children are also more likely to experience lucid dreams than adults, and the ability seems to diminish with age. Another study showed that 63 percent of 10-year-olds experienced monthly lucid dreams, while 58 percent of the 11-year-olds and only 36 percent of the 12-year-olds experienced monthly lucid dreams.

One thing to remember about lucid dreaming: While you can control how you react in a dream, you may not be able to control the dream itself. You can influence what happens by changing your reaction—say, from fear to confrontation—but you probably won't be able to change the basic landscape of the dream. The unconscious mind is powerful and in control during dreams. However, some people believe that you *can* learn to control where you go in dreams; this is the development of astral, or out-of-body, travel.

So put on your safari garb and go take a nap!

The Least You Need to Know

➤ Philosophers from ancient times to modern times have speculated on the nature of reality, the self, and dreams, including Plato, St. Augustine, Freud, Jung, Chuang-tzu, and the Dalai Lama.

➤ The sleep cycle, when measured on an EEG, contains similarities to meditation.

➤ Meditation contains elements of both sleeping and waking states, making it seem to be a fusion of the two states.

➤ Remembering your dreams and meditating upon the themes, images, symbols, and stories in those dreams can aid you in your quest for self-knowledge.

➤ Lucid dreaming is the ability to know you are dreaming during your dream and act accordingly.

Is Any Body Home?

We've been talking a lot about how meditation can improve the health and functioning of your mind-body. But we could just as well have said that meditation improves
the health and functioning of your *subtle body*. According to yoga philosophy, we are
much more than our physical bodies and our mental processes. We actually have three
bodies—the physical, subtle, and super-subtle—and only one of them shows up in the
mirror.

A Glimpse of the Three Bodies

Yoga philosophy states that when we consider all our physical, mental, and spiritual
layers, they contribute to what are called the three bodies. The three bodies consist of
the physical body you see in the mirror, plus two other layers that include and extend
out from it: the astral, or subtle body, and the causal, or super-subtle body. Throughout the subtle body are energy channels through which our life-energy flows.

From A to Om

The **physical body**, **astral body**, and **causal body** are all aspects of the whole self, including all its various layers and energy fields. The physical body is the body we see in the mirror. The astral body contains the realm of the mind and emotions, the chakras, and life force. The causal body contains the spirit.

Your physical body is the body you see in the mirror, and the body you can learn to control through self-discipline. The rules for living (yamas and niyamas) in Chapter 4, "Living the Good Life," physical exercise, such as yoga postures, and breath control are all ways to get the physical body underway so it doesn't interfere with your attempts to know your higher self.

The astral, or subtle, body is the realm of your mind and chakra energy system. The subtle body penetrates down though the physical body. Breathing exercises can also help to control the subtle body, as can the practice of sense withdrawal and concentration.

Last is the causal body, which is the finest body, the super-subtle body. The causal body contains the spirit itself and is your connection to the universe, God, and/or bliss. It penetrates down through the subtle and physical bodies. It's the body that understands the concept of "all is one." You can communicate with this body through meditation and the attainment of samadhi, or enlightenment.

The causal body (the spirit) is the finest and penetrates down through the astral or subtle (mind) and physical (gross) bodies. The astral or subtle body penetrates only down through the physical (or gross) body. So, the three bodies are interpenetrating—from the finest to the grossest levels.

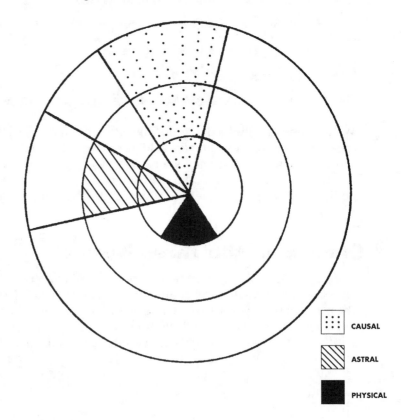

:::: CAUSAL

ASTRAL

PHYSICAL

Just as knowing ourselves includes delving into our unconscious minds, it also includes becoming familiar with and learning to maintain the three bodies.

Balancing Your Five Sheaths of Existence

But you are even more complex than your three bodies! Within these three bodies are five sheaths of existence, which are like envelopes or layers of energy, each containing and governing different aspects of your body. Learning to control these layers, one by one, will eventually clear the way for productive meditation. The five sheaths of existence include:

➤ The *physical sheath*, or actual physical body

➤ The *vital sheath*, or layer of prana surrounding and flowing through and from the body

➤ The *mind sheath*, or your emotions and thoughts, with energy extending slightly beyond the vital sheath

➤ The *intellect sheath*, or realm of higher knowledge and unclouded thought, which extends beyond the mind sheath

➤ The *bliss sheath*, or realm of divine energy that houses our potential for inner peace and happiness

The five sheaths of existence are similar to the three bodies—each of the finer sheaths penetrates down through the less fine, all the way through the physical. See the following table to discover how the three bodies relate directly to the five sheaths of existence.

The Three Bodies and the Five Sheaths of Existence

The Three Bodies	The Five Sheaths of Existence
Physical Body (*Sharira*)	Physical Sheath (*Anna-maya-kosha*)
	Prana Sheath (*Prana-maya-kosha*)
Astral Body (*Sukshma Sharira*)	Mind Sheath (*Mano-maya-kosha*)
	Intellect Sheath (*Vijnana-maya-kosha*)
Causal Body (*Karana Sharira*)	Bliss Sheath (*Ananda-maya-kosha*)

Meditations for the Physical Realm

First let's look at the most familiar of your bodies, your physical body. The physical realm contains two sheaths of existence: the physical sheath and the vital sheath. The physical body is your body itself. The Sanskrit word for the physical body can literally be translated as "food envelope." (Tells you how much they esteemed the mere physical body!) The vital body is your breath sheath, or layer of prana that flows through and from you. This second, vital sheath extends slightly beyond the physical sheath. The vital sheath is often paired with the mind sheath as well; you can think of the vital sheath as a bridge between the physical and astral bodies, existing partly in each.

Diligent practice to keep each of these layers in check will make meditation easier, but you can also use these sheaths of existence as subjects of focus (concentration) for your meditation sessions. We'll give you some suggestions:

1. The Physical Body: Housekeeping

Sit comfortably with your back straight and your eyes closed. Turn your attention to your feet and say or think the words:

➤ *Feet, be calm and tranquil. Wait here in peace until I need you again.*

➤ *Legs, be calm and tranquil. Wait here in peace until I need you again.*

➤ *Hips, be calm and tranquil. Wait here in peace until I need you again.*

➤ *Stomach, be calm and tranquil. Wait here in peace until I need you again.*

➤ *Chest, be calm and tranquil. Wait here in peace until I need you again.*

➤ *Back, be calm and tranquil. Wait here in peace until I need you again.*

➤ *Arms, be calm and tranquil. Wait here in peace until I need you again.*

➤ *Hands, be calm and tranquil. Wait here in peace until I need you again.*

➤ *Neck, be calm and tranquil. Wait here in peace until I need you again.*

➤ *Scalp, be calm and tranquil. Wait here in peace until I need you again.*

➤ *Face, be calm and tranquil. Wait here in peace until I need you again.*

Now, scan your body and feel how relaxed it is. If any part of you isn't "being" calm and tranquil, ask it again. Now, say:

➤ *Body, as you rest and wait, reveal your wisdom to me.*

Rest and wait. Be aware of your body. Is any part presenting itself to your attention? Listen to what your body has to tell you. Did you notice until now that your knee aches? It needs your attention. Is your neck revealing its stiffness? It needs your attention. Are you hungry or tired? You need to eat or sleep. Now, say:

➤ *Body, I will attend to you. Now, I need you again. Thank you for your wisdom.*

Bliss Byte

To keep your physical body in control, it helps to emphasize personal hygiene. We're sure you are perfectly clean, but a little extra attention to cleanliness, including a good daily scrub-down, a high-fiber diet to keep your insides clean, breathing exercises designed for cleansing, and keeping your clothes and external environment clean will help to keep your body maintained and less distracted during meditation.

2. The Vital Body: The Breath

Sit comfortably with your back straight. Close your eyes. Imagine your vital body, the body of life-force energy emanating from your physical body. Imagine how you look sitting where you are and how your vital body looks as it holds and encompasses your physical body. Imagine you can see life-force energy flowing in and out of you through your nose, your mouth, and your skin. Imagine it swirling and dancing around you.

Now, visualize your physical body. Imagine how good it would feel if it were even more intensely suffused with life-force energy. You can fill yourself with this beautiful and vibrant energy simply by breathing.

Slowly inhale through your nose to a count of five. Imagine the life-force energy flowing into you as you inhale, filling your legs, your body, your arms, and your head, and gathering up all the stagnant energy that's been lingering in the corners and crevices of your physical body for too long. Now, to a count of 10, exhale even more

Relax

If you're overweight, you can use breath meditation as a "vital" part of your fitness program. Concentrating on the breath promotes mindfulness and helps increase your lung capacity. Let that diaphragm muscle gently but fully expand and contract during deep breathing exercises—as it, and the surrounding abdominal muscles, grow stronger, you'll notice your body begin to change. Remember, no "body" is perfect. Be comfortable where you are and feel your breath move. Don't be intimidated by deep breathing exercises. Dive in!

slowly through your mouth with pursed lips. Let the exhale make a whispering sound and imagine you are shooting out all the stagnant energy that is now transformed, purified, and revitalized in your body as positive life-affirming energy that you are releasing for the benefit of others. Breathe in again in the same manner to a count of 10, and exhale in the same manner to a count of 20. Once more, inhale to the count of 20 and exhale to a count of 40.

Now, let your breathing return to normal again and feel the life-force energy swirling and dancing inside you, healing and freeing the systems of your body and filling your being with joy.

Bliss Byte

As we age, our breathing tends to become more shallow, and we use less of our lung capacity. Conscious practice of deep breathing—filling up the abdomen and lower chest first and not involving the shoulders during the inhalation—can help to maintain efficient and effective breathing through our entire lives. Watch your profile in a mirror as you breathe. If your shoulders rise and fall, your breathing is too shallow. Place your hands on your stomach and, as you breathe in, consciously expand the abdomen to fill with air. Some experts believe that deep breathing itself increases longevity. So use those lungs—all of them!

Meditations for the Astral Realm

The astral body is the realm of your mind and emotions. It's your *feeling* body, and it extends slightly beyond your vital body. Everything you think and feel lives as energy in you and around you, out as far as the astral body. Perhaps that is why people can sometimes "sense" each other's feelings. When you stand next to someone, you are closer to that person's astral body than you are to his or her physical body.

The astral body contains two more sheaths of existence, the mind sheath, or layer of thoughts and emotions, and the intellect sheath, the layer of higher understanding through which you can begin to see the true nature of reality. Just as the vital sheath is considered a bridge between the physical and the astral bodies, the intellect sheath is considered a bridge between the astral (subtle) body and the causal (super-subtle) body. You can learn to control the mind and intellect sheaths through breath control (which helps to center the mind), the practice of sense withdrawal, and concentration exercises. You can also include these layers as the subject of concentration for your meditations.

3. The Mind Sheath: Feeling

Sit comfortably with your back straight. Turn your attention to your heart chakra, the life-force energy vortex behind your heart. Imagine this chakra beginning to turn gently and slowly, pulling with it all the emotions and feelings that sit inside your chest. Imagine them swirling gently and ordering themselves around the slowly spinning chakra. Now, imagine that the diameter of the swirling chakra is growing as it picks up more and more emotions. It expands to fill your entire chest, then becomes wider and wider, like a hurricane on a weather map but gentler and smoother.

Now the spiraling wheel has extended beyond your chest, and its edges encompass your neck and head. Imagine the rays of the spiral catching up all the thoughts in your head and pulling them along, like debris in a mild, peaceful cyclone. There they go, riding on the waves of your emotions.

Imagine this spiraling wheel growing beyond the boundaries of your physical body, and then beyond the boundaries of your vital body, extending past breath and energy. Now, imagine the spiral growing and enveloping your physical and vital bodies in a warm, rosy, pink aura of emotion and thought. Everything you feel and think is reflected in and protected by this rosy halo.

Feel the projection of your emotions and thoughts into the space around you and marvel at their simple existence. Don't judge them. Just see them. There they are, as much a part of you as your ankle or your shoulder blade. No more important, no less.

Bliss Byte

Some people find color easy to work with during meditation, but for others, sound makes more sense. Others find the sensation of touch an easier point of focus, while for others, a thought works best. Chinese meditation balls are a good tactile source of focus (see Chapter 19, "Mantras: Sacred Formulas to Live By," for more). It all depends on your particular orientation. Experiment to see which of your senses provides the most effortless point of concentration.

4. The Intellect Sheath: Understanding

Sit comfortably with your back straight. Breathe normally and notice your breath. Now, close your eyes and casually notice your physical body. Visualize where it starts and where it stops. Next, recall your vital body, how it extends beyond the physical body in a swirling dance of energy. Next, recall your mind sheath, a glowing pink encompassing your physical and vital bodies.

What is beyond the mind sheath? Visualize the edges of the mind sheath. What do you see? Nothing at first, but then you begin to see a pale yellow color extending beyond the mind sheath. What is it? You can't quite see it. You can't quite get there.

Bring your attention back to your mind sheath. Visualize tiny bright green shapes floating around inside your mind sheath. Some are circles, some are triangles, some are squares, and some are random polygons with no names. Sometimes they bounce against the edges of the mind sheath but they seem to be stuck inside it as if in a bubble.

These green shapes are your thoughts and feelings. They live in the mind sheath but can't go beyond it. They are content to live there. But wait—one triangle doesn't seem content. It keeps bouncing against the mind sheath, as if trying to break through the bubble. Follow this triangle. Is it a thought or an emotion? What is it about?

Suddenly, the triangle breaks through the boundary of the mind sheath, and the intellect sheath shows itself in sunny yellow. Ah-ha! you think. Now I understand! You've reached a new level, a new understanding of some aspect of reality you've been struggling with. The true nature of your problems, your self, and your world are suddenly clear. You've encountered the intellect sheath.

To further open the chakras and free the breathing in the astral body, try the pose illustrated here. A soft pillow on the floor under your head and upper back allows your breath to flow without constriction. Feel your chest and your heart chakra relaxing and opening. Place your hands in prayer pose over your heart and concentrate on the way your heart lifts on every inhalation. Feel your breath and your mind clearing and expanding.

Open the Saturn and Jupiter chakras by allowing your knees to fall open, supported once again by soft pillows. Let your legs open only as far as they can comfortably go— don't press them toward the floor to the point of a painful stretch. This should feel good and liberating, not stressful!

As you breathe, feel all of your chakras opening and rising.

Meditations for the Causal Realm

The causal realm is so called because this is the realm where everything originates. Although you may be able to access it last, it was the first "you" before you descended into the physical body (according to reincarnation theory). Think of the causal realm as your spirit. It pervades you and extends from you, beyond all the other bodies. It is you, the whole you, and the you who you will be after your body has worn out. It is also the you who is the same as the universe, as God, as nature, and as all being. It is the universal, divine you. Yes, right there in front of you (and behind you and above you, etc.).

The only sheath within the causal realm is the bliss sheath. To get in touch with this sheath of existence is to gain true inner peace. Unlike the other sheaths of existence, this sheath is thought to be beyond space and time, pervading all reality.

5. The Bliss Sheath: Om

The following meditation is the most advanced of all the five-sheath meditations. Don't be discouraged if you can't get a feel for it. With practice, including the practice of many of the other meditations in this book, the bliss meditation will soon become second nature (or, more accurately, *first nature!*).

Sit comfortably with your back straight. Close your eyes and breathe normally. Focus on your breath. Listen to it. Visualize it. Feel it moving in and out of your nostrils. Stay with the breath for five minutes or more.

Now, visualize the word "Om." According to yogic theory, Om is actually a sound meant to represent the original sound of the vibrating universe. Om is like the sound of the origin of all things, and the continuing sound of all things that are one. It is the sound of divinity, unity, and the only true reality.

Now, try the sound. Begin softly, and let the *MMM* part of the word vibrate and linger. Repeat the word in a slow rhythm. As you murmur it, imagine the slow turning of the Earth, the galaxy, and the entire universe. Imagine you are making the sound of the universe breathing. Feel it expand and contract with every breath, feel it rotate with every Om. Focus on nothing but the sound of the origin of the universe. If other thoughts surface, blow them away gently with the sound of Om. Listen, speak, listen, speak, listen, and speak, until you see how you are able to make

Mindful Minute

The more you read and study meditation, the more often you might notice that many concepts having to do with meditation are expressed in Sanskrit, an ancient Eastern Indian language. Yoga philosophy and Buddhism originated in India, and meditation is more central to Indian philosophies than most others. Even though Sanskrit is not used today as a conversational language, many sacred texts were written in Sanskrit and so the terminology survives.

the sound of Om because you are the universe and the universe is you. You are divinity and divinity is you. You have always made the sound of Om, and you will always make the sound of Om. You are the sound. And look—the bliss sheath isn't a sheath at all. It is everything.

Be a Buddha

To reach the realization that all is one—not just to think it or know it intellectually—but to truly realize it (when it happens, you'll know) is what it means to be a Buddha. It can happen to you. It has happened to many before you and will happen to many after you. Experiencing this realization doesn't mean you cease to exist, of course. But typically, it results in an overwhelming and abundant sense of compassion for all sentient beings. The compassion is so strong that it becomes the focus of life and duty, to relieve the suffering of others.

Maybe you don't want to be a Buddha. Still, we'd like you to know that if Buddhahood is something you feel is the right path for you, it is an attainable goal. It may take years of work, but it can be achieved, and you don't have to be a Buddhist to do it. If you are of some other religion, you might not even feel comfortable saying you are journeying toward becoming a Buddha, but perhaps you can feel comfortable saying you are seeking true knowledge through service to humankind.

Are You Brave Enough for the Bardo?

Aside from happiness and contentment in this life, is there any point to becoming a Buddha, or achieving enlightenment? True knowledge of the nature of things, of God, or of the universal way may be incentive enough. But what about reality beyond this life? Does enlightenment have anything to do with that?

From A to Om

The **bardo** is the intermediate state between death and rebirth into the next life, according to reincarnation philosophy.

You can bet your past lives it does! For those who believe in reincarnation, achieving enlightenment means freedom from the endless cycle of birth and death we all undergo in order for our spirits to grow, learn, and become whole.

But before we plunge into a reincarnation discussion, we'd like you to consider first the experience and process of death. No, we don't mean to bum you out by talking about death. Far from it. Death isn't an end, it is a transition, and making the most of that transition can be your final act of self-actualization in this life.

Bardo is a word Tibetan Buddhists use to describe the transition time between death and rebirth in the next life. It is a sort of limbo during which the soul gets to regroup, look over what it has learned in life, and get ready to "play it again, Sam." If you ever saw the movie *Defending Your Life* with Albert Brooks and Meryl Streep, you may remember the scenes in which they got to see movies of the major events in their lives and defend themselves if they didn't act in a good or worthy manner. Then, at the end, they each got on different buses going to different places, stages, and levels. This could be an interpretation of the bardo.

Other interpretations can be found in descriptions of near-death experiences. The bardo is thought to last no longer than about 49 days. Before entering it, the soul is thought to experience the clear light of death. The soul moves through the light, into the bardo, and then at last, is born again.

The *Bardo Thödol* or *Tibetan Book of the Dead* is an instruction manual for death meant to be read to someone as they die and move into the bardo so they know what to do. According to this book, which gives a detailed explanation of what happens after death, the soul moves through several stages in the bardo, then back through the same stages toward rebirth. During sleep, the sleeper goes through four progressively deeper stages of sleep, then back up to stage 1 into dream sleep. The *Tibetan Book of the Dead* likens these two states, referring to sleep as a rehearsal for death, and also compares these two states to the stages through which one progresses during meditation.

The Transforming Experience of Death

Why rehearse for death, as the *Bardo Thödol* or *Tibetan Book of the Dead* suggests? Because death, whether or not it leads to rebirth, is an amazing opportunity for the soul. Death is a profound (we won't say final) lesson in nonattachment and the futility of materialism, mundane concerns, and the illusion of possession. (Life is also a bardo, however, and many life experiences—the act of meditation, just to name one—can be rehearsals for death, the ultimate act of letting go.)

In death, we gradually loosen our hold on the world and on the temporary reality we experienced as life. Our senses fade, and we move to a new stage of existence. The experienced meditator already knows what it is like to let go of attachments, escape the hold of the senses, and become one with the universe. How like death, yet how fulfilling and wonderful! If death is like enlightenment, then we have nothing to fear.

Reincarnation: Our Lives Are Like Beads on a String

But what about reincarnation? Is it true? Have we really been here before? Some say yes, some say no. Some have very strong opinions on both sides. We leave the question to you, to decide for yourself.

But those who believe in reincarnation compare us to beads on a string. We are the same evolving soul—the string—through our many lives, but the outer trappings, including the body and mind, change with each new life. Our souls learn something with each life. We have free will and sometimes we make good choices, sometimes bad choices. Our choices determine what we learn and how much our soul grows (or loses) in each life. This in turn determines how we come back next time.

Some believe we are only reincarnated as people. Others believe we can come back as animals, birds, insects—just about anything. Belief in reincarnation isn't necessarily specific to any religion. Even religions that traditionally discount it have members who suspect or believe it is true.

Have you lived before? Try our past life meditation and see what comes to you. If you do "remember" a past life, you might consider that it is another side of your personality, a part of you in your unconscious mind, or simple vivid imagination. On the other hand, also consider that you may actually be remembering a past life. Either way, the experience will be instructional and teach you a little bit more about who you are.

Bliss Byte

Do you recycle? Are you concerned about pollution, waste, and living an Earth-friendly life? Consider the possibility that you will be coming back to this Earth for many more lifetimes, and you may have to reap the consequences of environmental destruction. The time to start caring about the future of your environment is now.

Do Your Preferences Equal a Previous You?

Before we start the actual meditation, consider the following questions and whether they might be clues to past lives you've experienced:

➤ Have you always been particularly interested in a certain country, culture, or region of the world, although you never really knew why, such as ancient Greece, medieval Spain, or turn-of-the-century Paris?

➤ Is there a place you feel sure you would never want to visit, although you aren't sure why?

➤ Have you ever met someone and had the feeling you knew him or her from somewhere, even though you had never met before (at least in this life…)?

➤ Do you have unexplained fears, such as drowning, small spaces or crowds, or storms or heights?

➤ Is there a specific time in history that interests you more than others, such as the Victorian era or the Middle Ages?

➤ Have you ever visited a place that was very familiar even though you've never been there?

➤ Have you ever dreamed you were someone else?

Any of the above could obviously occur for reasons other than past lives, but maybe they are evidence after all.

Remembering a Past Life

If you would like to try to remember a past life, even if you don't really think they exist, try our past-life meditation. If nothing else, it will tell you something about yourself.

Sit comfortably with your back straight and close your eyes. Imagine yourself walking through a beautiful green field bordered by forest on all sides. The grass is brilliant green and dotted with small blue flowers. Suddenly in the middle of the field you come upon a rise of hill. Into the hill is set a massive wooden door with a heavy, round, gold door-pull. You approach the door and put your hand on the heavy, glossy wood. There you see your name carved in the door. You must be meant to enter!

Relax

Past-life meditations can be fun, fascinating, and yes, even addictive. Some people become so obsessed with finding out the details of their past lives that they completely miss the point of the exercise: How to improve this life and help your soul to grow in this stage.

You open the door to feel the air become damper but also lighter, like fog or mist. You feel as if you are walking through a cloud as you step into a round room. The room is encircled with doors, and each door has a gold nameplate on it. Turning in circles, you wonder which door you should enter.

Suddenly, one door begins to glow, and you notice a light on behind it. You go to the door and look at the nameplate. It has your name on it, and beneath it, another name. You know that this was your name in a past life. Look closely until you can read it. (It may be in another language or alphabet you don't understand.)

You open the door and step into a small chamber filled with blue mist. In front of you is a large wooden table holding a large book with a blue silk cover. You open the book and look at the page. At the top of the page is the name of a place. At the bottom of the page is a date. Look at the page until you see the place name and date clearly. Then, a picture forms in the middle of the page. It is a portrait of a figure with a half smile. You gaze at it and realize it is you in a past life. Study the picture until you can see it clearly.

When you look up from the book, you see the room is filled with shelves, cabinets, and drawers. Each one contains things that belonged to the person in the book, things that were meaningful, things from that person's life. Explore the room for as long as you like. Pick up objects, feel them, smell them, examine them, and remember their stories. Get to know the past you.

Now, go back through the door and into the room with the many doors. Know that you can return and work through all the doors at your leisure. When you open the door that leads into the field, open your eyes. Write about your experience so you don't forget the person you met there!

The Least You Need to Know

➤ The physical body is only one of three bodies; it is interpenetrated with the astral body, the realm of the emotions, thoughts, and understanding; and the causal body, the realm of the spirit.

➤ According to those who believe in reincarnation, the bardo is the intermediate state between death and rebirth.

➤ You can explore the possibility of your past lives through past-life meditation.

Part 4
Prepare Your Self
for Meditation

How stressed are you? Perhaps more stressed than you realize. It's easy to mistake a stressed state of being for "normal" when stress is present over long periods of time. In this section, we will help you to determine your own stress level and will offer you some coping strategies, including a technique called mindfulness, that can help wake you up to your life and really enjoy what you do each moment, even if you are washing the dishes or commuting to work.

We'll also give you some tips on where to meditate and how to create a meditation space indoors or outdoors (or both). Then we'll actually get you meditating, and we'll show you how to use your breath to enhance your meditation, your health, and even your longevity.

Chapter 11

Stress: Is Your Mind Too Full?

In This Chapter

➤ Stress: Living with it or without it

➤ How stressed are you? Take our quiz

➤ The physical and mental effects of stress

➤ If stress is the question, mindfulness is the answer

Spiritual layers or no spiritual layers, sometimes you may feel like nothing more than an exhausted heap of overtaxed muscles, joints, and emotions. Meanwhile, your brain is running at 110 miles per hour. What do you need to do today? When do you need to do it? How are you possibly going to do it all? Did you forget anything? Did you do a good job? Are you capable? How does *anybody get through the day*?

Are you stomped by stress? Most people are, at least some of the time. The responsibilities and challenges of life sometimes overwhelm even the laid-back types. Knowing how to let life's challenges roll off your back isn't easy, and sometimes it isn't practical, either. Stress helps you to take action when action is required. But sometimes, you may feel like screaming, "Enough is enough!"

Relax

Stress can cause serious health problems, so if you suffer from chronic stress or severe acute stress that you can't seem to relieve through meditation, don't hesitate to see a doctor or holistic health practitioner. You can't fix everything yourself. You may need medical treatment.

This Isn't Stress, It's Just Life!

To some extent, stress is a necessary evil (and sometimes, a necessary good) of modern life. But it isn't, or at least shouldn't be, the dominating force in your life. If acting under stress seems to be your modus operandi, however, it's time to re-evaluate your responses to life, your overloaded schedule, your stress-management techniques (or lack thereof), and your routines for mental maintenance (or lack thereof).

But first, let's evaluate how stressed you really are.

How Stressed Are You? A Self Quiz

Choose the one best answer for each of the following questions, to determine your stress level (for question 10, choose as many answers as apply):

1. Find a mirror and look in it. What is your facial expression at this moment?

    A. Slightly clenched jaw and slightly furrowed brow.

    B. I look tired.

    C. I look like I'm concentrating on something interesting.

    D. I've got a half smile and look relaxed.

2. What is your first reaction when the phone rings?

    A. Expectation.

    B. Thank God for caller ID.

    C. Panic. What if something awful has happened?

    D. Disinterest. I'll answer if I'm not busy, but if I'm involved in something, I'll check my messages later.

3. Who do you feel is dependent on you for their basic needs?

    A. Nobody.

    B. Just my children (those under 18).

    C. One or more adults (adult children, spouse or partner, parents).

    D. My children and my parents—I'm responsible for the generations on both ends!

4. How do you feel about your job?

   A. It pays the bills, but I have other pleasures in my life.

   B. I hate going to work each morning.

   C. I feel I have found my true calling, and my work is a joy.

   D. It's often unpleasant, tedious, or stressful, but at least it gives me status and money.

Bliss Byte

Sometimes the fastest and easiest way to diffuse a stressful situation is with laughter. Laughter is healing, relaxing, and a great way to put things into perspective. In fact, there is even a form of meditation, aptly named laughing meditation, that is based around laughter. In India, large groups of people gather together in parks and common areas, make funny faces, stretch, move, and laugh together. Some advocate waking up each morning and laughing for five minutes before the day begins. The laughter may be forced at first, but will soon become genuine as you realize how wonderfully funny life can be. Revel in it!

5. Are you:

   A. Single but looking.

   B. Happily unmarried.

   C. Recently divorced or separated.

   D. Happily married.

   E. Unhappily married.

6. During the time when you are home and awake, what percentage would you estimate you have the television turned on?

   A. 75–100 percent.

   B. About 50 percent.

   C. I watch maybe an hour a day.

   D. I rarely watch television.

7. How would you describe your financial situation?

   A. I have all the money I could ever spend and then some.

   B. I could always use more, but I get by just fine.

   C. I never have enough left by the end of the month.

   D. I try to live simply and get by on less. I make enough to meet my needs and that's all I need to make.

   E. I can barely get by, have already filed or am considering filing for bankruptcy, have huge debts, and/or worry about money constantly.

8. I feel:

   A. Content with who I am.

   B. Deeply dissatisfied with who I've become.

   C. Okay about myself but I'm striving to become a better person.

   D. I like the inside me but not the outside me.

   E. I like the outside me but not the inside me.

9. I also feel:

   A. Like I have no control over my life and what happens to me.

   B. Like I have only a little control over my life and what happens to me. I tend to blame circumstances, bad luck, or other people for consequences I've had to face.

   C. Mostly in control of my life, though major life events often give me the feeling I've lost control.

   D. I understand that I reap what I sow. I make my own luck and my own choices, and in general, I know that the consequences are my own responsibility.

10. How many of the following have you experienced in the last year?

    A. A move to a different state.

    B. Pregnancy, childbirth, or adoption of a child.

    C. A job change, including a hiring or firing.

    D. A major change in financial circumstances (good or bad).

    E. A trip out of the country.

    F. The death of a parent.

    G. The death of a child.

    H. The death of a friend or other relative.

    I. The death of a beloved pet.

    J. A major health problem.

K. Major surgery.

L. An accident resulting in serious injury.

M. A marriage.

N. A divorce.

O. A separation.

P. Divorce or separation of your parents.

Q. Health problems of your parents if they are under your care.

R. Graduation.

S. Being the victim of a crime.

T. A natural disaster (flood, tornado, hurricane, etc.).

U. A bout with depression.

V. More than two panic attacks or episodes of severe anxiety.

W. The development of an irrational fear.

Now, score your quiz by giving yourself points according to the following:

1. A: 3   B: 2   C: 1   D: 0
2. A: 1   B: 2   C: 3   D: 0
3. A: 0   B: 1   C: 2   D: 3
4. A: 1   B: 3   C: 0   D: 2
5. A: 2   B: 1   C: 3   D: 1   E: 3
6. A: 3   B: 2   C: 1   D: 0
7. A: 1   B: 1   C: 2   D: 0   E: 3
8. A: 0   B: 3   C: 1   D: 2   E: 2
9. A: 3   B: 2   C: 1   D: 0
10. One point for every answer circled.

If you scored between 25–40 points: If your stress level hasn't already affected your mental and/or physical health, it may well affect either or both very soon. Get help immediately. Delegate responsibility to other family members or friends. Find someone to talk to (friends and/or a licensed mental health professional or counselor) about your feelings. Realize you can't shoulder the burdens of the world on your own. If you aren't involved already, begin a program of moderate physical exercise like mindful walking or movement meditations such as yoga. You need to engage in some serious mental and physical maintenance that slows down the pace. (But remember, in times when you're feeling very low or depressed, physical activity through movement meditation may be better than sitting meditation.)

If you scored between 10–24 points: You certainly have stress in your life, and your stress levels are probably comparable to those of most active, involved people. Sometimes you feel completely overwhelmed by what life throws your way. Other times, you feel proudly in control of your life and circumstances. Meditation is the perfect mental maintenance activity to incorporate into your daily routine. It will strengthen your reserves and help you to handle those over-the-top days with grace and serenity. It will also help you to appreciate and live your life more fully, since you sometimes tend to switch on the auto-pilot to function.

If you scored between 0–9 points: Somehow you've managed to create a life of ease and relaxed attention. You feel good about yourself and your life, and when stressful events happen, they don't usually make you feel out of control. Maybe you're already meditating, and that's your secret! If you aren't, give it a try. Your frame of mind is such that you are primed for spiritual growth. All that daily junk isn't getting in the way. Also, you never know what the future has in store for you. Adding resources to your already formidable stress-management arsenal will assure continued success in dealing with the challenges of life.

What Stress Does to Your Body (and Your Mind!)

People experience two types of stress: chronic and acute. Chronic stress is experienced over a long period of time. An unhappy relationship or long-term financial problems are examples of situations that can cause chronic stress. Acute stress may be triggered by a sudden event, such as a car accident or getting fired from a job (if you become seriously injured or can't find work again, you might suffer from both acute and chronic stress).

From A to Om

The **fight-or-flight reaction** refers to the body's response to extreme stress, allowing it to react more quickly and with greater strength and speed so that it can fight or flee from a perceived threat (see Chapter 7, "Neurophysiology: This Is Your Brain on Meditation").

When we experience either type of stress, our bodies react in what we call the *fight-or-flight reaction*. This reaction can be observed in nature. When an animal is threatened by a predator, it has two choices: stand up and fight, or run for its life. Which method it chooses has to do with a lightning-fast appraisal of the situation. Would fighting be worth the risk? Could the animal flee fast enough? What is the size, strength, and nature of the threat?

We do the same thing. Although the development of stress in humans doesn't usually involve being chased by wild animals anymore (like it once did), it's just as real. Work deadlines, family members in trouble, life changes—physical or emotional crises of all kinds confront us, often on a daily basis. What happens to your body when the fight-or-flight response kicks in?

Lots of things, all designed to help you act more quickly and with greater strength. Even when your stress response is triggered by a threat that doesn't require a physical response, such as the death of a loved one or losing your job, the result is the same. Your body doesn't know the difference, and here's what happens:

➤ Stress hormones such as adrenaline and cortisol are released into your system and heighten your perception of a situation and your ability to react.

➤ Your heart beats faster and harder to deliver more nutrients and blood to muscles, in case you need to perform some physical action.

➤ Blood is diverted away from the gastrointestinal system toward muscles (have you noticed you are often completely without an appetite when you are under a lot of stress?).

➤ Your pupils dilate so you can see better.

➤ Your hair stands on end and your skin becomes more sensitive to vibrations.

➤ Your breathing rate quickens, delivering more oxygen to your body.

If you've forgotten that your presentation is due tomorrow, stress will serve you well, revving you up to get the work finished. But if you live under stress all the time, your *autonomic nervous system*, the source of all these changes, can easily become overtaxed. The signs of an overtaxed autonomic nervous system are chronic muscle tension, often in the form of tense shoulders and neck, furrowed brow, clenched jaw, and hunched posture; sweaty palms; elevated heart rate and/or blood pressure; and digestive problems.

From A to Om

The **autonomic nervous system** is responsible for bodily functions such as heartbeat, blood pressure, and digestion.

There are, of course, effective ways to manage chronic stress. People don't always choose the best ways, however. Instead, they may choose stress-management techniques that, while temporarily effective, eventually result in increased stress and decreased vitality, even compromised health.

Are you managing your stress through what Jon Kabat-Zinn, Ph.D., calls "maladaptive coping"? Check any of the following responses you sometimes have to stress:

➤ *Denial.* "Problem? What problem? I don't have a problem," or "This kind of thing may bother most people but it doesn't affect *me.*"

➤ *Workaholism.* It's easier to throw yourself into your work than to face problems in your personal life.

➤ *Chemicals.* A cocktail after work, a pot of coffee in one-mug doses during the workday, cigarette breaks, sleeping pills, and over-the-counter stimulants can all alter your mind-body in a way that can keep you functioning during periods of stress. Whether they help you to forget, keep you from feeling, stimulate you when you're feeling exhausted, or relax you when you are tense, chemicals may temporarily address the symptoms of stress but don't deal with the cause and may pose a risk to your health. (Always consult your physician before beginning any regimen of vitamins, supplements, or over-the-counter medications.) Plus, the effects, side effects, and after-effects of drugs can desensitize you to your own energy, making body scans ineffective and deflecting efforts at mindfulness. If you can't read your own body energy, you can't know as easily what needs fixing, and meditative focus will suffer, too.

➤ *Food.* Even though your digestion tends to shut down during periods of stress, that doesn't mean you'll stop eating altogether. In fact, the reverse may be true: Compulsive eating under stress is a common problem and may result in excess weight gain, ill health due to the low quality of foods consumed, and even eating disorders. Binge eating (eating more at one meal or sitting than is generally appropriate) and bulimia (binge eating followed by purging with laxatives or vomiting) are two eating disorders associated with compulsive eating.

Maladaptive coping mechanisms may help you in the short run but in the long run, may compromise your health and your ability to deal with stress on your own. What coping mechanism should replace these less-than-ideal stress responses?

We (and plenty of others before us) suggest *mindfulness*.

From A to Om

Mindfulness is a way of being. It means being completely aware of, though not necessarily emotionally involved with, the present moment.

Do the Right Thing

Have you ever wondered if, in any given situation, you are doing the "right" thing or the "best" thing? We're not talking about morality, here. We're talking about that gnawing feeling, deep down, that perhaps you've made a "wrong" decision, or are headed in the "wrong" direction. "Should" you have helped that kid who fell off his bike, even though you were late to a meeting? "Should" you have driven this way to work, or would the other way have been shorter? "Should" you have ordered the chicken, or would you have enjoyed the pasta more? Worrying about what we do and how we do it—even to the minutest and most trivial degree—is one of the major sources of stress for many people, but it doesn't have to be. Mindfulness holds the answer.

How? The answer is simply, "now." What "should" you being doing? You should be doing what you are doing right now—so really do it! Who "should" you be helping, who "should" you love? You should be helping and loving the person in front of you right now. So help and love that person! Where "should" you be? You should be where you are right now, so really be there! What "should" you eat? You should eat, and really enjoy, whatever food is in front of you. When "should" you start living your life? Now! Right now.

Sure, we understand that whatever you are doing at any given moment may not be the most conducive to your given schedule or efficient for the time you have. Maybe you "should" have helped that kid, but you didn't, and the moment is gone. Make note of the experience and maybe next time, you'll decide to help.

Maybe you're reading a magazine instead of balancing your checkbook, when you really "should" be balancing the checkbook. But look at it this way. If you aren't balancing your checkbook and have chosen, for whatever reason, to read a magazine instead at that moment, *read the magazine!* Don't sit there vaguely reading and thinking about what you should be doing. Or, *go balance your checkbook*. And really pay attention.

The point is to really do what you are doing, really address and experience each moment as it comes rather than letting part or most of your mind linger in the past or future. Live, and everything you do will have more meaning, more punch, more energy. "Should" can become a word that doesn't have much meaning for you because you're always doing just exactly what you are doing, and that's that. And stress? Well, what's the point of that?

The great thing about mindful living is that when you really experience each moment, you will eventually begin to seek out more meaningful moments to experience. That doesn't mean you have to be saving the world or doing something "worthy" every second of your existence. In fact, washing the dishes is just as "worthy" in its way as spending an afternoon painting the porch of the elderly lady who lives next door. But you may find that because of the joy and vitality it brings, you'll be more interested in helping your neighbors, or anyone else who needs your help. It may not happen right away, and shouldn't be forced. It is a natural evolution. Mindfulness helps you to live, and a big part of living is helping others to live, too.

Bliss Byte

Pick a daily chore that you would normally find tedious—for example, filing, paying bills, folding laundry, filling the car with gas, or commuting to work through rush-hour traffic. Decide to do that chore today with complete and total mindfulness, without thinking of getting it finished and out of the way, and without looking forward to what you'll do after you are done. Really *do* the work and feel the pleasure in performing the task—note how the papers or clothes or steering wheel feel in your hand, noticing every detail of your task. See it anew, and find the fun in it.

Thich Nhat Hahn's Mindful Miracle

But what are you supposed to do when stress really has you in its grip? How are you supposed to remember that only the now matters? You've got a job to do, perhaps a family to support, and obligations. You've got to keep it all in your head at once. You've got to plan for the future, learn from the past, organize, schedule, network. You can't just drop everything and live only in the "now," can you?

Living in the "now" doesn't mean forgetting the past or remaining oblivious to the future. Whatever you are doing in the present moment can be fully experienced, even if what you are doing is mapping out a retirement plan or writing in your journal how you feel right now about neglecting to help that kid who fell off his bike. Whatever you are doing, whatever you have to do, you can make that the most important thing to do, *at that moment*, whether it's doing the laundry, paying bills, washing the dog, preparing that expense report, eating dinner, waiting for a bus, planning for the future, or reconciling yourself with the past—you get the picture.

Living mindfully takes some training, however. Mindfulness meditation is the perfect training. It may also be the most powerful meditative technique for dealing with stress. Touted as an effective treatment for pain relief as well as an eye-opening way to live every day of your life, mindfulness has many proponents and many incarnations.

A study conducted by the Stress Reduction Clinic at the University of Massachusetts Medical Center shows how powerful this technique can be. The study followed 23 people in two groups, all with psoriasis (a skin disease) undergoing ultraviolet light treatments. One of the groups practiced the technique of mindfulness meditation taught in the clinic, which required them to focus on their breath and physical sensations during the treatment, eventually visualizing that the ultraviolet light was slowing down the disease process. The other group received the treatment without the mindfulness meditation. After 12 weeks, the skin patches on the group of meditators were healing much faster. Of the 13 meditators, 10 had clear skin after 40 sessions. In the group of 10 nonmeditators, only two had clear skin.

But medicine is only a small part of the mindfulness gift. According to Thich Nhat Hahn, an exiled Vietnamese monk and peace activist (nominated for the Nobel Peace Prize by Martin Luther King, Jr., in 1967), living mindfully is the only way to live. Each task of life should be performed with the sole purpose of performing that task. He uses the example of washing the dishes (he can imagine a machine to wash clothes, but can't imagine why anyone would want a machine to wash dishes!). When a visiting friend once asked him if he could do the dishes after a meal, Nhat Hahn agreed on the condition that he do the dishes in the right way. He must do the dishes *to do the dishes*, not to get them finished and get on with something else.

Nhat Hahn also suggests that everyone devote one day per week to mindfulness. Awake mindfully, noticing how you feel, how your surroundings look, what you hear and smell and taste. Go through your day slowly, quietly, with minimal talking, no television or radio, not even singing, and perform your daily chores with complete and total attention. Eventually, he says, you'll learn how to live every day mindfully, and your life will be transformed by peaceful awareness.

Bliss Byte

Mindfulness while performing the simple tasks of life will help to cultivate mindfulness that can get you through the more stressful events of life—major life changes, tragedies, etc. Much of the stress of major events involves dwelling on the past and the future. Because mindfulness deals only with the *now*, your list of worries diminishes.

Mindfulness, Buddha-Style

The Buddha has provided us with a special meditation to help attain a mindful state. The following exercise is part of a longer sutra, the *Sutra on the Full Awareness of Breathing*, and it provides a mean to help you increase mindfulness by calming and centering the breathing. Memorize it and use it to help you relax when life becomes overwhelming (the following excerpt is translated by Thich Nhat Hahn):

Breathing in, I know I am breathing in.

Breathing out, I know I am breathing out.

Breathing in a long breath, I know I am breathing in a long breath.

Breathing out a long breath, I know I am breathing out a long breath.

Breathing in a short breath, I know I am breathing in a short breath.

Breathing out a short breath, I know I am breathing out a short breath.

Breathing in, I am aware of my whole body.

Breathing out, I am aware of my whole body.

Breathing in, I calm my whole body.

Breathing out, I calm my whole body.

Repeat the Sutra of Mindfulness for 10 to 20 minutes, and you'll soon experience a pervading calm. As Thich Nhat Hahn says, "Your thoughts will have quieted down like a pond on which not even a ripple stirs."

From A to Om

A **sutra** in yoga philosophy is a precept or maxim, or a collection of these, such as Patajali's *Yoga Sutras*. Sutras use the fewest words to convey the teaching. In Buddhism, a sutra is a scriptural narrative, usually a discourse of the Buddha, such as in the *Sutra on the Full Awareness of Breathing*, where a disciple recounts a sermon of the Buddha. *Sutra* is a Sanskrit term translated as "simple truth," "thread," or "bare bones."

Surrender!

For mindfulness, one of the keys is surrender. We don't mean surrender as in "Oh, just give up. You'll never have control!" We mean surrender as in "Don't try to control what you can't control." Mindfulness means being acutely aware of your being in the present moment, but it also means not being emotionally involved with that awareness. An unbiased and indifferent observer is better able to take in the entirety of a situation. You can be that unbiased and indifferent observer in your own life.

Westerners sometimes have a problem with the idea of indifference and detachment. To us, those nouns sound like bad things. We tend to hear "indifferent" with the connotation of "uncaring" and "detachment" with the connotation of "cold and heartless."

But this isn't what we mean at all. On the contrary! Only by becoming detached can we truly express our care, love, and compassion for our fellow sentient beings. Nothing on this Earth is ours, at least not for very long. To make the most of the time we have together on this magnificent and lovely planet, we must see that things aren't ours to own. They are only ours to experience. Life is a gift, but a gift with strings attached. We need to help each other, love each other, and make the most of the gift by really living in full awareness. We need to extend our love and compassion beyond our immediate circle so that it encompasses the world. Rise above the petty details of ownership, jealousy, grasping, desire, and materialism to the miraculous level of higher consciousness where the gift of life blossoms into something far more exquisite than it was before. Like a lotus blossom with its roots in the mud at the bottom of a cloudy pond, we, too, can come into full flower if we keep moving upward and reaching toward the heavens.

Accepting Who You Are Right Now

Of course, if you're dissatisfied with who you are, you'll never be able to surrender your grasp on the world. You'll keep looking for answers, something to "fix" you or make you "better."

We've got a secret for you. Lean down close. Shhh. You are already perfect. Yep! It's true. You are a perfect, beautiful soul spending a little time here on Earth in order to learn more about the nature of reality. The Earth is fraught with difficult lessons, but they all come to the same thing. Life teaches you who you are.

Bliss Byte

A recent study by the U.S. government revealed that the typical American spends 84 percent of his or her time inside, and that over one-third of our waking hours are spent at an indoor workplace. But to truly enjoy your mindful awareness, try to get outside as often as possible and breathe the fresh air. Drink your morning coffee on the front steps, take your lunch break outside, walk barefoot in your yard, swim in a lake or the ocean, go for a picnic and sit on the ground, take a walk in the country, and perhaps most fulfilling of all, hug a tree! Really! The energy from a tree is strong and renewing.

Again we'll say it: That doesn't mean you can't improve yourself. But here's the thing: You aren't improving your soul. Your inner self, the pure you, is already perfect. What you are improving is your ability to recognize that perfect soul. Sometimes it's pretty difficult to see, buried under all these physical and emotional layers, but it's there, and it has great potential. When realized, it can flow out of you and around you. It can become you. Then, you are truly free.

Listening to Your Body: Crafting Your Stress Response

Remember all the things we told you happen to your body when you experience stress? Muscle tension, increased heart rate, increased breathing, blood flow away from the stomach and into the muscles, etc., are natural responses, but if you're living mindfully—and experiencing stress mindfully—you can moderate these responses in an effective way so they don't become the cause of chronic conditions. Here are some keys to crafting your stress response:

➤ Whenever you feel yourself becoming overwhelmed by stress, stop what you're doing and take a few deep breaths, then focus your attention on what your body is feeling. Don't judge or try to change anything just yet. Just notice. Is your heart beating fast? Have you lost your appetite? Do you have "butterflies" in your stomach? Is your mind racing? If possible, do a quick version of the mind-body scan in Chapter 3.

➤ Now, turn your attention to the cause of your stress. What is the trigger? Did your teenager just tell you he'll have to repeat the ninth grade? Did your boss tell you that your presentation is moved up to tomorrow morning? Did you realize you forgot to pay the electric bill? Did someone criticize, insult, or ignore you?

173

➤ Next, consider what would happen if you simply let the trigger go. What if you didn't let it bother you, realized it wasn't your problem, or simply decided to take care of it without getting emotionally involved? Would that be possible? What would happen? (This is often the easiest option.)

➤ Or, consider how you could modify your thinking about the event. Is there another way to see the problem? Think of all the options, no matter how absurd. List the possibilities in your mind or write them down. Remember, most stress triggers are only stressful because of the way we see them and the emotions we attach to them. Where can you revise?

➤ Next, think about what you might do about the trigger. Think about action strategies. Could you talk to your son about attending summer school or getting a tutor, or about learning to live with consequences? Could you ask your partner to take over dinner and the kids tonight so you can prepare your presentation? Call the electric company and explain that you forgot? Talk to the person who has hurt your feelings or angered you? Or even decide not to let the snub bother you? Again, list the possibilities in your mind or write them down.

➤ Now, do another quick mind-body scan. If you've got any tension left, imagine breathing into the area to relax it.

Now doesn't that feel better?

Vipassana: Insight Meditation

Vipassana meditation, also known as insight meditation, is a popular form of mindfulness meditation that anyone can learn easily. Originating in India with the Buddha, the technique became the basis of the Southeast Asian Theraveda Buddhism tradition. However, it is a technique—and a fairly easy one—not a theology. Anyone can practice it. The most important key to remember is that Vipassana meditation doesn't involve concentrating on one point of focus, like the breath, a mantra, or a candle flame. It is simple awareness, noticing everything you feel and everything in your environment, letting your mind drift around toward whatever catches your attention, but without becoming emotionally involved with it.

From A to Om

Vipassana meditation or insight meditation is a type of meditation grounded in the meditational aspect of Southeast Asian Theraveda Buddhism. *Vipassana* means "insight," and the technique is considered a meditation method the Buddha himself taught. It is simple, requiring only mindful awareness, which leads to insight.

Insight Exercise

Although you may want to take a class with a reputable teacher of insight meditation, you can try meditation that follows the basic concept on your own:

Sit comfortably with your back straight. Relax and breathe normally. Imagine the word "I." What does it mean? What is I? Become the I. Open your awareness as an I. Observe. What do you feel, hear, see, smell? Imagine that your awareness is one of those wispy dandelion seeds that blows through the air. Don't attempt to concentrate on any one thing. Simply let your mind go where it will. Don't become emotionally involved with anything you observe, just observe.

For instance, you might notice your breath for a while, then your awareness might shift to your sore neck muscles, then to that itch behind your ear, then to your list of chores for the day. When you get to that list of chores, don't dive into the thought and start planning. Be uninvolved. Just watch the thought. "There is a thought about my list of chores." "There, a feeling of pain." "There, a cold sensation in my feet." As you become the I, let the I observe these sensations like a bystander. For example, your awareness might shift something like this:

➤ *Thought*: I, I, I.

➤ *Thought*: I is me.

➤ *Thought*: Me, me, me.

➤ *Thought*: Me bored. I bored.

➤ *Feeling*: Sadness. Happiness. Sadness and happiness mixed. (Note: Avoid thinking, "Why are they mixed? What's wrong with me?")

➤ *Feeling*: Soreness in my knee.

➤ *Thought*: I, I, I.

➤ *Feeling*: Air on my face.

➤ *Thought*: What time is it?

➤ *Thought*: Sound of dog barking.

➤ *Thought*: Smell of geraniums.

➤ *Feeling*: Stiff back.

➤ *Thought*: Sound of silence, I in silence.

You get the idea. We don't intend for you to follow the above sequence. Instead, follow your own awareness. Practice this type of meditation each day and soon you will see your thoughts and feelings as small parts of you, but not *you*. They'll be manageable because they won't define you. They'll be of some interest, but they won't control you. *You* will control you. I, I, I. Who are you? Listen and find the answer.

Feeling more centered? We are! And we hope you are, too. Now that you've tried some techniques and really gotten your feet wet, let's get structured. Read on to learn how to integrate meditation into your daily life.

The Least You Need to Know

➤ Stress may be inevitable, but it doesn't have to compromise your health or clutter your mind.

➤ Mindfulness meditation can teach you to live in full awareness, experiencing every moment.

➤ Mindfulness meditation can also relieve pain, restore a positive attitude, and help you to accept who you are right now.

➤ You can control your stress response through mindfulness meditation.

➤ Insight meditation—following your awareness without a point of concentration (other than your own awareness!)—can help you to gain self-knowledge and control over your thoughts and feelings.

Where to Meditate

So you're under stress. What a shocker! What else is new in the modern world? Right now, you're probably good and ready to start doing something about it, so let's get down to some practical details that'll help you establish a regular, structured meditation practice.

In this chapter we'll help you find the perfect place to meditate. Technically, you can meditate anywhere, but there's no question that some places are more conducive to meditation than others. We'd like to help you survey the space you have and guide you in the creation of a perfect meditation space that is all your own.

Creating a Meditation Space in Your Home

Ideally, you could devote an entire room in your home to meditation, making it into a spiritual sanctuary. Unfortunately, not many people have an extra room to spare for this purpose. (If you happen to be in the process of designing a house to build, however, why not consider adding a small meditation room?) If you live in a limited space, however (like most of us), that doesn't mean you can't carve out the perfect spot for your daily meditation.

First, let's look at what's available in your home. Take the following list and walk through every room in your house. Check any spaces that might make possible meditation spaces:

Living Room/Den:

❑ Is your living room or den L-shaped? Could one end of the L be set apart with a curtain or stand-up screen for meditation?

❑ Do you have a spacious coat closet? Do you really use it, or could coats be relocated to an attractive coat rack or set of hooks by the door?

❑ Do you have any small areas like nooks, window seats, or closets?

❑ Do you have a home office or separate den that isn't completely full or only used occasionally?

Bliss Byte

Sometimes you may find yourself meditating in a less-than-ideal environment. If distracting sensory stimuli seem impossible to tune out, try an exercise in sensory withdrawal. Close your ears with your thumbs, your eyes with your index fingers, your nostrils with your middle fingers, and your lips with your ring and pinkie fingers. Open your nostrils for each inhalation and exhalation, closing them in between for a few seconds. Keep this up for five to 10 minutes. Turning off the senses gives your mind nowhere to turn but inward.

Kitchen/Dining Room:

❑ Do you have an enclosed pantry? Could you clean it out, throw out all the junk, and relocate food to the kitchen cabinets?

❑ Do you have a breakfast nook set off from the main kitchen?

❑ Do you have an enclosed formal dining room that rarely gets used?

Bedrooms/Bathrooms:

❏ Do you have a walk-in closet? Could clothes and shoes be relocated to a shallower closet or a stand-alone wardrobe?

❏ Any window seats, nooks, or extra floor space that you could surround with a drape or stand-up screens?

❏ Is your bathroom extra-large and comfortable (one of those bathrooms that is more "room" than "bath")? Could you devote a corner to meditation?

❏ Do you have a guestroom that isn't regularly occupied?

Indoor/Outdoor:

❏ Do you have a large screened-in porch or small porch that isn't used much?

❏ Do you have a garage or garden shed that isn't overwhelmed with junk or that could be cleaned out and made comfortable?

❏ Any balconies, decks, or roof areas made to walk on?

❏ Do you have a beautiful garden, tree or group of trees, corner of a hedge, or water source that would make an aesthetically appealing spot for meditation?

❏ Are there any unattached structures, such as gazebos, arches, arbors, trellises, or even a fenced-in corner or niche?

Now look at your list and the items you checked. Which seem the most practical, and also, the most private? Think about which area you'd like to use, talk to other family members about it if necessary, and get to work making the space your own.

Meditation Doesn't Mean Deprivation!

Once you've chosen a meditation space, the next step is personalization. Maybe you thought meditation was the stuff of ascetics and your meditation space must be spartan. Far from it! In fact, for the beginning meditator, comfort is extremely important. Otherwise, you may be setting yourself up to give up before you even get started.

How do you make your meditation space comfortable? First, it would help if you could regulate the temperature. If you can't or if you like to meditate outside, keep a soft blanket or quilt nearby to wrap yourself in. Hypothermia during meditation

Relax

Not having a designated meditation space is no reason to give up on the idea of meditation. You can always sit on your bed, on the floor in the middle of the living room (with the TV off!), in any comfortable chair, or even on top of the kitchen table, if it will hold you.

may help keep you awake, but it sure isn't conducive to sitting in one place for 20 minutes or more!

Likewise, if your meditation space is too hot, the heat will probably become distracting. Make sure the area has sufficient ventilation. Although natural cooling is preferable (open windows and fans, for example) during mid-summer, especially in warmer climates, we'll admit the A/C can feel really good. If blasting the air conditioner is the only way you can stand to sit there, then by all means, blast away.

Om Sweet Om: Setting Up

Next, consider aesthetics. Maybe the only space you can find to be alone is the attic, the basement, or the garage. That's great—unless just looking at these places depresses you. If your meditation space is cluttered with junk, you'll have a hard time clearing your mind. Our surroundings are often reflective of our internal housekeeping and changing our surroundings can alter our internal sense of ourselves. So before you meditate in your meditation space, make sure the space is ready.

Relax

Don't get *too* comfortable! If you feel too cozy in your meditation space, you may well fall asleep before you can say "Om." If it helps, keep the temperature a little on the cool side and sit up straight.

First, you'll want to clean your space really well. Clean from top to bottom and everything in between. Get rid of cobwebs, sort through junk and organize, throw away everything that you haven't used for one year and that doesn't have any significant personal meaning for you. Sweep, scrub, scour, polish, and shine.

You also might want to consider cleansing the energies of the room:

➤ First, make sure the space is immaculately clean.

➤ Open a window, a door, or both, so negative energy has somewhere to go.

➤ Declare your intention by standing or sitting in the middle of the room and concentrating on cleansing the energies of the room for the purpose of making it a spiritual space, a relaxing space, or both. If it helps, speak your intention out loud: "I will cleanse the energies of this room to make it a suitable space for meditation."

➤ Walk slowly around the room with a burning incense stick or *smudge* with a sage *smudge stick*, waving it into all the corners and crannies where energy could get "stuck." (You can buy smudge sticks at many organic grocery or health-food stores and other shops and boutiques that carry meditation tools.)

➤ Begin in the middle of the room and walk in a spiral as you ring a bell. The sound waves from the bell can purify the energy. Keep walking a tight spiral until you are walking around the edges of the room. Repeat if the sound of the bell still sounds muffled. You can even clear the space by walking around the room clapping your hands.

➤ Sprinkle water that you've blessed as you walk mindfully around the room. You might want to have a lit candle in the room during this cleansing procedure.

➤ Once you've cleansed the room, walk slowly around it to see if you can feel any "sticky" spots, or areas that don't feel right. Not everyone is in tune with this kind of energy sensation, but with practice it gets easier. If you sense any place where the energy still feels stagnant, repeat your cleansing procedure in that area. Corners are typical offenders. That's why round rooms are ideal for meditation.

➤ When you feel that the space is very clean, walk around one more time with your cleansing tool (the incense, the bells, your hands, etc.). But this time, project the intention of a spiritual haven, to attract energy conducive to concentration and spirituality.

From A to Om

A **smudge stick** is a bundle of dried herbs (sage is one of the most common) tied together and burned for the purpose of purification. The burning and purification process is called **smudging**, and it is a traditional Native American purification technique.

Bliss Byte

Before cleansing the energy of a room or house, it helps to be very clean yourself and to have an empty stomach and a clear mind. Don't eat on the day of your cleansing (you can drink water or juice), and take a long, thorough shower or bath. Then, relax as completely as possible for at least five minutes before beginning. When your physical body is cleansed and open, you'll be more in tune with your environment and setting the beneficial energies of your special mediation space.

After your space is clean, make your space comfortable. Cover hard cement or cold linoleum floors with soft, comfy throw rugs. Clean, fluff, or even recover old, lumpy furniture and pillows. Make sure your room has lots of pillows, mats, bolsters, or whatever else will make meditating more comfortable. Several companies sell meditation mats, meditation pillows and cushions (traditional kinds are called *zafus*), and small meditation benches.

You'll also want the place to have the right ambience. Light candles, burn incense, play relaxing music. Decorate with colors that make you feel tranquil (blues and greens are good) or joyful (orange and yellow are good). Hang the walls with tapestries or pictures showing symbols, figures, or scenes that relax and inspire you. You can even construct a personal altar on which you keep items of spiritual significance to you.

Personal altars can provide you with a sense that your meditation space is truly yours. They can also provide items to use as points of concentration during meditation and can inspire you to maintain a reverent and spiritual frame of mind. All your altar need be is a small table, shelf, or cabinet. Fill it with items that mean something to you:

➤ If you feel close to nature, keep pinecones, seashells, fresh flowers, pine branches, glass bowls of seawater, a miniature fountain, even a small fish tank on your altar.

➤ If you're devoted to a specific religion, keep statues, sacred texts, symbols, or other representations of those beliefs on your altar. (For example, statues of Buddha, of Hindu gods like Krishna or Ganesha, a crucifix or picture of Jesus, a Bible, a cross, a picture of the Om symbol, etc.)

➤ If you are inspired by music, keep a collection of instruments on your altar: small flutes, chimes, gongs, drums, whistles, rattles, and bells.

➤ If you are inspired by art, cover your altar with prints, photos, sculptures, or paintings you find meaningful and inspiring.

➤ If you admire and emulate a particular spiritual leader, include a picture of him or her on your altar.

➤ If you feel centered and grounded by considering the four elements, keep a bowl of water, a stick of burning incense or a burning candle (for fire), a bowl of salt or a beautiful crystal (for earth), and a wind chime (for air) on your altar.

Sounds, Sights, and Smells

Ideally, meditation involves withdrawal of the senses. Complete sense withdrawal isn't easy, however, especially for beginners. In fact, your senses can actually work for you, to help you train yourself to concentrate. The trick is not to bombard them, but to focus on them one at a time.

To help with this pursuit, you can fill your meditation space with tools and equipment that can help you with concentration techniques. You can spend thousands of dollars on fancy meditation and relaxation tools, but you needn't spend a penny. Consider some of the following:

➤ A cassette or CD player to play relaxing, tranquil music such as classical music or any of the many CDs designed for relaxation or meditation.

➤ A wind chime hung near an open window or in the current of a fan.

➤ Small mechanical fountains to provide the peaceful sound of flowing water.

➤ The sounds of bells, gongs, chimes, rattles, flutes, and drums can all be used as points of focus.

➤ Light/sound devices consisting of computerized glasses or masks that provide a light and sound show designed to ease the brain into a relaxed state.

➤ Candles, candles, candles, for use as a point of focus and also to give the room a warm glow.

➤ Mandala artwork, other spiritually inspired artwork.

➤ Incense and incense burner.

➤ Essential oil warmers or diffusers.

➤ Drape walls with fabric in tranquil colors (but keep any draped fabric away from candles and incense!).

Bliss Byte

For the perfect portable meditation space, find a beautiful stone somewhere outside. Make it sacred by blessing it. For example, you could hold it between your palms and bring your palms to your heart, saying, "I fill this stone with tranquility." Carry the stone with you so that whenever you pull it out of your pocket or purse, you create your own sacred space, wherever you are.

Honoring Your Meditation Space

Once you've created your meditation space to be a true embodiment of you (not of some generic idea you have about meditation), it should feel comfortable, not foreign or strange. Entering it should fill you with tranquility and satisfaction. If your intention is to have a relaxing space, your space should make you feel relaxed just stepping into it. If your intention is to have a spiritual haven, you should feel spiritually inspired by your space.

This is Joan's meditation room. Joan wanted to feel surrounded by sky, nature, beauty, simplicity, and love. Her meditation space is large enough for practicing yoga, or to be used as a healing space for Joan's massage clients—using a massage table or chair. The room is blue in color to evoke the peacefulness of a natural setting and sparsely furnished. Candles for soft lighting, plants, and moveable pillows create a functional and calming environment. A window allows for fresh air. Joan removes her shoes before entering her meditation room. You'll want to craft your own meditation space, one that's just right for you!

Now that you've crafted your space, honor it. Keep it sparkling clean. Periodically replace burned-down candles and wilted flowers. Clean up incense ash, shake out pillows and mats, dust your altar. Also, every so often, especially when you seem to have hit a meditation plateau, cleanse the energy of your space again, as directed above. Remember to open the windows and doors.

Also, when in your meditation space, you can honor it and maintain the atmosphere by behaving with reverence. Take your shoes off at the door. Speak softly. You might even consider saying a blessing each time you enter or exit the door or entrance to the space. A few to try:

➤ *I honor this space.*

➤ *Thank you for this haven.*

➤ *May truth be present here.*

Feng Shui: Beneficial Energies for Your Home

The ancient art of *Feng Shui* (pronounced *fung shway*) originated in China thousands of years ago but has become suddenly "in." Feng Shui is the art of arranging interiors—furniture and other items—and landscaping to make them more conducive to greater health, prosperity, love, spirituality, or other higher goals. Donald Trump hires experts to decorate his buildings using Feng Shui techniques. Bookstores are brimming with books on Feng Shui and in most cities you can find a Feng Shui master to help you arrange your living space to best facilitate the flow of energy.

The idea makes sense: Just as bodies contain life-force energy that flows through certain channels, the rest of the world flows with energy, too. Call it prana, chi, or whatever you like. It's everywhere, and it enlivens our cities, our towns, our neighborhoods, our homes, our workplaces, our gardens, and our meditation spaces. Or if those spaces are arranged so that they block and stagnate or drain the energy, it deadens them.

> **From A to Om**
>
> **Feng Shui** is the ancient Chinese art of placement. It involves arranging interior spaces and placing houses and buildings within a landscape to best facilitate the flow of energy and ensure health, prosperity, wisdom, and other positive qualities to the inhabitants.

We won't pretend to be Feng Shui masters, but we can tell you a couple of basic principles you can use in your meditation space (and in your home, too). In general, keep in mind that energy is affected by everything around it, including objects and also including the moods, attitudes, emotions, and actions of the people it surrounds. (Another reason to behave with reverence in your meditation space!)

Also keep in mind that although general principles do exist, Feng Shui is to some extent an individual matter. Arrange things so they "feel" right to you, even if you don't know why. Trust your instinct.

Try the following Feng Shui techniques in your meditation space:

➤ Placing mirrors in corners, nooks, and other spaces where swirling energy could become trapped helps to loosen the energy and keep it moving.

➤ Living things (plants, fish, flowers, pine branches, etc.) and clean crystals help draw in energy and keep it moving.

➤ Square shapes hold energy while round shapes move energy (so you might consider a square altar in a round room, or a square meditation mat or pillow with pictures of round mandalas on the walls).

➤ Keep the area outside the door or entrance to your meditation space clear (also the space outside the door to your home) so energy has an open channel through which to enter the room. Also, if your door opens to a wall, place a mirror on the wall to push the energy into the room.

185

➤ Your kitchen is indicative of your financial situation. A dirty kitchen (especially a dirty stove) indicates financial problems.

➤ Corners, beams, pillars, posts, and large pieces of furniture in the middle of rooms disturb energy flow. Keep the space clear and give energy a "river" to flow through.

➤ The ideal place in your home for a meditation space is the lower-left corner when standing in the entranceway of your house. This is the part of the house related to self-realization, introspection, and meditation. The center of the house is also good. This space represents health and energy.

➤ Crystals hanging in the windows focus and intensify energy.

Creating Outdoor Meditation Spaces: Sacred Geometry

If your meditation space is outside, you can still make certain changes to create the perfectly personalized meditation space. Filling your yard with living plants, flowers, and trees will bring it to life, even if you only have space for potted plants. Limit or eliminate the use of chemical pesticides and fertilizers. Try organic gardening methods instead to have a truly Earth-friendly space. And whenever you get the chance, plant a tree. Trees are like wise old souls and make excellent meditation partners. You'll feel grounded sitting over those deep roots and sheltered by the tree canopy.

Mindful Minute

Clear quartz crystals are good for purifying energy as it enters a room. Periodically clean your crystals with water (rinse well). Also, re-energize them every few months by placing them outside in direct sunlight for several hours. Sun is very important to a crystal's energetic properties. The crystal absorbs, reflects, and heals through the sun's energy.

Zen Gardening

Zen gardening can be as easy as filling a bowl with sand and rocks, and as comprehensive as specially landscaping your entire property. Zen gardens are meant to serve as meditation spaces. They typically reflect the ideas and spirit of the culture, so your Zen garden should reflect you more than, say, Japan (unless you are from Japan, in which case it could do both!). Zen gardens are typically dry, and use sand and rocks to represent water. Sand represents the ocean, and plants or trees could represent vast forests. Dry streambeds made with stone are a common feature. Sand may also be raked in geometric patterns. Zen gardens are miniature representations of natural or spiritual phenomena.

Before crafting your own Zen garden, think about what you would want your meditation space to represent. How could you represent your ideas, your self, in a garden?

But sand in a bowl designed with circles and streams of pebbles or raked in patterns can be a Zen garden, too, and a garden this small could fit on your personal altar.

Take a look at Chapter 27, "Om Away from Om: Spiritual Travel," where you'll find many sacred places discussed, including Japanese Zen gardens.

Pond and Water Spaces

Water can be inspiring, grounding, uplifting, refreshing, and purifying. The sound of water makes an excellent point of focus for meditation, and the sight of a bubbling fountain, a pond surrounded by flowers and filled with bright orange koi (large Japanese goldfish), or even a beautiful birdbath can be the perfect addition to an outdoor meditation space. Check your local garden center for supplies. Many companies also sell water gardening equipment of fine quality in unique designs.

Choosing a Meditation Class

If, in despair, you just can't find a good meditation spot, or if you've created the perfect spot but you'd like a little in-person guidance about what to do there, you might consider taking a meditation class. Although meditation is a highly personal experience, a meditation class, or even a simple meditation group, may give you just the motivation you need to sit still in silence for a significant length of time. Being in the company of others who are also interested in the "inner journey" can inspire you to stick with your program. Discipline is an important aspect of meditation and is sometimes easier when you've got like-minded friends around you. *Satsung* is a Sanskrit word used to describe the company of like-minded spirits and the strength possible through their companionship.

Mindful Minute

Nature has a profound effect on healing. A 1984 study by a researcher at Texas A&M found that hospital patients whose windows revealed a view of a courtyard with plants and greenery healed faster than those whose rooms showed mostly man-made structures. The patients with the views of nature had shorter hospital stays, received fewer negative notes on nurse reports, and requested fewer pain medications.

Relax

Are you too busy to meditate? Can't find the time to join a meditation class? Even if your life doesn't afford the opportunity to have a time or place for sitting meditation, you can take a regular activity and turn it into a mindfulness meditation (see Chapter 11, "Stress: Is Your Mind *Too* Full?").

A meditation class "in action."

Meditation classes may be difficult to find or may be short-term or even single-session classes designed to teach a specific technique. If you can't find a meditation class that appeals to you or makes you comfortable, consider starting your own meditation group. If you attend a place of worship, you can likely find people who would be interested in joining you. Or, ask people in your yoga class, ask around at your natural food store or an alternative bookstore, or ask your massage therapist. Chances are someone near you either knows of something like what you seek or knows others who would be interested in meditating together.

If you do take a class with a teacher, be wary of anything that seems overly costly, that requires more money to learn additional "secrets," or that makes you uncomfortable in any way. Many wonderful meditation teachers exist to help you in your journey, but like any other field, there are always a few who are not so well intentioned. Keep your eyes open (figuratively), use your common sense, and sprinkle that with a healthy dose of intuition. When you've found someone you can trust, learn all you can. A good meditation teacher is a great gift.

We hope you are happy with the meditation space you have created, or are at the very least inspired to find and create the perfect space. Once you feel serene about your surroundings, you're ready to get meditating!

Bliss Byte

Can you see your meditation teacher's aura (see Chapter 8, "Energy Central," for instructions)? If it is yellow or gold and very clear, your teacher is spiritually advanced and could serve as a worthy spiritual advisor, according to proponents of auric sight. (However, we advise that you should never substitute aura for intuition. If you think someone's aura looks bright and clear but you have a feeling you don't trust them or they make you uncomfortable, go with your intuition.)

The Least You Need to Know

➤ You can create the perfect meditation space in your own home with a little cleaning, rearranging, and personalizing.

➤ The way you arrange your meditation space and your home can influence the flow of energy through the room and, by extension, the quality of your meditation.

➤ Outdoor meditation spaces can be beautiful havens, too. Try a Zen garden, an outdoor pond, or a fountain.

➤ Consider the variety of meditation classes available, for a meditation space away from home and a new perspective on meditation.

Starting Your Meditation Practice

By now, you've learned a lot about what meditation can do for you, what stress does to you, and even about a lot of different types of meditation. But what kind of picture do you have in your own head about your meditation practice? Do you see yourself focusing on breathing? Are you more interested in forms of moving meditation? Do you like the idea of spiritual exploration? Are you just looking for some effective stress relief? Are you nervous? Confused? A little scared? Or are you eager to start reaping the benefits?

For goodness sake, how do you actually *start*? That's what we'll discuss in this chapter.

What Do You Want from Your Meditation Practice?

You've started. You've begun the learning process and have been presented with lots of ideas that have you thinking about how you would like to use meditation in your own life. But until you address this question, you won't get the most from your meditation practice.

Relax

Just as too much physical activity without a good warm-up and without getting in shape first can cause injury and soreness, trying to meditate for too long or expecting too much at first can lead to frustration and meditation burn-out. Slow down!

You can devote some serious thought to what you want from meditation, but perhaps a better way to address the question is to write. As the famous novelist E. M. Forster once said, "How can I know what I think until I see what I say?" Writing down your thoughts and then reading them a day or two later can sometimes help to clarify and solidify your intentions.

If you don't like writing, you can speak into a tape recorder or talk over the question with a friend. To get you started, we'll give you a little structure.

A Meditation Essay Test You Can't Fail

Answer the following questions as fully and truthfully as you can. Don't worry about correct grammar, spelling, or style. Just write what you feel after reading each question. There are no right or wrong answers. The point is to form your intentions and bring them into your conscious mind so that your meditation practice has a structure and a purpose.

1. Before reading this book, the first thing I thought of when I heard the word "meditation" was:

   _____

   _____

2. Now that I've read some of this book, I am most surprised by the fact that meditation is/can:

   _____

   _____

3. I am reading this book because:

   _____

   _____

4. The aspect of meditation that interests me the most is:

   _____

   _____

5. The people close to me have or will probably have the opinion that meditation is:

   _____

   _____

6. I feel the most stress in the areas of my life having to do with:

   _____

   _____

Bliss Byte

If discipline is very difficult for you and you can't seem to get yourself to write down your meditation goals, try setting a timer for your allotted meditation time—say five or 10 minutes. When the timer sounds, write the first word in your mind. Do this for a few weeks. What do your accumulated words tell you? Look up each of the words in the dictionary and use the definitions as the subject of concentration for future meditation sessions. Consider the words as a group—are they nouns, verbs, adjectives, or adverbs? Are they positive or negative, nurturing or critical, stressed or relaxed, passive or active? Does looking at the word(s) you've written make you feel more or less comfortable about your meditation practice?

7. Meditation fits into my spiritual beliefs in the following ways:

_____

_____

8. I'm not sure I understand or feel quite comfortable with the following aspects of meditation:

_____

_____

9. I envision myself meditating in the following location(s):

_____

_____

10. I envision myself meditating by concentrating on:

_____

_____

11. I envision myself struggling during meditation with:

_____

_____

12. I envision myself trying different types of meditation, especially:

_____

_____

13. When I have to sit still for a long time, I tend to:

_____

_____

193

14. My feelings about meditating in a group are:

15. I believe meditation could make a difference in my life by:

16. I am a little bit afraid of meditating because:

17. I think meditation could make me more:

18. When comparing the idea of meditation versus the idea of prayer, my feeling is:

19. The thing I'm most looking forward to in beginning a meditation practice is:

20. I would like to formally state my commitment to a meditation practice, in my own words:

Once you've finished, put your answers aside. Don't read them over just yet. Wait a day or two and read them when you have a few moments to yourself. What do they reveal to you that you might not have recognized before?

Now, imagine how you might summarize your feelings about meditation in one sentence. For instance, you might realize:

➤ "I'm afraid I won't be able to meditate, but I want to try."

➤ "I am afraid of confronting myself during meditation, but I want to try."

➤ "I am committed to expanding the limits of my spiritual life."

➤ "I just need to find an effective way to relax!"

Write your summary statement here:

My Meditation Summary Statement:

Meditation Perspectives

	My Stress Perspective	My Spiritual Perspective	My Health Perspective	My Self-Knowledge Perspective
What do I hope meditation will bring to my life?				
What feelings dominate my life right now?				
What do I want to learn about myself?				
What do I feel I can and can't control?				
I feel best when:				
I feel worst when:				
My breathing tends to be:				
My mind and body don't communicate very well when:				

Break It Down: Uncovering What Meditation Means to You

Now that you've gone over your answers again and summarized your general *perspective*, break down the different categories a bit further. Are you primarily drawn to stress relief, spiritual fulfillment, health benefits, or enlightenment itself? Are you attracted to the aspects of meditation from other cultures, or how it will best fit into your own cultural heritage? Use the following table to help you take a closer look.

Bliss Byte

Meditation may bring up painful memories or hurt in your life. If you continue to meditate, you won't be able to run away from these because meditation increases your awareness and sensitivity. Meditation helps you to roll up your sleeves and deal with the ups and downs of life constructively and with balance. Consider complementing your meditation practice by discussing any persistently troubling thoughts and feelings with a counselor or mental health professional. A therapist may be able to help you to focus and direct your meditation to help you achieve resolution and may also contribute insights and suggestions you may not have considered on your own.

Answer each question four times, according to your feelings or experiences regarding stress relief and relaxation, spiritual life, health, and self-knowledge. These answers can be very brief—a few words, a phrase, a sentence. If you get stuck on one because you can't see how, for you, the question applies to a particular column, just leave it blank or mark it with an X. If you'd like to answer more comprehensively, write your responses on a separate sheet of paper.

There are no right or wrong responses. Each person has his or her own unique experience of meditation. Use this exercise to help you determine what a regular meditation practice means for *your* life. And consider this, as you begin to meditate, your reasons for meditating will evolve and grow as you do—and in ways that may surprise and delight you! In fact, in the beginning you may not know exactly *why* it's important to you to meditate regularly, only that you want to do it.

Just the fact that meditation isn't something that's taught in school or practiced by everyone in our society can make it feel unfamiliar at first, or even awkward. But, like any skill, meditation takes time to get the hang of, but the experience of meditating itself will soon become reason enough to continue doing it. Soon, you'll realize what a wondrous thing meditation is, and this will draw you back to your meditation practice again and again.

You're Not Alone

People meditate for a variety of reasons; there are no goals in meditation, or preset requirements. If finding like-minded meditators is important for you, look for groups that don't necessarily advertise meditation but are based around the same interests you have.

For instance, attending a stress-management course, a prayer group, a seminar on Buddhism, a yoga class, or a self-improvement workshop might put you in contact with other people who are either already meditating or would be interested in forming a meditation group. You might even look for a support group where you don't actually meditate, but discuss your life experiences and interests.

From A to Om

Perspective means "point of view." Meditation does have many benefits, but the real purpose of meditation is not to accomplish things. It is an expression of who you truly are. Use meditation to help you discover your perspective—on your *self*.

When to Meditate

So now you know the why of your meditation practice. (And if the big "why" question is still elusive—that's okay, too!) What about the when? Meditating at random times each day is better than no meditation, but it isn't ideal, either. Many philosophies postulate that a regular schedule is best for a calm mind and good health. For example, Indian Ayurveda prescribes a regular routine for people who suffer from health problems, which they see as imbalances of internal forces (see Chapter 26, "Rx: Meditation").

If you're schedule-resistant, adopting a regular schedule may seem impossible and even undesirable. Maybe you like your free-wheelin' lifestyle! But a regular time for meditation, if for nothing else, will help to keep you grounded and centered. Although you may at first dread anything you

Mindful Minute

Many cultures consider the time between 5:00 and 5:30 a.m. the perfect time to meditate. This time, just before or at sunrise, is a time when peacefulness, awareness, and a calm state of mind are easiest to uncover. Think you can't possibly get up that early? Try going to bed an hour earlier, then setting your alarm. It might be hard at first, but it's largely a matter of habit.

have to do every day at a certain time, look at it as a welcome oasis rather than a chore or a burden. Sure, sometimes you won't feel like it. But discipline is the first step to freedom. (Really!)

To find the ideal meditation time for you, check the items in the following list that apply to you:

Energy Factor:

- ❏ My energy peak seems to be in the early morning.
- ❏ My energy peak seems to be in the late morning.
- ❏ My energy peak seems to be in the afternoon.
- ❏ My energy peak seems to be in the early evening.
- ❏ My energy peak seems to be late at night.

Time Factor:

- ❏ I have to be at work very early in the morning.
- ❏ I get home at least an hour or two before dinner.
- ❏ I have a free space in the middle of the day.
- ❏ I am completely swamped with responsibility until everyone goes to sleep at night.

Believe it or not, it is better to meditate during times of peak energy than in times of low energy. Even though your meditation practice may involve sitting or lying down, you'll need a lot of energy to channel into the effort of mindfulness, concentration, and awareness. If you are in an energy slump, you'll probably just fall asleep.

But time, of course, is the crucial factor. When it comes to energy, it doesn't matter if you are a morning person if you already get up before dawn and immediately launch into an award-winning effort to get everyone in your family, including yourself, dispatched to their proper locations before school buses and carpools leave, meetings begin, and time clocks hit their designated hours. If your only possible free time is your lunch hour or that precious interval between when the kids are asleep and when you collapse in bed, you'll probably find that evening is your best meditation time. Ideally, of course, your energy peak and your free time coincide, but we recognize that it isn't a perfect world.

Whatever time works, pick a time and stick to it whenever possible. Keep that time sacred and instruct the people who live with you to respect your meditation time. Turn on the answering machine, go to your meditation space leaving all other responsibilities behind, and be at peace.

Start Slow

Now you've probably got a pretty clear idea of what your priorities are for your meditation practice, when to do it, where to do it, even how to do it. "Can I finally get started?" you may be pleading to the pages of this book. All right, all right, let's do it! But don't expect us to rush into anything. Indeed, rushing is contrary to the very nature of meditation. Remember the fable of the tortoise and the hare? Slow and steady will get you there.

When you first sit down (or lie down or stand up or whatever form you are trying), make your goal a good five minutes of meditation. For first-timers, this may be the longest five minutes you've ever experienced! Your nose might itch, your muscles might twitch, and you'll probably run down every

Relax

Don't let your back be your enemy! Posture is important, even when seated. An erect spine keeps the energy circulating through the body and keeps the chest open, allowing for fuller breathing. Imagine a rope pulling the crown of your head toward the sky. Bring your shoulders back to open the chest and breathe.

to-do list on your agenda before you remember to remind yourself that you are meditating. Don't worry. That's usually how it is at first. It will get better.

Stick with five-minute sessions for three days, then move up to seven minutes the next day, eight minutes the following day, nine minutes the next day, then on the seventh day, 10 minutes. Stick with 10-minute sessions for one week, then move up to 15 for a week, then 20 minutes.

Bliss Byte

Sometimes stress is purely a matter of mismanaged time. When you spend too much time dwelling in the past or worrying about the future, you waste a lot of time in the present. Meditation helps to bring your awareness back to the present, opening up an eternity in the now. That's why it's so important to let go of your worries, fears, and even hopes and joys when you meditate. Focus only on the present in its calm "hereness."

Twenty minutes twice per day is the recommended meditation schedule according to many instructors, but if you can only manage it once, that's great. In one month, you're there! If you can eventually work up to 30, 45, or even 60 minutes, that's great, too. Eventually, the goal is to be able to maintain a mindful, meditative state all the time, but here's our suggested schedule for beginners:

Day two	5 minutes
Day three	5 minutes
Day four	7 minutes
Day five	8 minutes
Day six	9 minutes
Day seven	10 minutes
Week two	10 minutes
Week three	15 minutes
Week four	20 minutes

To keep track of the time, set a timer. If you're looking at a clock every minute or so, not only will the time seem interminable, but the clock will keep you from concentrating on your point of focus, and time will become too high a priority in your awareness. With a timer (a simple kitchen timer or egg timer with a bell will do), you can forget about the time until you hear the signal. Try to use a timer with a gentle ring and without a loud tick, tick, tick.

Bliss Byte

If you are having a lot of trouble keeping your mind focused on your breath, your mantra, or your visual point of focus, try counting. According to Zen master Thich Nhat Hahn, counting is a great meditation technique for beginning meditators. Breathe in and count "one," breathe out and count "one," breathe in and count "two," breathe out and count "two," etc. Counting helps to keep the mind from wandering, but varies just enough to keep the novice meditator involved.

Be Diligent

Diligence is another important quality to cultivate when beginning a meditation practice. Without perseverance and discipline, you'll soon give up. Maybe your parents used to tell you that nothing worth having comes easily. That's usually true, and it's true here, too. Meditation takes time to yield its benefits.

In many ways, our modern society is an undisciplined one. We don't want to wait for anything. We have fast food. We have drive-thru banks, dry-cleaners, pharmacies, even drive-thru quick shops! (As if quick shops aren't quick enough.) We want everything that might be a little tedious done for us. We're glad to pay money for it, but what spiritual price are we paying as we shell out the big bucks? Sometimes it may seem like no one wants to work for anything anymore. It's easier to buy a lottery ticket than earn your own living. (But not easier to win!)

But you can change all that, at least for yourself. (And perhaps the world can change, too, slowly, person by person.) One step at a time, one aspect of your life at a time, cultivate discipline. Be diligent about the very task of living. Meditation can be the groundwork of that diligence. You can do it! You can change your life, one Om at a time.

A Little Progress on a Long Road to Samadhi

The road to enlightenment—whatever enlightenment means to you—is a long one, fraught with obstacles. But you can find your bliss, little by little. Although meditation won't result in immediate, dramatic benefits, it does yield tiny treasures along the way. One day, you may suddenly realize that your work demands don't get to you the way they used to. Or your spouse's annoying little habits aren't so annoying. Maybe you find that you are seeing a brilliant sunset or a snowy forest or a bed of pink tulips for the very first time, and the sight fills you with sudden joy.

Maybe you will look in the mirror one day and will, quite unexpectedly, love what you see, and it will have nothing to do with your external appearance. Maybe your movements will develop more grace, your speech will become more relaxed, or your demeanor will suddenly radiate composure. Maybe one month, day by day, your life will look more and more like a garden every day. Then you'll see how worthwhile a daily meditation practice can be.

Relax

Expectation can be a hindrance to meditation. If you are expecting drastic change after just a few sessions, you'll be disappointed and may discontinue your meditation practice. Live in the moment when meditating, rather than looking forward to the future benefits.

Leave Your Pride on the Doorstep

In this competitive world, the idea of pouring your time and energy into something that has nothing to do with competition, "besting" anyone, or winning may seem a little hard to swallow. But meditation isn't about being the best, but only about learning to be the best that you can be. Can you imagine a competitive attitude applied to meditation? "Check me out—I'm *way* more relaxed than you'll *ever* be!" "Ha! I attained enlightenment *first*!" Pretty ridiculous, huh! The whole point of meditation is to remove stress-inducing mentalities and ideally, to come to the realization that we are all one. And if we are all one, then competition is pointless.

If you are naturally competitive, let your nature help your personal journey rather than hinder it. Meditation on a regular basis will soften the "winner/loser" aspects of competition. You may find your focus shifts to finding "win/win" situations for everyone! Indeed, everyone is a winner in meditation, a highly personal journey of self-discovery.

Mindful Minute

Many eating disorders can be traced to a sense of competitiveness and wanting to be "perfect," often coupled with a desire to gain control. A steady meditation practice in conjunction with professional help from a licensed therapist can help to encourage a noncompetitive nature, as well as the acceptance of oneself and a recognition that we only have control over ourselves.

So let your meditation practice occur in a "no-pride zone." Let all that rat race, one-up-manship, keeping-up-with-the-Jones, I-can-do-it-better-and-faster-and-for-more-money business float away like all your other distracting thoughts, and just be. No pride, no worries.

Going the Distance

Meditation is a journey, just like life. It's a long journey, but a rewarding journey. Be ready to persevere and be patient. Some stretches on this road go on for miles, like a trip across the desert. Yet, even the desert, though it looks dry and brown at first glance, reveals its wonders when you really concentrate on the view.

Of course, no journey begins until you take that first step, so when you're ready (and you are), sit down, take a deep breath, and begin. To borrow a slogan from a company that thrives on appareling competitive bodies, "Just do it." Make meditation a part of your lifestyle, of who you are.

The Least You Need to Know

➤ Your meditation practice will be more focused if you consider why you want to try meditation and what your meditation priorities are.

➤ Begin your meditation practice slowly, just a few minutes at a time to start. Don't expect immediate dramatic effects, either. Long-term, regular practice will yield the best results.

➤ Meditation takes diligence but not pride. Competitiveness is antithetical to the spirit of meditation.

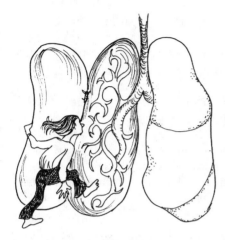

Enter the Breathing Room

Before we jump into the actual meditation process any further, we'd like to cover one more very important process. We've talked a lot about meditation techniques that involve following the breath or focusing your attention on your breathing, but are you breathing the right way?

You may be skeptical that there is a right way to breathe. If your breathing is keeping you alive, you're doing it right, right?

Not necessarily. As infants, most of us were able to breathe effortlessly, deeply, and in the way that best nourished our bodies with oxygen. As we grow older, however, tension, stress, bad posture, diet, and other factors begin to hinder proper breathing. According to many proponents of breathwork and of natural health care in general, the breath may be the most important factor in increasing and maintaining good health and longevity. And that's what we'll discuss in this chapter.

The Breath of Life

Remember all that talk about prana, the life-force energy that can suffuse our bodies more fully if we learn how to draw it into us through the breath? Maybe prana is the reason breathwork is so important. Many languages and traditions have linked breath with spirit, divinity, wisdom, and the creative spark. The word *inspiration* literally means "to breathe in," while the word *expiration*, meaning "to breathe out," is sometimes used as a synonym for death. In Tibetan Buddhism, breath is sometimes called "the vehicle of the mind." In Sanskrit, the word for breath is *prana*, which also denotes universal life-force energy. In the Bible, God breathed into clay to create man, and the Holy Spirit is said to "inspire." In Judaism, the word for breath also means "spirit of God." In Greek, the word *pneuma* meant breath, soul, air, and spirit. The Chinese character for breath consists of three different characters that mean "of the conscious self or heart." In Latin, *anima spiritus* means both breath and soul, and in Japanese, *ki* means both air and spirit.

Or maybe breathwork is important because of the benefits more oxygen brings to all the systems of the body—the muscles, heart, lungs, brain, digestion, even our attitudes, emotions, and energy level. Have you ever wondered why children have so much energy? Perhaps it is because they still know how to breathe. Perhaps that kind of energy could be yours.

And So I Asked My Teacher, "How Do I Breathe?"

Maybe you are under the impression that breathwork is for amateur meditators. Meditation 101, right? Actually, although breathwork is an excellent way to ease into meditation, it's nothing less than a lifetime pursuit. Zen masters are still working on perfecting the nuances of breathing. Breathing may be easy, but breathing *well* is another matter. Remember the student of meditation who thought breathwork was boring (see Chapter 5, "The Soul Has Many Mansions")? Experienced meditators will tell you that learning to breathe can be a lifelong journey.

Relax

When you realize you're under stress or overwhelmed, simply "Remember to breathe."

Breathing is, in itself, both a beginning and a highly advanced form of meditation. The breath is a multi-layered, highly complex, yet pure and simple process. It suffuses the soul with vitality. It delivers oxygen to the brain. It is as mundane as panting, as sublime as the nature of reality. To control the breath is to control life itself. You could simultaneously ponder it and practice it for a lifetime. And many have.

The Psyche, the Breath, the Soul

Breath is life. We can live for a number of weeks without food, about two or three days without water, but only a few moments without breath. Breathing properly will fill you with vitality. Allowing your body, your mood, or anything else to interfere with right breathing only interferes with your vitality. Guard your breath, master the breathing process, and you will be filled with life, energy, and inspiration.

Breath has plenty of physical benefits, but it has benefits for the psyche, as well. Conscious deep breathing has the amazing capacity to calm us, even in the most stressful situations. From calming the nerves before a test to bringing tranquility to the mind of someone who is dying, deep breathing transforms us. Or perhaps "transform" is the wrong word. Actually, deep breathing *reminds* us of how we are meant to feel.

Bliss Byte

Try this simple calming exercise: Double the length of your exhalation to your inhalation. For example, breathe in to a count of four, then breathe out to a count of eight. Work up to an inhalation on the count of six and exhalation on the count of 12, eight and 16, nine and 18, 10 and 20. Never strain the breathing process. If you feel strain, intersperse the rhythm with some normal breaths.

That feeling is the source of a new sort of self-control. Deep breathing reminds us that although we may not be able to control the world, we can control our reaction to the world. We can control our selves. Consider a newborn baby. Newborn humans have less control over themselves and are less able to survive on their own than any other newborn animal. They are helpless for longer than any other newborn, as well. Yet, are they stressed out about it? Nope. Sure, they'll make a fuss when they want something, but as soon as their needs are met, they are calm and happy again. (As long as their needs are met, which may be a key as to how we all lose this ability to breathe mindfully.) Infants know how to breathe, and with each breath, their bodies experience the present moment, wherein everything is just fine.

Just think how much more self-control you have than a baby, and how much more control you have over your own circumstances! If, in addition to this added skill, you could retain the ability to breathe like a baby, you'd probably find yourself sleeping like a baby, smiling like a baby, eating like a baby, loving like a baby, and...happy as a clam.

The Physiology of Breathing

Why does breath have such a pervasive influence on your mind-body? For one thing, our entire body is made up of cells, and cells are nourished through breath (as well as through the food we eat).

To truly understand how significant breath is for life, it helps to know a little bit about the actual process of breathing, and what happens in the body with each breath. When you inhale oxygen, it flows into your lungs and attaches to *hemoglobin* (part of red blood cells). It then travels into the capillaries of the body, where it diffuses into your body tissue to nourish and replenish it. The blood cells, having dumped their oxygen load, pick up a load of carbon dioxide, travel back through the capillaries to the veins, and flow into the heart, where they are pumped back to the lungs. The carbon dioxide is expelled by the lungs via the exhalation of the breath. Another inhalation delivers more oxygen to the lungs, and the cycle continues. Talk about a circle of life!

The cardiovascular, respiratory, and circulatory systems flow oxygen through its circle of life.

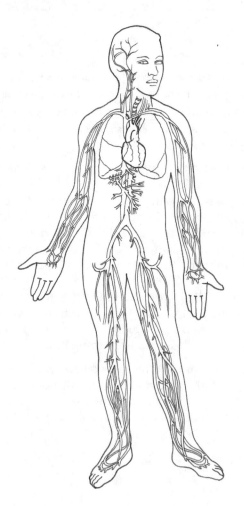

The oxygen is able to keep entering this lung-heart-lung system because your body has certain muscles that keep moving it in and out of the body, including the diaphragm muscle and abdominal muscles. For deep breathing, the diaphragm may be the most important muscle over which you can exert a great deal of conscious control.

Actually, you've got several diaphragm muscles, but the largest one and the one most instrumental in breathing (although the others play a part, too) is the large, bowl-shaped muscle that lies at the bottom of your chest, just above your abdomen. When you inhale, the diaphragm expands downward to give your lungs and chest more room to hold breath. Imagine the cup of the bowl filling up and dropping downward to make more room for air. With each exhalation, the bowl inverts, its cup pushing upward to push air out. Ideally, this process comes off without a hitch. Realistically, however, we often manage to get it all wrong. Sure, we keep breathing. We stay alive. But we no longer maximize our breath potential.

From A to Om

Hemoglobin is a molecule in red blood cells responsible for carrying oxygen from the lungs to the tissues and carbon dioxide from the tissues back to the lungs.

Breathing at Its Worst

Life has taught us to mess with a good thing. Most adults have developed breathing patterns that restrict the flow of oxygen, and the inevitable result is undernourished tissue, including muscle tissue and brain tissue. Restricted oxygen flow may also result in a greater sense of anxiety, a lower tolerance for stress, and an inability to think and react quickly. Unhealthy breathing patterns come in several forms.

One of the most common forms of unhealthy breathing is shallow deep breathing. This kind of breathing is what many people do when they *think* they are breathing deeply, as in, "Everybody take a deeeeeep breath!" As they suck in air, these

Mindful Minute

Deep breathing is being used more frequently as an actual medical therapy. The Stress Reduction Clinic at the University of Massachusetts Medical Center teaches its clients deep breathing exercises and uses breathing as a focus for mindfulness meditation.

misbreathers hike up their shoulders and raise their chests. But what do your shoulders have to do with breathing? If anything, they should be moving outward, away from your body, not up around your ears. Even our diaphragm muscles can become involved in this pseudo–deep breathing. If you're accustomed to holding your stomach in all the time (as do many of us, conditioned as we are to try to look thinner), your diaphragm may get confused, thinking that upon inhalation, it should push upward, forcing air into the upper chest. Upon exhalation, it then collapses downward.

Bliss Byte

Breathing can be more interesting than simple inhalation and exhalation. During meditation, try a variety of techniques. A few powerful breathing methods: 1) Inhale with a series of small breaths, then exhale with a *SSS* sound. 2) Inhale through pursed lips and exhale with a whistle. 3) Breathe in through one nostril while holding the other closed, then switch and exhale through the opposite nostril. Repeat the other way. These techniques can increase your vitality and alter your consciousness. Deep breathing can even create a natural buzz! A drug is defined as any substance taken into the body that effects change. Oxygen is no different.

But this is backward and counterproductive to an efficient intake of oxygen. When this kind of breathing becomes chronic, it interferes with the workings of the whole mind-body system. Common problems associated with this type of breathing are indigestion, muscle tension in the upper body, confusion, and a feeling of being uncoordinated. If your very breath is uncoordinated, it is only natural that your mind-body will follow suit.

We block our breathing in other ways, too. Chronic muscle tension and chronic pain can tend to make people hold their bodies in a chronic clinch. Overall muscle tension doesn't allow the entire body to expand and contract with the breath. Bad posture doesn't allow the lungs and diaphragm to expand and contract sufficiently. Stress can cause rapid, shallow breathing, which brings in less oxygen and causes the loss of too much carbon dioxide. The system becomes out of balance and in the extreme, *hyperventilation* occurs.

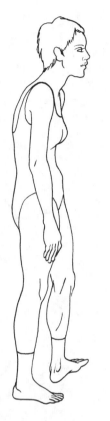 

The hunched shoulders and collapsed chest characteristic in poor posture restrict breathing and inhibit the correct action of the diaphragm muscle. Lift and open your heart chakra, creating space for the flow of breath into and through the body and allowing the diaphragm muscle to function at its best.

Breathing at Its Best

Nobody wants to hyperventilate, of course, but who wouldn't want to maximize their physical and mental power through something as easy as breathing? But how do we regain our ability to breathe fully, deeply, and with the whole body?

Correct breathing comes in many forms, depending on what you are doing and what your body's needs are. Your breath will necessarily change with each passing moment. But ideally, you should be breathing deeply.

During deep breathing, your diaphragm presses downward and your abdomen extends on the inhalation, rather than your chest rising and shoulders lifting. Also, your lower back expands outward (this movement is subtle but real), and your rib cage expands to allow room for your expanding lungs. On the exhalation, the diaphragm should rise, causing your

A to Om

Hyperventilation is "overbreathing," or breathing too rapidly and shallowly. It is characterized by a feeling of not being able to get enough air, as well as dizziness, racing heart, fainting, and muscle cramps.

abdomen to fall inward, your lower back to contract slightly, and your ribcage to move back to its normal position. Your shoulders shouldn't move at all during proper deep breathing, and you might have noticed we don't mention your upper chest. Try to keep it still and focus your attention lower. If you focus on your upper chest, you may tend to begin breathing more shallowly again. Remember: inhale, abdomen, lower back, and rib cage expand. Exhale, abdomen, lower back, and rib cage contract, returning to normal position and helping to push the breath out of the body.

Breath pours in, dia-phragm moves down. Breathe pours out, dia-phragm moves up. It's a mantra!

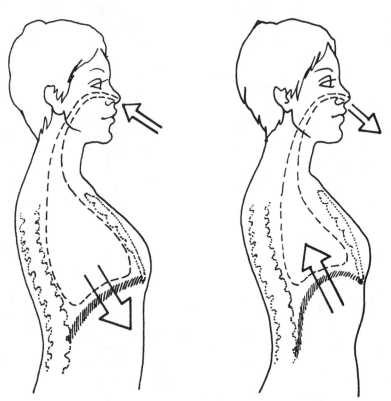

This action is contrary to how many adults are used to breathing because shallow breathing is a common malady of adult life. In shallow breathing, the chest rises and falls, and sometimes the shoulders follow. In deep breathing, the shoulders stay still and the abdomen and stomach move first, filling up before the upper chest, and then these lower areas are the first to begin pushing the breath out on the exhalation.

If you are a shallow breather (like many people are), you may find deep breathing counter-intuitive and extremely difficult at first. It helps to lie down and put your hand on your stomach. As you inhale, try to push your hand out with your stomach as you feel your lower back and ribcage expanding, too. As you exhale, push your stomach in with your hand, all the while trying not to engage your shoulders, but instead focusing on the lower half of your torso and ribcage contracting. Eventually you'll get the hang of it. Then you'll be able to try it standing up, and before long it will be second nature once again.

Another way to encourage proper deep breathing is to concentrate on breathing "out of" your entire body. Rather than visualizing air filling your lungs and moving back out, visualize that with each inhalation, air flows in through every pore on the surface of your skin and expands your entire body. With the exhalation, air flows out through your skin again. Feel your entire body slowly inhaling, exhaling, inhaling, exhaling. Your feet, your legs, your stomach, your back, your shoulders, your arms, your head. Now you're breathing!

Mindful Minute

Holotropic breathwork is a psycho-spiritual bodywork technique developed by Stanislav Grof, M.D., and his wife, Christina, in 1976. It combines rapid breathing with loud music, meant to invoke an alternate state of consciousness that loosens psychological barriers and frees repressed memories and emotions.

How Do You Breathe? A Self Quiz

For this quiz, wear clothing that allows you to see your body shape (or, if you are comfortable, strip down to your skivvies or wear no clothes at all!). Stand in front of a large mirror, preferably a full-length mirror. Pick the one best answer for each question.

1. Take a deep breath without thinking too much about it. As you inhale, what moves?

   A. My shoulders move up and my chest rises. My stomach caves in.

   B. My stomach expands and my chest sinks slightly. My shoulders don't move.

2. Now, exhale. What moves?

   A. My shoulders sink back down and my chest falls.

   B. My stomach sinks back in. My shoulders and chest don't move.

3. Take another deep breath, both inhalation and exhalation. What sounds do you hear?

   A. Louder inhale than exhale.

   B. Louder exhale than inhale.

4. Take another deep breath and concentrate on the muscles in your chest. Are you exerting more effort:

   A. On the inhale than the exhale?

B. On the exhale than the inhale?

5. Turn so that you see your profile in the mirror. Stand normally and look at your stomach. What do you see?

    A. Tightly contracted stomach muscles.

    B. A stomach just hangin' out.

6. Still in profile, take a deep breath. What moves?

    A. My chest.

    B. My stomach.

7. Place one hand on your chest and the other hand on your abdomen. Breathe 10 normal breaths. Which hand moves more?

    A. The chest hand.

    B. The abdomen hand.

8. Still in profile, look at your back. What do you see?

    A. I look pretty slumped. I should probably stand up straighter!

    B. A nice straight line from the crown of my head to my heels.

9. Pretend you are hyperventilating by breathing quickly with shallow breaths. (Don't do it for more than 10 seconds.) How does it feel?

    A. Not so bad—kind of natural.

    B. Horrible and unnatural.

10. Without changing your breath rate, count how many total breaths (inhalation and exhalation) you make in one minute. Did you count:

    A. More than 15 breaths.

    B. Less than 15 breaths.

Now, count how many As and how many Bs you have.

If you have more than five As: You definitely have some serious restricted breathing habits. Consider making breathwork a priority during your meditation sessions, as well as any time you need to relax. Becoming conscious of your breathing and practicing good breathing are the two most important keys to retraining yourself. Once you learn to breathe the way your body is meant to breathe, you'll probably be astounded by the changes you will experience. You'll feel better, have more energy, and your thinking will be sharper.

If you have more than five Bs: You have either relearned or never forgotten how to breathe deeply and fully. Of course, if you have even one A, you've got room for improvement. Who doesn't? Make breathwork a priority, especially since deep breathing comes easily to you. Capitalize on those good breathing habits to maximize your physical and mental well-being.

Sutra on the Full Awareness of Breathing

Learning how to breathe well is by no means a "New Age" phenomena. Breathing has been the cornerstone of meditation for centuries, and an ancient Buddhist text, called the *Sutra on the Full Awareness of Breathing*, or the *Anapanasati Sutra*, is considered by many to be among the most important meditation texts in existence.

In this sutra, a disciple of the Buddha tells the story of the Buddha instructing his disciples on the importance of breathing in full awareness, which will eventually "lead to the perfect accomplishment of true understanding and complete liberation." Part two of the sutra contains the excerpt we offered in Chapter 11, "Stress: Is Your Mind *Too* Full?" to help you with mindfulness, as well as an explanation by the Buddha of how breath can lead to enlightenment. According to the Buddha, full awareness breathing is the first step toward perfection (translation by Thich Nhat Hahn):

Relax

Asthma affects one in 20 adults in the United States, and the numbers are increasing. If you have asthma, a condition in which the tubes in the lungs spasm, contracting and making breathing difficult, regular deep breathing exercises are particularly important. Deep breathing improves the tone of all your breathing mechanisms and also has a relaxing effect that can help to lessen the severity of an asthma attack.

> *When the practitioner can maintain, without distraction, the practice of observing the body in the body, the feelings in the feelings, the mind in the mind, and the objects of mind in the objects of mind, persevering, fully awake, clearly understanding his state, gone beyond all attachment and aversion to this life, with unwavering, steadfast, imperturbable meditative stability, he will attain the first Factor of Awakening, namely mindfulness. When this factor is developed, it will come to perfection.*

Breathing Exercises

Breathing exercises make a wonderful warm-up for meditation, as well as becoming a point of focus during meditation. Below are some breathing exercises to try, adapted from many traditions:

Om Exhalation

This exercise calms and quiets the mind and invokes a feeling of oneness with the universe.

➤ Sit in your favorite meditative pose and close your eyes.

➤ Inhale deeply, feeling the breath filling you from your lower abdomen upward.

➤ Open your lips and softly begin to make the sound Om.

➤ Allow the sound of Om to encompass your entire awareness.

➤ Draw out the O sound, then let the M sound vibrate.

➤ Repeat several times.

Diaphragm-Building Breath

This exercise is designed to strengthen and loosen the diaphragm muscle so it can become your ally in effective breathing.

➤ Lie on your back on the floor or bed with one pillow under your back and two pillows under your head, so your body is just slightly inclined.

➤ Place your hands at the base of your rib cage with fingers spread. Imagine your diaphragm inside you at the base of your ribs, like a big, upturned salad bowl.

➤ Begin to breathe slowly and deeply into your rib cage. Feel your hands moving out with the inhalation, in with the exhalation. Imagine your diaphragm expanding downward and outward with the inhalation, up again with the exhalation.

➤ Now, with each inhalation, apply a slight resistance with your hands to the ribcage. Make the pressure very light, just enough to force your diaphragm muscle to work a little harder to expand the rib cage.

➤ Breathe 10 long, slow breaths using this resistance, then release your hands, place them at your sides, and breathe 10 more long, slow breaths without resistance. Imagine your diaphragm becoming stronger and more flexible.

Spaced-Out Breathing

Between inhalations and exhalations, we naturally pause for a second or two. In this exercise, consciously expand that pause and use those seconds as a meditative moment to contemplate the space within breath as a space for enlightenment and greater knowledge to enter into your consciousness.

➤ Sit comfortably with your back straight. Inhale deeply and slowly through your nose to a count of 10.

➤ When your lungs feel completely full, hold your breath to a count of five.

➤ Exhale through pursed lips to a count of 20. Imagine you are imitating the sound of the wind. On the count of 20, quickly and sharply blow out the last of your breath.

➤ When all the breath is blown out, wait five seconds before inhaling.

➤ Repeat.

To make breathing a conscious and purposeful part of your life is to fill your life with vitality, energy, and peace. Don't let another breath go by without knowing it and living it. Then, cultivate your breath so that it becomes a tool for greater awareness and self-knowledge.

The Least You Need to Know

➤ Breath is life, and learning to breathe well may be the most important thing you can do for your mind–body.

➤ We are born knowing how to breathe well, but many of us lose the skill after years of bad habits and stress.

➤ The diaphragm muscle should move downward with the inhalation and upward with the exhalation.

➤ You can retrain your breath.

Part 5
Ready, Set, OM!

Now we're meditating! In this section, we'll introduce you to different techniques for sitting meditation, including the Zen technique of zazen, *various yoga meditative positions, and what to do with your hands (positions called* mudras). *Next, we'll walk you through walking meditation, including a technique called* kinhin, *which is Zen meditation on the move, and labyrinth walking, a newly revived form of walking meditation that involves following a maze-like pattern into a center and back out again.*

For the extra energetic, we'll introduce you to moving meditation, from the ancient forms of QiGong, T'ai Chi Chuan, and yoga, to the more modern forms of dynamic meditation and ecstatic dancing. Lie back and relax with us in shavasana, *the lying-down yoga "corpse pose" that embodies relaxation in its most supreme form. Last, we'll show you how to use sounds, including chanting and the repetition of* mantras, *to further enhance your meditations. And you thought meditation was going to be boring!*

Chapter 15

Seated Meditation: Finding Center

In This Chapter

➤ How to sit during meditation

➤ Flexibility: From easy pose to lotus pose

➤ Chair meditations

➤ Mudras: What to do with your hands

Although types, forms, and positions of meditation vary widely, when asked, most people would say that sitting is the meditation posture. Indeed, sitting is the most widely practiced meditation position and the position the Buddha was in when he attained enlightenment. If sitting meditation is good enough for the Buddha, it's certainly good enough for us!

Within the realm of sitting meditation, however, you still have a lot of options, which we'll explain in this chapter. Try them all, pick your favorites, then "Om" away to your heart's content.

Zazen: Seated Meditation

The type of meditation employed by Zen is called *zazen*. Zazen involves the entire ritual of seated meditation. The actual meditation technique employed in zazen varies according to the teacher, but many agree that for true zazen, the mind doesn't focus on any one thing. Counting, following the breath, or focusing on a mantra or a visual point are all meditation techniques, but they aren't zazen. For zazen, pure and uninvolved awareness of your thoughts, feelings, emotions, and sensations is the key.

From A to Om

Zazen is the word for the practice of sitting meditation in Zen Buddhism, with or without the practice of a koan (a Zen riddle that defies logic, meant to lead the mind out of ordinary thinking and into enlightenment).

From A to Om

A **zendo** is a Zen meditation hall. **Gassho** is a hand position similar to the yoga's prayer position, the mudra called **namaste**. (See page 233 to see an illustration of namaste and find out more.)

Zazen can be practiced anywhere, and if you aren't in a Zen monastery, you can practice zazen in whatever way works for you. In fact, part of Zen is finding your own way. But zazen does involve certain conventions, and if you ever decide to practice it in a *zendo*, or meditation hall, you'll want to know the "etiquette":

➤ Enter the zendo left foot first.

➤ Place your hands, palms together as if praying, a few inches in front of your chest with your arms parallel to the ground, a hand position called *gassho* in Zen Buddhism, and bow to the altar, which may be as simple as a burning stick of incense. Gassho is often used in conjunction with a bow, to greet others and to show respect. The position is similar to the namaste mudra in yoga meditation.

➤ When you walk across the room, turn corners squarely. Don't meander, and don't cross directly in front of the altar. When in the zendo, always move and turn clockwise.

➤ Place your hands in the gassho position again and bow toward your seat and to the people meditating on either side of you, who will respond with the gassho bow.

➤ Turn clockwise and face the people across the room, bowing in gassho to them. They also will respond.

➤ Sit down on your *zafu*, which may be placed on top of a thick mat or small futon called a *zabuton*.

➤ Turn clockwise toward the wall if *Soto* style (away from the wall if *Rinzai* style).

Zazen typically uses a three-point or tripod position of the body for greatest stability. The practitioner sits in the lotus position or kneeling position with both knees touching the ground or the zabuton (see the following figure). The third point is the zafu or small pillow the practitioner sits on. Small meditation benches can also be used and may be more comfortable for some.

At home, you can use a small pillow to achieve the zazen position of seated meditation. The position should be comfortable, not forced, so cross your legs in whatever manner is most natural for you at this time.

From A to Om

A **zafu** is a small pillow for sitting during Zen meditation. A **zabuton** is a thick meditation mat or small futon placed under the zafu. These items make meditation more comfortable and help to put the body into a three-point or tripod position for greater stability, the three points being the zafu and each knee when sitting in the lotus position or when kneeling.

Once you are seated, rock back and forth a bit to find the most stable position. Lift from the crown of your head as if a silk thread were pulling it up. Straighten your back and breathe easily. Lift your heart and feel your shoulders relax down. Place your tongue behind your upper teeth. Keep your mouth closed on the inhale, breathing through your nose. On the exhale, open your mouth slightly or exhale through your nose.

For zazen, keep your eyes slightly open but unfocused, angled about halfway between straight ahead and down. Don't actually look at anything. Take a few deep breaths, then breathe normally. Place your hands together, both upturned, your left hand cradling your right in your lap against your abdomen. The second joints of your middle fingers should touch, and your fingers should face each other and be parallel. Lift both thumbs and join them at the tips to form an oval. This hand position, or *mudra*, is sometimes called the cosmic mudra (see the illustration of the chalice mudra on page 236 for more).

The rest is simple: Don't concentrate. Observe your breath, your body feeling, your emotions, your thoughts, whatever, but don't concentrate on any one thing. If something captures your attention, acknowledge it, but stay emotionally

Mindful Minute

Zen Buddhism consists of two main sects, **Soto** and **Rinzai**. In Soto Zen, "just sitting" is the primary method of zazen, based on the idea that sitting like the Buddha when he attained enlightenment will eventually bring enlightenment. In the Rinzai sect, the primary mode of meditation is the consideration of the koan during zazen.

From A to Om

A **mudra** is a hand position that redirects energy emitted from the fingertips back into the mind–body by connecting the fingers and hands to each other in different ways.

disengaged from it. Let your emotions and thoughts be things separate from you. Watch them like balloons or dandelion fluff floating by you—with interest and appreciation, but without becoming them. Don't let them capture you. Watch them, and your body will gradually relax.

Zazen is, by it's very nature technique-less, so we can't really give you any zazen "tricks" or "rules." It is simply pure awareness. It is easy, yet it is also supremely difficult and takes years of practice to perfect. You don't have to do anything—but yet, you don't have to do anything! Now you're zazen-ing!

Chair Meditations for Home, School, or Office

We realize that seated meditation isn't always practical in every situation. You might not want your boss walking into your office to find you sitting on the floor. But that doesn't mean you can't meditate at the office. You'll probably enjoy your job better (and perform it better, too) if you find a few minutes here and there for meditation. (A quick five-minute session in lieu of a coffee break will do wonders for your workday—set your watch alarm or bring a small timer to work. And if you smoke, a mini-meditation break is a great, healthy substitute for a cigarette break!)

Your desk chair is a fine place for meditation as is any comfortable chair at home that has a firm seat for support. Learning a few quick steps for chair meditation will make meditation even more accessible because you can practice it daily at work, at school, or even at your own kitchen table.

➤ Sit up straight in your chair. Depending on the shape of the chair, you may not be able to use the backrest. Shift around until you find a steady, stable position centered over the hips that feels comfortable. Keep your feet flat on the floor to stay grounded. Rest your hands on your knees.

➤ Take a cue from zazen and close your eyes only partially. That way, if something demands your immediate attention, you'll be able to adjust more quickly than if your eyes were closed. Of course, if you don't have to worry about distractions (which is ideal), you can close your eyes completely.

➤ Take three very deep breaths originating in your lower abdomen. Breathe in through your nose, out through your mouth.

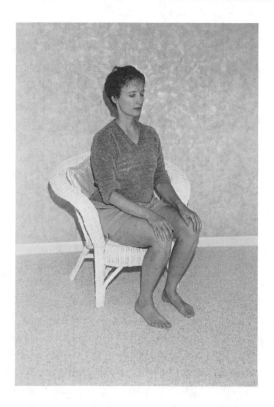

Joan demonstrates seated meditation at home. Place your feet firmly on the ground. Remember to lift your heart and relax your shoulders down. Good posture is essential to the chair meditation pose. Keep your back straight and slightly away from a swayed chair's back.

Notice Joan's bare feet; if you're practicing chair meditation at the office, it's a good time to kick off your shoes. Removing your shoes is a way to humble yourself to your surroundings and is also symbolic of removing your Earth worries and concerns.

Bliss Byte

If the chair you choose has a reclining back, sit straight up on the edge of the chair and don't use the back. If your chair has a firm, straight back that can support you with your feet still planted on the floor, go ahead and make use of the extra support.

Now choose your favorite meditation option from the following list. If varying techniques will keep you meditating more regularly, pick a different method each day:

➤ Focus on the feel of your breath as it moves in and out of your nostrils. Refuse to let other thoughts and feelings engage you. Don't fight them. Acknowledge them, then go back to the breath.

➤ Focus on sound. What do you hear around you? Notice all the sounds of your office, your classroom, your kitchen, or wherever you are. Do you hear air coming out of the vents? Copy machines? Ringing phones? The low murmur of conversation? Focus on the pure sound, not the meaning of any of the sounds.

➤ Focus on an object on your desk. Whenever your mind wanders, bring it back to the contemplation of the object—say, a stapler. What does the stapler do? What parts does it have? How often does it need to be maintained? What is its purpose? What would the world be like without it? How have you used it in the past? And if you're really getting into it: What might the stapler represent in your life? Does it symbolize something for you? Does it have a cosmic meaning? Why did you choose it? What is your awareness trying to tell you about yourself? About the nature of reality?

➤ Focus on the mantra: "Now." If you can't say it out loud (say you're meditating in a doctor's waiting room), repeat it in your mind. Now. Now. Now. Become the present moment. There is no past. There is no future. There is only now, and you are completely present in the now.

➤ Do a quick sitting body scan. Move your awareness from your toes slowly up your legs, your body and arms, your neck, and your head. Imagine your awareness is a warm, rose-colored ring of light moving upward, then moving back down again. As it moves up, it warms and relaxes your body, concentrating its heat in your body at the place where you hold the most tension. As it moves back down, from the crown of your head to your toes, imagine the sensation that your body is melting into total relaxation.

Seated Meditative Poses

If you're going to sit while you meditate, it helps to know how to sit. The position you choose can mean the difference between sticking to it and giving up after a few uncomfortable minutes.

Mindful Minute

Today is a gift. That's why it's called the "present!"

We've already explained the traditional sitting position for zazen (sitting on a zafu in the lotus position or sitting with the knees touching the floor for a tripod-like stability). Meditating yogis (and lots of other meditators, too) use several other positions. We'll show you a few of the most common.

Comfort and good posture are keys to seated meditation. A slumped back constricts your breathing and keeps energy from flowing through your body to stimulate and open your chakras. If possible, try your seated meditation pose in front of a mirror to check your posture and correct it, if necessary. Seeing is believing! If your legs and lower back are not comfortable, use a small pillow to support your back and rest your knees on the floor, as is done in zazen.

Easy Pose

This pose is perfect for the beginning meditator. This pose is called *sukhasana* in Sanskrit, which literally means "joy pose," and joyful is just how you'll feel when you sit in this stable yet simple pose. The easy pose helps to quiet your mind and bring your body to stillness. It requires far less flexibility than some of the more advanced poses.

Joan demonstrates easy pose. Sit in a simple cross-legged position with either leg on top. Lift the crown of your head and feel your spine straighten. Rest your hands on your knees, palms down, and relax into the pose, rocking back and forth slightly to find the perfect center of stability. Photo by Saeid Lahouti.

But even though this is called "easy pose," it's not easy for many Westerners to do. If your spine is not comfortably straight in this pose, you should sit higher—on several folded firm blankets or a bolster—and even give the knees support if necessary. If this makes the pose a bit "easier" for you, go ahead and try it.

Kneeling Pose

The kneeling pose is one of the most common poses held by Zen Buddhist monks. It can be uncomfortable for the beginning meditator, especially on the knees, but sitting on a pillow or zafu (as shown) eases the discomfort considerably. This is also the pose to use with a meditation bench.

In Sanskrit, this pose is called *vajrasana*, which literally means "thunderbolt pose" or "diamond pose." These names suggest the pose's power. The pressure from sitting on the feet helps to stimulate circulation to the feet. This pose also opens the chest and relieves pressure on the diaphragm, making for more breathing room.

Joan demonstrates kneeling pose. Sit back on your heels, keeping your knees and heels together. Or place a pillow or small meditation bench (or even a thick, sturdy book) between your ankles and sit on it. Or place a larger firm pillow across your ankles and sit on it. Keep your spine straight, lifting the crown of your head. If you feel uncomfortable pressure on your knees, go back to the easy pose for awhile. Photo by Saeid Lahouti.

Regular yoga practice will help to make you more flexible, and eventually, this kneeling pose will feel great. Don't rush it! Meditative poses must feel good so that your body isn't a distraction.

Hero Pose

The hero pose, or *virasana* in Sanskrit, is a more advanced version of the kneeling pose. This pose can also be hard on your knees, so don't force it or do anything that hurts. With time, stretching, and regular yoga practice, you'll relax into it eventually. Again, you can sit on a firm pillow, zafu, bench, or book to ease the knees.

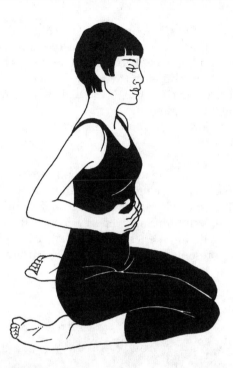

Sit back on your heels, then gradually separate your feet until you are sitting on the floor between your ankles. Feel your breath move in and out of your body. Then, place your hands on your knees.

Lotus's Many Petals

The most classic meditation pose, and the pose most people envision when they picture someone meditating, is the lotus pose. In Sanskrit, this pose is called *padmasana* (meaning lotus pose), and the posture represents the lotus flower open to the light. This posture keeps the spine straight and is the most stable of the poses. It keeps the body still, and when the body is still, the mind eventually stills too. In fact, you can even fall asleep in this position and not fall over! This posture keeps your chest open, gives you lots of breathing room, and opens your Venus chakra (heart chakra).

According to legend, the Buddha once stood before his disciples and held up a lotus flower without speaking. He held it and held it until one of his disciples exclaimed that he understood! The sutra doesn't say what he understood, but many have interpreted the meaning of the Buddha's action. A common interpretation is that the lotus flower, which grows in muddy water, has its roots

Mindful Minute

In 1983, a Detroit chemical manufacturing firm instituted a meditation program for their workers. According to owner Buck Montgomery, after three years, 52 of the 100 employees at all levels were meditating for 20 minutes before work and 20 minutes in the afternoon during work (yes, they were paid for the time). Productivity rose 120 percent, absenteeism fell by 85 percent, quality control rose 240 percent, injuries dropped by 70 percent, sick days fell by 16 percent, and profits soared 520 percent.

229

in slime but ascends to the top of the water where it opens its beautiful and untainted flower. This symbolizes enlightenment, wherein the enlightened one is unaffected by the imperfect world, remaining pure and perfect. Another interpretation is that the lotus flower shifts across the surface of a pond with the wind, yet stays rooted, symbolizing stability in the face of an unpredictable world. All these ideas are represented by yoga's primary meditative pose, the lotus pose.

Full Lotus (Padmasana)

Sit and take a few deep breaths. Bring one ankle up over the opposite thigh, then bring the other ankle over its opposite thigh. For some people, putting the right leg on top is easier. For others, putting the left leg on top is easier. Your right leg is linked with your left brain and represents yang, solar energy, and male energy. Your left leg is linked with your right brain and represents yin, lunar energy, and female energy. Whichever leg feels more comfortable on top represents which energy force is stronger in you.

Joan demonstrates yoga's lotus pose. Remember, first and foremost, it is always important to be comfortable. Relax back into the easy pose if lotus proves too demanding for this meditation session. Try again tomorrow! Photo by Saeid Lahouti.

Bliss Byte

A common problem for beginners in sitting meditation is that the legs fall asleep, especially when seated in the full lotus position. If the lotus position is uncomfortable or painful in any way, change into a different position. The lotus position is meant to be very comfortable and stable for those who are flexible enough to hold it easily. If you can't, shift your position and try again another time. The more you practice this position and yoga poses that increase flexibility, the sooner you'll find the lotus pose, or padmasana, as comfortable as your favorite easy chair. (For some, the lotus pose is never very comfortable. No problem! It isn't necessary for enlightenment!)

Meditation teachers often recommend practicing more often in the less comfortable position to balance the body until either leg is equally comfortable on top. Some say that men are usually more comfortable with the right leg on top and women with the left leg on top, but there are many exceptions. Find what feels more comfortable for you regardless of your gender, then work to balance yourself by periodically practicing in the less comfortable position.

And remember, if the lotus pose is uncomfortable or painful, be gentle on yourself and go back to the easy pose or try the half lotus until your body is accustomed to the posture.

Half Lotus (Ardha Padmasana)

The half lotus has similar benefits to the lotus pose. In the half lotus, one foot is placed on the opposite thigh, but the opposite foot stays on the floor. If your sitting bones are stable and moving down into the floor, your body shouldn't lean but will remain straight. Half lotus pose is easier than the lotus pose and is a good way to work up to the full lotus if you periodically switch the foot that rests on top of the opposite thigh.

Relax

Many meditation teachers recommend that a meditation pose not be held for longer than three hours.

Bound Lotus

Once you've mastered the full lotus, you can move on to the bound lotus pose, or *baddha padmasana*. This pose requires good arm and shoulder flexibility, as well as good leg and hip flexibility, but it offers an incredibly solid base and opens the chest even further, facilitating breathing and a deeply relaxed peacefulness.

Sit in a full lotus position. Cross your arms behind your back and hold your right foot with your left hand and your left foot with your right hand. With enough practice, you'll be as relaxed in this pose as Joan is! Take it one day at a time. Photo by Saeid Lahouti.

Mudras to Channel Chakra Energy

Once you've got your sitting position mastered, consider what you'll do with your hands. In the previous section on zazen, we described one hand position, but there are actually many. These hand positions are called mudras, and their purpose is to rechannel energy, which is thought to emanate from the fingertips, back into the body.

Each of the five fingers releases a different kind of energy and corresponds to different aspects of our mind-bodies. Therefore, making "circuits" out of different combinations of fingers will have different effects on the subtle interplay of energies in the body during meditation. Each of the five fingers is representative of the following:

➤ The thumb is a symbol of divine energy, unaffected by our thought patterns or actions.

➤ The index finger is the Jupiter finger and symbolizes our ego, or self, energy, and the energy controlled by our subconscious mind.

➤ The middle finger is the Saturn finger. This energy is very strong and stabilizing.

➤ The ring finger is the Sun finger. It emits solar energy and is related to personal strength.

➤ The little finger is the Mercury finger. It emits energy related to intellectual and worldly pursuits.

Yoga practitioners developed many different hand positions to be used during meditation, but here are a few of our favorites.

Bliss Byte

Placing your hands palms-down on your knees during meditation helps to center and ground your energy. Placing your hands palms-up on your knees helps to open you to the energies around you.

Namaste Mudra: Honoring You

The *namaste mudra* is achieved by placing the palms together with fingers extended as in the Zen gassho hand position, with thumbs and fingers parallel. In the namaste mudra, however, the arms are bent with elbows down. Like gassho, the hands are brought close to the chest at the level of the heart. This mudra shows respect and humility. When you perform the namaste mudra (as well as when you say the word "namaste"), you are symbolically saying something along the lines of, "I recognize the light in you" or "I honor the divinity in you." The "you" also contains the implication that all is one.

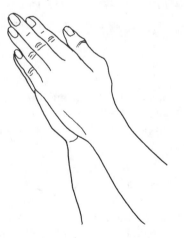

The namaste mudra indicates respect and humility.

Om Mudra: Divine You

The *Om mudra*, or divinity gesture, is commonly used while in the lotus position. This mudra brings the tips of the thumb and index finger together to form a complete circle. Your hands are then placed palms-up on your knees.

Because the thumb represents divine energy and the index finger represents self energy, the Om mudra joins divinity and the self into one continuous circuit of energy. With the Om mudra, self and the divine become one.

The Om mudra joins divine energy and the self.

Bliss Byte

Om (sometimes spelled *aum*) is the sound of the universe in yoga literature, and it is said that the entire world is manifested from this one sound. Om is all, and all is Om. When you practice the Om mudra, try to feel your inclusion in this oneness.

Gnana Mudra: Wise You

The *gnana mudra*, or wisdom gesture, also joins the thumb and index finger, but not tip to tip. Instead, the index finger touches the first joint of the thumb. As with the Om mudra, place your hands palms-up on your knees.

This mudra symbolizes enlightened individuality. Within the awareness of oneness with the divinity is the awareness that you are still you. You are aware of the illusion of the ego, and the part of the thumb extending above the index finger represents this awareness of your oneness with the universe. Yet, you still have your own personality and your own methods for living. This mudra is excellent for people who are having trouble with the concept of the loss of ego, but who still want to find oneness. The best of both worlds!

The gnana mudra symbolizes enlightened individuality.

Buddhi Mudra: Enlightened You

The *buddhi mudra*, or enlightenment gesture, is often associated with the Buddha and is a good mudra for centering and calming. Bring your thumb and index fingers together, tip to tip, as in the Om mudra. Then bring both hands together, knuckles touching, and rest your hands against your lower abdomen at your Jupiter chakra. This makes perfect sense: The Sanskrit name for the Jupiter chakra, *svadhisthana*, means "dwelling place of the self."

This mudra represents divinity and the self becoming one, but also joins all the other energies, too, which are then brought to rest against the chakra that represents the action and the self. Performing this mudra quiets the mind, stills action, and enlightens the self to its divinity within. It is a good mudra to practice when you are feeling tense or rushed.

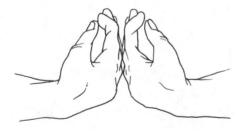

The buddhi mudra reminds us of the divinity within.

Chalice Mudra: A Cup of Bliss

The *chalice mudra* is very similar to the cosmic mudra frequently employed in zazen. It is a powerful mudra, making a circuit of the entire hand and joining the two thumbs, which emanate divine energy.

Use this mudra when meditating in the lotus or half lotus position. If your right foot is on top, place your right hand inside your cupped left hand. If your left foot is on top, place your left hand inside your cupped right hand. Then, forming an oval, join the thumbs, tip to tip, and place your joined hands in your lap.

The chalice mudra is a mudra of blissful energy.

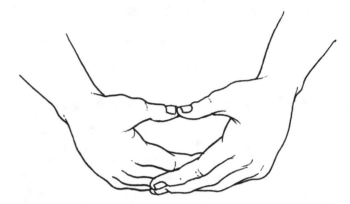

Shanti Mudra: Bless You

The *shanti mudra* is used to bless anything you wish to bless and has traditionally been used to bless food before it is eaten. Place your middle finger on the fingernail of your index finger, then touch the object to be blessed while saying (out loud or in your mind), "Om, shanti, shanti, shanti." *Shanti* means peace, and this blessing sends positive vibrations.

The shanti mudra is a gesture of blessing.

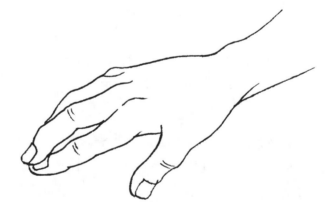

Gomukha Mudra: Unified You

The *gomukha mudra* or interlocking gesture is a good mudra to use while meditating when your energy feels scattered. It symbolizes unification of body and mind. Interlock your fingers together to form a cup. Note how your two hands become one. The thumbs can lie on top of each other, or you can touch them tip to tip, which symbolizes that you are functioning equally through both your body (represented by the right thumb) and mind (represented by the left thumb), and that the essential you—your spirit—is comprised of both.

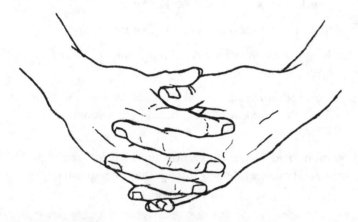

The gomukha mudra symbolizes the unification of body and mind.

Prithvi Mudra: Stable You

The *prithvi mudra*, or Earth gesture, represents sending the energy into the Earth, then receiving it back into the Saturn chakra. This mudra results in a feeling of great stability and oneness with the Earth. Put your hands in the position of the gnana mudra (wisdom gesture), but separate the fingers and turn the palms downward. The fingers may rest on the knees.

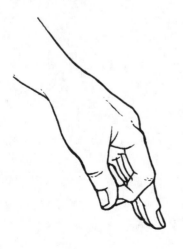

The prithvi mudra represents oneness with the Earth.

You needn't practice the same sitting position or mudra each time, although some people have their favorites. Matching your meditation positions and gestures to your flexibility level, your moods, and your individual needs for the day will add a degree of flavor to your routine and customize your meditation sessions to be most effective.

You've assumed the position. You've got the gestures. You're ready to go. Have a wonderful 20 minutes (or more!).

The Least You Need to Know

➤ Zazen is the form of seated meditation practiced in Zen meditation.

➤ Chair meditation is also great for work breaks, school breaks, or short breaks at home. No flexibility necessary!

➤ Yoga has developed many other meditative positions, each requiring different degrees of flexibility and with different effects, including the venerable lotus pose.

➤ Mudras are hand positions held during meditation and used for greetings and blessings. Mudras rechannel energy released through the fingertips back into the body.

Chapter 16

Walking Meditation: Peace Is Every Step

In This Chapter

➤ Can you meditate if you're busy walking?

➤ How, when, and where to walk mindfully

➤ Labyrinths and pilgrimages: Sacred walks for everyday people

➤ Moving along the life path

Sitting isn't the only way to meditate! It's a good way to meditate, make no mistake. But walking can be an incredibly powerful and enlightening technique for meditation. Yes, walking—that same thing you do to get in shape, that thing you do when you have to get somewhere, that thing you've known how to do since you were approximately one year old.

Walking meditation is probably about as old as the first person who ever had to walk somewhere by him- or herself. Solitary walking seems to encourage a meditative state. Many artists claim they get their best and most inspired ideas while walking. Walking through nature can be awe-inspiring and can invoke an appropriately meditative sense of wonder. Walking needn't be for the purpose of "getting somewhere."

In many traditions, walking takes a more formal turn, following specific patterns or directions. Whether walking the path of a labyrinth while engaging in meditative prayer or following the clockwise path around the zendo altar in walking zazen (called *kinhin*), walking can be accomplished solely for the purpose of being in the moment while walking.

Even though the awareness is intensely focused, walking meditation does involve movement and so makes a nice alternative to sitting meditation, especially when you have a lot of energy and just feel like moving.

Kinhin: Walking Meditation

Kinhin is zazen performed while walking. While the top half of your body retains the posture of sitting meditation, the bottom half is in motion. In Buddhist zendos (meditation halls), while some sit in meditation, others walk, always clockwise, around the altar in the practice of kinhin. Sometimes walking and sitting meditations are practiced in alternation. Kinhin is typically performed very slowly, at the rate of one step per full breath (inhale and exhale—yes, that slowly), although in some traditions, it's slightly faster than this.

Slow walking allows for complete awareness of every movement and every motion. The awareness continues to move, too, but experiences every aspect of the movement. Kinhin can also be performed outside in a circle or in a straight line, back and forth.

Where Are You Going? And How Do You Get There?

But you needn't call it kinhin to enjoy walking meditation. Many traditions have practiced and contemplated walking as a meditative form. One thing they all have in common is to abolish the thought of destination from the process of walking so that only the walking remains. That doesn't mean you can't have a destination when you practice walking meditation. But if you do have a destination, it doesn't concern you during your meditation because you are living wholly in the present moment, and that moment is all of your awareness.

From A to Om

Kinhin is zazen performed while walking. While the upper body is held in the position used for sitting meditation, the lower body moves, very slowly, with complete and total awareness of the movement. **Zazen** is the Zen Buddhist form of sitting meditation in which the meditator sits in pure, unengaged awareness. A **zendo** is an informal meditation hall for the practice of zazen and kinhin. It contains an altar which is usually in the center of the room but may also be against a wall.

Bliss Byte

If appropriate, perform your **kinhin**, or walking meditation, barefoot. Even more ideally, walk barefoot outside. The closer your foot comes to making contact with the earth, the more vivid will be your experience and the Earth energy you can utilize. Feel each part of your foot as it makes contact with the ground beneath you—from heel to toe. Pause for a moment in your walking, just to feel the solid strength of your feet evenly supporting your body weight. Lift your toes off of the ground and plant each one down again, firmly, one at a time. Give thanks for the joy of walking and begin to move again.

Ideally, meditative walking should be undertaken solely for the purpose of the walk. Where can you walk? Anywhere—but some environments are more conducive to meditation than others. Why not try:

➤ A hike through a national, state, or city park

➤ Walking around a beautiful flower bed, whether in your own yard or in a park

➤ A circle around the block of your own (or someone else's) residential neighborhood

➤ Walking the perimeter of a peaceful room in your home

➤ Walking slowly back and forth down the length of a long hallway in your home

➤ Organizing a nature walk or labyrinth walk (see below) with friends, or, if you practice an organized religion, with members of your church or temple group

Bliss Byte

Do meditative walks work in groups? Walking with a friend can make meditation difficult because you will likely be distracted by conversation unless you both agree to make the walk a meditative one. Walking in groups can be a wonderful way to practice communal meditation, with everyone walking in his or her own meditative manner.

Wherever you decide to walk during meditation, in beautiful surroundings, or in ordinary ones, outside or inside, in a sacred space or a living space, the most important thing is to be in the moment and experience the walking with full awareness. Where are you going during meditation? Right where you are. And how do you get there? You are there.

Taking Your Time: Mindful Walking

To walk mindfully is to walk knowing you are walking, experiencing every step, every movement, every contact with air and earth. In his book *Peace Is Every Step*, Zen master Thich Nhat Hahn offers a few beautiful tips for mindful walking:

> *"Although we walk all the time, our walking is usually more like running. When we walk like that, we print anxiety and sorrow on the Earth. We have to walk in a way that we only print peace and serenity on the Earth."*

> *"Each step we take will create a cool breeze, refreshing our body and mind. Every step makes a flower bloom under our feet."*

Walking mindfully through nature is both an inner process and an outer process. As we walk toward greater self-awareness in peace and appreciation of beauty and nature, we also change the Earth beneath us with our steps and the world around us with the change in our attitudes. Walking is movement. It is action (even when you're walking veeeery slowly). Walking with love, reverence, humility, and joy will spread these energies over the Earth with every step.

Mindful walking is a great way to ease into a practice of meditation. Stressful thoughts melt away as you concentrate on your movement, breathing, and the beauty of the world around you. Where you are going, and where you have been, fade in importance. What matters now is where you are!

Walk to change the world by walking to change yourself—or more accurately, by walking to find yourself. You are the true destination! As you walk, you symbolically act out your inner journey on life's path, and if you do so mindfully and with full awareness, you'll know exactly what path you're on.

Bliss Byte

If you've got access to a safe natural body of water, take a meditative water walk for a change of pace. Put on your bathing suit and walk parallel to the bank of a lake or the beach of the ocean, hip deep to waist deep in the water. Really soak in the natural surroundings and feel how different it is to walk in water. An added benefit for meditation: The water will force you to slow your pace.

Country Walks

Walking in nature can be a powerful experience, whether you're walking through a beautiful flower garden on a warm, sunny day, or a muddy path on a drizzly, gray day. Maintaining contact with the natural world is crucial to human survival. If you live in the country, country walks are easy. Just step out your front door! If you live in the city but aren't too far from the country, take a mini-vacation every week or two, drive out into the country, and walk.

Country walking is different than walking in well-manicured parks, gardens, or nature centers. In the country, nature is in control. The beauty tends to be rawer, neater, and less structured. It has a more free-wheeling and uncontrolled quality to it that many "city" people find uncomfortable. If you're one of these people, you may find that you will feel more balanced and centered if you face this discomfort and get to know the country outside your city a little more intimately.

Bliss Byte

Are you strapped for nature in your neighborhood? Take a stroll through a local upscale garden center. Sure, the nature may be in pots, but it's still beautiful. You may have to tell a salesperson you are "just browsing," but other than that, you probably won't be disturbed.

You can't, of course, walk without permission on other people's property, but you can probably find a back road where you can park and take a walk. Or, if you live near the mountains, a forest, or the beach, walk in these magnificent environments. And why not substitute your regular vacation for a camping trip or other wilderness outing? You'll have continual chances for meditation walks in nature, and you may come back from your vacation more rested than if you'd just returned from the fanciest spa in Europe.

If you aren't sure how to begin meditating while walking, follow these steps (literally!) for a tranquil country meditation walk:

➤ Begin by matching your steps with your breath. Don't force a rhythm that doesn't feel right. For a slow pace, try one to four steps for every deep inhalation and one to four (or two to eight) steps for every long, full exhalation.

➤ Bring your awareness to your feet. Feel them as they make contact with the earth. Do they touch the ground heel to toe? How does it feel to touch the earth? Can you feel the movement of your weight shifting along the length of your foot as it touches the ground from heel to toe? Are you slamming your heel into the ground instead of placing it softly? (If the weather and environment permit, it helps to go barefoot or wear very soft shoes, such as moccasins, to better feel the contact.)

➤ Now, in your mind, tell yourself what you are doing. Examples: "I am walking on this country road." "I am walking down this mountain path." "I am walking along this beach." Repeat this phrase in your mind again and again, not automatically, but to remind yourself to experience the present moment. Whenever your mind starts to wander away from your actual walking experience, bring it back to your chosen statement. Pay attention. Pay attention. Pay attention.

➤ What do you see? Notice the colors, the textures, the patterns, and the movements of nature.

➤ What do you hear? Notice the sounds of nature.

➤ What do you smell? Notice the aromas of nature.

➤ What do you feel? Stop occasionally to put your hand on a tree, feel a beautiful flower petal, brush your fingers through the grass, examine a lovely seashell, take in an incredible view. Then continue on.

➤ The point of meditative walking in nature isn't to completely internalize your awareness. It is, instead, to completely experience your awareness and make contact with nature again, to re-energize and replenish your soul. We are all nature-hungry to some degree. Feed yourself!

➤ Walk for at least 20 minutes. An hour is better. An hour every day is best!

City Walks

If you live in the city, youwon't always have the opportunity to drive out to the country for walking. But that doesn't mean all your meditation sessions have to entail sitting still indoors. (And if you live in the suburbs or the country, a city walk can be stimulating and invigorating meditation.) Walking meditations in the city involve different types of stimuli from country walks. Each will have its own message and lesson for you. Choose a route where you can avoid walking in the city street (safety first!), don a good pair of walking shoes to protect your feet and joints from the impact of hitting concrete, and off you go.

Every city has its own rhythm, personality, flavor, and spirit. Learn the spirit of your own city by walking whenever you can. Know thy city, know thyself!

➤ As soon as you step outside, look up and notice the sky. City or country, wherever you are, when you are outside, you can almost always see the sky. Notice the color, the light, the presence or absence of clouds. Appreciate the infinite beauty of the sky.

Mindful Minute

One more advanced form of walking meditation involves walking with the head down and awareness internally directed for a pre-set amount of time. When the set time is over, the walker looks up and takes in his or her surroundings. If you try it, exercise caution so you don't bump into anything!

Mindful Minute

"Me? Hug a tree? I'm no tree hugger!" Why not? Put your arms around a tree—the bigger and older the better—and give it a solid, long, firm hug. The carbon dioxide you exhale, the tree breathes in. The oxygen the tree exhales, you breathe in. You are joined in a lovely symbiotic relationship symbolized by your hug. You might be surprised how reassuring it feels to hug a tree!

➤ Begin walking by matching your steps with your breath. Don't force a rhythm that doesn't feel right. For a slow pace, try one to four steps for every deep inhalation and one to four (or two to eight) steps for every long, full exhalation. What pace are the city's inhabitant's keeping? Is it a mindful pace? Do you find yourself moving in sync with the city's pace or to a pace of your own?

➤ Bring your awareness to your feet. Feel them as they make contact with the ground. How far beneath your walking surface is the Earth? Can you sense its vibrations? Walk gently on concrete to ease the stress on your feet and joints. How are your touching the ground—gently or violently? Can you feel the temperature of the ground through your shoes?

➤ Now, in your mind, tell yourself what you are doing. Examples: "I am walking on this sidewalk." "I am walking down this cobblestone hill." "I am walking along this boardwalk." Repeat this phrase in your mind again and again, not automatically, but to remind yourself to experience the present moment. Whenever your mind wanders away from your walking experience, bring it back to your chosen statement. Pay attention. Pay attention. Pay attention.

Bliss Byte

Try this exercise in mindfulness: Set a timer for 60 seconds. From inside your home or office, look out a window until the timer sounds. After 60 seconds, look away from the window and write down in detail all the things you saw. Not the thoughts you had, but only what you visually observed. The more you do this exercise, the longer your list will be, as you learn how to watch mindfully. Repeat the same exercise recording only the sounds.

➤ What do you see? Notice the colors, the textures, the patterns, the movements of the city around you. What colors come from natural sources, such as trees and flowers? Where are the human-made colors? The colors of cars, buildings, the clothing worn by the people who are passing you? If you come across a fantastic view during your walk, stop and see it.

➤ What do you hear? Notice the sounds of the city. Can you hear honking, car engines, bus engines, truck engines? The rumble of a motorcycle, the clatter of a jackhammer, people's voices, sirens, doors opening and closing, music?

➤ What do you smell? Notice the aromas of the city. Cooking food, dust, exhaust (don't breathe exhaust fumes if you can help it, of course), perfume, the smell of shops or homes as you pass their opened doors, flowers?

➤ What do you feel? Stop occasionally to put your hand on a tree, feel a beautiful flower petal, and touch any incarnations of nature that grace the city. Also, feel the solidity of that fire hydrant or sign post, brush your fingers along a rough brick or smooth marble wall, stop to pet a friendly cat or dog (make sure that dog is friendly—don't chance it if you aren't sure), then continue on.

➤ The point of meditative walking in the city isn't to completely internalize your awareness. It is, instead, to completely experience your awareness and make contact with your environment. We can all use a good look around once in a while. Who knows what the world might be trying to teach you—about life and about yourself. Wish each person you pass on a busy city street the gift of inner serenity and mindfulness. Bring your own gift of rhythm, peace, and mindfulness to the city pace surrounding you.

➤ Walk for at least 20 minutes. An hour is better. An hour every day is best!

Sacred Walks

Sometimes, meditative walking has a more internalized flavor and isn't meant so much for experiencing the present moment as for symbolizing a journey into the self. Not surprisingly, many formalized sacred walks are associated with particular religions or religious institutions, but sacred walks don't "belong" to any creed. They are universal, spiritual tools that anyone of any belief can use for self-discovery.

The Labyrinth

One type of sacred walk that has become popular in recent years is the *labyrinth*. Labyrinths have been around for thousands of years, but they've never been as portable and well-traversed as they are today. Labyrinth patterns are in evidence on artifacts up to 4,000 years old, from all over the world, including India, Egypt, Sumatra, Peru, Afghanistan, England, and the American Southwest.

Relax

Although night can be a beautiful and peaceful time for a meditative walk, these days, we can't recommend walking alone at night, especially in larger cities. Unfortunately, the world isn't always a safe place. If you do want to walk at night, make sure you walk in a safe place and take a buddy along with you.

Labyrinths are somewhat like mazes, and mazes are sometimes called labyrinths. However, a classic *unicursal* labyrinth has only one path, as opposed to a maze, which has many paths and is designed to challenge the intellect to find the center. The labyrinth is meant to represent the spiritual journey into the interior self.

From A to Om

A **labyrinth** is a maze-like pattern or structure consisting of a single or **unicursal** path leading to the center. Typically, the pattern consists of seven interconnected concentric circles.

Perhaps the most famous labyrinth is the labyrinth of Greek mythology belonging to King Minos of Crete, in which the Minotaur lived. According to the myth, King Minos liked to sacrifice seven young Greek men and women on a regular basis to be devoured by the dreaded Minotaur, a creature half bull and half man. According to the myth, Theseus, the son of King Aegeus of Athens, entered the labyrinth to save his friends and was successful, thanks to King Minos's daughter, Ariadne, who was smitten with Theseus. Ariadne gave Theseus a ball of twine so he could find his way back out of the labyrinth. Curiously, labyrinths at this time were unicursal (containing only one path), and King Minos's labyrinth, as represented on Cretan coins, is the classic seven-circle unicursal labyrinth, so why Theseus needed help finding his way out becomes a symbolic mystery, a metaphor for his journey.

Labyrinths typically consist of seven or 11 concentric circles containing a winding path that leads, quite indirectly, to the center. Walkers step into the labyrinth and slowly follow the circuitous route to the center while meditating, praying, reading scriptures, breathing consciously, or simply walking with slow deliberation. Frequently, evocative music plays in the background—classical music or Gregorian chants, for example. How transforming could the experience be? Incredibly, many who walk labyrinths claim they experienced incredible emotional or spiritual upheavals.

According to Reverend Lauren Artress of Grace Cathedral in San Francisco in her book *Walking a Sacred Path: Rediscovering the Labyrinth as a Spiritual Tool*, "To walk a sacred path is to discover our inner sacred space: that core of feeling that is waiting to have life breathed back into it through symbols, archetypal forms like the labyrinth, rituals, stories, and myths."

Dr. Artress is largely responsible for the recent popularity of labyrinth walking. In 1991, she walked the 11-circle labyrinth at the Chartres Cathedral in France and understood the process as a spiritual tool and a universal archetype of our culture. According to Dr. Artress, all cultures have the concept and imagery of life as a path, and the labyrinth is an actual, usable representation of this path. She soon constructed a 35-foot replica of the Chartres labyrinth, painted with purple paint on a portable canvas, for her San Francisco church. Since first making that portable labyrinth available, Grace Cathedral has constructed a 36-foot-wide wool tapestry labyrinth in its nave and a 40-foot-wide terrazzo labyrinth on its grounds. Over a million people have walked the labyrinths at Grace Cathedral.

Dr. Artress also travels around the country with her portable labyrinth, making it available via workshops and conferences to a wide variety of religious groups. Grace Cathedral has formed a Labyrinth Network so that people who contact them can find a labyrinth to visit and to walk. Or contact them if you are interested in building your own labyrinth and registering it with the Labyrinth Network. Call the Veridatis Labyrinth Project, Grace Cathedral, at (415) 749-6356, or e-mail veridatas@gracecathedral.org.

The experience of walking the labyrinth may surprise you—what starts out as pure fun and discovery transforms into a profound exploration of the self; one that you share with the other labyrinth walkers as they wind in and out of your ritual path.

The Pilgrimage

A *pilgrimage* is a completely different kind of sacred walk. Actually, it's more like a sacred journey, but it needn't be an elaborate, across-the-world kind of journey. Choose a destination that is sacred to you, whether a known sacred spot like Stonehenge or Sedona, Arizona; or a personal sacred spot, like that rock that juts out over the bay a few miles from your home, or that beautiful, ancient Cathedral in a neighboring town. (See Chapter 27, "Om Away from Om: Spiritual Travel," for more on spiritual travel and visiting sacred places—whether as an arm-chair, virtual, or "real" traveler.)

To make your pilgrimage, plan ahead. Travel there in a reflective frame of mind, preparing for the experience and asking for insight and a spiritual awakening.

Mindful Minute

An 11-circle religious labyrinth also arose in the Middle Ages in Europe. One of the most famous labyrinths is a 41-foot-wide labyrinth laid into the floor of the Chartres Cathedral in France. Labyrinth walking has recently become popular, largely due to the efforts of Reverend Lauren Artress, canon at Grace Cathedral in San Francisco.

Visit the spot with complete awareness and mindfulness, and with respect for the culture and religious traditions that define the place and its original (or even current) purpose and use. Meditate while at the spot, if possible. Walk through and around the area in walking meditation. As you walk, imagine the history of the ground you are walking upon. Ask the place for guidance. Don't expect some miraculous "sign," but do remain keenly aware of what is happening around you. What might the experience reveal to you? Before you leave, ask for a blessing from your sacred spot and offer your thanks. Leave with a reverent sense of gratitude.

249

Reflect on your experience as you return home, then meditate on the experience. What did you feel? What did you learn? What did you discover?

Graduations

Life is full of opportunities for walking. Most of them involve getting somewhere, some of them don't. Others are the *big* walks that symbolize a life transition. For these moments, mindful walking is especially important. These are the moments you'll want to remember for as long as you can, but they also tend to be the moments in which we don't focus because we are so overwhelmed with stress, emotion, or organizational details. Once your life-transition walk has begun, however, let everything past and future disappear. Live fully and wholly in the now when you:

From A to Om

A **pilgrimage** is a journey to a shrine or holy place.

➤ Walk across the stage to receive your diploma

➤ Walk down the aisle to get married

➤ Walk to the podium to give a speech or presentation

➤ Walk out of an old home for the last time

➤ Walk into a new home for the first time

➤ Walk into or away from any life-changing situation: a birth, a death, walking toward someone you love, leaving someone you love, walking into a new job, walking away from an old job, waking up and walking out of your bedroom on your birthday, etc.

Students at Washington College in Chestertown, Maryland begin the ritual walk marking their graduation. It's all in the feet! Courtesy Washington College, photograph by Trisha McGee.

Live your defining moments, and gradually you'll learn to live all your moments—because really, the only moment that truly defines you is *this* moment.

Walking seems like such a mundane act, yet it can be a spiritually intense or profoundly relaxing experience. Learn to walk just for the sake of the walk, and your journey will become your destination.

The Least You Need to Know

➤ Kinhin is the walking form of zazen (the Zen form of seated meditation) in which the meditator walks in a slow circle around an altar in a meditation hall while letting the mind be open in pure awareness.

➤ Mindful walking means walking for the sake of walking—with one-pointed focus and concentration on the walk itself—not for the sake of a destination.

➤ Both the country and the city can provide good environments for walking meditation.

➤ Walking the ritual path of a labyrinth to reach the center is symbolic of journeying to the center of the self for greater self-knowledge.

➤ A pilgrimage to a sacred place can offer another sacred space in which to practice sitting or walking meditation.

➤ Major life walks are enhanced via mindful walking.

Chapter 17

Movement Meditation: Get Your Groove

In This Chapter

➤ Meditation in motion

➤ Yoga, T'ai Chi, and QiGong

➤ Dynamic meditation

➤ Dance, whirl, and shake your booty!

If sitting can be meditation and walking can be meditation, can anything be meditation? Yes, anything *can* be meditation. With practice, you can maintain a state of mindful awareness 24 hours a day. So, once you've learned to meditate while sitting and meditate while walking, expand your meditation practice to other areas of movement. Or, if movement is more your style, get out your energy with dynamic meditation *before* you attempt sitting meditation.

For centuries, various cultures have attempted to extend the meditative state into other areas of physical activity, resulting in many forms of mind-body-spirit fitness programs, from yoga to whirling. Each of these systems is designed to nurture, maintain, strengthen, and actualize the entire self and is best practiced in a state of mindfulness, to reap the maximum benefit.

Whether you're looking for an interesting variation to your regular fitness program or want to immerse yourself in the spiritual dimension of your favorite tradition, read on for more about the many forms of movement meditation.

Fitting the Body to Free the Mind

You are an individual. Yes, even though we keep saying "all is one," that doesn't mean you aren't you. You have your own likes and dislikes, preferences and abilities. While your best friend may be crazy about her yoga class, you might feel a stronger affinity to a long jog in the park. Or maybe you love the idea of learning all about T'ai Chi or martial arts, but your partner is far more interested in a ballet class.

Don't force yourself into a form that doesn't fit. You won't be comfortable, and if your body isn't comfortable, your mind certainly won't be at ease. Sure, eventually you can expand your repertoire of physical and spiritual pursuits, and in some cases, purposefully working on something that isn't comfortable can help you to become more balanced and to grow. But at first, while you are still mastering the fine art of self-discipline, go with your inclinations. You'll be more likely to keep it up.

Bliss Byte

All set for sitting meditation but you just can't sit still? Maintain your upper body in your sitting meditation pose, stand up, and slowly walk around the perimeter of your meditation space, focusing on your breathing.

Yoga Is More Than Exercise

These days, yoga is big news. Yoga classes of all types are popping up everywhere. Some of the more high-profile yoga teachers have become minor celebrities, while major celebrities are turning to yoga more often as their favorite fitness method. Fitness gurus like Kathy Smith and Jane Fonda have put out best-selling yoga videos, and Madonna claims she no longer engages in any fitness program except yoga. In fact, Madonna's CD *Ray of Light* was largely inspired by her yoga practice.

Of course, popularity isn't a reason to engage in anything. Yoga isn't just a passing fad. It has been around for thousands of years, and we're betting it will be around for thousands more. It only happens that society's current whim is to embrace it. If you are interested in yoga, try it out. Maybe it's for you. Maybe it's not. But before you decide yoga's not your cup of tea, give it a chance. It's more than exercise, and it isn't just stretching. It is a complete program of mind-body maintenance, including physical exercises, breathing exercises, and an important relaxation technique called *shavasana* (see Chapter 18, "Shavasana: It's Not Just Lying Around!" for more on shavasana).

Yoga doesn't have to be static, either. Although many of the yoga poses are moved into and then held, yoga also contains *vinyasas*, or flowing sequences of postures. Rather than holding each pose, the yogi moves through the poses, sometimes quite vigorously. Vinyasas can be a real workout and have so charmed the public that a whole new type of yoga, called Power Yoga, is now all the rage in health clubs, gyms, and yoga classes around the country. Power Yoga is a highly aerobic form of Astanga Yoga that also employs vigorous but flowing movements through sequences of postures.

QiGong: Live Long and Prosper

QiGong (also known as *chi kung*) is another centuries-old system of mind-body maintenance originating in China and based on many of the principles of Taoism. QiGong is sitting or standing meditation; exercises for stretching, releasing energy, and purifying the body; massage; breathwork; and certain targeted movements to correct imbalances or disease.

QiGong is based around the concept of chi (or Qi) and the meridians through which it flows. It also deals with the energy field around the body. QiGong exercises are designed to purify and open the meridians so energy can flow freely through them to heal the body. Its exercises are simple and many are designed for people who are ill or injured. Meditation is an important part of QiGong, but many QiGong practitioners meditate standing up. The mind should remain in a meditative state during the exercises. QiGong also has a form of walking meditation.

T'ai Chi: The Restorative Power of Slow Motion

T'ai Chi is a martial arts form that developed out of QiGong. It involves slow, flowing movements also designed to free the passage of life-force energy through the body's meridians and, in the case of its martial arts aspect, use this life-force energy in combat. T'ai Chi movement sequences are commonly practiced in China, often outdoors

From A to Om

Yoga means "union" and comes from the Sanskrit root *yuj*, meaning "to yoke or join together." It is a centuries-old system for mind-body health designed to gain control over the body, breath, and mind so that enlightenment can be attained. **Vinyasa** is a steady flow of connected yoga postures linked with breathing exercises in a continuous movement.

From A to Om

QiGong means "energy skill" and is sometimes translated as "empowerment." It is a 5,000-year-old system of health and life-force energy maintenance and also a healing art. It is the forerunner of T'ai Chi and the other martial arts systems from China. QiGong typically exists in three forms: martial, medical, and spiritual.

in the morning. In the West it is gaining popularity, too, as a gentle, slow, yet exhilarating form of exercise. Although the sequences of movements are more difficult to learn than those of QiGong, they aren't strenuous and can be performed by anyone, young or old, healthy or ailing.

From A to Om

T'ai Chi means "way of the fist" and is a martial arts system and fitness method developed from QiGong. Today, T'ai Chi has evolved from its martial arts origins into a practice of movement meditation for peaceful purposes.

Relax

Most forms of moving meditation, including yoga, QiGong, T'ai Chi, and dynamic meditation, are best practiced under the guidance of a capable and experienced teacher. A teacher can guide you, address your individual issues, and help to keep you from injuring yourself.

And You Thought You Wouldn't Sweat!

Many other systems for moving meditation exist as well. Some of them, including dynamic meditation, ecstatic dancing, and whirling, are incredibly intense, both physically and emotionally. The point of these high-intensity moving meditations is to shake the holds on the mind by shaking and completely exhausting the body. When the physical barriers have been dissolved, the mental barriers fall away, and the mind is free. These moving meditations, which are actually more like meditation preparations, aren't for everyone. But if you want a good workout that is emotionally intense and will facilitate sitting meditation, give them a try.

Yoga's Devotional Vinyasas

If you're interested in exploring the yoga path but enjoy more vigorous physical activity, yoga vinyasas may be the perfect choice for you. On those days when you feel too restless for sitting meditation, move through a few yoga vinyasas with complete mindfulness. You'll get a healthy workout for both your body and your mind.

In Tune with the Rhythm of Life

Many yoga poses are meant to capture the spirit of animals or objects in the natural world such as mountains and trees. By stringing these poses together in a natural flow, vinyasas imitate the rhythm of nature. When performing a vinyasa, go at the "right" pace. In other words, move through the poses at a pace that feels natural for you. Some days, you may find yourself moving fast, other days you'll move more slowly. Follow your natural rhythms and fall in step with your mind-body.

Bliss Byte

When performing yoga vinyasas, coordinate your breath to the movement. In general, exhale when going into a forward bending or contractive pose and inhale when going into a backbending or expansive pose.

Sun Salutation

Probably the most well-known vinyasa is the sun salutation. Our solar system revolves around the sun, and the sun powers our planet. This vinyasa offers thanks to the sun for all it gives us and is most appropriately performed outdoors at sunrise, facing east (although you can, of course, perform it any time, anywhere, for a quick pick-me-up). This vinyasa will give you an all-over workout.

As you move through this solar meditation, keep a picture of the sun in your mind and contemplate its effects on the world. Think of how it feels shining on your skin, how it changes the look of the world around you, and what it has meant to you in the past. Stay attuned to the feel of the sun salutation movements as your body flows through the postures. Feel the sun's energy flowing into you as you perform this vinyasa, filling you with vitality.

➤ *Stand with your feet together, back straight, hands together in front of your chest as if in prayer.*

➤ *Inhale and raise your arms up and slightly behind your head, leaning back slightly to look toward the sun.*

➤ *Exhale and bend forward, dropping your hands toward the floor.*

➤ *Inhale, place your hands on the floor, and step back with your right foot so your right leg is extended behind you.*

➤ *Exhale as you bring your left leg behind you and hold your body up as if about to do a push-up.*

➤ *Exhale further and touch your knees, chest, and chin to the floor.*

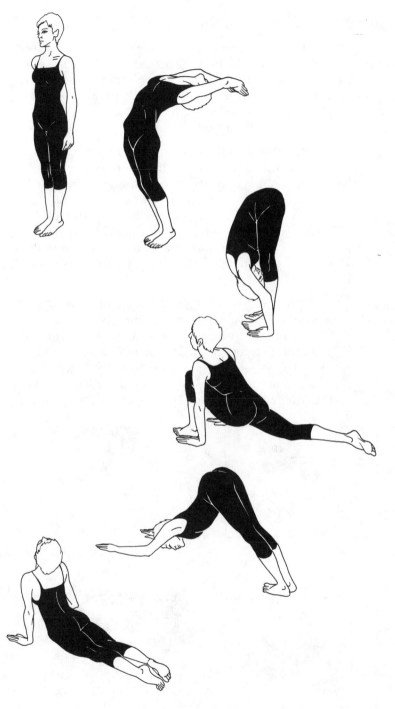

➤ Inhale and lift the front part of your torso off the ground. Look up.

➤ Exhale, lifting your hips so that your body forms an upside-down V.

➤ Inhale and bring your right leg forward, leaving your left leg extended behind you.

➤ Exhale and stand up but leave the front part of your torso hanging forward.

➤ Inhale as you bring your torso up to stretch slightly back, arms up, looking again toward the sun.

➤ Exhale and stand straight and tall with hands to your sides.

➤ Repeat again, bringing the left leg back first.

Lock in the Energy: Bandhas

Yoga vinyasas and postures fill the body with prana and activate the internal life-force energy. Yoga literature stresses the importance of holding prana in the body to keep the body healthy and balanced. How can you keep prana from escaping once you've activated it? And can you intensify it as it meanders through its channels, or *nadis*?

Yoga has the answer: Heat it up and lock it in with specific movements called *bandhas*.

Bandhas aren't drastic movements. They are little movements, but they can be incorporated into your meditation program. The three bandhas are best used in conjunction with *pranayama*, or deep breathing exercises. As prana infuses the body, bandhas lock it in, intensify it, even reverse its subtle direction along the internal channels in ways that make it merge with itself, heat up, and strengthen (to simplify an advanced yoga theory).

Try using bandhas during your next deep breathing session (go back to Chapter 14, "Enter the Breathing Room," for more on breathing exercises and techniques), as preparation for meditation, or during meditation itself. You may find your meditation experience intensified. Practice the following bandhas in order, as specified, over a two-breath cycle, or work on one at a time.

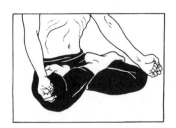

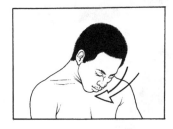

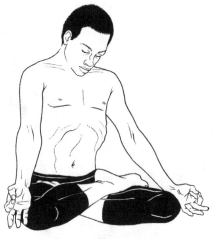

Practicing the three bandhas together is a powerful, advanced yoga technique for optimizing the positive affect of prana in the mind-body. Try it—gently. If lotus pose is too uncomfortable, relax into easy pose.

> **From A to Om**
>
> **Bandhas**, literally "to bind" or "to lock," are muscular locks used during yoga postures and breathing exercises to intensify the energy of prana in the body. The three primary bandhas are mula bandha, uddiyani bandha, and jalandhara bandha. **Nadis** are the internal channels or pathways through which prana flows in the body.

➤ **Jalandhara bandha.** Inhale deeply, slightly raising your chest, then as you hold the breath in, place your chin gently into your chest to prevent the escape of prana from your upper body. Hold for a few seconds (be sure not to strain your neck—the hold is firm but gentle), release this bandha, and lift your head before exhalation.

➤ **Uddiyana bandha.** After you have exhaled completely, pull your navel up and back toward your spine. This action works the diaphragm muscle and forces prana up one of the nadis, when it would naturally be moving down, intensifying its energy. Release.

➤ **Mula bandha.** Inhale deeply, then contract the perineal muscle (the muscle you sit on, in the area between your rectum and your genitals). This lock prevents the escape of life-force energy from the lower body, pushing it back up. If you can't isolate your perineal muscle, contract your anal sphincter and the whole general area down there. Eventually, you'll be able to tell the difference between the different muscles (no hurry—that kind of muscle isolation is quite advanced).

Don't expect to feel anything dramatic at first. The effect of bandhas is subtle but real. Eventually, as you become more internally sensitive and self-aware (the inevitable result of meditation!), you will be able to detect the energizing effect of bandhas.

Bliss Byte

Bandha contractions should be light. Don't wrench your muscles into unnatural contractions. Place your chin gently on your chest, pull your navel back lightly, contract your perineal muscle with about the same effort you would make to close your eyes. Bandhas aren't meant to be strenuous or severe. It doesn't take massive physical action to internally redirect prana—just a little nudge from the mind-body. Although advanced yogis practice the bandhas to a more intense degree.

QiGong's Cultivation of Health

QiGong, as we said above, consists of several meditational aspects. Sitting or standing meditation is an important part of QiGong. So are simple, easy, chi-directing exercises designed to heal and revitalize. You could study QiGong for years with a master, but we'll just give you a small sampling of the possibilities.

Healing the Body, Nurturing the Spirit

One of the primary uses of QiGong is for healing and also to train people who want to learn energy healing. QiGong, using many of the principles of *traditional Chinese medicine* (TCM), prescribes certain exercises, massages, and meditations for particular problems. For QiGong, health problems are mind-body imbalances of chi related to five different areas, which TCM views as reservoirs of chi:

➤ Kidney energy imbalances

➤ Liver energy imbalances

➤ Heart energy imbalances

➤ Spleen energy imbalances

➤ Lung energy imbalances

Or combinations of any of the above. Energy imbalances can mean too much or too little chi in any of the above organs.

By balancing and replenishing the flow of chi, or life-force energy, in the body, QiGong helps the body to heal and the mind to settle.

Bliss Byte

One specialized breathing technique sometimes used in QiGong is "reversed breathing." Unlike incorrect reverse breathing, this type of breathing is conscious and mindful, engaging and strengthening the lymph glands, the descending aorta, and the sacral lumbar area, as well as the diaphragm muscle. Place your hands on the lower abdomen. As you inhale, press your hands in and contract the abdomen. As you exhale, push your abdomen out and relax. Repeat for 50 breaths.

QiGong offers a full program of health to address a variety of ailments. For example, perhaps you suffer from indigestion, ulcers, or other digestive ailments. According to TCM these are related to an imbalance in spleen energy. For someone with a spleen imbalance, QiGong recommends:

➤ Eating a healthy balanced diet, including a lot of fresh vegetables, cooked to make them more digestible.

➤ Eating small amounts of food more frequently instead of large amounts less often.

➤ Stomach massage.

➤ Exercises to revitalize and energize the spleen, to restore proper functioning, such as the Earth exercise (an exercise involving a firm wide stance and twisting back and forth at the waist) and the Tiger Plays with Ball exercise, which Joan demonstrates in the photograph on page 265.

➤ The stimulation of the Three Yin Crossing Point (an acupressure point) with the thumb, located about three inches straight up from the ankle joint on the inside of each leg.

Obviously, it is out of the scope of this book to give a detailed explanation of the entire program that is QiGong, but read on for a sample of meditative exercises based on QiGong principles. For even more information, read *The Complete Idiot's Guide to T'ai Chi and QiGong* (Alpha Books, 1999).

Mindful Minute

Thousands of people in China practice QiGong and T'ai Chi in public parks beginning early in the morning, around 5:30 a.m.

Medical QiGong Exercise

Every illness addressed by QiGong is addressed in many ways, as you can see from the list of prescribed actions for digestive problems. However, we can give you a brief sampling of the ways in which QiGong could address your individual health concerns:

➤ **Suffering from fatigue, lethargy, lower-back pain, or osteoporosis?** You could have a kidney energy imbalance. Sit in a chair, place your elbows on your knees, lightly clasp your hands, and bend forward until you feel a stretch in your lower back. Direct your attention to your kidneys, then ask your body, "What are you afraid of?" After that question, wait mindfully and observe what happens. Breathe deeply and allow your feelings to bubble up. If fears arise, acknowledge them. Don't judge, just observe. Now, make the sound "fffuuu." Extend the sound, allowing it to resonate and vibrate through your body. Make the sound "chu-whaaay." Let your fears stir and flush from the kidneys with the rush of cleansing vibration. As the fear leaves you, feel how clean and open and light your body feels. Sit up straight and smile!

➤ **Suffering from insomnia, heart palpitations, overheating, or shortness of breath?** You could have a heart energy imbalance. Stand with your feet slightly wider than shoulder-width apart, back straight, lifting the crown of your head toward the ceiling. With your hands loosely at your sides, begin to sway your hands together backward and forward. As your hands sway back, exhale. As they sway forward, inhale. Hold your shoulders in a relaxed position and let the swaying motion gently rock your entire body. As you swing your arms forward, imagine inhaling pure, clean, white energy. As your arms sway backward, imagine exhaling negative, toxic energy transformed as clear joy. Feel the negative energy being transformed and flung away from you out of your fingertips as positive energy. Continue to sway for two minutes, mindful of the changing feelings in your body. You should feel relaxed as muscle tension dissolves, and your hands will feel warm and tingly.

Bliss Byte

Deep QiGong practice involves moving chi in the body in a pattern called **xiao zhou tian**, which means "small universe." By keeping the movement of chi in the small universe flowing and open, illness is prevented.

➤ **Suffering from a stiff back?** Your primary river of energy may be dammed up. QiGong includes lots of great stretching exercises that, when practiced mindfully, can relax the body, calm the mind, and loosen the joints and muscles. To loosen the spine, stand with your feet a little wider than shoulder-width apart. Very slowly allow your body to drop from the waist and hang forward. Imagine your vertebrae folding over, one at a time. When you are hanging down, try to completely relax your torso and head so that the weight of your head gives the spine a nice stretch. Hold each elbow with the opposite hand and breathe deeply. Swing your torso back and forth slightly to loosen your hold on your spine and neck. Stay down for about one minute, then slowly rise back up, vertebrae by vertebrae.

➤ **Suffering from lowered or lack of energy and vitality?** Try the following meditative exercise, called Tiger Plays with Ball. Stand with your feet a little wider than shoulder-width apart. Bend your knees slightly and take a few deep breaths. (This exercise can also be practiced in a chair—just follow the directions for the upper body.) Now, imagine a great ball of bright energy in front of you at waist level. The energy comes from you but glows in front of you like a miniature planet. You can control this ball of energy. Grasp the ball with your arms and hands. Move your hands around it. Feel its radiating electricity and heat. Explore the ball, play with the ball. It is yours. (This exercise is also great for a boost in self-confidence.)

Joan demonstrates the QiGong exercise, Tiger Plays with Ball.

Spiritual QiGong Exercise

Although QiGong serves several purposes, it is difficult to separate it out into health and spirituality exercises because every exercise, massage, and meditation aspect serves both purposes. Your intention in using them may change, of course. For a psycho-spiritual energy lift, modify the Tiger Plays with Ball exercise described above to practice the Heavenly Eye exercise:

Stand with your feet a little wider than shoulder-width apart, back straight, knees slightly bent, head lifted. Lift your hands up in front of you as if you are lifting the energy ball in the previous exercise. Spread your fingers and allow your palms to face you, elbows slightly dropped. Imagine your palms are pointing to your third eye, or sun chakra, the spot in the middle of your forehead. Relax and breathe deeply. Feel your arms floating, lifted by the energy, as if you can hold them up effortlessly. Let stress flow down and away from you as white light, pure spiritual energy flows into you. Imagine your third eye opening so that you see the true nature of reality. Feel joy flooding your body as you recognize truth.

QiGong is a wonderful program for overall health, combining meditation with fitness and good health habits.

Bliss Byte

Many energy movements involve holding the arms and hands above heart level. This increases the circulation to the heart, as well as gathering energy in the center of the body, where it can be fully directed. Need a quick energy boost during the middle of the day? Hold your arms straight up for one minute. If you have a heart condition, however, check with your physician before practicing this exercise.

T'ai Chi's Principles of Force

T'ai Chi, a martial arts form that grew out of QiGong, isn't normally thought of as a martial art in the West. Here, T'ai Chi fans are attracted to the principles of T'ai Chi more akin to QiGong—the gentle, slow, easy movements designed to heal the body and still the mind. In fact, T'ai Chi is often called "movement meditation."

T'ai Chi is centered around the idea of gravity and moving in harmony with the force of gravity (as well as the force opposing gravity). Although today many forms and even more opinions exist about how T'ai Chi "should" be practiced, a few basic principles apply to any T'ai Chi method. To understand these principles, it helps first to understand three intimately related principles: Sir Isaac Newton's Three Laws of Physics.

What? You don't remember them from high school? We'll refresh your memory.

➤ Unless something exerts a force onto an object, the object will stay at rest. By the same token, an object will move at a constant speed unless a force is applied to it.

➤ Force = mass × acceleration. In other words, as force increases, acceleration will increase at a proportional rate.

➤ To every action there is an equal and opposite reaction.

How do these principles relate to T'ai Chi? T'ai Chi is all about gravity. Gravity pulls us to the Earth, and the spinning of the Earth exerts centrifugal force on us, pulling us away from its center. Somehow, it all balances out, and we are able to walk around and function without getting sucked into the ground or flying off into space.

According to T'ai Chi, these two forces meet in the approximate area of our abdomens, what we sometimes call the *center of gravity*. But not every body is in harmony with gravity. Sometimes, gravity gets the best of us, pulling us down, bending and misaligning us. T'ai Chi's aim is to help the body become perfectly balanced in relation to gravity. When you move one part of your body in a T'ai Chi exercise, another moves in an equal and opposite reaction. If your body is in motion, T'ai Chi helps it to remain in motion, and acceleration in T'ai Chi movements is related to your mass and the force you apply, so that everything balances perfectly.

Balance is the key to T'ai Chi. In T'ai Chi literature, it is said that when the practitioner of T'ai Chi is in perfect harmony with gravity, a leaf falling on his or her hand will cause that hand to sink like a scale from the weight of the leaf. A high level of sensitivity is apparent. T'ai Chi's four principles are:

➤ Just the right amount of force is used to bring about the result—no more, no less.

➤ No movement will go against the structure of the body and no movement will be extraneous.

➤ Be in constant awareness of the force of gravity.

➤ Also be in constant awareness of gravity's counter force.

T'ai Chi is a complex art form, and we won't get into the many movement series here. If you like the idea of T'ai Chi, find a good teacher near you. Then use these four principles in conjunction with Newton's Three Laws as anchor points in your T'ai Chi practice. And don't forget—remain mindful!

Meditation in Motion

Meditation is a challenge, but for some people it seems like an impossibility to sit in one place for 20 minutes. The modern world is so overwrought with stress that stillness may be counterproductive for much of our society, at least until we can peel off some of that negative energy. Meditation teachers have developed an answer: meditation that really moves!

Dynamic Meditation

Dynamic meditation is meditation with movement. Yoga vinyasas, QiGong, and T'ai Chi are meditation with movement, too, but dynamic meditation has no other purpose than to facilitate meditation. What is it, exactly? Dynamic meditation can mean seated meditation during which the meditator simply moves his or her hands and arms slowly and mindfully, remaining aware of the movement. On the opposite end of the scale, it can mean rapid breathing, frantic crazed thrashing dance movements, and total collapse to the floor after the body has become completely exhausted. Different teachers have developed different methods, but if you are a mover and a shaker and find it impossible to sit still, consider trying dynamic meditation.

Bliss Byte

Movement can be meditation, but it can also be preparation for meditation, getting rid of excess energy and excess thought before attempting meditation. If you are feeling too "wound up" to meditate, try some high-energy dancing, whirling, jumping up and down, shaking out your body parts, or even taking a quick sprint around the block first. If you tire out your muscles before, meditation may be easier, especially if you are used to a lot of activity and find it difficult to sit still.

The point of exhaustive movements is actually to prepare the body for stillness. When past traumas, present stress, and dread of the future armor the body with tension, it can be extremely difficult to let the body relax, let alone be open to enlightenment. Dynamic meditation shakes loose this armoring, stirs up the internalized emotions, and rattles them around until they come loose. Participants may end up laughing hysterically, sobbing, or simply so exhausted that they have no choice but to lie still. After the movement session, dynamic meditation usually involves a period of complete stillness, allowing the mind to discover what is happening in the body.

Sound interesting? Try the following dynamic meditation exercise:

➤ If you desire, put on music, preferably instrumental-only and high-energy.

➤ Stand with feet about shoulder-width apart, arms loose. Roll your head from side to side, shake out your arms and legs, and breathe easily.

➤ Now increase your breath rate so it is rapid but inhalations remain very deep. Don't make any attempt to regulate the breath to any rhythm. Just suck it in, then blow it out. Continue for two minutes.

➤ Next let your body begin to move. Don't follow any patterns or move in a way that you think would "look right." Feel the movement. Let your body move the way it wants to move. Let the movement be organic, originating from inside your body, not from your brain. You may want to close your eyes so you aren't as conscious about how you look.

Relax

Shallow rapid breaths could cause hyperventilation. When trying rapid breathing as preparation for dynamic meditation, keep those breaths deep and full. If you become dizzy, breathe normally for 30 seconds, then continue.

➤ Allow your body to pick up the pace if it wants to. Really go crazy. Thrash your arms around, jump up and down, let out any sound that comes to you. A hearty "Ha!" or "Hoo!" or "Ho!" is good, but whatever comes out of you is good, too. Be mindful of what your body is doing, don't just let your mind drift away. But do let everything go. Don't hold back anything. Continue dancing in this way for 20 to 30 minutes, or until you are too exhausted to continue (the amount of time depends on your level of exertion and your fitness—a shorter time doesn't mean you did it wrong).

➤ Now, let your entire body collapse to the floor and lie there in whatever position you landed, utterly still. Be completely present in your body. Feel what has happened to it. Notice all the sensations. Feel whether any emotions have released, whether you feel good, upset, cleansed, or angry. All are possible. Just stay in stillness and mindfulness for 10 minutes.

Dynamic meditation can be an intense experience, but it can also be darned fun! And it really does make sitting meditation a lot easier.

Relax

It is important for practitioners of movement meditation to have enough room to move in and also to feel safe in their movements. If you practice these techniques in a class, make sure you have enough space between yourself and others. If you practice at home, make sure the room in which you practice is free from obstacles that could hurt you or be broken.

Ecstatic Dancing

Ecstatic dancing is similar in theory to dynamic meditation. It exists in various forms in many indigenous cultures, but you can practice it in your own living room. Put on music and let yourself go. Really dance. Dance up a storm. Cut that rug in two. Dance nonstop with everything you've got for 20 minutes, then relax into a seated meditation in easy pose. Ahhhhhhhhhhhhhooooommmm.

Whirling

Whirling is most often associated with the Sufis and a related sect, the dervishes. (You've probably heard of whirling dervishes.) Sufism is a mystical version of Islam, and meditation is an important part of the Sufi way. Whirling is a way to spin off negative energy and exhaust the body so it doesn't interfere with the spiritual journey. It also puts your body into a transformed state. You can do it, too—just make sure you don't try it in a room where you could knock anything over or get hurt! Outside in a big yard (with no trees) is a good option.

Relax

Whirling can be fun and a great meditation technique, but if you have a medical condition that involves dizziness, suffer from vertigo (dizziness) or tinnitus (ringing in the ears), whether associated with another condition or not, or if you are taking any medication for which dizziness is a side effect, leave the whirling for the dervishes and practice a different form of dynamic meditation instead.

➤ Stand relaxed with arms down and knees slightly bent. Slowly begin to spin in a circle, counter-clockwise (or clockwise if counterclockwise seems unnatural).

➤ Spin faster and faster, to music if it helps, with eyes unfocused to prevent dizziness. Don't try to see anything.

➤ Remain mindful. Notice how your body feels, every sensation as you whirl.

➤ Keep spinning until you are going as fast as you can, and go as fast as you can until your body naturally falls over. (Remember, do it in a room where you can fall over and not get hurt.)

➤ Once you've collapsed to the floor, lie in perfect stillness and feel the Earth moving below you. Notice how you feel and whether your awareness has changed in any way. Is it sharper? Duller? How is it different?

➤ Eventually work up to about 20 minutes or so of whirling.

Moving meditation may not always seem like meditation, but if it is always mindful, it will be meditation. It will also help to calm, strengthen, control, and quiet your body so that sitting meditation is easier. So get moving!

The Least You Need to Know

➤ Many cultures have developed forms of moving meditation such as yoga, QiGong, T'ai Chi, ecstatic dancing, and whirling.

➤ Yoga vinyasas, such as the sun salutation series, are flowing sequences of yoga poses.

➤ QiGong is a Chinese system of life-force-energy management for better health.

➤ T'ai Chi is a martial arts form based in QiGong.

➤ Dynamic meditation, ecstatic dancing, and whirling can exhaust the body so that it doesn't interfere with meditation.

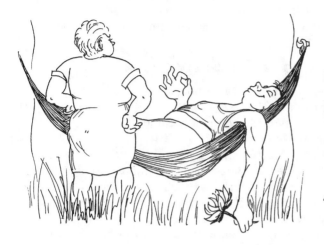

Chapter 18

Shavasana: It's Not Just Lying Around!

In This Chapter

➤ Shavasana: Yoga's ultimate relaxation meditation

➤ It's not as easy as it looks

➤ Being and nothingness

Despite what you think about the complexities of—and flexibility and/or strength required for—advanced yoga poses, the most difficult yoga pose of all doesn't take any flexibility or boundless physical strength at all to hold. It's the most important of all the yoga poses, the perfect preparation for meditation, yet it entails only lying on your back on the floor and...that's it! Lying on your back on the floor.

Actually, *shavasana* is more complicated than lying down. While lying on your back on the floor, you have to relax. (Tough.) You have to slow your thinking through meditation. (Tougher still.) And, at last, you become able to transcend your body and your mind to commune with your true self. (Now that's challenging!)

Concentrate on Relaxing

You could probably spend a lifetime working on step one of shavasana, relaxation. Relaxation is a fine art, and shavasana is the perfect canvas. But to lie on the floor in a way that facilitates relaxation takes a little forethought.

First, you'll want to find a place where you won't be disturbed for the duration of your shavasana meditation session (20 to 30 minutes is nice). Second, you'll want a comfortable but firm surface. Clean carpeted floors, floors with mats, or the Earth itself are perfect. Third, you'll want to choose the right time for shavasana.

Where to Do Shavasana

Unless you have a very understanding boss, you probably can't do shavasana on the job. ("What happened to Mary? Why is she lying on the floor? Oh, Mary? Are you awake?") To keep from falling asleep, you probably shouldn't practice shavasana on your bed, plus a bed doesn't offer the support that's optimal for performing the pose (although shavasana in bed is a good way to cure insomnia and to fall asleep in slow and relaxed fashion). The kitchen floor isn't the best place, unless you don't mind looking at that dirty refrigerator vent close-up. So where is the best place to practice this all-important yoga pose? How about:

➤ Your living room floor when no one else is home

➤ Your bedroom floor, with a "do not disturb" sign hung from the outside door-knob

➤ On a soft blanket on the grass in your backyard or out on your deck (the neighbors will think you are sunbathing)

As long as your chosen location is comfortable (but not *too* comfortable), supports your body firmly, and is free from distractions, you've got your spot!

From A to Om

Shavasana literally means "corpse pose" and is the most important of all yoga postures, designed to bring the body into total, conscious relaxation, using meditation to remove both physical and mental distractions.

Bliss Byte

Shavasana is the perfect pose for people who, due to health reasons, find it painful to sit upright for long periods of time without back support. The elderly and chronically ill may find the benefits of a steady practice of this pose relaxing and stress-reducing. However, shavasana shouldn't be practiced to the exclusion of any movement exercises or physical therapy regimen that's recommended by your physician or physical therapist.

When to Do Shavasana

When you do shavasana largely depends on you. Shavasana in the evening after an exhausting day may catapult you straight into dreamland. On the other hand, it might be just the pick-me-up you need to get dinner ready and the kids to bed. Same thing with early morning shavasana. The only way to know when your body will respond best to shavasana is to try it at different times of day to see what works best for you:

➤ As soon as you wake up in the morning, yawn, stretch, get out of bed, and lie down on the floor. If you tend to fall right back to sleep, this isn't a good time for shavasana.

➤ After your morning exercise and a shower but before breakfast (shavasana is best performed on an empty stomach). Still falling asleep? Morning probably isn't your best time. (Or you're not getting enough sleep. If you always *thought* you were a morning person, try going to bed an hour earlier and give it another go.)

➤ Mid-morning, about an hour or two after breakfast. This is a high-energy time for many people and a good time to practice shavasana if you have a stressful day ahead of you.

➤ Lunch break. If you go home for lunch (or are already home for lunch), try shavasana for 20 minutes before you eat. You'll probably find you can eat your lunch more slowly and with greater mindfulness after a satisfying shavasana session.

➤ Mid-afternoon is sleepy time for most people and not the best time for shavasana (although a great time for a cat nap). And if your nap and shavasana practice blend together, so much the better. Eventually, with practice, you'll learn to stay alert in shavasana.

➤ Late afternoon, right after school or work, is a great time for shavasana if you aren't too tired. It can calm you and ease the tensions from your workday, helping you to make the transition from work to home. After shavasana, you can concentrate fully on your home life without suffering what the Chinese call "monkey brain" (in other words, incessant mental chatter).

➤ Early evening is another high-energy time. A few hours after dinner when you are feeling calm and relaxed, take a 20-minute shavasana break. Later, you'll sleep like a baby.

➤ If you're a night owl, late night might be the best time for you to practice shavasana. If your awareness is sharpest when the moon is highest, falling asleep may not be a problem.

Whenever you practice shavasana, don't feel too bad if you do fall asleep. You probably needed the cat nap. Try again at a different time.

The Mind-Body Scan Becomes Your Meditation

Joan takes a break to prepare for meditation at home in supported shavasana. People with lower-back problems will find it uncomfortable to lie flat on the floor. Place a pillow or rolled blanket under your knees to take pressure off that sensitive lower back. You can also support your head and neck with a small pillow.

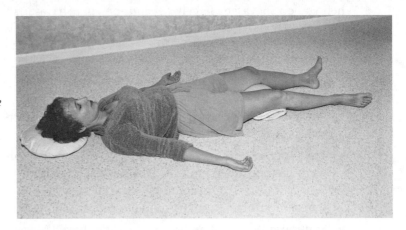

Remember the various mind-body scans we've included in this book? Here's another one that incorporates the practice of shavasana. This time, the sole purpose of the mind-body scan is to relax your body. First, lie in the shavasana position, flat on your back on the floor, arms slightly out, legs slightly apart and relaxed. Try not to "hold" anywhere. Breathe and feel your spine sinking into the floor. On each of the following contractions, hold for a slow count of three. Now:

Relax

If you are worried you'll fall asleep during shavasana, set a timer! Try to focus completely on relaxation, even if only for a few brief moments. If you know the timer is set, you won't have to worry about the time in the back of your mind.

➤ Bring your awareness to your left foot. Flex your ankle and fill your foot with tension. Hold, then relax, letting all the tension flow from your foot.

➤ Flex your calf muscle and hold, then release, letting tension flow out of your lower leg, out through your toes.

➤ Bend your knee just slightly and contract your thigh muscle tightly. Imagine all the tensions and negative or stagnant energy in your left leg gathering in the thigh muscle. Then, release and visualize this negative energy and tension flowing down your leg and out your toes, transformed as positive, life-affirming energy. Notice the relaxed feeling in your left leg. Does it feel more relaxed than your right leg?

➤ Repeat with your right leg, then note whether both legs feel equally relaxed. Stay mindful!

➤ Squeeze your buttocks together as tightly as you can. Release and feel the tension flowing away.

➤ Squeeze your abdominal muscles as tightly as you can. Release and feel the tension flowing away.

➤ Bring your awareness to your spine. Imagine the tension trickling down your spine and flowing out of your tailbone. Feel each vertebrae becoming heavier and looser, sinking into the floor.

➤ Contract your upper abdominals, under your ribcage, drawing your navel back toward your spine as far as you can, then release, allowing all the tension in your torso to flow out of your tailbone.

➤ Contract your chest muscles as tightly as you can, then release, feeling the energy flow down your spine and out of your tailbone.

➤ Now, bring your awareness to your left shoulder. Tighten your shoulder muscle, lifting it slightly off the floor with the effort. Then release, letting the shoulder sink into the floor. Imagine the negative energy and tension flowing down your arm and out of your fingertips, again, transformed as pure joy.

➤ Tense your upper arm muscles (biceps and triceps) as tightly as you can, lifting your upper arm slightly off the floor. Then release, and feel the tension flowing down and out of your fingertips transformed as joy.

➤ Tense your lower arm, lifting it slightly off the floor. Release, and feel the tension flowing down and out of your fingertips transformed as joy.

➤ Make a tight fist out of your left hand. Squeeze, then release, letting the tensions flow away.

➤ Now, spread the fingers of your left hand wide and hold. Release, then feel all the remaining tension in your left arm flowing away out the ends of your fingers. Notice the feeling of relaxation in your left arm. Does it feel more relaxed than your right arm?

➤ Repeat with your right arm. Then notice whether both arms feel equally relaxed. Stay mindful!

➤ Pull your chin back toward your neck, tensing the muscles of your neck and throat. Release and imagine the negative energy and tension flowing down your spine and out your tailbone, transformed as pure, positive joy.

➤ Clench your jaw tightly and scrunch up your whole face, then release. Feel the negative energy flowing out of the crown of your head, transformed as joy.

Mindful Minute

Shavasana has measurable physical benefits on the body. It calms the nerves, lowers blood pressure, improves blood flow to the heart, and lessens fatigue. Shavasana is a great pose for opening the chakras to free the flow of prana through the body.

➤ Open your eyes and mouth as wide as you possibly can, hold, and release, feeling the negative energy flowing out of the crown of your head, released as pure, positive energy that your body has gathered and transformed.

➤ Now imagine your awareness is a warm, glowing ring of light. It begins around your toes and moves slowly, slowly up your body from your toes to your crown, searching for tension. Whenever it senses tension, it glows red, alerting you to tense areas. Let this "scanner" move up and down your body several times. Whenever it senses tension, tense the area again, then release, until all tension is gone. Imagine the ring of light gradually turning a calm, tranquil blue as you progressively relax.

➤ At last you should be feeling completely relaxed. Imagine your body melting into the floor or ground. Breathe deeply and with each breath, feel your muscle fibers dissolving and loosening. Remain completely mindful and aware. Try not to let your mind drift away into sleep. Notice everything. Let your consciousness vibrate with the intensity of your awareness.

➤ Remain in that still, relaxed position for 10 minutes or so, then slowly imagine your body separating from the Earth and becoming itself again, lighter, easier, and freer.

➤ Sit up slowly, stand up slowly, and voilà! No more stress.

The mind-body scan moving into shavasana is a way to help you relax, but it is more a shavasana prelude than the actual practice. The real shavasana comes during that heavy, sinking, dissolving stage when you feel as if your body is, well…a corpse.

Bliss Byte

Did your parents ever tell you that patience is a virtue? It is certainly a virtue in shavasana, and one that can be cultivated. If you find your mind racing, try counting very slowly to 10, then starting back at one again. Repeat until you feel better able to relax. You can also visualize your body slowly sinking into the floor or your muscles relaxing and melting. If you get an unbearable itch, give it some time, but don't torture yourself. If it won't go away, scratch it, then relax again. You can do this! And with practice, shavasana really does become easier.

Shavasana: Yoga's Corpse Pose

The *corpse pose* is so named for more reasons than the fact that you lie as still as a corpse. In shavasana, you certainly aren't dead, but in many ways, you can be like the dead. Your body should become very still. Then your mind should become still. At last, only your awareness is left, the essential you, unencumbered by the fetters of body and mind.

According to yoga theory (and many other theories), this is what happens at death. Your soul is released from the trappings of body and mind and is free to be itself—at least until it moves into another body to be reborn. Shavasana allows your soul to get a little taste of that freedom, and a short break from that sometimes troublesome body armor and worrisome brain.

Being and Nothingness

To borrow the title of a work by the famous French existentialist playwright and author Jean-Paul Sartre, shavasana is a little like "being and nothingness." You *are*, yet you are nothing. And you are everything. Your body lies there, yet it does nothing. Your mind is there, but it is still. Your true being—your soul—is set free by the temporary nothingness/everythingness of your body and mind.

To get to this stage of shavasana wherein body and mind dissolve into each other and into the world around them—stepping out of the soul's way to allow for full commune with the universe—isn't easy. We're not saying you'll be able to do it the first time around. But that is what you are moving toward as you practice shavasana.

Another advantage to allowing your body and mind to become nothingness for a little while is that they both get a well-deserved rest. They work hard keeping you functioning in the world, and if you can turn them both off for a short time once or twice a day, you'll find that they return to you in much better condition, like an overheated motor that is allowed to cool off.

Taking Root in the Earth

During pure shavasana, your thought slows and, ultimately, thought will be suspended. But to get to that point, it sometimes helps to engage in thought that moves you in the right direction. Shavasana can be effectively visualized in many ways, but we'd like to suggest two: as the body merging with Earth, and as the body merging with sky. The total suspension of thought for any length of time only occurs in the advanced stages of samadhi, but you may experience a slowing down or momentary suspension of thought early on in your meditation practice.

Bliss Byte

Especially for children and teenagers, some pre-meditation energetic activity like running, aerobic dance, or Hatha Yoga postures can make the shavasana pose easier to maintain. Shavasana is an excellent activity for children and teens. It teaches focus, concentration, balance, centering, patience, and stress management—qualities many children no longer possess (or never learned) in our fast-paced world. Practice shavasana with your kids and teach your teenager, too. Shavasana can be a way for your children to gain a sense of control over their bodies and minds, which will cultivate self-esteem—and everyone can use more of that!

For the first option, try the following visualization to ease you into shavasana:

Lie down on your back on the floor, arms slightly out from the body, legs slightly apart. Shift your body until you find a comfortable position. Close your eyes and breathe deeply.

With each breath, imagine you are inhaling peace, and peace feels cool, soft, and heavy. This peace gathers up the body's chaos, chatter, and distraction. On the exhalation, all is exhaled as peaceful, positive energy. In with peace, chaos transformed, out with joy. In with peace, chatter transformed, out with calm.

With each inhalation, feel your muscles relaxing and your bones becoming heavier. Imagine that your spine is falling with the weight of gravity. Feel your foot bones, leg bones, hip bones, shoulders, neck, and head growing heavier, melting, joining with and rooting into the Earth. Relax into the arms of Mother Earth. Breathe in peace, breathe out peace.

Soon, your muscles, bones, and entire body have sunk gently into the Earth and you feel cool and relaxed. Your breath is easy and soothing. You are completely supported, nurtured, and rocked by the spinning planet. You feel complete comfort and ease. All your thoughts have given up trying to distract you and flow away with your exhalations. Only cool, heavy, wholly relaxing peace remains.

Stay in this position for 10 to 20 minutes, then slowly offer a blessing to the Earth. Feel yourself becoming lighter. Feel your thoughts returning, relaxed and easy now. Slowly sit, then stand. Carry your awareness of your communion with the Earth throughout the rest of your day.

Floating Like a Cloud in the Sky

The other visualization option to help ease you into shavasana is to imagine your body going up instead of down. Try this one:

Lie down on your back on the floor, arms slightly out from the body, legs slightly apart. Shift your body until you find a comfortable position. Close your eyes and breathe deeply.

With each inhalation, imagine you are breathing in pure, white, playful light. Imagine that the light gathers up and soothes all the heaviness, stress, pain, negative emotions, and darkness lingering in your body and mind. With each exhalation, the transformed energy leaves your body as pure joy. In, white light to gather up heaviness and pain. Out, heaviness and pain, transformed as joy and lightness.

As you continue to inhale the light, imagine it filling your body as helium fills a balloon. First, the light fills your toes, your feet, and your legs. Imagine it cleansing your body, dancing inside you. Imagine it is airy, joyful, laughing light as it fills your torso, your arms, your neck, and your head.

Imagine the last of the negativity purified to flow out with your breath as healing, positive energy. The white light is taking up all the space now, and it begins to glow, and you begin to glow with it. Imagine the lightness radiating from your body, from around your head like a halo, from out of the tips of your fingers and toes, encircling your body so that you feel safe, calm, happy, and completely at home.

Mindful Minute

Some physicians claim that stress is the original source of all illness. Even in cases where illness or the source of pain isn't caused by stress, stress-reduction techniques can promote healing and reduce the experience of pain. In one study conducted by the Stress Reduction Clinic at the University of Massachusetts Medical Center, after an eight-week training period in the clinic in which patients were taught a variety of stress-management relaxation techniques, 75 percent of patients with chronic pain achieved a 33 percent reduction in their pain (according to how they rated their pain on a questionnaire), and 61 percent of pain patients achieved at least a 50 percent reduction in their pain. In addition, most showed an improvement in their ability to engage in normal activities and a drop in negative mood states. You can benefit, too—incorporate shavasana into your life and zap that stress!

Bliss Byte

Visualizing colors from nature can have a calming effect on the body. The grass is green and the sky is blue. Blue and green are naturally relaxing colors that calm the nervous system. Consciously incorporate colors like blue and green into your visualizations to make them more effective. You may find yourself more in tune to seeing the auras of people and things around, you, too (see Chapter 8, "Energy Central," for more on seeing auras).

Now, the light is becoming even lighter. It washes over your arms with a rush like a spring zephyr, and you feel your arms begin to lift. It rushes over your legs and feet, and your legs and feet feel as if they are floating, too. The light wraps your body with its comforting arms and cradles your head. Gravity no longer has any effect on you. Up you go, floating, flying, hardly able to keep from laughing with joy.

Imagine floating effortlessly through the roof of your house and into the sky, surrounded by light. Suddenly, the blue of the sky is all around you and it is beautiful, airy, light blue. Then you feel the cool mist of a cloud surrounding you. You realize you are resting in a cloud, and no place could be safer or more beautiful. The cloud sparkles with gold light and rocks you gently, softly. You recognize that you are pure spirit. Your old, clunky body is waiting for you far below. Your busy thoughts are rattling around down there, unable to get past the ceiling of your house. And here you are, rocked in light, embraced by peace, serenely safe in the sky.

Stay here for 10 to 20 minutes, basking in pure, unhindered awareness. Then, slowly offer a blessing to the cloud and feel yourself, bit by bit, ounce by ounce, becoming heavier. Float gently earthbound through the heavens, through the roof of your home, and back into your waiting body. In your absence, you notice, your body has become relaxed. Your thoughts have stopped chattering around the ceiling and have floated back into you, slower, quieter, and relaxed. Open your eyes and slowly, mindfully aware of your body, sit up, then stand. Carry your awareness of your communion with the sky throughout the rest of your day.

Breathe to the Center of Peace and Tranquillity

You may have noticed that most of the space in the above exercises has been taken up with the visualizations used to get into the state of shavasana, but not much space is spent describing the state of shavasana. That's because, for the most part, shavasana is an indescribable state. It is the soul communing with the universe, the true nature of the self revealed. These things can hardly be described in ordinary language.

Bliss Byte

Visualizing yourself surrounded by a beautiful white light may bring out your best, but it can help your relationships with others, too. The next time someone is troubling you, imagine they're surrounded by a white light. How does your perception of the person—and consequently, your actions toward that person—change?

But when you are in shavasana, it may not always match this ideal. Your thoughts will probably keep trying to infringe on your peace. What business does a thought about whether the pest-control guy is coming today have to do with the true nature of you? No business at all, but thoughts are notorious for going places that aren't any of their business! To keep them at bay, as well as the intrusive body sensations you'll probably also experience (the familiar itching, twitching, cramping, and aching), keep in mind one thought. Return to it whenever your mind or body behaves out of turn: *Breathe to the center*. (And if itches are a real problem, give yourself a break and scratch them, then return to your thought. If you think you can't scratch, you'll itch even more!)

Imagine that each breath comes and goes from the very center of your being, where only peace and tranquility live. Breathe in peace, breathe out peace. Your breath will be deep and long and full because each breath comes from so far inside you. Imagine that the center of yourself is a planet all its own, the planet *you*, and your body and mind are its galaxy. Come back to the image again and again, and breathe, breathe, breathe. Before long, your body and your thoughts will get the hint and learn to behave. Prana, or life-force energy, will move through you and in and out of you more freely, revitalizing your physical, astral, and causal bodies (see Chapter 10, "Is Any Body Home?"). You'll have more physical energy as you move through life, but you'll also have more energy on the other, more subtle levels that are also you. And then, what a glorious communion you can have with the true you!

You Are the Universe: Paint the Sky with Stars

Many ancient cultures believed (and many still believe) that we are more than just the world. We are microcosms of the universe. Our bodies are like mini universes, and the big universe around us is really just us in macro scale.

If this is true—and let's just postulate for a moment that it is—then nothing true or real can threaten us, harm us, or destroy our lives. Sure, things can affect and drastically change the course of—or even spell the end of—the lives we experience in these physical bodies. But our true life (our soul life), and our true self (our soul self) can't be hurt by anything that happens. Even if our energy transforms into something else after our bodies are gone, even when our energy no longer takes the shape of "us," it still remains intact as an essential ingredient of the universe.

And what can hurt the universe? The universe is everything, and the Earth is just a tiny, tiny portion of it. And it is us, so we are everything, and our physical bodies going through our daily lives are just a tiny, tiny portion of who we are. That's power. And that's also a fantastic opportunity.

You have the opportunity to make the most of your personal universe. You can ignore it, pretend it isn't there, even deny it or get angry at it. Or, you can live in it, watch it, love it, nurture it, experience it, and paint it with stars. The choice is up to you. We suggest you grab your paintbrush, lie down on the floor, and relax into meditation.

The Least You Need to Know

➤ Shavasana is the easiest yoga pose, physically, but also the most challenging because it involves true and total relaxation and a dissolving of the body and mind.

➤ Visualizations and breathwork can help to relax your body and mind to better facilitate meditating in shavasana.

➤ The quality of your existence is your own responsibility. You have the power to make it beautiful.

Mantras: Sacred Formulas to Live By

You've heard the word "Om" from us and probably from other sources. You might recognize it as something that someone repeats while meditating. But does it have any purpose other than being a point of focus for meditation? Is it no different than looking at a spot on the carpet or following your breathing during meditation? That's what we'll explore in this chapter.

The Meaning of Mantra

The sound Om is what is called a *mantra* in meditation. Actually, mantras are much more than points of concentration, although they do serve that purpose during meditation. Mantras also use the power of sound to cleanse the body and mind of negative thoughts and energy, invoke spiritual power, and even heal. Mantras can be chanted, spoken, sung, thought, and even written. They are powerful meditative tools you can use in your own meditation practice.

The mantra itself is a sound or collection of sounds, usually vowel-dominated, that create certain vibrations. Mantras can be like prayers or appeals to a higher power. They can be intense points of focus to bring the mind to single-mindedness. They can also be healing sounds projected toward others.

Chants: From Gregorian to Native American to Tibetan

Chanting is the most prevalent way to use a mantra, and it is common to virtually every world culture in one form or another. Not all traditions use the word "mantra," but repeating certain vowel sounds and an intense focus on the vibration of sound, called *harmonics*, and/or *overtones*, is a common thread in many of the mystical and occult traditions around the world.

Gregorian chanting, part of the tradition of the Catholic Church, makes use of sound vibrations, and overtones are audible in Gregorian chants. Sufis chant vowel sounds for spiritual communion and for healing. Chanting the names of God is part of Kabbalah. Shamans in Mongolia practice a tradition called *hoomi* (also *choomig* and *xoomij*), which is type of throat singing that produces overtones.

The Aborigines in Australia blow through an instrument to produce a sound with overtones similar to those made by chanting. Native American shamans chant using vowel sounds during their rituals. Tibetan Buddhist chanting is so advanced that some monks can produce a three-note chord with a single voice. Even the original religion of Tibet, called Bon (prior to the arrival of Buddhism from India) was based around chanting, and the word "bon" actually means "to chant" in Tibetan.

In Hinduism, mantras are thought to have originated with ancient seers, the mantras given to them as gifts from the divine spirit. These mantras have been passed down for millennia from guru to student, and when a guru gives a student a mantra, they must both chant that mantra throughout their lives—linking them together and also to that mantra's aspect of God. Repeating the mantra in the exact way, with unaltered melody and notes from the original, will preserve the mantra's incredible vibrational power to cleanse negative energy and put the chanter in direct communion with God. Each person supposedly has a mantra that is just right for him or her, which can be found or, ideally, given by that person's guru.

In Transcendental Meditation (TM), the meditator is given his or her own mantra after taking a class, and chanting that mantra is an integral part of TM. In Buddhism, chanting is used to focus the mind, and the Heart of Great Wisdom Sutra, a distillation of the Buddha's teachings, although really too long to be a mantra, is chanted by Buddhists worldwide.

In Tibetan Buddhism, mantras are charged with spiritual power, and chanting them releases this power. The more times a mantra is chanted, the stronger the spiritual energy. Tibetan prayer wheels contain large numbers of mantras written in very small letters on pieces of paper. Each spin of the prayer wheel is thought to be the equivalent of chanting the mantra as many times as it is written. For example, if a prayer wheel contains a mantra written 1,000 times, 10 spins of the prayer wheel would offer the same benefits as chanting the mantra 10,000 times.

Mindful Minute

When a mantra is spoken, it is known as Vaikhari Japa. When it is whispered or hummed, it is known as Upamsu Japa. When the mantra is repeated mentally but not spoken out loud, it is known as Manasika Japa. When the mantra is written, it is called Likhita Japa. In Likhita Japa, the mantra is sometimes written again and again in very small letters so that the words form a picture, making it an art form.

Chanting helps to prolong the exhalation of the breath, calms the mind, slows the heart, and after long periods, helps to bring the meditator into an alternate state of consciousness. Whether this is due to the effect on breathing, the effect of one-pointed thinking, the effect of the repetition, the vibrations of the mantra itself, or (most likely) a combination of the four hasn't been proven. Different traditions believe different things. But chanting or reciting mantras does seem to be a highly effective form of meditation for people of many beliefs, traditions, and cultures. It might be just the technique for you.

Six Aspects of Mantras, According to Mantra Yoga

Name	Description
Rishi	The ancient seer to whom the mantra was originally revealed thousands of years ago
Raga	The main melody line of the mantra, which should be imitated exactly to preserve the specific vibration of the mantra
Devata	The individual aspect of God associated with the mantra
Bija	The essence of the mantra that gives the mantra its energy
Kilaka	The force required by the yogi to persist in working with the mantra
Sakti	The dynamic creation energy released in the yogi through repetition of the mantra

Many mantras are Sanskrit words (like Om). Sanskrit is considered a sacred language because its sounds actually signify what they refer to—the vibration of the things represented by the sound. Om is actually thought to *be* the sound of the universe. But mantras don't have to be in a foreign language. Any word that contains spiritual meaning for you and feels right to you will work, especially if it is a word that has been repeated by many people throughout history (increasing, it is thought, the spiritual power of the word). Every word has its own meaning but also its own sound, its own vibrations. When meaning and vibration both resonate for you (something you may be able to sense intuitively), you've found your mantra! Some possibilities:

➤ Amen

➤ Shalom ("peace" in Hebrew, pronounced *shah-loam*)

➤ Hallelujah

➤ Hail Mary

➤ Ave Maria (pronounced *ah-vay mah-ree-ah*)

➤ Our Father

➤ Maranatha ("come to God, come to Jesus" in Aramaic, pronounced *mare-ah-nah-thah*)

➤ Love

➤ Yahweh (a Hebrew name for God, pronounced *Yah-way*)

➤ Sun

➤ Moon

➤ Allah (Islamic name for God, pronounced *Ah-la*)

➤ La ilaha ilia Allah ("there is no God but Allah"—the Sufi mantra used during ecstatic dance rituals; pronounced *lah ih-la-ha ih-lee-ah Ah-la*)

➤ Light (inhalation), love (exhalation). Love (inhalation), light (exhalation).

➤ One is all, all is one.

➤ Om, shanti, shanti, shanti ("all is peace, peace, peace"; pronounced *aum shahn-tee shahn-tee shahn-tee*)

Longer chants can also be used. According to some, longer chants are mantras, but according to others, a mantra shouldn't be more than you can keep in your mind at once. If you like the idea of a longer chant, look for short poems, hymns, prayers, Zen koans, or other

Mindful Minute

According to the yoga of sound, called Nada Yoga, the mantra you choose is very important because there is a particular sound vibration that corresponds with your spiritual nature. Your body will respond better to that vibration than to other vibrations, so the wrong mantra won't affect you, while the right mantra can have a profound spiritual impact. How do you find the right mantra? Either your spiritual teacher will give you the right mantra, or you'll know through intuition (the mantra that "seems right").

passages of writing, songs, prayers that resonate for you. Also, take up the reading of sacred texts from various cultures. The Bible, the *Yoga Sutras*, the *Tao Te Ching*, the *Kabbalah*, the Buddhist sutras, the *Tibetan Book of the Dead*, and the *Bhagavad Gita* (to name a few) are full of passages with mantra potential. Here's one from the Buddha:

> The thought manifests as the word;
> The word manifests as the deed;
> The deed develops into habit;
> And habit hardens into character.
> So watch the thought and its ways with care,
> And let it spring from love
> Born out of concern for all beings.

Bliss Byte

Try using beads to keep track of the number of times you chant a mantra, as do many meditators in a variety of traditions. In Hinduism, the chanter moves the beads between thumb and ring finger with each recitation of a mantra. A rosary is a string of beads divided into different groups, with different short prayers, such as in the Catholic faith with the Hail Mary, the Lord's Prayer, and the Fatima prayer, corresponding with each group (see Chapter 23, "Meditation Mix and Match: Adapting the Great Traditions").

Silence versus Sound

Don't forget the flip side of the mantra: silence. Silence can be just as powerful as the mantra itself and is indeed an integral part of practicing mantra meditation. Listening to the silence between mantras is like turning your awareness to the space between inhalations and exhalations of the breath. Silence has its own energy, and that energy can empower you if you tune in to it. If you've ever been alone in a soundproof room, you may have felt the energy of silence—surprising, strong, and capable of altering awareness. But how often are we truly present in silence? (And how often do we get to sit and meditate in a soundproof room?)

Try sitting in silence for a while before you begin reciting your mantra. Don't make a sound, just listen. Chances are you can hear something. What do you hear? Listening is a fine art, far different from hearing. Hearing happens. Listening requires mindfulness.

Are You Listening?

When you aren't used to cultivating your listening skills, you may find listening difficult. But listening can be a great way to meditate, and good listening skills can improve other areas of your life, too. For example, how often do you listen when someone talks to you? How focused are you on what they are saying? Are you waiting for your turn? Are you thinking about other things? Or are you really tuned in with complete mindfulness? When you learn to listen to what people say, you may be surprised at what you hear!

Bliss Byte

After repeating any mantra, spend time in silence. This silence is very important to allow the vibrational aspects of the mantra to settle within your stilled self where they will resonate through the chakras to stimulate and awaken them. Vibration and sound are intimately joined in the human body. To understand just how important vibration is, breathe in deeply and hum out one long consistent note. Feel the strong vibration in your throat at the Mercury chakra—the seat of communication. Consider how this sound is experienced by someone who is Deaf—the Deaf person will interpret and process the sound solely as vibration; they *feel* the sound. See how the quality and placement of the vibration changes as you hum different musical notes.

But even when no one is saying a word, you'll find much to hear. Try this meditative listening exercise to cultivate your listening skills before you try chanting a mantra:

1. Sit comfortably with your back straight, your legs crossed, and your hands open, palms up, on your knees (symbolizing openness and willingness to listen). Breathe a few deep breaths, then allow your breathing to become normal. Shift your awareness away from your breathing. Close your eyes so visual impressions don't mingle with sound impressions. Listen.

2. Don't analyze what you hear, simply listen. As you hear sounds, list them in your mind. If you don't know what they are, describe them. Let your awareness move freely from sound to sound to sound, nonjudgmentally, but mindfully. Don't preface the items on your list with "I hear…" because that involves an act and the ego. Your mental list might go something like this:

➤ Car driving by

➤ Bird singing

➤ Air from vents

➤ Refrigerator compressor

➤ Voices

➤ Distant music

➤ Heart beating

➤ Buzzing

➤ Whirring

➤ Whispers

➤ Computer hum

➤ Running water

➤ Breathing

Mindful Minute

According to French physician Alfred Tomatis, M.D., many of the cranial nerves lead to the ear, including a nerve that also affects the organs of speech and breathing, the heart, and the gastrointestinal tract. This suggests that a great many bodily functions could be affected by what we hear, including what sounds we are able to make.

3. Keep listening for 10 to 20 minutes, then open your eyes. Try to keep the sense of listening with you throughout your day. The more you practice this meditation, the keener and more sensitive your hearing will become. You'll hear sounds beneath sounds, layers of sounds, subtle sounds, barely audible sounds. You'll hear mindfully, and what you hear will take on more meaning.

Are You Really Listening?

Some people believe that you can train yourself to hear the harmonics, or overtones, of sounds. The more sensitive your hearing becomes and the more aware you become of layers and nuances of sound, the better you will be able to hear the sounds above sounds and above those sounds.

In some cases, overtones are easy to hear. In Gregorian chanting, when musical instruments are played a certain way, or in other types of singing, overtones sometimes pop out quite evidently. But according to some who have studied the subject, overtones exist for every tone, and hearing them is merely a matter of training the ear. (This type of training can be likened to training your eye to see auras.)

Conversely, the ability to produce harmonics and overtones is an art that supposedly can be taught. Monks of many faiths typically engage in chanting and singing, and some are able, through diligent practice and guidance, to produce audible harmonics with their voices (such as the one-voice chords produced by some Tibetan monks).

Healing Sounds

Mantras and other sound vibrations are also thought to have a healing effect on the body in two ways: Listening to harmonic tones and music induces a relaxed state and promotes healing, and chanting or singing harmonic tones produces a similar response.

One study showed that the repetition of a single word actually lowered blood pressure, slowed heart rate, reduced respiration rate, and calmed brain wave activity in the test subjects, increasing alpha waves (the brain waves associated with drowsiness, relaxed attention, and meditation states).

An interesting anecdote about the power of chanting involves a Benedictine monastery. A new abbot had the monastery's monks stop their six to eight hours of daily chanting, thinking the chanting served no purpose. Soon afterward, the monks became fatigued and depressed. Various doctors had suggested the monks change their diets and made other recommendations, but nothing worked. Finally, the leaders of the monastery approached the French otolaryngologist, Alfred Tomatis, M.D., who specialized in the study of ear function and of listening. Dr. Tomatis, who believed that the cortex of the brain is charged with energy via sound waves, suggested the monks return to chanting. Their symptoms soon disappeared, and they easily resumed their schedules, which included only four hours of sleep. Many sound researchers believe that disease is simply the body being "out of tune" and that sound can be used to tune the body so that it can heal. Some work with computers that produce specific sounds meant to heal, even to change the molecular structure of the human body. Some also believe that producing vocal sounds, especially using harmonics, combined with the intention to heal, will produce healing.

In Hinduism, the mantra *Hari Om* is the healing mantra. Hari (pronounced *ha-ree*) means "to take away" and Om (pronounced *ah-oh-m*, or *aum*) refers to the Hindu trinity of creation, preservation, and destruction. Hari Om calls on the preservation aspect of God to preserve health. Many traditions believe that reciting a mantra for someone who is sick will send healing vibrations into them, and that even chanting a mantra when you hear about someone who is sick or injured, even if you aren't with them or don't know them, will send healing energy their way. Such is the power of the mantra!

Resonating the Chakras

Many traditions also associate different sounds with each of the chakras. Sound researchers in the West have been studying the effects of various mantras and vowel sounds on the chakras, for healing, for energy, and for spiritual well-being. Chanting the correct sound can resonate within the chakra, helping to open it and free the energy.

Different traditions and researchers have associated different sounds with each of the chakras.

Chakra Sounds

According to both yoga philosophy and Tibetan Buddhism, each chakra contains a "seed sound" (or *biji*) associated with that chakra. These sounds can be used as mantras when meditating on the chakras. As you chant the sounds, allow them to vibrate into the chakra with which they are associated, and feel the sound vibration activating the energy of the chakra.

Although several Western researchers have developed their own systems for chakra sounds, the traditional Sanskrit sounds are as follows:

➤ Saturn chakra (at the base of the spine): LAM

➤ Jupiter chakra (lower abdomen): VAM

➤ Mars chakra (behind the naval): RAM

➤ Venus chakra (behind the heart): YAM

➤ Mercury chakra (in the throat): HAM

➤ Sun chakra (the third eye, in the middle of the brow): OM

➤ Thousand Petalled Lotus (the crown): OM

Creating Your Own Mantras

Maybe none of the mantras we've mentioned appeal to you. That doesn't mean you can't create your own. The best way to know if a mantra is right for you is to use your intuition. Does it feel right? Do you like the sound of it? Do you like to say it? Does it energize you or put you in a spiritual or reverent frame of mind? Does it make you feel good?

Listen for mantras as you go through your life. Listen for words, songs, and sounds that "strike a chord," so to speak. Or simply experiment with sounds using your own voice. What resonates for you? Which vibrations feel good?

Try the vowel sounds—A, E, I, O, U. Try variations—AH, AYE, EE, OH, OO. Try vowel sounds from other languages, sing simple melodies using vowel sounds, or, as we've said before, pick words you love. String them together in combinations. There is no harm in trying lots of different mantras, both established and of your own making. When you find one (or more) that you love, write them down, memorize them, keep them close to you.

Having trouble getting started? Try this create-your-own-mantra exercise:

Write down one word that begins with each of the following letters. The word should have a pleasant connotation to you and make you feel relaxed or invoke a beautiful or soothing image. For example, A: air, B: bliss, C: crystalline, D: dune. If you can't think of a good word for one of the letters, just fill in the word "one."

A: _____   N: _____

B: _____   O: _____

C: _____   P: _____

D: _____   Q: _____

E: _____   R: _____

F: _____   S: _____

G: _____   T: _____

H: _____   U: _____

I: _____   V: _____

J: _____   W: _____

K: _____   Y: _____

L: _____   Z: _____

M: _____

Now, make the following mantras by combining words on your list as follows:

| _____ | _____ | _____ | _____ | _____ |
| A word | C word | D word | T word | R word |

| _____ | _____ | _____ | _____ | _____ |
| E word | B word | G word | L word | P word |

| _____ | _____ | _____ | _____ | _____ |
| H word | I word | Z word | M word | O word |

| _____ | _____ | _____ | _____ | _____ |
| N word | S word | U word | C word | U word |

Now try your own combinations:

_____	_____	_____	_____	_____
_____	_____	_____	_____	_____
_____	_____	_____	_____	_____
_____	_____	_____	_____	_____

Some may come out sounding silly, some so-so, and some, perfection! We hope you find something perfect to add to your mantra repertoire.

Bliss Byte

Try focusing on the following sounds during meditation to help purify your mind of negative energy: waterfall, ocean waves, bells, the sound of the sea in a conch shell, thunder, echoes, bass drum, rainfall, whistling wind, or the sound of a flute. You say it isn't convenient to meditate by a waterfall, a beach, a rainforest, or in the vicinity of a talented musician? These sounds are widely available on CDs and tapes. Check your local enlightened bookstore or music store. Rolling meditation balls in your palm also makes a nice, cleansing sound for meditation, and releases extra tension, too.

Bells, Gongs, and Chimes

As long as we're on the subject of sound, chanting a mantra isn't the only way to use healing vibrations. Bells, gongs, and chimes can also help to dispel negative energy, both in your environment and in you. They can help to clarify and purify your thoughts in preparation for meditation and can serve as a periodic reminder to bring the mind back to stillness during meditation. (In fact, Vietnamese Zen master Thich Nhat Hahn suggests that whenever you hear any bell as you go through life, you can consider it a reminder to be mindful.) Meditation balls, those metal balls with chimes also used to exercise the hand muscles, also make a soothing sound that dissolves tension.

Bells, gongs, and chimes can also be beautiful additions to your personal altar and can clear the energy in a room before you meditate. Look for quality instruments that will last. Better materials make for more resonant and purifying vibrations. For example, a cheap aluminum bell won't sound nearly as beautiful or powerful as a bell made from silver, brass, bronze, or high-quality metal combinations.

Whatever your favorite meditation technique, don't neglect the power of sound for healing, spiritual renewal, and a direct line to the divine!

Meditation makes use of visual and auditory sources of focus for the mind-body, from the steady flame of the candle to the sound of a bell or chime sounded before, during, or at the end of your meditation session.

Chinese meditation balls make a soothing sound but also stimulate your sense of touch during meditation.

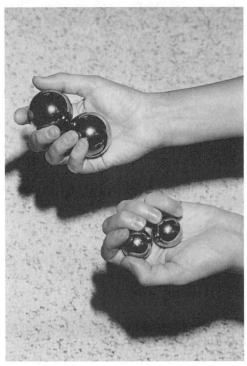

The Least You Need to Know

➤ Chanting and the repetition of certain words and syllables are traditions utilized by most major and many minor world religions and cultures.

➤ Silence is as powerful as sound, and both can be used during meditation.

➤ Sound has healing power as well as spiritual power.

➤ Sound can resonate the chakras, releasing chakra energy.

➤ You can use an existing mantra or create your own.

Part 6
More Ways to Meditate

As if you don't have enough options, in this next section we'll show you how to meditate with mandalas, those beautiful works of art traditional to Tibetan Buddhism and commonly used as meditation focal points. We'll show you how to find mandalas in the world around you, contemplate your own body as a mandala, even create your own mandala works of art.

Next, we'll introduce you to guided imagery and creative visualization, techniques that use the power of your imagination to help you fulfill your dreams and change your life. We'll show you how drawing, writing, and the sports you love can be forms of meditation. And last of all, we'll introduce you to meditation techniques from the great traditions of the world, from Europe and Africa to the Middle East and Native America, so you can find the method that works best and feels most right for you.

Chapter 20

Mandalas: The Circle of Life

In This Chapter

➤ Mandala meditation

➤ What mandalas mean: The circle of life

➤ How to make your own, personalized mandala

For the visually inclined, *mandala* meditation can be a welcome change from focusing on the breath or the repetition of a mantra. Mandalas are beautiful circular designs that can be used as a point of focus and for contemplation during meditation, but they are far more than pretty pictures. Mandalas are rich with symbolism and an important part of the sacred rituals of many cultures.

What Do Mandalas Represent?

Mandalas's circular designs represent the nature of both the universe (in macrocosm) and the body (in microcosm). Classic mandalas (such as the Cretan labyrinth) usually consist of seven or more concentric circles in quadrants aligned with the four directions, and contain a square center, often with a representation of a God or other symbol of purity or perfection.

Other mandalas are based on 11 circles (such as the labyrinth at Chartres cathedral in Paris and the elongated mandala of the Tree of Life from the Kabbalah). The Hopi medicine wheel is based on the number four, and Tibetan mandalas may have different numbers of circles, representing the chakras, for example, or the elements, or protective deities. Mandalas are archetypes. They appear in all cultures and all ages. The body itself is a sort of mandala, and so is the universe.

Mindful Minute

Tibet is located in the upper elevations of southwest China. Since 1965, the Tibetan government has been under the rule of Communist China. Tibet's Dalai Lama lives in exile in Dharamsala, India, where he presides over Tibetan Buddhism, as well as the Tibetan nation-in-exile. (See Chapter 27, "Om Away from Om: Spiritual Travel," for more about visiting sacred places.)

The culture most famous for its mandalas and one of the likely origins of the mandala as we know it today is Tibet. These days, Westerners are increasingly well-versed in Tibetan culture, as Tibetan Buddhism gains in popularity. With its emphasis on mindfulness and its colorful and decorative rituals, the mandala is perhaps the most characteristic symbol of Tibetan Buddhism.

In Tibet, mandalas are often painted on paper or dyed into cloth. An important part of the Tibetan monk initiation ritual is the formation of highly intricate, amazingly beautiful mandalas made by pouring colored sand on a flat surface with very fine tools (this takes about eight days). The ritual presents the mandala, the meditators, and other offerings to the guru, to the deity, and to the Three Jewels (the Buddha, the Buddha's teaching, and the community of monks). The ritual also involves purification, protection, and other basic elements of Tantric Buddhism initiation (the foundation of Tibetan Buddhism). Then, these spectacular works of transitory art are swept up, put into a jug clothed as adeity, and poured into the river.

Of course, you don't need to be entering a monastery to use a mandala. Meditators use mandalas or figures like them all over the world as a way to focus the attention. They all serve as an inspiration and a source of contemplation: What does the mandala say about who you are?

Planet Mandala: World Without End

But what do mandalas symbolize? Typically, a mandala consists of seven concentric circles divided into four quadrants, with openings on each side lined up with the four directions (north, south, east, and west). In the center of the mandala is a square, and in the square is a deity or other sign of purity or perfection.

Many variations on this basic structure exist. Some mandalas are simple circles with a sacred object in the center. Some are missing the four openings, some are even missing the sacred center object (which the meditator is then meant to project into the mandala as part of the meditation practice). Mandalas can be two-dimensional or three-dimensional, large or small, beautifully simple or beautifully complex. Mandalas can decorate walls, ceilings, or floors. They can be used to walk on or gaze at. But mandalas typically represent two things: the universe and the body.

A *yantra* is a figure similar to a mandala and the two are often confused and, in some representations, even combined. However, a yantra is primarily linear in nature, consisting of straight lines forming a roughly circular shape (rather than curved lines).

Yantras often have syllables or short written directions in the center, and unlike mandalas, which are often considered transitory constructions, yantras are often used repeatedly, sometimes as amulets or as diagrams to be buried in protection rituals.

The point of the mandala's dual representation of universe and body is this: The universe and the body are one and the same. In symbolizing both universe and body, the mandala brings this oneness to light. The universe and the human body

From A to Om

A **yantra** is a linear symbol similar to a mandala, often with a symbol or written words in the center.

have in common an inner center of divinity and successive outer layers retaining different qualities. (Remember the three bodies and the five sheaths of existence from Chapter 10, "Is Any Body Home?") The body is a microcosm of the universe, and the Buddhist representation of the universe has the general shape of a body.

Goin' Round in Circles

The circle itself—the mandala's primary shape—is an archetypal symbol, occurring in the art of cultures worldwide for thousands of years. Considered a sign of life, eternity and/or divinity in many cultures, the circle in both simple and complex forms is everywhere. Of course it is—because it's everywhere in nature (the sun; the moon; the Earth; a tree trunk; a tree canopy; stones; the sky; ripples of water around any object dropped into the water; spots on the leopard, on a butterfly, on a fish; etc.).

Although mandalas are thought to have originated in Tibet, China, or India, the depiction of circles is universal. Carl Gustav Jung, the Swiss psychologist we mentioned in Chapter 9, "Are You the Dreamer, or the Dream?" on dreams, believed that the circle was one of those deeply ingrained archetypes in the human collective unconscious. Jung interpreted the mandala's many circles as representing different aspects of the personality. Although he incorrectly mixed several traditions into his mandala interpretations (not being an expert on Tibetan Buddhism), he did understand their basic purpose: to help the meditator become aware of the divine within, which will free him or her from the illusion of individuality.

Many of the yoga mudras (hand positions; see Chapter 15, "Seated Meditation: Finding Center") bring the fingers or hands into a circle to redirect energy back into the body. On a much grander scale, many cities throughout the world employ a circular design, even placing the city's most respected or sacred spot in the center, like a mandala: Rome, Jerusalem, and Baghdad, to name a few.

Bliss Byte

In addition to the human body itself as mandala, many circles exist within the body. The Circle of Willis at the base of the brain equalizes cerebral circulation. The eyes, the nostrils, the open mouth, and the face itself are all roughly circular. The passage of oxygen into the lungs, into the blood, through the heart, back into the lungs, and out again is circular. Sit in stillness and feel the circle of life at work in your own body.

Circles are integral parts of religious traditions around the world. Although links between circles and the sacred are too numerous to mention, here are a few significant ones:

➤ Aztec calendars

➤ Navajo creation paintings

➤ Halos around angels

➤ Tibetan prayer wheels

➤ Depictions of the four elements from many cultures

➤ Depictions of the four directions from many cultures

➤ Earth itself

And the list goes on.

Mindful Minute

Even the hard drive of your computer is a circle. If you store mantras on the hard drive of your computer, your hard drive can serve as a kind of prayer wheel, spinning the mantra and purifying your home. Why not make use of technology for spiritual ends?

Circle of Life: Beyond the Lion King

Many cultures have many versions of the concept of the circle of life. We are born, we live, we die, we are reborn. Or, we are born, we live, we die, we become part of the Earth, which in turn provides nourishment for new life. Parents bring children into the world, then the children become parents, then their children become parents. We are spirit, then flesh, then spirit. Whatever your personal version, few can deny life has a distinctly cyclical nature.

Native American Medicine Wheels

The Native American medicine wheel is another sacred circle meant to represent the circle of life. In Native American culture, the word "medicine" refers not to pharmaceuticals, but to anything that helps to grow the soul, leading to higher self-knowledge and awareness. Medicine wheels are circles made from stones or other natural materials that attract spiritual energy. They contain sacred points, such as the four directions or the elements. To meditate inside a medicine wheel is to create a sacred space, a mandala for which you are the center.

You can create your own medicine wheel mandala, outdoors or indoors, for use during meditation. Go into your yard or another outdoor place where you can collect stones. Walk around and look for stones that feel or look special to you. Collect four large stones (not so large that you can't carry them) and between four and 16 smaller stones. You can also collect other natural materials—pine cones, beautiful leaves, feathers, bits of coral, seashells, fossils, wood, and flowers.

Bliss Byte

Labyrinth mandalas (see Chapter 16, "Walking Meditation: Peace Is Every Step") painted on canvas are being used in hospitals and other health care facilities with phenomenal results. Patients and staff alike walk the winding paths to the center of the mandalas and out again. Some feel utterly transformed, others just incredibly relaxed. The labyrinth mandala walk seems to have a particularly positive effect on patients with mental health problems.

Plant a stake in the ground tied with a string of between three and six feet long, so your circle will be perfect. Place one stone at the northernmost point of the circle, one at the southernmost point, another at the easternmost point, and another at the westernmost point. Fill in the rest of the circle's border with your other stones and natural items, using the string as a guide.

Now, enter your circle from the east and walk to the center of your circle. Ask a blessing from each of the four directions, facing each direction as you ask. Each direction is associated with an element, so you might say something like:

➤ Spirit of the East, spirit of air, bless this circle that it may be sacred.

➤ Spirit of the South, spirit of water, bless this circle that it may be healing.

➤ Spirit of the West, spirit of fire, bless this circle that it may be purified.

> ➤ Spirit of the North, spirit of earth, bless this circle that it may impart inner strength.

Now, sit in the center, facing whichever direction seems right for your needs at the moment (for example, if you need strength, face north; if you need healing, face south). Sit with mindful awareness and allow nature to speak to you.

You can also make a small medicine wheel for the inside of your house, which you can use as a point of focus during meditation, just as you would a mandala. On any flat, clean surface, place a circle of natural items (they may remain more stable if you first cover the surface with sand or moss). You can leave the center open or fill it with a crystal, beautiful shell, or other meaningful object.

Use the medicine wheel in a way that feels right for you. Following your instincts is more important than exactly replicating a tradition from another culture. Focus on the sacred and eternal nature of the circle and let the circle's wisdom guide you.

The Outer Mandala: The Universe

In Tibetan Buddhism, the mandala is thought to represent the cosmos. Three-dimensional mandala models reveal the Buddhist idea of all of creation. Although models differ in their construction, most have a few things in common. The base of the cosmos consists of circles or disks lined up with the four directions (north, south, east, and west) and stacked vertically. The highest point of the structure is the most sacred point and the base of the structure is the most mundane point (and in some representations, depicts the eight hot and eight cold layers of hell, not unlike Dante's *Inferno*). The top of the three-dimensional mandala structure has the rough shape of a head with a pointed topknot, representing the universe as roughly human-shaped.

Mindful Minute

Buddhists place the human-inhabited Earth along the margins of the cosmos. The center of the cosmos is occupied by the gods. The cosmos is structured like the human body, and through meditation, one attempts to return to the center of all things, where divinity lives.

The Inner Mandala: YOU

Just as the cosmos is shaped like a body, so is the body structured like the cosmos. The body itself is considered to be a mandala in the Tibetan tradition. In fact, the three-dimensional mandala can be overlaid on a picture of the human body to show the correspondence. The disks forming the base of the mandala ring the feet, lower legs, upper legs, and hips, forming the realms of air, fire, water, and earth. The torso represents the realm of the chakras and the energy that moves through them, containing the potential for enlightenment. The head is the center and uppermost point of the mandala, minutely centered around the third eye.

Other representations of the body as mandala have also been formulated. One model, for example, demonstrates the movements of the different energies and bodily fluids through the body's meridians in a pattern that resembles a mandala. Also consider the layers of subtle bodies in yoga philosophy (see Chapter 10), the aura (see Chapter 8, "Energy Central"), or even your eyes, those mandala-like windows to your soul. The subject is interesting to study, but to consider yourself a mandala, all you need to know is that you are a sort of energy spiral and your deepest, truest, most spiritual self lies in your center. Through meditation, you can wind your way inside and discover that center.

Relax

If your head is spinning trying to understand the sacred history and theory behind mandalas, relax! Mandalas are meant to be visually grounding and calming. Go look at one for a while and you'll see what we mean.

Creating Your Personalized Mandala

You don't have to be a talented painter or skilled with the intricate tools Tibetan monks use to create their sand mandalas to create your own personal mandala. Although you can probably find beautiful representations of mandalas in books, on posters, on tapestries, or from other sources, a mandala you make yourself can mean more and hold more spiritual power than the most intricate and artful construction in the world.

To make your own mandala, tape a blank sheet of paper on a flat, hard surface, or use a photocopy of our mandala template, below. If you aren't using our template, draw a large perfectly round circle, either by tracing something circular or by tying a string to a pin in the center of the page and tying the other end to a pencil (or use a drawing compass). Using the center of the circle for a guide, measure points one to two inches or more (depending on how big your circle is) above, below, to the right, and to the left of the center. Using a ruler, connect the points to form a square in the center of the circle. Next, bisect the circle vertically and horizontally so it is divided into quadrants.

Now you have your mandala outline. The center can contain a picture, symbol, or mantra that is sacred and meaningful to you and your personal quest. The rest of the mantra can be decorated in whatever way you like, whether you decide to fill it with ornamental concentric rings or simply fill it with a solid color. Give it a border, make designs or pictures at each outer corner, whatever moves you. Don't worry about making it artistically impressive. This is a personal project, for your eyes only if that's the way you want it. Use color, or not. Use rulers and stencils, or not. Use stickers, paints, markers, cut out pictures from magazines, or just a plain black pencil. Make several. Make a whole book of them, if you like. (And check out Chapter 22, "The Art and Sport of Meditation," to see how creating art can be a meditation in itself.) Then, when you have created your own personal mandala (or two or three...), place it on your altar, frame it and hang it on the wall in your meditation room, or, as we suggested, create a book full of your mandala art to use in your meditation practice.

Photocopy this template and use it to create your own mandala. Simple or intricate, let your mandala creation reflect your own spiritual nature. You are the artist!

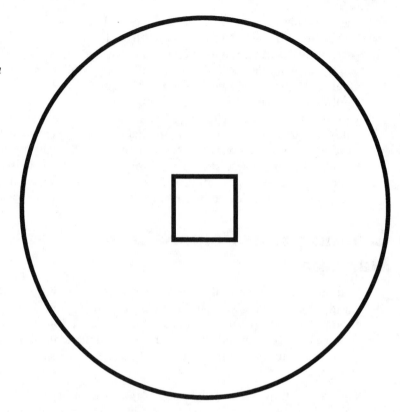

Bliss Byte

Remember the "Magic Eye" art, that huge fad from a few years back? First you see an evenly patterned design, but if you stare just right, your vision shifts and you see a three-dimensional picture. These are a sort of pop-culture, modern mandala. They induce an intense state of focus and concentration, and some are surprisingly beautiful, too, in their own way (though they are computer-generated, quite unlike the painstaking sand art of Tibetan monks).

Meditating on the Circle

Meditating using a mandala can take several forms. You can contemplate the mandala in your mind: the universe as mandala, the self as mandala, or the universe as the self, and vice versa. You can sit inside a mandala, such as a medicine wheel. You can walk the winding course of a mandala, as in a labyrinth, whether in Chartres Cathedral or on a painted canvas (see Chapter 16), symbolically travelling to the center of yourself. Or you can place or hang a picture of a mandala in front of you.

Using a pencil, trace the path of the Chartres Cathedral labyrinth.

To use a mandala as a visual point of focus during meditation, make sure the mandala is easily viewed from your meditation position. Ideally, it should be four to six feet away from you at eye level if it is a large (poster-sized) mandala, or directly in front of you on the ground if it's smaller, in which case you can look down at it. Depending on the nature of your mandala, you can:

➤ Gaze at the mandala's center.

➤ Travel the winding paths (in labyrinth-types) with your eyes.

➤ Look at the edges and let the mandala draw your eyes naturally toward the center.

➤ Look at the entire picture and contemplate how it represents you and your spiritual search.

➤ If you have created your own mandala with a yantra-like mantra or affirmation in the center, you can gaze at the center while repeating the words written there.

➤ Or simply contemplate the mandala's beauty and mindfully await impressions or guidance that may come to you.

However you choose to use mandalas, they can be a beautiful, symbolic, inspiring, and sacred addition to your meditation practice.

The Least You Need to Know

➤ Mandalas are an integral part of Tibetan Buddhism.

➤ Mandalas come in many forms, from simple circles to highly intricate artwork.

➤ The circle is a symbol of life, eternity, and divinity in many cultures and can be considered an archetype, or common symbol, to all of humankind.

➤ Mandalas represent the cosmos in macrocosm and the human body in microcosm, symbolizing how the two are one and the same.

➤ You can design your own personal mandala to use in your meditation practice.

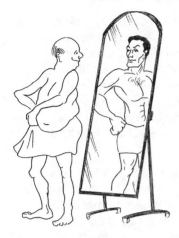

Chapter 21

Seeing Is Believing: Guided Imagery and Creative Visualization

In This Chapter

➤ The difference between imagining and doing

➤ How to reawaken your imagination

➤ Taking a tour of the inner you

➤ Fine-tuning your visualization power

Remember "The Little Engine That Could"? He was just a little engine, but when he saw that steep hill ahead of him, a seemingly impossible obstacle, he kept telling himself, "I think I can, I think I can, I think I can," and he pulled all his train cars over the hill. You know the moral: The power of positive thinking and all that.

But positive thinking can go further than simply telling yourself "I think I can." Seeing yourself accomplishing the things you want to accomplish may actually bring those things into your reach.

Our human brains are storehouses of potential. Who knows what our human limits are when it comes to accomplishing the amazing? We haven't discovered them yet. So what is holding you back from having the life you always wanted, being the person you dream of being? Only your mind holds you back. If you can retrain your mind so that it pushes you forward you can do anything. In this chapter, we'll show you how.

The Power of Thought to Transform Reality

Perhaps you're skeptical. "How," you ask yourself, "can thinking actually change the nature of reality?" Well, first of all, we aren't saying that if you concentrate on that spoon in your hand it will suddenly bend in two or that you can make a chair slide across the floor simply by staring with all your might. But changing your life, improving your health, finding personal happiness and success, becoming your ideal self—these things are far more complex and affected by far more factors than a spoon or a chair. Humans are also so complex that it would be virtually impossible to break down every factor involved in why someone is happy and someone else isn't, or why someone is sick and someone else is healthy.

If you get a cold, for example, you might say, "Oh, it's because my daughter brought it home from school," or "If that client hadn't sneezed in my face, I wouldn't have this cold!" Sure, cold germs may have been introduced into your system in one of these ways. But why wasn't your immune system able to fight it off? Your child's teacher isn't sick. Your business partner got sneezed on, too, but she's feeling great.

Bliss Byte

Start directing your thoughts and energies toward realizing your goals and dreams for the future. Doing something as simple as writing down a list or chart containing your goals for the week, the month, and/or the year will trigger amazing creative processes within yourself that will help you make your goals a reality. Don't be afraid to dream big dreams, either: As long as you're honest with yourself and realize that it will take work to reach your goals, the power of your mind can get you started on the right path.

And how often do you find a way to blame yourself for that cold? Sure, you got the cold. But now what are you going to do about it? Did you think as soon as you saw your daughter's runny nose that you'd surely catch a cold *again*? Although it's hard to prove (or disprove), your attitude and your thoughts about yourself and your life may actually have a subtle (or not-so-subtle) effect on your immune system. How can you take advantage of this relationship?

Thinking in a positive way and visualizing in a positive, pleasant, and life-affirming manner may help you to ward off complications of that cold (pneumonia, bronchitis, ear infection), may speed your healing, and if nothing else, will make your cold seem a whole lot more bearable.

Although it's true that some things are definitely beyond your control, recent research indicates that the way you think and feel at any given moment has specific physical effects on your body and soul. Simply changing your thinking in favor of a positive outcome could dramatically increase your mind-body's healing power. Please do remember that *no one* is responsible for bringing on their own illnesses; we don't want you to feel you need to take the blame or responsibility for getting that cold. What we *do* want you to do is to use your mind's natural healing power to send beneficial thoughts and messages that will speed your body's return to health—and your mind-body's return to a state of balanced well-being.

Mindful Minute

An affirmation is a verbalized desire stated in positive terms. Affirmations are most effectively stated in terms of the present, such as "I open myself to the joy and happiness of life," or "Thank you patience, for teaching me your lesson." Repeating affirmations on a daily, even an hourly, basis can significantly influence your reality. If you change your mind, you change your life.

Welcome to the Imagi-Nation

Remember what an important part of your life imagination played when you were a child? Adults tend to underestimate the power of the imagination, and thus neglect to exercise their imaginations like they did as children. What a waste! Adult life sometimes leaves little time or space for indulging your more fanciful instincts, but your imagination is an amazing resource that can change your life for the better—including making it a whole lot more fun!

If you haven't visited the imagi-nation lately, however, you may find that you don't remember your way around. Before you launch into *guided imagery* or *creative visualization*, get your imagination back in shape with a few simple exercises. Think like a kid again, and with some practice, you'll be ready for some serious visualization work.

Try one of the following exercises every day for two weeks:

➤ Go outside on a clear day, spread a blanket on the lawn, lie on your back, and look at the clouds. What do you see? Animals? People? Monsters? Castles? Angels?

➤ Set aside 20 minutes for daydreaming. If you could be anybody in the world, just for a day, who would you be? What would it be like?

From A to Om

Guided imagery is meditation facilitated by another person (or your own voice on a tape). **Creative visualization** is a one-person affair in which the meditator imagines that the conditions or things he or she desires are already manifest, helping to bring those conditions into being.

➤ Did you ever have an imaginary friend? Invent one! We can all use another friend to talk to now and then, especially one who is such a good listener. Imagine your friend, then talk—pour out your heart!

➤ Suck on a piece of hard candy. Really concentrate on the candy, its taste, and texture. Make it last as long as you can. And if you can't resist that temptation to bite down, really experience and enjoy that burst of flavor that comes along with it!

➤ Go to a local park and swing on the swings.

Mindful Minute

A 1998 study printed in *Alternative Therapy Journal* showed that relaxed attention to oneself via relaxation techniques, meditation, and imagery techniques enhanced connectivity between the brain and the body.

➤ Rake leaves and jump in the pile. Or shovel snow and jump in that pile. Make a snowman. Build a fort. Wear red mittens!

➤ Walk around your house on your hands and knees. What different perspective do you get? Next, walk around your house looking down into a hand-held mirror pointed at the ceiling. Pretend you are walking on the ceiling.

➤ Pretend you are your favorite animal. How would you move? What sound would you make? What would you do all day? Try moving like your favorite animal. (This is a great game to play with kids.)

➤ Take a walk and imagine you are hiking through a foreign land. Imagine everthing familiar is something exotic and new. Or imagine you are a foreigner seeing your neighborhood for the first time.

➤ Play with kids. If you run out of ideas for imaginative games, they'll always be able to think of more.

Guided Imagery: A Self Tour

Guided imagery allows you to get inside yourself. With the help of a voice that tells your mind where to go, you can explore your inner landscape like a pioneer. Your mind-body can reveal a lot of information if you are willing to listen. In fact, it may just be waiting for you to pay attention.

In the following guided imagery meditations, either have a trusted friend read the script for you (after which you can reciprocate the favor) or tape your own voice. Read slowly in a soothing voice, pausing where it seems appropriate, or where you see an ellipses ("…") in the script.

Introduction to Yourself

This first guided imagery experience is a good introduction to guided imagery. Think of it as an "imagination warm-up."

Close your eyes and breathe deeply. Let your breath fill you with peace, and breathe out tension with every exhalation until you feel very relaxed…

Now, think of a place that is special to you, a place where you feel comfortable, secure, and loved. It can be a place you have been many times or a place that exists only in your imagination. Imagine yourself in that place. See the place in your mind. What do you see around you? What colors and shapes do you see? What textures can you feel? What aromas do you smell? Do you hear sounds? Let yourself observe the place with all your senses for a moment, feeling safe, secure, and comfortable…

Now, from that place, imagine yourself getting up and walking. Walk through your place until you see a large oak door. You can see white light glowing around the door. Walk up to the door and open it to reveal a beautiful, glowing light. Step into it and walk through it. As you step through the light, you see you are now on a white beach and the ocean is a brilliant sapphire blue. You are standing among some small dunes dotted with sea oats and pink flowers. You walk through the dunes and onto the beach itself. The sand is soft and warm. The sun is warm on your skin, and a light breeze gently caresses you. You walk along the line of the surf, and friendly waves foam around your feet. The water is warm, too. You look out over the ocean, and the pale blue sky seems to merge with the bright blue sea so that you can hardly tell where they meet.

Far off in the sea, you see a school of dolphins jumping high into the air. A flock of bright white pelicans soars high above you. It is just you and nature. Look around. Feel the place with all your senses…

Then you see another door, set into a sand dune. Curious, you walk back up the beach and open the door. Again you see the white light. You walk into the light and as you step out of it, you hear the rustle of leaves underfoot. You are in a beautiful forest of tall green trees. In front of you is a winding, leaf-covered path. You walk slowly down the path, looking around.

Sunlight filters through the leaves and dapples the path with light. Wind plays in the leaves, and their gentle rustle soothes you. Somewhere nearby you hear the sound of water. The path veers off to the right, and you follow it down to a brook filled with smooth, colored stones. Along the banks are bluebells, and a stately weeping willow tree dangles its fronds into the water. Water splashes and tumbles over the stones. A few large stones protrude from the water. Using them as stepping stones, you step easily across the brook.

The path continues up the opposite bank, and then the forest opens into a bright green glade. The grass is covered with a sea of yellow daffodils. Carefully, you walk through the glade and sit in the middle of the flowers. The trees surrounding the glade are a silvery green in the light. You sit and take in the place using all your senses…

Then you see a little house on the other side of the glade. You get up, walk over to it, and open the door. You walk through the familiar white light and find yourself back in that place you love. You smile, happy to be home. You lie back, relax, close your eyes, and think about the beautiful places you have been today. Then slowly, when you are ready, open your eyes.

Bliss Byte

If visualizing is hard for you, perhaps one of your other senses might work better. For example, hold a flower, close your eyes, and stroke the petals. Stay with the feelings that come from this. Or smell the flower and let the fragrance linger silently in your mind, bringing forth whatever impressions it might. If you have a hard time visualizing in images, just allow yourself to feel the instructions in any way that makes sense to you. You don't have to "see" them.

The Self-Healing Body

The next guided imagery exercise is for those of you who are ill, injured, or need any type of physical healing. You're more intuitive about what is going on in your body than you might realize, so give your body a chance to tell you what is wrong and what you should do about it. Again, lie back comfortably, relax, breathe, and close your eyes.

Close your eyes and breathe deeply. Let your breath fill you with peace, and breathe out tension with every exhalation until you feel very relaxed…

Now think of that special place where you feel comfortable and loved. It can be a place you have been many times or one that exists only in your imagination. Imagine yourself in that place. See the place in your mind. What do you see around you? What colors and shapes do you see? What textures do you feel? What aromas do you smell? Do you hear sounds? Let yourself observe the place with all your senses for a moment, feeling safe, secure, and comfortable…

Now turn your attention inward. Ask your body to continue to relax. You are safe here and have no reason to hide anything. Imagine that your body has its own consciousness. Ask it "What is wrong?" Listen. Imagine your body responding. What part of you wants to talk? Your stomach? Your head? Your knee? Your heart? Keep listening until part of your body stirs and speaks to you…

Ask the part of you that is speaking how it feels. Is it in pain? Is it angry with you? Is it feeling neglected? Are you paying too much attention to it? Listen for what it wants to tell you...

Ask it what it wants you to do. Does it want you to leave it alone? Does it need medical attention? Does it need you to stop ignoring it? Does it need some TLC? Does it need you to eat better, to nourish it, or exercise more, to allow it movement? Listen for what it wants to tell you...

Now imagine yourself speaking to your body. Tell it you are sorry you haven't been listening. Tell it you will now do what it requires so it can heal. Make a promise to nurture your body in the way it needs you to nurture it. Feel loving kindness toward your body. Thank it. Thank yourself. Breathe, reflect on what you have learned about yourself, then slowly open your eyes.

The Happiness Trip

Guided imagery can also help you to confront the emotional issues in your life that are keeping you from being happy. Try this guided imagery exercise when you feel low self-esteem or that your life has gone off-course.

Relax

Don't rely on guided imagery to cure your medical problem. The mind is powerful, but you can't expect to know how to use that power immediately, without years of practice. Guided imagery can help to point you in the right direction and can help to make subtle shifts in your health and healing processes, but if your symptoms disturb your daily life or otherwise alarm you for any reason, please visit your health practitioner as soon as possible. Don't ignore your body's signals because you are trying to do everything with your mind!

Close your eyes and breathe deeply. Let your breath fill you with peace, and breathe out tension with every exhalation until you feel very relaxed...

Now think of a place where you feel comfortable and secure. It can be a place you have been many times or one that exists only in your imagination. Imagine yourself in that place. See the place in your mind. What do you see around you? What colors and shapes do you see? What textures do you feel? What aromas do you smell? Do you hear sounds? Let yourself observe the place with all your senses for a moment, feeling safe, secure, and comfortable...

Imagine yourself standing up because you hear someone coming. You feel a sense of happy anticipation as you hear the small footsteps of a child coming toward you. Suddenly, a little child appears. You smile at the child, step forward, and it reaches its hands up for your embrace. You take the child into your arms and give it a long, loving hug...

Now you put the child down and together you walk, hand in hand, through your safe place. You show the child around and explain why the place is special to you. The child listens with interest, then the two of you sit together. Suddenly, the child begins to weep softly. "What's wrong?" you ask with concern, stroking the child's hair. The child crawls into your lap and, feeling ultimately safe, begins to tell you. Listen. What does the child say?...

Think about what the child has told you. Then take the child in your arms again, hold it close to you, and promise the child that everything will be okay. No matter what has happened, you are here now, and as an adult, you have greater control of your life. Promise the child you will take care of it from now on and that nothing in the past can hurt it anymore. Promise it the love, the safety, the security, and the attention it may not have gotten before. All that is over. You are in charge now. Promise the child. Promise yourself...

The child looks up at you with a smile, and you know everything will be fine. The child leans toward you and whispers in your ear: "It's me!" You look closely at the child's face and you realize that the child is you, as a child. You smile because it makes so much sense that this child is you. As the child stands, kisses you on the cheek, says thank you, and skips away, you know you will see this child again soon. Take a few moments to contemplate all you have learned, then open your eyes.

Mindful Minute

Until the 1850s, only half of the children in the United States reached five years of age. Today, almost 98 percent surpass the age of five and live to adulthood.

Creative Visualization: You Are What You See

Creative visualization is a lot like guided imagery except you do it on your own, without the help of an outside voice to guide you. Creative visualization is a little like a full-color, three-dimensional daily affirmation. Instead of beginning each day by saying "Every day in every way I'm getting better and better," or whatever other daily affirmations you may have heard, creative visualization helps you to see and experience yourself "better and better," with the help of your imagination.

The purpose behind creative visualization is to change your thinking and, by changing your thinking, change your life. Use the following visualization exercises below as springboards and fill them in with your own hopes, goals, dreams, aspirations—in other words, shape these exercises so they follow the path of your own personal evolution.

Bliss Byte

Daily affirmations can be like a "quickie" visualization. Try repeating any of the following 10 times each morning:

I am becoming happier. The core of my being is at peace. Each experience I have is an opportunity for greater growth. There are no mistakes in life, only lessons. I forgive all who have hurt me. I forgive myself for all I have hurt. I go forth in love and peace. I embrace the universe. I send loving thoughts to all human beings and wish for their happiness and well-being.

You're Already Living Your Dream!

First, make a list, and not just in your head—write this list on paper. At the top of your list, write a short paragraph describing your dream (or one of your dreams). Be specific. For example, you might write, "I want to be running my own business within two years," "I want to have a healthy, strong body," "I want to become an architect," or "I want to learn to paint." If you have more than one dream (as most of us do), concentrate on just one until you reach it, to keep your energies concentrated.

Next, list seven things you can do to get you to your dream. For example, "Save money for business capital," "Take a yoga class," or even "Move to Paris and spend my days painting on the Left Bank." Now you've got a week's worth of visualizations!

Each day, pick one item on your list, set a timer for 20 minutes, relax, sit comfortably, close your eyes, and visualize yourself living your dream. For example, say your ultimate dream is to be healthy, in-shape, strong, and confident. Perhaps you feel your lack of confidence lies in your lack of health or strength, or your weight. Your list might contain the following items:

➤ Eat only fresh, healthy foods

➤ Take a walk in the fresh air every day

➤ Learn yoga

➤ Devote 30 minutes each morning to personal care

➤ Get a massage

➤ Find friends who are working toward the same goals

➤ Meditate every day

317

For each item, imagine every detail required to carry out that step toward your dream. For instance, on the first day, you might imagine yourself eating a delicious fresh salad, a bowl of strawberries, or a steaming vegetable stew. Imagine your health improving, your energy rising, your body becoming healthier and stronger. Imagine the new "healthier you" going through life eating well. Then the next day, visualize the new you walking in all kinds of different places. The day after that, imagine yourself in your new yoga class. Visualize performing the yoga poses, getting to know the teacher, etc. You get the picture.

The point is to personalize your visualization and to perform it every day. If you think it, it *can* come true. If you think it all the time, it *will* come true. You can make it happen.

Everything You Ever Wanted

What do you want? Health? Wealth? Love? Success? Happiness? Beauty? All of the above? Creative visualization can help you to achieve everything you ever wanted. No, it won't magically cause you to win the lottery or reconstruct your flawed nose. But it can subtly change your thought processes, which will change your motivations and actions, which will change your energy, which will attract good fortune and repel bad fortune.

Every morning before you get out of bed and every night before you go to sleep, spend 10 to 20 minutes visualizing yourself with everything you ever wanted. Imagine yourself living in your dream house, maintaining your ideal weight, becoming an overnight business success, falling in love with the perfect mate, being in perfect health. Imagine all the details. How do you look? How do your surroundings look? What do you do? What do you say? Don't waste time during these visualization sessions worrying about how impossible the vision is or how you couldn't possibly attain it. Expend your energy on nothing but the richly detailed visualization of you with your dreams fulfilled.

Interestingly, the more you practice creative visualization, the more you may find that what you really want is different than what you thought you wanted. For example, maybe you think you want great wealth. Money is certainly a handy thing to have, especially if you're usually in short supply. But the more you imagine having a lot of money, including all the details, implications, and effects, the more you might become bored. So you can buy whatever car you want—so what? What else is there?

Eventually, your visualizations may take on a more spiritual tone. You'll imagine yourself truly happy, truly content, truly interested in the world around you and humankind's spiritual quest. You'll be more concerned with achieving the dreams for the inner you rather than the outer you.

But you can achieve them all—the inner goals and the outer goals—as long as they are truly important to you. We aren't saying it is easy, but if you are committed enough to visualize every day, you will become committed enough to adjusting your life in ways that will make your dreams come true. Visualization helps you to define your dreams, pinpoint your goals, and work out strategies for achievement—even without realizing it on a conscious level. Commit yourself to creative visualization, and watch your life transform. Before you know it, the only thing left to visualize will be reality!

Bliss Byte

Claims have been made that we use only about 10 percent of our brains. The left side of our brains is logic-oriented, the right side is artistic- and intuitive-oriented. Where does the majority of your 10 percent lie? Think about the way you tend to see things. Do you remember how to get from place to place because you have a sense of where to go (right-brained) or because you remember landmarks or directions (left-brained)? Do you enjoy poetry (right-brained) or learning languages (left-brained)? Are you more intuitive (right-brained) or logical (left-brained)? Wherever your tendencies, make a habit to try to develop those parts of you that don't come quite as easily and you'll be more balanced. And whatever your inclinations, remember that you've still got a heck of a lot of brain power left (or right)!

Seeing the Light: Candle and Flame Meditation

Using the imagination is easier for some than others, but everyone can improve their "mind's eye" by training their physical eyes. One way to strengthen your eyes is through a special kind of meditation using a candle or a flame.

In yoga, this meditation is called *trataka*. To perform this meditation, light a candle and sit about two feet away, with the flame at or slightly below eye level. Be sure to sit far enough away that you can look at the flame easily without feeling cross-eyed. Blink several times to moisten your eyes and fix your gaze on the flame. Concentrate on this visual point of reference and acknowledge and then dismiss any other thoughts that come to mind. Look at the flame for as long as you can without blinking. (If the room is drafty and the flame won't stay lit, try this exercise substituting a paper with a large dot—about $1^1/_2$ inches in diameter—taped to the wall.)

Joan demonstrates the focused concentration of meditating on a single steady point of light in a candle flame.

From A to Om

Trataka is a yogic eye exercise/ meditation involving gazing at a candle or flame and designed to strengthen the inner vision.

When your eyes begin to water and you must blink, go ahead, then resume your gaze. The first time you try trataka, you'll probably only be able to go for a minute or so before you have to blink, but the more you practice, the longer you'll be able to last, and the stronger your eyes will become. Keep this up for 10 to 20 minutes, then rinse your eyes with cool water or a light saline solution.

According to yoga literature, trataka strengthens the inner vision and sometimes even induces *clairvoyance*, the ability to perceive things not in the physical realm. You might also like to practice trataka in front of a larger flame, such as a fireplace or a campfire. Through the ages, monks and spiritual sages have worked with the dawning sun this way. At about 5:30 a.m. when the sun rises, it is not yet strong enough to hurt the eyes. Meditative reflection and focus on the rising sun can lead to spiritual insight.

Creating the Mood: Aromatherapy and Meditation

A truly relaxed state and a feeling of safety and security is essential for guided imagery and creative visualization. To help create a soothing atmosphere, try a little *aromatherapy*. Aromatherapy is the therapeutic use of essential oils for healing, calming, energizing, and relaxation. Essential oils can be applied to the skin, as in massage, inhaled, or diffused into the air, which is the ideal method for meditation.

Essential oils can be diffused into the air of your meditation room via several methods. For a low-tech method of diffusion, you can purchase a metal ring consisting of a shallow trough that fits around the top of a light bulb. Fill the ring with oil, turn on the light, and as the ring warms, the essential oil warms, filling the room with fragrance. For a high-tech and highly efficient option, an essential oil diffuser permeates the room and doesn't alter the oil through heating. Proponents claim that everyone in a home where a diffuser is operating (even pets!) will be pleasantly calmed, relaxed, or energized, depending on the oil being used.

Essential oils can be purchased at natural-food stores, bath stores, certain specialty stores, or via mail-order. The following oils are good choices for use in a diffuser or a light-bulb ring during meditation or to spritz around your altar with an atomizer:

From A to Om

Clairvoyance is the psychic ability to perceive things that can't be seen physically.

From A to Om

Aromatherapy is the therapeutic use of essential oils, either applied to the skin or inhaled, for healing and mood alteration. Essential oils are aromatic oils distilled from plant sources such as flowers, leaves, and bark. Pure essential oils are produced by steam distillation. Different scents are thought to have different effects on the mind–body.

For Calming	For Energizing
Bergamot	Eucalyptus (*E. globulus*)
Cedarwood	Fir
Eucalyptus (*E. citriodora*)	Grapefruit
Frankincense	Jasmine
Lavender	Juniper
Mandarin	Lemon
Myrrh	Lemongrass

continues

continued

For Calming	For Energizing
Orange	Patchouli
Rosewood	Peppermint
Tea tree	Pine
Yarrow	Rosemary
Ylang ylang	Spearmint

We hope you've found some inspiring and creative (and aromatic) ways to reawaken your imagination and make it work for you. We are strong advocates of the cultivation of imagination. How easy it is to forget what power we have—the awesome power of a child at play. What better role model could we find? Who could be happier, more content, and more fascinated with the magic of life on earth than a child living deep in the heart of the "imagi-nation"?

The Least You Need to Know

➤ What you think helps you become what you are.

➤ Cultivating the power of your imagination can help you make your dreams come true.

➤ Guided imagery uses a vocal guide to help you toward greater self-knowledge, healing, and happiness.

➤ Creative visualization helps you to live the life you've always wanted—today!

➤ You can cultivate and enhance your imagination and inner vision through candle meditation and aromatherapy.

Chapter 22

The Art and Sport of Meditation

In This Chapter

➤ Achieving flow

➤ Automatic writing as meditation

➤ Automatic drawing as meditation

➤ Sports as meditation

We've said it before: Anything can be meditation. In fact, when you practice mindfulness during work and play, you may find your performance, not to mention your concentration, improves dramatically. Mindful sports, mindful art, mindful reading, mindful creativity—you may be surprised at the heights you can reach when you focus all your attention on what you are doing, instead of half your attention, like most people do, most of the time.

Perhaps you've heard of the concept of *flow*. Flow occurs when you immerse yourself in any task and become completely absorbed in it. Time and space seem to disappear. Only you and the task you are absorbed in—whether your tennis game or your drawing of a still life—exist to you in those moments. Flow is really just mindful meditation while doing. It is an amazing experience that can enrich your life and bring out talents, creativity, and skill you never knew you had.

Achieving Flow

Did you ever burn a hole in a piece of paper by focusing the sun's rays through a magnifying glass or a pair of eyeglasses? That's a little like flow. The sun itself can't burn paper, but when *concentrated* through a magnifying glass, it becomes much hotter and more intense. Your concentration can act like the magnifying glass, focusing your skills, attention, and abilities. You probably never thought you could burn holes in your work, your play, your daily activity—but you can! (Figuratively, anyway.)

From A to Om

Flow is a state of total concentration leading to complete absorption in an activity, whether sports, creative pursuits, work, or even working a crossword puzzle.

Flow comes easily to kids. Have you ever watched small children engaged in a game of pretend? Coloring with crayons? Making animal shapes from Play-Dough? If you try to get their attention, it may take a minute or two. They're so absorbed in their work that they may not hear you at first. Kids haven't been exposed to the levels of stress and responsibilities familiar to adults, so they are less easily distracted. They know how to concentrate. We've lost this art of concentration as we've become consumed by the thousand details of daily living.

But achieving flow is a skill worth cultivating because being able to live in a state of flow is highly satisfying. It allows you to perform at full capacity. Regaining the ability to achieve flow isn't easy, but it can be done with practice. Basically flow is more easily achieved when you have control over your mental state, and to gain control, you need to work out your mind. Just like bodily control, mental control comes through exercise.

The Optimal State of Peak Performance

Even if you can't control when it happens, you've probably experienced flow before. Have you ever:

➤ Been playing sports (from basketball to billiards) and suddenly could do no wrong, every move and every play executed with perfection?

➤ Been writing a report, a short story, or a diary entry and lost complete track of time because you were so focused on your writing?

➤ Been giving a speech or a presentation and suddenly, every word was perfect, your jokes were a big hit, and even when you ad-libbed, you were a sensation?

➤ Been playing or singing music when suddenly the sound seemed to change, and you played or sang better and with greater skill than you ever thought you could?

➤ Been making repairs on your house or working in your garden with such absorption and single-mindedness that the whole day went by without any sense of time passing?

➤ Been painting, drawing, sculpting, or even doodling, when time seemed to stop, and suddenly you looked at your creation and thought, "How could I have made such a beautiful thing?"

➤ Been reading a novel or a poem and been so completely transported into the story or imagery that you didn't notice distractions around you?

Relax

If your flow seems as if it's flown the coop and you're continually frustrated by attempts to get it moving, perhaps you have a physiological upset that a regular check-up with your doctor can mend or therapy with a professional counselor can address. Through it all, keep that beautiful mind of yours open to new possibilities for inspiration. They are all around you!

We could go on and on. Examples are endless because flow can happen no matter what you are doing. When it happens, you know it. Afterward, you think, "Phew! That was amazing!" You find yourself with a feeling of *being* the project, speech, garden, painting, music, baseball, whatever it is that you're experiencing so fully. In another way, you can view it as the subject of your absorption flowing through *you*, the garden, painting, or baseball moves through your experience of it while you maintain a sense of detachment. That's flow.

What if we could achieve flow whenever we wanted it? What if every moment of our lives could be similarly amazing? Such a state of being is the reward and result of cultivating mindfulness.

The Zen of Being in the Moment of Doing

We've talked about mindfulness before, of course, but it's worth repeating in terms of flow. To achieve flow during your everyday activities, one thing and one thing only is necessary:

Do for the sake of doing, not for the sake of the end result.

Sound familiar? This concept is integral to the Zen way of life, the Buddha preached it, and it is the ideal state for the practice of many different spiritual pursuits, from moving meditations, such as yoga, to daily seated meditation. The aim of flow and the aim of meditation isn't to *accomplish* things, but to experience them. The idea sounds simple, but it's easier said than done. As soon as you begin to live mindfully in the moment, your mind-body resists. You fidget, grow restless; your thoughts wander into the future, back to the past, anywhere but now. But when your mind-body wanders, *you are missing the now*, and *now* is when *everything happens*. Don't miss your life. Live mindfully, and you'll step into the state of flow.

Lazy Brain Syndrome

But as we said before, learning to live in the moment and do for the sake of doing takes practice. It also takes an active brain, ready to engage in active pursuit.

Do you have a couch-potato brain? Lots of us do. How many of the following statements are true for you?

❏ After a long, difficult day, I usually watch TV to relax.

❏ I'm uncomfortable with silence. If I'm alone in the house, I have to have the TV or radio on.

❏ I like to read magazines or the newspaper, but books take too much concentration.

❏ I don't even try to understand poetry.

❏ The last time I learned a new word was in school.

❏ Sometimes I do crossword puzzles, but I never finish them.

❏ Conversation is only for exchanging information.

❏ I get impatient listening to music.

❏ If people around me start talking about philosophical subjects, I tune out.

❏ Now that I'm not in school and have a good job, I don't need to learn things anymore, unless they are directly relevant to my job.

❏ I don't have any hobbies.

Relax

Too much exercise can be just as unhealthy as not enough! If you work in a stressful job all day then go to the gym and run at top speed on the treadmill for hours to blaring music and lights, you're gearing your body and mind up for sensory overload. A quiet run in the park, followed by 20 minutes of seated meditation, may be more suited to your overworked body and mind.

If you checked one or two boxes, your mind is respectably active. More than that, though, and you've got couch-potato mind. Make no mistake: We're not saying you're unintelligent. Being lazy has nothing to do with intelligence. It could simply be the result of unhealthy habits. Or it could be a side effect of overwork and not enough rest—common ailments in our fast-paced, information-packed society. Will changing take effort? Of course. Will you enjoy it? Not always.

Having a lazy mind may seem much easier than having an active, toned mind, just like it's deceptively easier to lie on the couch than to go on a brisk five-mile walk or an aerobics class. But those people who do exercise—both body and mind—will tell you that once you get into the exercise habit, the lazy habits are far less desirable and far less tempting. And what seems "easy" can be more painful to your mind-body in the long run; not only does it make us feel less alive and connected to others and to ourselves, it opens the door to premature aging and the potential for illness.

How do you break lazy habits? The key is to set up some guidelines for yourself and stick to them. Just knowing, in some vague way, that you need to be more mentally active won't be much help. If you've set up some hard-and-fast rules, however, you'll know exactly what you need to do. Changing your thinking patterns will be easier and finally within reach.

Rule 1: Not all activities are equally conducive to flow. Once every day, spend at least 30 minutes on stimulating, mind-stretching, creative activities that engage you and challenge you, such as writing, painting, drawing, sports, making music, dancing, or games such as chess or word puzzles.

Rule 2: Find pleasure in complex thought. The next time someone starts a conversation about some philosophical, hypothetical, or historical subject, join in. The next time you see an article or run across a book on a subject you don't know anything about but that strikes your fancy, read it—all of it. You might find that the effort is worthwhile.

Rule 3: Revive the lost art of conversation. Once each month, invite friends over just to talk. No television, no rented videos, just interesting, animated conversation. Have everyone come armed with three topics meant to spark discussion.

Rule 4: Revive the lost art of letter writing. In the telecommunications age, it's easy to forget the pleasure of a written letter—and e-mails, though efficient, often contribute to our sense of isolation and sound-byte communication instead of bringing us a feeling of shared intimacy. Put thought, care, and effort into your letters to far-away friends and relatives. You'll get just as much out of the writing as they will out of receiving your letters. Try to write a letter to someone once every week.

Rule 5: Allot one hour every weekend purely to mind play. Do the Sunday crossword puzzle. Work a jigsaw puzzle. Play bridge. Solve some math problems, just for fun! (Really! It can be fun if you don't *have* to do it.) Read poetry and make an effort to understand it.

Rule 6: Create no-TV zones. Choose a day or a daily period of time in which the TV absolutely cannot be turned on. Watching TV can be fun and educational, but it also tends to be a mind-numbing activity that many use to fill up silence so their minds don't have to engage. Have you ever found yourself watching TV and, although you aren't enjoying the program, find yourself unable to turn it off? Do your brain a favor. Turn it off.

Rule 7: Create a silence zone. Spend one hour of every week in complete silence. No talking, no listening to television or radio, no communication with others. Ask the other members of your household to respect your hour of silence. Although you can't keep away every noise, don't focus on the noises you do hear. Make an effort to cultivate the stillness within. Get used to the silence of you.

Bliss Byte

The French psychological anthropologist Roger Caillois divided pleasurable activities into four categories. **Agon** includes competitive games, including sports and other athletic events. **Alea** describes games of chance, such as bingo, blackjack, or fortune-telling. **Ilinx** refers to consciousness-altering games such as amusement park rides or high-risk activities like skydiving. **Mimicry** describes imaginative games in which an alternate reality is created, such as acting in the theater, painting, writing, or other artistic endeavors. All these activities have the potential to induce flow.

Zen and the Art of Athletics

Sports are an art. Whether you prefer ballet or baseball, high jump or hackey-sack, mindfulness and complete absorption in your performance will bring out your highest skill and, more importantly, help you to experience the true joy of the game.

Mindful Minute

Home run record-holder Mark McGwire of the St. Louis Cardinals has this to say about the art of flow in hitting homers: "See the ball. Nice and easy. Get a pitch to hit." How's that for a baseball meditation mantra?

But if you're an athlete (even just on Saturday afternoons), you know that you don't experience flow during every practice, every drill, and especially not during every game. If only you could! Flow in sports often seems like an elusive miracle. Sometimes you've got it. Sometimes you don't. And when you see it happen—when you witness a teammate or watch a pro enter the flow state of mind-body excellence in sports—wow, what a wonderful sight!

You *can* have more control over when your athletic performance peaks and when it doesn't. Being healthy and in shape helps, of course. Practice helps. But the real key is mindfulness. When you're out there, on the court or the green or the field or the rink or the dance floor, you won't perform at your peak capacity unless you are completely absorbed in the *now* of your performance. When you do become one with your sport, your ability will leap higher than a ballerina, or a high jumper, or a pole vaulter! You'll make shots you never imagined you could make. You'll execute moves like a legend. You'll be "in the zone." And it will feel so good.

When you experience flow while playing sports, you have the opportunity to experience something rare: You'll *be* poetry in motion. You'll *remember* because you were paying attention. You were paying attention to such a degree that you became the game. And when you are the game, your ego dissolves, your worries about who is watching or how you are playing dissolve, even time and space dissolve. All that is left is *the game*, and the game is you, and suddenly, you know exactly how to play. It's easy. It's almost effortless. Or, at least, it suddenly seems that way.

To refine your powers of concentration and mindfulness during physical activity, try the following exercises, which are all forms of meditation-in-action:

➤ Dribble a basketball and see how many times you can dribble before you mind wanders. Keep practicing and watch your time increase.

➤ Play a game of catch with a friend, using a football, a baseball, or even a Nerf ball! Never take your eye off the ball, even for a second. See how long you can go before your eyes shift away.

➤ Go running and time your breath with your steps. For example, inhale for five steps, exhale for 10 steps. How far can you run before you lose track of the breath? (If you become short of breath, decrease the number of steps per breath rather than giving up the count.)

Relax

Before you start any new fitness program, be sure to consult your doctor. If you've never considered yourself particularly athletic but are interesting in getting "physical," you might want to try gentle moving meditations such as yoga. A daily practice of moving yoga meditation can be a great way to prepare for an athletic flow state.

➤ Hold a prop from your sport during meditation. Whether a volleyball or a ballet slipper, focus on the object. Turn it around in your hands. Notice everything about it. Imagine it being used in your sport. Imagine using it yourself. Pour your energy into the object and try to discern its energy. Concentrate until you feel like you have become one with the object. (It may take more than one meditation session.)

➤ Spend 15 to 20 minutes every day sitting quietly and visualizing yourself performing your sport well. Watch how perfectly you execute the plays, the steps, the moves. See yourself totally absorbed in your performance. Feel how it feels. If you think it, you can do it!

Cultivating flow in your athletic performance may take a little time and concentration, but you'll be glad you did. You'll be a better athlete, and a more awake and alive human being.

A Rose Is a Rose Is a Rose Is...

Sports isn't the only activity in which you can cultivate flow. Ideally, you could live in flow, and the more you practice, the more it will happen to you. Two of the best activities for helping your mind to achieve flow are automatic writing and automatic drawing. Whether you consider yourself a skilled writer doesn't matter. The point of these automatic processes is to free the normal constraints on your thinking and let your subconscious mind peek through. It's a great way to engender creativity, get you out of creative ruts, and open up new ways of perception.

Bliss Byte

If you find yourself in a creative rut, here are a few tips to help you get all four tires back on the road again: skip, run in the rain, take a shower and as sing as loud as you can, face toward people in the elevator (as opposed to the door), smile at everything. When you return to your creative project, you'll have a fresh perspective and awareness to bring to your efforts. Hey, you could even take a 20-minute, mindful walking meditation break!

Automatic Writing: What's on Your Mind?

Gertrude Stein (1874–1946) was an eccentric and avant-garde American writer who lived in Paris and was most famous for her stream-of-consciousness writing. (She is the author of the phrase borrowed for the title of this section, "A rose is a rose is a rose...") To Stein, writing should illuminate the present moment, and the present moment can only truly be described using fragmentation, repetition, and simplification. Stein wrote from her subconscious. Following is a sample of her automatic writing, from *Tender Buttons*, 1914:

GLAZED GLITTER.

Nickel, what is nickel, it is originally rid of a cover.

The change in that is that red weakens an hour. The change has come. There is no search. But there is, there is that hope and that interpretation and sometime, surely any is unwelcome, sometime there is breath and there will be a sinecure and charming very charming is that clean and cleansing. Certainly glittering is handsome and convincing.

There is no gratitude in mercy and in medicine. There can be breakages in Japanese. That is no programme. That is no color chosen. It was chosen yesterday, that showed spitting and perhaps washing and polishing. It certainly showed no obligation and perhaps if borrowing is not natural there is some use in giving.

It doesn't make sense, you say? Of course not! It doesn't have to make sense, and neither does your automatic writing. But it may make sense to you, and it may reveal you to yourself.

To practice automatic writing as meditation, start an automatic-writing journal. Every day for at least 20 minutes, sit down and write without stopping. Write anything that comes into your head. It can be clever, it can be silly, it can be nonsense, it can be the same word over and over. It can be, "I don't know what to write I don't know what to write I don't know what to write" for three pages. Believe us—after a few days or

Mindful Minute

Stream of consciousness refers to an unchecked flow of thoughts, either spoken or written, as a literary technique designed to portray the preconscious impressions of the mind before they can be logically arranged. Therefore, stream-of-consciousness expression usually appears nonsensical, lacking cohesiveness and logical sequence. Famous writers to use the technique are Gertrude Stein, James Joyce, William Faulkner, and Virginia Woolf.

perhaps weeks, you'll know what to write, some of the time. When you don't, write what you are feeling, thinking, seeing, hearing…whatever. Don't judge it, don't analyze, don't interpret. Just let the words flow from your soul. You don't even have to read it when you are done. But if you look back on it a few weeks, months, or years later, you'll see clues to who you are, and your journey toward greater self-knowledge will advance another step or two.

Primal Pictures

Many of Gertrude Stein's colleagues were painters, and she was particularly fond of the cubists (including Pablo Picasso, who painted her portrait). Any great painter, at some point in his or her experience, begins to draw automatically—the articulateness of the painter is transferred to the hand. Automatic drawing can also be a part of Zen meditation. Automatic drawing makes an excellent meditation because during automatic drawing, ideally the "I" or ego expands to encompass what you are drawing so that you become the drawing process. You are your subject and your subject is you. You become one with the process. You are meditating—and creating, too!

Another unique advantage of automatic drawing is that it forces you to become articulate in another system of symbols of expression and communication, that is, you begin to think in images, not in words. This process helps to free the mind of its usual baggage of thought clutter and become absorbed in a new way of understanding—a visual one.

Drawing meditation does more than help you to lose yourself for a short time each day. It also teaches you how to see. As you draw what you see, and as it absorbs you and consumes you, you begin to see the extraordinary in the ordinary. As you go through life, you'll begin to see in terms of subjects for a drawing, and everything will look different—more beautiful, more miraculous.

Bliss Byte

Before you set pencil to paper, try what Frederick Franck, author of *Zen Seeing, Zen Drawing*, calls a "dry run." Trace the basic shape of your subject on your paper with your finger, creating an imaginary white space for your drawing. This helps you to focus on your task and keeps your drawing the size you desire. Scared of that white space? Just dive in. Automatic drawing is about free expression, not about artistic talent. What you draw doesn't have to be representational at all (though it can be). Blob down colors or make shapes that appeal to you. Keep a special sketchbook for your automatic drawings. Or, if you'd like to create your own illustrated book, combine your automatic writing diary and your sketchbook—nineteenth century artist and poet William Blake is famous for his poems annotated with watercolor drawings!

Automatic Drawing: What Do You See?

To try automatic drawing, keep a drawing pad or journal and each day, for at least 20 minutes, sit down, look around, and draw something you see. Don't worry about how good your drawing is. Don't worry about whether your subject is a good subject. Don't worry about what others might think of your drawing. Don't even worry about looking too closely at the paper. Just draw from within. See the object and let what you see travel into you so that you become it and it flows from your pencil. Maybe your drawing will be awkward, maybe it will barely resemble what you see—at first. But keep it up. Teach yourself how to see that vegetable or tree or child playing or daffodil or sleeping cat or blue pitcher. Draw, and lose yourself in your art so that you become the act of drawing.

Another way to stimulate creativity in automatic drawing is to try sketching with your nondominant hand. By using the hand you don't write with, you're further distancing yourself from that world of words, language, and control your hands are accustomed to. You may find you're better able to let go and let your subconscious thoughts and feelings surface in your automatic drawing. And you may also become less concerned about the quality of your drawing and more interested in the freedom of the experience.

We asked our illustrator Wendy Frost to contribute an automatic drawing to our book. Always the professional artist, Wendy's first question was, "What do you want me to draw, and what style do you want it in?" Anything, we answered. Draw whatever you want, however you want to, for 15 minutes. Then stop. Wendy chose to draw her two cats, Earl Grey and Bob Cat, who make a habit of lying on her drawing table as she works.

We asked Wendy to comment on the drawing afterward. She chose to draw the cats, she said, because they make her feel happy and contented. We believe Wendy's feelings of joy and affection for the animals made the automatic-drawing exercise that much more pleasant for Wendy. She chose an artistic flow experience that promoted an inner sense of calm and happiness. What a nice meditation break! And what a wonderful picture of two comfortable cats.

Our illustrator Wendy Frost's automatic drawing of Earl Grey and Bob Cat.

The Least You Need to Know

➤ "Flow" is the state of total absorption in an activity.

➤ You can achieve flow more often and with more intention if you train your brain.

➤ Sports can become an art form when performed during flow.

➤ Automatic writing and automatic drawing are good ways to practice achieving a state of flow and mindfulness.

Chapter 23

Meditation Mix and Match: Adapting the Great Traditions

In This Chapter

➤ Learning about other traditions

➤ Christian traditions

➤ A Kabbalah meditation

➤ Suitable sutras

➤ Native American traditions

➤ An African altar

Meditation in one form or another is practiced in every major world tradition. For a little variety, you can adapt the great traditions for use in your own meditative practice. Trying out meditation techniques doesn't mean you are "betraying" your own beliefs, religion, or philosophy—or that you need to accept the beliefs and traditions of the religion or culture that created those meditation techniques. It only means you are open to learning, growing, and understanding all your fellow sentient beings and the greater, wider path of humankind's spiritual journey, as a whole, throughout time and into the future. We'll help you explore this wide world of meditation in this chapter. Happy sampling!

Sacred Circles

From the Native American medicine wheel to the Tibetan prayer wheel, Catholic rosary, or yogi's mala, religious, cultural, and meditative traditions make use of the circle, bead, or wheel as an aid for meditative ritual and prayer. The image connects meditators of all traditions to the sacred universal significance of the perfect circle, Om.

Beads on a String

Let's take a closer look at the Catholic rosary and the yogi's mala.

The Catholic rosary is a string of beads used to keep track of the prayer cycle. Praying the rosary is a sort of multistepped mantra that can give structure and grounding to a meditative practice.

The term "rosary" is sometimes used also to refer to the sequence of prayers itself. The rosary consists of groups of 10 beads with dividers and a section extending from the loop, usually with a crucifix or cross pendant. Catholics believe that saying the rosary will achieve specific benefits for the person performing the ritual and for the subject of the prayer's meditation. A *chaplet* is a complete cycle of prayers through the entire rosary, consisting of working through one group of five divine mysteries. A *decade* is a group of 10 beads on the rosary.

Bliss Byte

The repetition of a mantra generates spiritual power according to many Eastern religious traditions. The Tibetan prayer wheel makes the repetition of mantras even faster by literally spinning the mantras, an equivalent to speaking them. The greater number of repetitions, the greater the power. The same principle applies to the rosary. The more rosary prayers recited, the more spiritual power is invoked. Of course, the repetition of any mantra needs to be done mindfully and with the proper attitude (devotion) to be effective; mindless repetition won't do.

The act of saying the rosary becomes a verbal, mental, and physical meditative practice through the mantra of the recited prayer and the use of the hands to finger the beads. The supplicant progresses through the circle of prayers that the physical rosary itself represents as a whole object.

The yogi's mala serves a similar purpose of facilitating meditation. Malas contain 108 beads, including a larger bead called the *meru*. The mala is held in the right hand, and the beads are rolled one by one between the third finger and the thumb as the mantra is recited. When the meditator has come full circle to achieve the meru bead, the sequence is reversed in the opposite direction. For yogis without malas, a sequence of finger movements to count through each of the 108 repetitions can be performed.

The yogi's mala is used in the recitation of mantras.

As the Tibetan Dalai Lama has called our past and present lives beads on a string, the use of the rosary and the mala in meditation reflects the joining of individual and collective prayers in a striving toward perfect enlightenment: the circle and the divine sound of the universe. "Om," "Aum," "Amen," "Hum," "Amin"—sacred words to Jews, Christians, Egyptians, Greeks, Romans, Tibetans, and Muslims—are each based upon the all-encompassing sound.

The Sanskrit representation of Om.

A Prayer a Day...

Praying every day or several times per day at regular times gives a spiritual structure and regularity to your life. Just as Christian monks and nuns pray during eight structured times of day to keep God foremost in their minds, and just as Muslims pray five times each day to keep focused on Allah, you, too, can devise a regular prayer schedule. In the morning, express your thanks and hope for the day to come. Throughout the day, remind yourself of your purpose. At the end of the day, express your thanks for the opportunities you have been given and your hope for the next day. Cultivate mindfulness of your day's progress in your prayer life—whether you practice any particular organized religion or not, and those qualities of gratitude, love, and generosity will become part of your everyday outlook and experience of life, as well as a worthy foundation for self-awareness in your meditative practice.

Many people find it helpful to use a daily prayer book or book of daily affirmations to supply ideas and information to stimulate and/or focus contemplative thought. Your local bookstore is full of affirmation books with both secular and religious themes—everything from affirmations for new mothers to affirmations for African Americans to affirmations for prayer from Pope John Paul II. Use whatever kind of prayer book or daily affirmation collection seems to speak to you directly and compellingly.

A daily sequence of meditation and affirmation becomes its own circle of experience, giving shape and considered meaning to each day's events, thoughts, and feelings.

The Meditative Prayer Schedule of Monks and Nuns

Prayer	Timing	Purpose
Vigils, or Matins	Early morning before sunrise	To anticipate an event or the coming of a new day
Lauds	As the sun rises	To celebrate the arrival of the new day
Prime	The hour when duties for the day are assigned	To pray for and meditate on the work to be done
Terce	Mid-morning	A prayer break!
Sext	Noon-time prayer	To renew the day's purpose
None	Mid-afternoon prayer	All are assembled to consider the day together in prayer and meditation
Vespers	The hour of dusk	To encourage a release of the tension of the day that has just passed
Compline	Before sleep	To look over the progress of the day, ask forgiveness for mistakes, and make new resolutions for the coming day

Kabbalah's Tree of Life Meditation

Kabbalah, that mystical sect of Judaism, is largely based around a symbol of the universe, the body, and the journey of meditation called the Tree of Life. This "tree" consists of a branched shape with seven circles on the bottom and three circles on the top. Much has been made about the meaning of these 10 circles, each of which contains a different name and power or energy:

➤ The *Kether*, or Crown: The top circle is the highest power, representative of divinity and divine understanding. This is the power that governs and balances all the others.

➤ The *Binah*: The intelligence circle.

➤ The *Chokmah*: The wisdom circle.

➤ The *Geburah*: The severity circle (the energy that hinders evil, also called the death star).

➤ The *Chesed*: The mercy circle (also called the star of life).

➤ The *Tepereth*: The unity circle, the mediator between creator and creation; this is the center circle of the tree.

➤ The *Hod*: The thought circle, in which mind conquers matter.

➤ The *Netsah*: The emotion circle, in which justice triumphs.

➤ The *Jesod*: The identity circle, which is the foundation of all belief and philosophy.

➤ The *Malkuth*: The circle at the base of the tree, this is the body circle, representing God's creation of both body and universe.

Mindful Minute

According to the Old Testament of the Bible, the Garden of Eden contained two trees, the Tree of the Knowledge of Good and Evil (from whence the infamous apple came) and the Tree of Life. Although Genesis doesn't say much about the Tree of Life, it is thought that this tree is symbolized by the Kabbalah Tree of Life.

Many philosophies link the tree of life with the body's chakras (see Chapter 8, "Energy Central"), the body's form, and the hierarchy of the universe. The circles also represent the steps of meditation, wherein the meditator begins in the body, works up through increasingly higher stages of consciousness, and at last opens the third eye or crown of the tree and attains enlightened understanding.

To use the Tree of Life in meditation, you can gaze upon it as a whole (using it as a mandala), you can concentrate on each circle in succession, or you can simply contemplate the idea of the Tree of Life. But according to the teachings of Kabbalah, you must first light the tree by speaking one of the 25 names of God. You must pick the correct name for the process to work. To find the name that will work for you, slowly scan the following list and say each name to yourself, contemplating its meaning. Whichever one feels right, especially if it floods you with a positive feeling, is the one for you. (The most commonly used names are *Yod He Vav He* and *Ahavah*.)

➤ *Abicha*: Our Father

➤ *Abir*: Mighty One

➤ *Adonoi*: Lord

➤ *Ahavah*: Love

➤ *Ehyeh*: I Am

➤ *Elohi*: Great Living One

➤ *Anochi*: I

➤ *Eshda*: The Firey Law

➤ *Gabor*: Mighty

➤ *Gadol*: Great

➤ *Ha Tzur*: The Rock

➤ *Chaim*: Life

➤ *Kabud*: Honor

➤ *Masika*: Messiah

➤ *Nora*: Full of Awe

➤ *Olam*: Everlasting Worlds

➤ *Tsaddik*: Saint

➤ *Zion*: Place of God

➤ *Kodosh*: Holy One

➤ *Ra 'a Ya*: Shepherd

➤ *Shalom*: Peace

➤ *Torah*: Law

➤ *Tehom*: Great Deep

➤ *Tamim*: Perfect

➤ *Yod He Vav He*: Brilliant Name of Fire

Once you've chosen a name, sit quietly in meditation and repeat the name over and over like a mantra. When you begin to feel a warm glow inside, the Tree of Life is lit for you. You can then meditate on the tree. Use your chosen name for God for meditation any time, especially when you need to feel centered and calm.

If you still aren't sure which name to choose, want to know how to pronounce all the names, or want to learn more, classes in Kabbalah are popular and widely available in larger cities. And please remember that in adapting the traditions of any religion to your own meditative practice, it is proper to pay the appropriate respect to the source of that devout ritual. Upon completing your meditation session, offer thanks to that particular tradition for inspiring your meditation and creating a ritual to benefit the welfare of humankind.

Mindful Minute

In the Muslim tradition, five rules govern daily practice:

1. Believe in Allah, and Muhammad, his Prophet.

2. Pray five times each day.

3. Be kind and charitable to those in need.

4. Observe the Islamic fasts.

5. At least once in your life, make a pilgrimage to the holy city of Mecca (in Saudi Arabia, the birthplace of Muhammad).

Sutras to Suit Ya'

Both Buddhist and yoga traditions contain sutras as part of their literature. These sutras contain kernels of wisdom, parables, and figurative language to teach about the nature of reality. To use a sutra for meditation, take the text to a quiet place, sit comfortably, read the sutra several times to yourself to get it in your head, then either repeat it like a mantra or meditate on its meaning.

Meditation on Lovingkindness

This Buddhist sutra is full of power. Supposedly originating from the Buddha himself, its purpose is to kindle a feeling of lovingkindness in the heart of the meditator, toward oneself, toward loved ones, and even (especially!) toward one's enemies. Repeat this adaption of the Meditation on Lovingkindness to yourself again and again, especially when you are angry, until you begin to feel the melting joy of forgiveness in your heart:

May I be healthy and happy. May I be free from hatred. May I be free from ill will. May I be free from distress. May I be free from suffering.

May my parents be healthy and happy. May they be free from hatred. May they be free from ill will. May they be free from distress. May they be free from suffering.

May my siblings be healthy and happy. May they be free from hatred. May they be free from ill will. May they be free from distress. May they be free from suffering.

May my teachers be healthy and happy. May they be free from hatred. May they be free from ill will. May they be free from distress. May they be free from suffering.

May my friends be healthy and happy. May they be free from hatred. May they be free from ill will. May they be free from distress. May they be free from suffering.

May my relatives be healthy and happy. May they be free from hatred. May they be free from ill will. May they be free from distress. May they be free from suffering.

May those whom I have difficulty loving be healthy and happy. May they be free from hatred. May they be free from ill will. May they be free from distress. May they be free from suffering.

May all those whom I know be healthy and happy. May they be free from hatred. May they be free from ill will. May they be free from distress. May they be free from suffering.

May all those whom I don't know be healthy and happy. May they be free from hatred. May they be free from ill will. May they be free from distress. May they be free from suffering.

May all living beings be healthy and happy. May they be free from hatred. May they be free from ill will. May they be free from distress. May they be free from suffering.

Mindful Minute

Kahlil Gibran wrote, "Your pain is the breaking of the shell that encloses your understanding." When meditation, prayer, visualization, guided imagery, or any other form of inner exploration turns up memories or feelings that are difficult, go slowly while considering that perhaps this difficulty will open your awareness to new levels and insights.

Sutras from Patanjali

Use any of the following bits of yoga wisdom from the *Yoga Sutras* of Patanjali (as translated in the book *The Heart of Yoga* by T.K.V. Desikachar) for a mantra or focus of meditation and/or contemplation:

➤ *The more intense the faith and the effort, the closer the goal.*

➤ *What decays is the external. What does not is deep within us.*

➤ *The result of contentment is total happiness.*

➤ *Anything can be understood. With each attempt, fresh and spontaneous understanding arises.*

➤ *Freedom is when the mind has complete identity with the Perceiver.*

Native American Life Meditations

The Native American tradition views everything on earth as imbued with spirit. People, animals, plants, rocks, mountains, water, even human-made items like clothing, bowls, weapons, and jewelry have their own spirits. Above all is Great Spirit, a divine fusion of male and female energy (yin/yang balance once again!).

Some Native American tribes also believe that each person has a totem. A totem is usually an animal but can also be a plant, a rock, or other item from nature. Your totem has knowledge and inspiration to offer you and can help you through your life if you are open to its wisdom. One way to discover your totem is to go on a vision quest (see Chapter 2, "Meditation Power: Beyond Words"), which allows your totem to reveal itself to you.

Totemism does not believe in standing apart from nature, but rather in preserving the natural order. To quote a story reflecting this from the book *The World Religions* by Huston Smith:

> At one point, the art department at Arizona State University decided to offer a course on basketweaving and approached a neighboring Indian reservation for an instructor. The tribe proposed its master weaver, an old woman, for the position. The entire course turned out to consist of trips to the plants that provide the fibers for her baskets, where myths involving the plant were recounted and supplicating songs and prayers were memorized. There was no weaving.

Although a typical vision quest involves several days of fasting and sitting within a medicine wheel (see Chapter 20, "Mandalas: The Circle of Life") in nature, you also can take a "mini vision quest." Set aside an hour or two during which you go outside and find a place that feels comfortable and good to you. It can be in your own yard, in a park, or in any other natural setting. The fewer signs of civilization, the better.

Construct a medicine wheel out of rocks and other natural materials. Thank each of the four directions, then sit in the middle. Ask Great Spirit to reveal your totem. Remain mindful and wait. Soak in the natural surroundings, breathe deeply, and relax. Don't try to figure out what your totem might be. Just sit in mindfulness, open to anything.

Bliss Byte

One way to show your reverence for nature is to learn how to walk silently through nature and leave no trace that you were ever there. Make a habit of taking walks in the woods or other natural areas and practice walking without making a sound, so as not to disturb the natural order around you. Remember, however, to breathe deeply and relax your body and mind as you take in the beauty around you.

In many cases, an animal will appear. Sometimes it will remain shyly on the perimeter. In a few cases, animals have come into the medicine wheel to commune with the meditator. Or you may find your attention suddenly drawn to a certain plant, tree, stone, or other item. Wait, listen to the message from nature, and allow your totem to be revealed. If you can wait in mindful silence for two hours (rather than giving up after 20 or 30 minutes out of boredom), your patience will likely be rewarded.

You may see several animals while engaged in your quest, but the animal that is your totem will come closer to you or capture your attention more fully than the others. Or, perhaps a certain tree, rock, or other being will become central to your consciousness. Don't just assume the first animal you see or tree you notice is your totem, though it might be. Wait out the time, and by the end, you'll probably know.

Once your totem has been revealed to you—whether squirrel, blackbird, deer, eagle, oak tree, or other being or object—spend some time contemplating your totem. Imagine what it feels to be your totem. Continue to meditate on your totem as often as possible. Eventually, you will feel a oneness with your totem, and you will be ready for its guiding wisdom, which will also come to you during meditation, dreams, or contemplation.

Respecting the Earth

Native Americans also hold the Earth in the highest respect. The Earth represents the female energy of Great Spirit, and it has much to teach us. It shares its bounty and takes little in return. To share in this respect for the Earth, live your life in an Earth-friendly way. Don't litter, pollute, or waste. Try to make as little of an impact on the natural world as possible. Live in it, commune with it, but don't destroy it. Your life will seem easier, simpler, purer, and more loving when you don't spend your energy on destruction and waste.

You can also meditate on the Earth. For a twist on the normal meditation pose, go outside, lie down on your stomach on the ground, spread your arms out, and feel as if you are holding the Earth. Imagine that she in turn is rocking you. Feel at one with Mother Earth and imagine her energy filling you and your energy filling her. Stay in the position for 20 minutes, breathing deeply, and allowing the Earth to speak to you and heal you. Don't forget to offer your thanks for the Earth's blessing after your meditation is over.

Honoring the Ancestors

Native Americans also honor their ancestors and believe that the ancestral spirits are always available to offer counsel, inspiration, and strength to their descendents. You, too, can call on the power of your ancestors, even if you don't know anything about them.

➤ Sit comfortably with your back straight and breathe deeply.

➤ Raise your hands into the air, palms up, and say, "I call upon you, my ancestors, to offer me your wisdom so that I may live my life well."

➤ Lower your hands and leave them palms-up on your knees in the spirit of openness.

➤ Breathe normally and sit in mindfulness, open to any impressions that may come to you. If you are facing a particular life challenge or dilemma, imagine you see it in front of you, encased in a bubble with a big question mark on it.

➤ Continue to wait, mindfully. Perhaps a face or figure will come into your mind. Perhaps it will speak to you. Maybe it is someone you remember or maybe it is an ancestor from long ago. Even if it is only a figment of your imagination, be open to the suggestions from your subconscious that may or may not be influenced by the energies (and genetics) of your ancestors.

➤ Sometimes, rather than a figure coming into your mind, a voice or an idea will present itself as a solution to your problem or a direction to take. Listen, then spend time in contemplation of what has come to you or been given to you.

Relax

If you find that your mind is flooded with images and impressions, continue to repeat your mantra, either verbally or silently. With persistence, your mind will gain focus.

African Meditation: Altar-ed States

Altars are an important part of the religious tradition in African tribal cultures. Altars are outdoors, constructed at places thought to be boundaries between the material and spirit worlds. Although different religions use altars in different ways (for example, in Namibia, each altar is dedicated to a god), altars are typically decorated with objects thought to be magical, sacred, or otherwise spiritually powerful. Altar locations often coincide with natural boundaries, such as the edges of forests and the banks of rivers.

From A to Om

An **altar** is a natural or constructed platform or table used for sacred purposes, upon which sacred objects can be placed to aid in worship.

You can design your own outdoor altar, at the base of a tree, at the foot of a large rock, on a mountaintop, or wherever in nature seems like a sacred place to you (such a place may exist right in your own backyard). Stand in front of it and ask that your ancestors bless your altar. Dedicate your altar to one particular virtue, such as courage, health, or friendship.

Then, with your altar's virtue in mind, carefully place flowers, pinecones, beautiful stones, or other natural items on your altar space. Draw or paint a mandala or other symbol of spiritual significance to you on your altar. As you place each item on your altar, ask that your ancestors bless the item and endow it with spiritual power.

Draw or paint a diamond on your forehead over the area of your third eye, between and just above your eyes. Now, sit or kneel in front of your altar, relax, breathe, and ask for a blessing from your ancestors. Meditate on the virtue to which you have dedicated your altar. Let the spirits of your ancestors and/or the African gods speak to you through your intuition, revealing the best path to the virtue represented by your altar.

Meditating on Other Cultures

Sampling the traditions and techniques of other cultures can be fun, illuminating, and even enlightening! Wisdom comes in all shapes, sizes, languages, and disguises. If you can stop yourself from rejecting something just because you aren't used to it, you'll be surprised at what you might learn. Open your mind and watch it grow big enough to hold whatever you pour into it.

The Least You Need to Know

➤ You can vary your meditation practice by adopting aspects of meditation from many cultures.

➤ Prayer beads, from the rosary to the mala, are used by many of the world's religious traditions. Their circular ritual connects us to the universal circle of life.

➤ The Kabbalist Tree of Life can be a focus of meditation.

➤ The sutras are simple truths to meditate on within Buddhist and yoga traditions.

➤ A totem is a Native American concept representing unity with nature and can be an inspiration and guiding force during meditation.

➤ Altars are an important part of the religious tradition in many African tribal cultures and can be used for spiritual insight during meditation.

Part 7
Meditation for Your Life

Meditation doesn't have to remain a separate part of your life. You can design your life to enhance your meditation, and in turn, meditation will enhance your life. What you eat and how you eat it can directly affect your meditation efforts. We'll show you what foods and food attitudes will make meditation a breeze. We'll also describe how meditation can help ease you through the challenges of being a woman, a man, a family member, a kid, or a senior.

Meditation can help to enhance your health and address your health concerns. We'll offer some meditations to help your body heal. We'll show you how to meditate while away from home, and as long as you're planning a trip, why not make it a meditation vacation? We'll show you how.

Last of all, we'll introduce you to a wonderful and special form of meditation that helps you to see yourself as an integral part of a complex and amazing Earth consciousness, just waking up to the possibilities of its own potential. What a wonderful future we all have in store—and what a fine time we'll have getting there, awake and alive with the help of meditation!

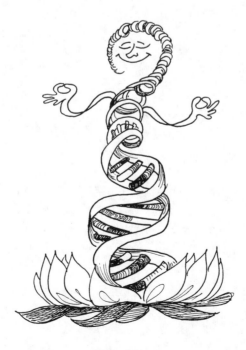

Chapter 24

Food for Thought: Fueling Your Body and Your Mind

In This Chapter

➤ Knowing what foods are healthful

➤ The pros and cons of meditation and being a vegetarian

➤ Foods that boost brain power

➤ All about supplements

➤ Fasting: Good or bad?

According to Rene Descartes, you think, therefore you are. We would like to take that one step further: You eat, therefore you think. (Which would lead, logically, to the conclusion that you are what you eat!) Everyone knows that too many calories and too much fat can increase the number on that bathroom scale, as well as clog your arteries and lead to a variety of health problems, but what about your ability to think, remember, solve problems, react quickly—all that brain-related stuff? Is your ability to finish that afternoon project related to what you had for lunch? Research clearly demonstrates that laboratory animals live longer when they consume fewer calories than the recommended daily allowances. Studies also show that people who consume a low-calorie meal can concentrate better than those who chow down. The way food affects your ability to concentrate—and thus to meditate—is exactly what we explore in this chapter.

Brain Food: The Theory

Food plays a crucial role in your brain's ability to function both over the short term and the long term. The meal you ate just a few hours ago directly influences the way your brain is working right now. And, over time, deficiencies in diet may lead to serious cognitive problems.

All this is directly relevant to meditation and also to cultivating a state of mindfulness and of flow in daily life (see the previous chapter). Why? Because if you've eaten the wrong thing for dinner, you might find it next to impossible to sit still or stay awake for your evening meditation. You might find mindfulness an incredible challenge after one kind of breakfast and a snap after another kind.

Could facilitating mindfulness and meditation really be as easy as making a few dietary adjustments? It sure can help. We'll explain how.

It is also very important to have your food prepared by someone with good vibes. The emotional and mental state of the food preparer goes right into the food. This is why it's a good idea to cook your own food as often as possible, putting positive energies into the food. Also, blessing the food is most beneficial to neutralize any negatives and put positive, healthy vibrations into the food you're about to eat.

Bliss Byte

While yoga philosophy advocates the consumption of a fresh, pure, vegetarian diet, it also insists that any food, when eaten with complete awareness and enjoyment, will nourish the body. Likewise, any food, no matter how healthy, will be unhealthy for the body if eaten in a rushed, tense, stressed, or angry manner. So maybe we shouldn't say "You are what you eat," but instead, "You are *how* you eat!" The next time you are preparing for a meal, make a conscious effort to relax and smile, then savor every bite.

Living Healthy in a Toxic World

Eating good food, breathing clean air, and drinking pure water used to be easy. You went out into your garden, your orchard, or the chicken coop, selected your dinner, scooped some water from the well, took a few deep breaths of air, picked some flowers for the table, and went on with your day, feeling refreshed and healthy. Back then, daily life also included quite a bit more exercise, most of it outside, than what we experience today.

Indeed, the world looks a lot different today, as we all know. Food is shipped from thousands of miles away, coated with wax, dyes, preservatives, and pesticides or injected with hormones, antibiotics, and chemicals. Food also comes packaged in boxes and preserved so that it can last and last and last on that supermarket shelf. Even locally grown produce tends to be sprayed with pesticides.

Our rivers, lakes, and oceans are filled with waste, our air is filled with smog, and in some cities, breathing can actually hurt as the polluted air oxidizes your lung tissue. Ouch!

Bliss Byte

Pollution exists on many levels. The lighting from our larger cities has drastically reduced the view of the stars. Since 1972, Tucson, Arizona, has fitted outdoor lights with shields that greatly reduce light pollution for the benefit of local observatories and the Tucson population in general. Tucson is one of the few cities where you can actually stargaze! When was the last time you saw stars for miles around you?

Never mind (for the moment) the disrespect for Mother Earth and future generations such anti-stewardship of the Earth has wrought. What about us, right here, right now? What *on Earth* are we stuffing into our bodies, and how does it impact our health, our mental state, and our spiritual selves?

Although it isn't as easy as it used to be, it is possible to live healthfully and eat well in a toxic world. An increasing number of consumers are demanding organic food, free-range meat and eggs, and locally grown produce. Because food with such high levels of preservatives, pesticides, and processing is a relatively recent occurrence, we have yet to fully witness the effects on the general population. Why take chances? Whenever you can, choose food closest to its natural state, organically grown, and with as little processing and packaging as possible. As you change your diet, you may notice that you are thinking more clearly and with more ease than you were on that diet of frozen dinners and diet soda.

Good Nutrition for Mind Power

Good nutrition and strategic nutrition are both crucial for optimum brain functioning. How much do you know about how food affects your brain? Take our true-false test to see.

True	False	Food for Thought
❏	❏	You'll probably think more clearly and more quickly if your breakfast consists of protein (peanut butter or turkey sandwich, an egg, a yogurt shake) than carbohydrates (bran muffin, cereal).
❏	❏	A cup of coffee in the morning ups your brain power.
❏	❏	A cup of coffee during a mid-afternoon break will pull you out of that slump and revive your brain power.
❏	❏	When you eat dinner, it's best for your brain power to eat the salad and bread first, then the main course protein source.
❏	❏	Everyone should start their day with breakfast as soon as they wake up in the morning to perform well during the day.
❏	❏	A candy bar or a chocolate-chip cookie is a good pick-me-up, offering a burst of energy.

Now, see how you did: The first three items are true, the second three are false. Really!

From A to Om

Serotonin is a neurotransmitter, a chemical in your brain responsible for transmitting messages, that has a calming, relaxing effect and can cause drowsiness. **Tyrosine** and **tryptophan** are two amino acids that come from protein that comes from the food we eat. If tryptophan gets to the brain first, you'll be more likely to become drowsy. If tyrosine gets there first, you'll be more likely to become more energized and alert.

Starting the morning with protein rather than carbohydrates will definitely provide for better mental activity. Protein contains an amino acid called *tyrosine*, which leads to increased energy and alertness. Carbohydrates, on the other hand, lead to the production of *serotonin*, a neurotransmitter that has a calming effect. Also, beginning a meal with carbohydrates (as in that salad and bread) actually allows an amino acid called *tryptophan* to reach your brain first, blocking the tyrosine from having its energizing effect. In addition, tryptophan converts to serotonin in your brain, making you even drowsier and less able to concentrate.

The effect is even more extreme in people over the age of 40. One study performed at the Chicago Medical School of 184 adults measured concentration, memory, and performance on mental tasks after a meal of either turkey (protein) or sherbet (carbohydrates). Those over the age of 40 had twice as much trouble with concentration, memory, and mental tasks when they ate the sherbet. The difference was less extreme in those under 40.

Several other studies also demonstrate the positive effects of protein versus the negative effects of carbohydrates on brain power. One study conducted at the Massachusetts Institute of Technology involved providing a turkey lunch containing approximately 3 ounces of protein for 40 men between 18 and 28 years old. The men were given complex mental tasks. On a different day, the men were given a lunch containing 4 ounces of wheat starch, which is almost pure carbohydrates. They then performed the same mental tasks. According to the study, after the wheat starch lunch, performance was "significantly impaired" compared to the protein lunch.

We aren't saying carbohydrates are bad. Far from it! Your body needs carbohydrates, especially the complex kind (found in fruits, vegetables, and whole grains), for fiber, vitamins, and minerals. The trick, when it comes to revving up your brain for clearer thinking, is to eat the protein *first*. And whole-grain, high-fiber cereal is a good breakfast, as long as you top it off with protein-rich milk. (That bran muffin probably has a lot of fat. Go for the cereal instead.)

And what about that coffee? Coffee isn't for everyone, and caffeinated beverages with lots of sugar, like soda or coffee or tea loaded with sugar and cream, aren't good for anyone. But a single cup of morning coffee actually has been shown to improve mental activity within minutes and the effects may last as long as six hours, according to a Massachusetts Institute of Technology study. The caffeine is the responsible party and has a similar effect when consumed in the mid-afternoon, when many people begin to feel drowsy.

Of course, like the Buddha, we like to preach moderation in all things! Drinking coffee from dawn 'til dusk is overusing caffeine, which can wreak havoc on your nerves. One cup will do. Or, if you don't like the idea of consuming any mind-altering chemicals (although technically, all the food we eat contains chemicals that influence the mind), stick with the high-protein breakfast and a peanut butter sandwich for a mid-day snack. (Remember that consuming caffeine and sugar can lead to a physical dependence on these substances.)

The news about coffee seems to change every few months. First, it's bad for your heart. Then it isn't. Then it can cause cancer. Then it doesn't. Then it contains substances that fight cancer. Because scientists still have much to learn about the effects of caffeine, coffee, and virtually all other foods and beverages on the body, go with your instincts. If you like coffee, have a cup or two, but be reasonable about your consumption. If you don't like it, don't start drinking it. And if you feel as if you are addicted to it and can't help drinking too much, you're probably better off quitting. Anything that becomes an addiction is best avoided because it doesn't allow you to practice sensible health habits and moderation.

Breakfast, studies show, isn't actually the necessity we once believed. For children, breakfast is crucial and boosts school performance. But for adults, who are better able to maintain stable blood sugar levels overnight, breakfast is an option. If you aren't hungry first thing in the morning, don't eat anything. When you get

Mindful Minute

For more on addressing your potentially destructive behaviors and breaking out of the old familiar patterns, read *The Complete Idiot's Guide to Breaking Bad Habits* (Alpha Books, 1998).

hungry later in the morning, have breakfast. Eating when you aren't hungry is a nasty habit, anyway. Learn to listen to your body. (And if you think it's telling you it wants chocolate doughnuts for breakfast, remember that's your negative habit talking, not your body.) Very often our bodies send us messages that may not be reliable, based more on our bad dietary habits than on genuine, healthful needs. Often we need to retrain our bodies to desire healthful foods!

Do You Have to Be a Vegetarian?

If you've studied the traditions of other cultures, you've probably discovered that many practice and advocate a vegetarian diet. The yoga principle of nonviolence necessitates a vegetarian diet because eating animals involves killing them first, and whether you or someone else does the killing doesn't matter to a yogi. Violence was involved. Buddhists, too, typically practice a vegetarian diet. The first of the five Buddhist precepts says, "I will refrain from harming any living beings," and that includes, of course, the killing of animals for food.

Bliss Byte

You can still get plenty of protein if you are a vegetarian. Dairy products, milk, yogurt, cheese, and especially eggs are excellent protein sources. Of course, many vegetarians refrain from all animal proteins. Brown rice, legumes, whole grains, nuts, and nut butters are also great protein sources. And don't forget soy, in its many manifestations—tofu, miso, tempeh, soy beans, soy flour, etc. Soy is not only protein-rich, but is now thought to be an excellent cancer fighter.

If you want to practice Zen meditation or yoga meditation, does that mean you have to be a vegetarian, too? Absolutely not. *But* (there's always a but), you may find that the more you practice your meditation, the less appealing meat will become. The problem with your question "Do I have to be a vegetarian?" is the "have to" part. If you feel that being a vegetarian is a "have to" kind of thing, an undesirable obligation or sacrifice that you despise (you'll know that's true if you find yourself wandering wistfully toward the meat counter whenever you are grocery shopping), then you aren't ready to be a vegetarian. Maybe you won't ever become one. But plenty of people who begin to meditate, especially those who study Buddhism or yoga, eventually decide to phase meat out of their lives.

In other words, vegetarianism is just one part of the meditation journey, and maybe you won't decide to take that path. *But* (another but), just for a little incentive, studies do show that vegetarians are generally healthier, suffer from fewer minor illnesses, and live longer than their meat-eating counterparts.

The 10 Best Foods for Meditation

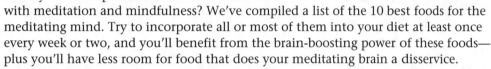

Mindful Minute

Countries with high meat consumption typically have correspondingly high cancer mortality rates. Coincidence? You decide!

So what exactly should you eat if you want to boost your brain power and have an easier time with meditation and mindfulness? We've compiled a list of the 10 best foods for the meditating mind. Try to incorporate all or most of them into your diet at least once every week or two, and you'll benefit from the brain-boosting power of these foods— plus you'll have less room for food that does your meditating brain a disservice.

Eggs. Eggs are an excellent, high-quality protein source, and egg yolks are a great source of lecithin, a fatty substance that provides choline to the brain, which is transformed into acetylcholine in the brain. Acetylcholine is responsible for the ability to learn and the ability to remember. Look for eggs from free-range chickens. They are healthier and taste better, too.

Oatmeal. Oatmeal has protein (even more when topped with milk) and is another good source of choline. Steel-cut or whole oats (old-fashioned oats) are better than instant.

Brown rice. Brown rice has both protein and choline plus a healthy dose of fiber and B vitamins. B vitamins are crucial for brain function because they are responsible for catalyzing many of the brain's chemical reactions. If you hate cooking rice, invest in a rice cooker to make the task easy.

Low-fat cottage cheese. Chock full of protein, but with very little fat, cottage cheese is fast, easy, and a real brain booster. It may also help to kill your craving for less healthy foods like chips because it has a salty taste. Nevertheless, low-salt varieties are healthiest.

Fish. Fish is low in fat and carbohydrates and high in protein. It also contains the much-publicized omega-3 fatty acid thought to improve brain function. Mackerel, salmon, and herring are good choices. Rich in omega-3, these cold-water fish are also less likely to be contaminated by environmental pollutants.

Soybeans and other soy products (like tofu). Soy is rich in lecithin, high in protein, and soybean oil contains polyunsaturated fat. In one study, rats fed a diet of soybean oil learned 20 percent faster and remembered what they learned better than rats on a regular diet. Look for organically grown soybeans and products.

Spinach. Spinach contains folate (a B vitamin), which the brain uses to make brain tissue and neurotransmitters. Spinach is also iron-rich, and iron helps your brain to receive oxygen and make neurotransmitters. It also contains manganese and magnesium, which help your brain to use energy from other nutrients. Look for organic spinach at your grocery store, health-food market, or local produce stand.

Lean meat. Chicken and turkey are excellent sources of protein, zinc, and iron, and they are low-fat, too. Tyrosine-rich, lean meat means more energy and alertness. Zinc is a mineral that aids the brain in transmitting its electrical impulses. Free-range meat is best. (If you choose to eat vegetarian, you can certainly find other good protein sources.)

Peanuts and peanut butter. Peanuts have protein, lecithin, and B vitamins. They are high in fat, though, so don't overindulge. A handful of peanuts or a couple of tablespoons of peanut butter on whole-wheat bread are acceptable snacks. Look for the natural types of peanut butter without added sugar.

Dried fruit. Raisins, dates, and prunes contain iron and boron, a mineral thought to be important for maintaining the brain's electrical activity. Look for dried fruit without added sulfites, available in health-food stores.

Relax

Watch your fat intake: High-fat foods take a lot more effort to digest than low-fat foods, diverting blood from your brain. Go for the low-fat meal, and you'll be in better shape to think, remember, concentrate, and react. When you choose fat, go for olive oil and canola oil, which may actually have a positive effect on your brain.

Of course, this list isn't exclusive. All healthy foods benefit your brain in one way or another, whether directly or by improving your general health. And remember, Earth-friendly eating will help you to feel more in harmony with the planet. You may notice a gradual peace come over you as you change your eating habits. Mindful eating will come naturally. Your cravings for junk food will gently decline until they disappear completely. Your body will become leaner, stronger, and more energetic. And your brain—why, meditation will be as easy as eating a delicious stir-fry of fresh, crisp organic vegetables over nutty brown rice!

Herbs and Botanicals to Grow By

As you visit your local health-food market, or even your local supermarket, you might notice that a good deal of the store is dedicated not to food but to lots of little bottles, jars, and packets of herbs and botanicals. Herbal remedies are big business these days, and even mainstream markets are looking for a piece of the herbal pie. In fact, in 1998, the American public was expected to spend $4.3 billion on herbal supplements.

But should you spend your hard-earned cash on *herbs* and *botanicals*? That depends on who you talk to, but more and more are saying yes—if you know what you are buying.

Because the sale of herbs and botanicals isn't yet regulated by the Food and Drug Administration (FDA), anyone can sell them and the products don't have to pass any standards. The only requirement is that labels on marketed herbs can't say they cure medical problems (even if they do sometimes bestow healthful benefits when taken properly in the correct amounts), unless they have gone through the rigorous, expensive, and time-consuming process of getting FDA approval.

So, an herb like ginkgo biloba, which is thought to have amazing effects on brain circulation and is thought to be a possible remedy for the symptoms of Alzheimer's disease, can't legally say it improves the symptoms of Alzheimer's disease. In addition, a bottle of pills marked "ginkgo biloba" may or may not have an amount of ginkgo biloba equivalent to amounts used in scientific studies. A pill could have hardly any ginkgo biloba at all but still advertise itself as a ginkgo biloba supplement. In fact, many herbal supplements don't even list their ingredients on the bottle. Who knows what you're getting!

In response to consumer protest, many companies are coming out with more explicit packaging, listing concentrations of the herbs in their products and making a good effort to prove that their products are of the highest quality. A few grassroots groups are rallying to demand better and more consistent herbal supplement formulas. But don't buy herbal products with your eyes closed. Read the labels and research the companies (you might be surprised to find out who really makes those herbs with the attractive earthy packaging and quaint company name). In other words, buyer beware. Or, to be even safer, learn about herbs on your own and grow them in your backyard! (But do your homework. Some herbs can be incredibly powerful and even toxic.)

From A to Om

Herbs are plants used for medicinal or therapeutic purposes (and also for cooking). **Botanicals** are formulas made from plant sources, which include herbs, herbal combinations, and substances made from various parts of plants.

Relax

Before beginning to take any herb or botanical in any form, consult your physician or a licensed natural medicine professional. Herbs and botanicals, though "natural," have effects on the body like any drug or chemical. Herbs, botanicals, and other supplements, such as vitamin supplements, may also interact with any drug treatments prescribed by your physician in potentially adverse ways. See your doctor first before you take anything!

Bliss Byte

If you have a window in your kitchen, try growing a few of your favorite herbs. Most varieties require minimal space and can be grown in small pots. Grow from seeds or buy small plants from a local garden center or herbalist. Easy varieties to grow in kitchen gardens are basil, oregano, thyme, parsley, cilantro, sage, rosemary, peppermint, lavender, and feverfew. Also try growing garlic bulbs and aloe vera plants. Keep plants in a sunny location, keep soil moist, and grow in well-drained pots.

Which herbs and botanicals are supposed to improve brain function and which might prove helpful supports in a meditation practice? Although what works for you might be different than what works for other people, we'll tell you a little bit about the big three, the herbs most known for their brain-boosting power. The following herbs have all been the subjects of scientific studies providing evidence that they do indeed provide health benefits (although not all studies were equally rigorous or accepted by the mainstream community):

➤ **Ginkgo biloba.** The number-one-selling herb in the United States today, ginkgo biloba has been used as a prescription medicine in Europe for years and is one of the most well-studied herbal remedies. Made from the leaves of the Ginkgo tree, this herb improves brain function and alertness, promotes blood flow and fights free radicals in the brain, and improves short-term memory, headache, depression, and other neurological disorders (as well as a host of functions in the rest of your body!). Many doctors in the United States are now suggesting their patients showing early signs of senility try ginkgo biloba.

➤ **Ginseng.** Made from a root, ginseng increases blood supply to the brain, lowers blood sugar levels, increases energy, and increases the body's resistance to stress.

➤ **St. John's Wort.** Sometimes called the "herbal Prozac," this herb, made from the plant's flowers and leaves, has been shown to have a significant effect on people suffering from clinical depression. It also relieves anxiety.

There are hundreds of other herbs and botanicals available in many forms, from pills to teas. To be safe, do your homework on any herbal remedy you think might help you, and/or consult a reputable herbalist.

Vitamins and Supplements: Are They Worth It?

As long as you're browsing the aisles for herbal remedies, why not pick up a few vitamin and mineral supplements? Are you wasting your money with these? Maybe, depending on what you buy. Your brain actually requires a wide range of nutrients, including many different vitamins and minerals, to keep it operating at its peak. You may not be able to get enough of everything every day, even with a healthy, varied diet. A complete vitamin and mineral supplement is a good insurance policy against deficiencies.

On the other hand, megadoses of vitamins and minerals may not do you any good and could even cause unpleasant—even dangerous—side effects. Most doctors and nutritionists who recommend supplements suggest taking a regular multivitamin and mineral supplement with doses at approximately 100 percent DV (daily value), unless you have a specific problem that might be addressed by higher dosages.

Yoga Foodies

Westerners have their way of looking at food—in terms of vitamin/mineral content, chemical substances, calories, fat, protein content, etc. Yoga teaches a somewhat different approach. According to yoga philosophy, food can be divided into three categories: tamasic, rajasic, or sattvic. *Tamasic* food tends to make you sleepy, lethargic, and inactive. It steals your ambition and your energy. *Rajasic* food revs you up a little too much. It promotes excess energy, even anxiety, agitation, and discontentment. *Sattvic* food is the "middle road." Sattvic foods fill you with vitality, strength, and peace of mind. They are "yogi foods."

Obviously, to facilitate meditation via this system, you'll want to try to eat mostly sattvic foods. If you do eat something rajasic, you can balance its effects by eating something tamasic, but this creates an unstable system tenuously balanced by two extremes, rather than a stable system, centered in the middle of the two extremes.

Relax

If you are pregnant or nursing a baby, you must be extra careful about any herbs you ingest. Levels of certain chemicals within herbs that would be safe for you might not be safe for a baby. Never take any herbs without the guidance of your physician or trained herbalist when you are pregnant, and don't drink herbal teas except those that contain only food-grade herbs, such as orange, lemon, cinnamon, peppermint, or ginger tea.

Mindful Minute

Due to a number of factors such as pollution and over-farming, American soil doesn't have the nutritional punch it once had, and so the vegetables and fruits grown from it are less nutritious than they once were, too. Just one more reason to pop that daily multivitamin/mineral supplement!

We hold the type of food we take into our mind-body in our own hands! Strive to achieve the balance best for your overall health and most productive for your meditative practice: sattva.

TAMAS   SATTVA   RAJAS

From A to Om

Yoga philosophy divides food into three categories: **tamasic** food (such as alcohol and highly processed food) promotes lethargy and inactivity; **rajasic** foods (such as meat, hot peppers, and caffeinated beverages) promote anxiety and agitation; **sattvic** foods (such as fresh produce, whole grains, and milk) promote vitality, strength, and peace of mind.

Tamas: Dull Mind

Tamasic foods are any foods that are addictive, intoxicating, stale, processed, or drastically changed from original form. To avoid laziness, fatigue, and lack of ambition, avoid foods such as:

➤ Microwaveable frozen dinners

➤ Canned food

➤ Packaged, processed food with lots of preservatives

➤ Alcohol

➤ Old produce

➤ Waxed, sprayed produce

Rajas: Sharp Mind

Rajasic foods are spicy, stimulating, sour, bitter, or have a very strong taste. Avoid rajasic foods if you are prone to anxiety or feel you need to remain (or become) calm and clear-headed. Rajasic foods can also make some people irritable and even aggressive. Examples are:

➤ All meat and fish

➤ Eggs

➤ Spicy spices, such as black and red peppers

➤ Caffeinated beverages like coffee

Sattva: Clear Mind

To keep your mind more easily in a clear, pure, mindful state, try to base your diet on sattvic foods such as:

➤ Fresh, organic fruits and vegetables

➤ Fresh whole-grain products

➤ Almonds and sesame seeds

➤ Milk, butter, and other milk products

➤ Legumes

➤ Honey

Once you've begun to change your eating habits, if you feel yourself starting to slip, let your meditation help you! Whenever you feel like eating something you know isn't good for you, go meditate first. Breathe deeply and visualize yourself pure, healthy, and strong. Stick with it for 10 minutes, and your craving will probably disappear. If it doesn't, go have a bite or two. It may not taste as good as you thought it would, and next time, you may be better able to resist.

Relax

Avoid foods that seem to give you a "quick-fix" and rev up your energy level such as coffee or a candy bar. They're actually tamasic in nature because that quick-fix is short-lived and soon results in an energy plummet that lasts.

Relax

Don't rush "rajasically" to your kitchen and throw away every food you see as remotely unhealthy. By gradually changing and balancing your eating habits and food choices, you'll find that healthier foods will naturally become more appealing to you.

Is Fasting Good for Meditation?

Many cultures include fasting as a part of their religious traditions or rituals. Jesus supposedly fasted for 40 days in the desert. Native Americans fast during their vision quests. Shamans and holy men in many indigenous cultures use fasting and meditation to sharpen awareness and sometimes to induce visions. Fasting is an important part of Islam. Regular fasting (for example, one day every week or three or four days out of every month) has even become a way to cleanse and purify the body for many Westerners.

But does it help meditation? Many people who fast get what is known as a "fasting high" on the second or third day of a fast, during which they feel as if their minds have become exceptionally clear. This may well be an ideal time for meditation. However, fast with caution. If you aren't in good health, it can further compromise your system. Juice fasts are safest, during which you refrain from solid foods but consume fruit and vegetable juice and vegetable broth.

Bliss Byte

By not eating at least four to five hours before sleep, you permit your body to fast naturally and cleanse itself while you sleep. When you awaken, don't shock your system with heavy foods. Start with a room-temperature or slightly warm glass of water (with a few drops of lemon juice if desired, to warm up the digestive process). Then, have some fresh fruit or whole grains.

Making dietary changes should be a slow, gradual process. Sudden changes usually don't stick. If you're committed to health and to helping yourself maintain the optimal mental state at all times, work on one area at a time. Even if it takes a couple of years, you can change your diet for the better, and any change for the better will be well worth the journey.

The Least You Need to Know

➤ You can eat well even in a polluted world.

➤ You don't have to be a vegetarian to meditate, but meditation may make you want to become a vegetarian.

➤ Certain foods are particularly good for boosting brain power and facilitating your meditation practice.

➤ Herbal and vitamin/mineral supplements may provide good nutritional support to a well-balanced, varied diet of healthy, fresh foods.

➤ Another healthy way to eat is to follow the yoga system and eat primarily sattvic, or balancing foods such as fresh produce, whole grains, milk, and honey.

➤ Fasting for short periods on occasion may clear your mind, making meditation easier.

Chapter 25

A Special Meditation Gift for YOU

In This Chapter

➤ Meditation's special benefits for women

➤ Meditation's special benefits for men

➤ Meditating as a family

➤ Kids and seniors, too

Now we'd like to give you something special. We know you're someone special: a woman, a man, a parent, young or old, growing, aging, and seeking. Not every meditation fits every person, but we'd like to tailor some meditations for your situation. We know you are out there, so read on! This one's for you!

For Women Only

Although it hasn't always been fashionable to say so, women are different than men. Beyond the obvious anatomical differences, women have many subtle physical and mental differences as well. Your hormonal make-up is different. Your brains are different. The area connecting the two hemispheres of the brain is larger in women than in men, suggesting that women integrate both sides more effectively. Women have better fine motor coordination and are better at doing many things at once.

One study showed that in a crowded room, men are able to carry on a conversation and completely tune out the conversations around them, while women tend to find this almost impossible and can't help hearing what others around them are saying.

(You aren't eavesdropping—you can't help it! It's the nature of your brains!) Women tend to be more left-brain dominated, which is the realm of language, and women are typically more verbal, talk earlier, and are more dependent on verbal skills for communication. You like to talk things out.

Because women tend to express themselves verbally and because you are so used to doing five things at once, meditation can be a real challenge. "What, sit there for 20 minutes without discussing it with anyone? Yikes! And can't I do the dishes while I'm meditating, or fold the laundry, or get some of that work done that I brought home?" Girlfriends, you may be ultra-efficient, but you are running those poor brains of yours ragged! Especially in this day and age, when women are often expected to do it all— have a great career, keep a sparkling home, keep our men happy, manage a family, and clip coupons—you can really use a daily meditation break or two.

Stress gets to you, but you don't like to admit it, or show it. You hold on and hold on, holding everything together, until suddenly you realize you've taken on too much and have to let go of everything at once. What a mess! (Ugh—more cleaning up to do!)

Let meditation become a part of your daily mental maintenance, and you'll be in much better shape to take it all on. Simplify your life and eliminate those aspects that aren't important. Take time to relax, enjoy your life, and breathe. And when you are folding that laundry, do it mindfully. Fold it for the sake of folding the laundry. How much sweeter life can be! (Especially when you realize that "male energy" can fold laundry, too!)

Bliss Byte

The universe operates in a balanced way. The planets maintain a certain range of distance from the sun, and the moon remains a certain range of distance from the Earth. In yoga, the sun/solar energy is viewed as male, and the moon/lunar energy is viewed as female. However, both principles—solar and lunar energy—exist within all people.

Meditation and Your Cycle

Until they reach the end of childbearing years, just about all women have to face the challenge and gift of monthly menstruation. Our culture views menstruation as a painful, negative time, shrouded in the mysterious "premenstrual syndrome" (PMS), which may, as far as nonmenstruating women know, turn them suddenly into unpredictable people on a seeming emotional roller coaster.

But women don't have to view the monthly cycle as a negative thing. In fact, when viewed in a positive light (as other cultures have done before us), PMS symptoms may actually lessen. The next time you begin to feel the first discomfort related to your monthly cycle, try the following meditation:

1. Lie flat on your back on the floor as in shavasana (see Chapter 18, "Shavasana: It's Not Just Lying Around!"). Place a small pillow under your lower back and another under your knees. Lace your fingers together and place your hands on your lower abdomen. Breathe deeply three times.

2. Visualize yourself standing on a beach at night. The sky is clear, the breeze is warm, and you can hear palm trees rustling behind you. The water is quiet and dark, and the waves lap rhythmically at your feet, spreading foam along the shoreline. Imagine a bright, white full moon is slowly rising above the horizon where the midnight-blue sky meets the ocean. Watch it rise slowly into the peaceful darkness until it is high in the sky. The dark, rhythmic ocean reflects the silvery light of the moon and the waves are painted with light.

3. Now, see the moon waning, gradually becoming eclipsed by darkness. Watch the bright area grow thinner and thinner until only a pale crescent remains in the sky. Feel the breeze blowing the salty air around you and breathe it in deeply. Feel the rhythm of the waves in your body. Now, imagine the moon waxing again, the dark area fading, and the brightness growing larger and larger until the moon is a full, bright disk again. Feel the moon's energy pulling on the waves and gently rolling them onto the shore. Feel the moon's energy in you, moving your internal physical structure to its own rhythm, which is also your rhythm. Feel at one with the rhythm of the ocean and the moon. Let the movement move you. Go with it. Don't fight it. It is you.

Mindful Minute

The ocean tides are created by the gravitational pull of the moon. That moon (read: lunar energy) has a lot of clout here on Earth!

4. Breathe deeply and feel the lunar rhythm for 10 minutes or more. Then slowly, open your eyes.

Meditation to Help Boost Fertility

For a woman suffering from infertility, it may seem that everyone around her is having children. Infertility can become consuming, making life a frustrating, heartbreaking, stressful battle. Fortunately, technology has come a long way in addressing infertility. Yet, approximately 10 million American couples of childbearing age are infertile, and technology may not be able to help them all.

If you are a woman and have been diagnosed as infertile, the most important thing you can do is love yourself. Being infertile isn't some divine punishment for anything in your past. It isn't due to some hidden agenda of your subconscious mind. It doesn't mean you are somehow faulty. But it could be, in part, related to stress.

Two organs at the base of your brain are largely responsible for releasing stress hormones in your body: the pituitary gland and the hypothalamus. The hypothalamus also releases chemical signals that stimulate the pituitary gland to produce two hormones that stimulate ovulation. An overproduction of stress hormones can disrupt this process and may cause menstruation and ovulation to become irregular or, in extreme cases, stop.

Mindful Minute

Preliminary results suggest that stress-reduction techniques may indeed enhance fertility. In one informal study conducted by the Faulkner Centre for Reproductive Medicine in Boston, 54 women were taught a relaxation technique and were asked to practice for 20 minutes twice per day for 10 weeks. Within six months after the program, 34 percent of the women became pregnant, an average higher than typical for women being treated for infertility.

Although women have conceived in the most stressful situations imaginable (even in concentration camps), if you have a physical problem that reduces your fertility, stress may be the factor to seal the deal, inhibiting your infertility. Eliminating stress will only increase your chances of conception, and at worst, it will help you to come to terms with who you are as a whole person, beyond the part of you who wants a baby.

If you're struggling with infertility, being treated for infertility, grieving about your infertility, or simply attempting to conceive, meditation is an important ally. Try to meditate for at least 20 minutes each day. Here is a meditation to help you on your way:

Sit comfortably with your back straight and your eyes closed. Rest your hands on your knees, palms up, to signify your receptiveness. Breathe deeply and slowly. Now imagine a beautiful, glowing divine presence. Perhaps it is God, perhaps it is Mother Earth, perhaps an angel. Imagine the presence surrounding you, emanating love. With each deep inhalation, you breathe in this love, and it fills your body until you develop a beautiful halo of rose light around your entire self. Visualize the presence lifting, effortlessly bearing your weight and gently holding you. You've never felt such all-encompassing love and acceptance. You hear a voice whispering, "I love you. You are perfect. I love you. You are perfect," over and over. Say the words along with the voice and say them to yourself: *I love you. You are perfect.* Know that you are loved and that you are perfect. Continue to breathe and relax into this complete and unconditional love and acceptance for at least 15 minutes.

Bliss Byte

Shavasana (see Chapter 18) is a wonderful technique for pregnancy. Use plenty of pillows to make yourself comfortable. Don't lie flat on your back after your twentieth week of pregnancy, however. You can cut off circulation to your extremities and possibly to the baby. Instead, lie on your left side with pillows under your head and at least one pillow between your knees. Then meditate your stress away and focus on the love that lies within and all around you.

Meditation for Pregnancy and Childbirth

Under the best of circumstances, pregnancy and childbirth are stressful events. The stress is often good stress, but good stress is still stress. Meditation during pregnancy is a great way to relax, reduce your stress level, and bond with your not-yet-born baby. Pregnancy tends to magnify any stress you already have, so manage that stress:

1. Sit in a comfortable chair with your feet up on a stool, ottoman, or stack of pillows. Get really comfy, then place your hands on your belly. Breathe deeply and relax. With each inhalation, imagine love flowing into your lungs, into your blood, and into your baby. With each exhalation, imagine your baby's love flowing back out to you.

2. Gently rub your hands over your belly and on the exhalation, make a soft, vibrating "mmm." Feel the sound vibrating through your body and let it be a sound of love your baby can feel. Your baby can't understand language, but it can feel this expression of your love. Continue to breathe, inhaling love into your baby, exhaling your baby's love into the air around you.

3. Perform this meditation every day.

During childbirth, meditation can be a great way to move through the pain of labor, but the most important thing for childbirth is mindfulness. Remaining completely aware and mindful through the experience will help you to remember every precious moment (even the painful ones will someday seem precious). Mindful awareness and objective observation of labor pains may make them more bearable, but even if you choose to have some type of pain relief, be mindful of every feeling, every sensation, and that fantastic feeling when the pain stops.

This squatting pose can help you to relax, open your hips, and prepare for labor. Stack pillows on the floor as high as you need for comfort. The squat is an active pose; don't strain your joints and muscles or push the pose to the point of pain or stress. After holding the pose comfortably for as long as you desire, relax down to a seated pose on the floor and continue your practice of relaxation and meditation.

When you first see that baby of yours, be there. Be awake and aware. Live that moment, and someday you can tell your child all about it because you'll *remember*.

Meditation and Breastfeeding

If you watch a breastfeeding mother, you may think it looks like the most effortless and natural act imaginable. And it is—after the first few weeks. Those first few weeks can be tough ones for many women, and many give up trying to breastfeed before they get over this hump. Experts agree, however, that breastfeeding is the best way to feed your baby; no formula can duplicate breastmilk, which is individually tailored for your baby's needs. Breastfed babies are typically healthier and suffer from fewer health problems.

But before you get the hang of it and before your baby has the hang of it, breastfeeding can be difficult, frustrating, and in those postpartum days, may sometimes

Mindful Minute

Stress can make a pregnancy more difficult, but some studies suggest that attitude is an even more important factor. One study found that pregnant women who had to work despite their desire to stay home were at a much greater risk of preterm labor and giving birth to babies with low birth weight—probably because of the extra stress working against their desires triggered.

reduce you (and baby) to tears. When you feel like you want to quit even though you know you don't *really* want to quit, try this meditation:

Lie back on a big pile of pillows or in a comfortable chair with your feet up. Hold your baby in your arms when it isn't particularly hungry and isn't crying. Hold it against your heart. Close your eyes and breathe in deeply, then breathe out. Imagine you and your baby are surrounded by a warm yellow glow that encompasses you both as if you were one being. Feel your baby against you. Feel its breathing. Then, match your breathing to your baby's, at a rate of approximately four of baby's breaths to one of your own (find a ratio that feels comfortable). Continue with this rhythm until it becomes as natural as breathing on your own, and until you feel like you and your baby are as in harmony as you were when your baby was still inside you.

Bliss Byte

Touch is crucial for babies, so bring your baby into your meditation practice. As your little one sleeps, rest its little hand upon your upturned hand and accept your baby's beautiful energy into your own energy. Send lots of loving energy back in return. Meditate on your baby's face, potential, and the bond between the two of you. When your baby gets a little older, let him or her continue to join you in your meditation practice. If baby sees you meditating each day and always feels a part of it, eventually your baby will make meditation a part of his or her own life. What a wonderful gift for a mother to bestow on her child!

Mom Meditation

Once your kids get past the newborn stage, chaos sets in. It will probably last for the next, oh, 20 years or so. You can't eliminate chaos completely in a house with kids, so you're better off learning to manage it. Stressed-out moms can use a little mothering. Whenever you start to feel the chaos rising, stop what you are doing, breathe in deeply, feel the strength of the ground beneath your feet, and as you exhale, say (or think) the following five-element mantra:

Mother Earth, breathe peace into me.

Mother Earth, let peace glow in me.

Mother Earth, flood me with peace.

Mother Earth, peace grows in me.

Mother Earth, your peace ascends.

Meditation to Ease Menopause

One segment of the arc of womanhood involves the winding down of the childbearing years. This time marks an important transition in the life of a woman. Symbolically, life's purpose can shift now. Even if your children have been on their own for a while or even if they aren't quite out of the nest yet, menopause marks that period of life when your life can at last become your own. It is a time to return to the world, a time when the capacity to love becomes greater, more galactic and inclusive, as your focus broadens beyond your immediate family to include the community. Balance, as ever, is the key between care of the self and care of the world.

Women are brought up in our society to be giving. But there is a time for giving and a time for living. Sure, you can do them both at the same time, but sometimes it's nice to focus solely on the latter. Finding your own strength, your own individuality, your own desires, journeying out into the world or into the soul, or both, is the promise of life-after-childbearing. Make the most of yours! And if menopause is accompanied by discomfort or difficult symptoms, see your doctor, but also, keep meditating:

Sit comfortably with your back straight and your eyes closed. Breathe deeply and prepare to count very slowly to 20. As you count, say and visualize the following:

1. I am a baby, playing, laughing, crawling, learning.
2. I am a small child, toddling, walking, loving, learning.
3. I am in school, making friends, living, learning.
4. I am in high school, making friends, exploring life, learning.
5. I am a young adult, finding a career, meeting people who will become important in my life (you can name them), learning.
6. I am in middle age, enjoying my friends, my family, still learning.
7. I am here today, beautiful, wise, loving, beloved, and still learning.
8. I am still learning—what am I learning?
9. I am still loving—who am I loving?
10. I am still learning—what am I learning?
11. I am still happy—how am I happy?
12. I am still learning—what am I learning?
13. I am still playing—how am I playing?
14. I am still learning—what am I learning?
15. I am still laughing—what makes me laugh?

16. I am still learning—what am I learning?

17. I am still making friends—who are my friends?

18. I am still learning—what am I learning?

19. I am still beautiful—see how beautiful I am?

20. I am still learning—what am I learning?

Now, relax and reflect upon how much you still have to learn, how much of life you have left, how your life has really just begun.

For Men

Don't worry, guys. We haven't forgotten you. You are unique, too, biologically, hormonally, and emotionally. You tend to be right-brain dominated, better at thinking spatially, such as knowing where one object is in relation to others. That's why you never ask for directions—you can find your way on your own! Your brain is typically bigger than the female brain (no snide comments, please), and you may be more likely to depend on a single area of your brain to help you accomplish tasks, making it easier for you to focus your attention on one thing to the exclusion of distractions.

Because you tend to be right-brained, you also tend to excel at reasoning and math problems, though verbal skills may take a little more practice. Of course, none of these biological factors hem you in. Maybe you're a fantastic speaker and/or writer. Maybe you're lousy at math or can't find where you're going without a map to save your life. We're all individuals, but we also have a lot in common, and one of those commonalities is the ability to benefit from meditation.

There's No Edge on a Circle

Men don't have it easy in the modern world, either. You guys are under a lot of pressure. You're supposed to earn a respectable living, but that's nothing new. In addition, however, you're now expected to be a caring, nurturing partner, be a loving and giving dad, help out with the housework, and look really good, too. At least, that's what we're all led to believe by television, movies, and the current literature. Yes, you're supposed to be Superman.

Of course, no one is really Superman, and chances are, like most men, you excel in a couple of these areas but other areas just aren't your forte. The result of trying to live up to such unrealistic expectations, however, is a lot of stress, and stress tends to set men on edge. Maybe you get angry,

Relax

Hey there guys! Meditation is not a competitive sport, so rein in your tendency to make meditation another aggressive activity. It is an inner process of growth and understanding. The practice of meditation, though, can improve one's athletic abilities by increasing focus and concentration.

irritable, or depressed. And speaking of edge, you may hear a lot about having the competitive edge, being on the cutting edge, edging out the other guy—it's enough to send a man right over the edge!

When life gets to be too much, there's nothing wrong with putting on the brakes and stepping back from the edge. You can set limits for yourself, and you can practice stress management. These days, it's almost a necessity. Take, for your symbol of calm, the circle. Circles don't have edges, and if you follow them with your eyes, they don't have a beginning or an ending. No finish line, no goal, just a continuous and eternal path.

Perhaps you find it frustrating to conceive of a journey without an end, without competition, without a *goal*. Step into that challenge and see where it takes you. Once you set aside the idea of a goal, you'll be far more able to practice mindfulness. With mindfulness, the joy and the experience is in the doing, not in the "getting to." Try this meditation to train your mind toward this different perspective:

1. Sit comfortably with your back straight and your eyes closed. Breathe deeply, then visualize a golden circle in front of you. The circle grows, flattens out, and becomes a circular path. Imagine yourself stepping onto this circular path. You begin walking, then you begin running. But what's this? You're going in circles! You're not getting anywhere! Imagine that you feel frustrated at first because you are running the same track again and again. What's the point? Then, quite suddenly, you stop in your tracks. You look around you. There is no "point." Yet, you haven't even noticed where you are! You look around again, and the air around you transforms into a beautiful landscape of tall green trees, bright blue lakes, snow-topped mountains. Where did this come from, you wonder? The circle is still beneath your feet, but as you stand still, you recognize it has a spectacular view to offer. What more might there be to see?

2. Start walking very slowly, and with each step, a new and magnificent scene surrounds you. A rocky cliff overlooking a dramatic seascape. Rolling hills blanketed with snow and trees encased in ice crystals. A brilliant red and purple sunset over a desert canyon. A sensational waterfall tumbling into a blue-green grotto. And then, something wonderful happens. The golden circle seems to come apart, falling, and as you look down, you see it has transformed into a spiral. Still circular, yet universes have opened up below you, and you see you are just beginning an amazing journey. And the journey is in the journeying.

3. Walk along the spiral and live each step fully and completely for as long as you like, at least 10 minutes. When you've seen enough for today, take a few more deep, slow breaths and say the words, "Live for this moment. And this moment. And this moment." Open your eyes and start living!

Meditation for Your Prostate (and the Rest of You!)

Your prostate certainly is not the only area of concern when it comes to men's health. It's just the area that gets the most press! Other men's health issues include heart disease, impotence, longevity, and hair loss, to name just a few. Can meditation keep you healthier, help you to live longer, make you more virile? Meditation can certainly facilitate your body's healing efforts, and perhaps even more importantly, it can change your mind about your body. And that's half the battle.

Each morning, begin your day with 20 minutes of seated meditation. Sit in mindfulness. Listen and feel your breath moving in and out of your body. When you are comfortable and feel calm, chant the following mantra: Say "Health in," then inhale deeply, from the lower abdomen (don't lift those shoulders or chest). Then say "Tension out," and exhale fully. Then say "Strength in," and inhale deeply, "Hesitation out," then exhale fully. Then say (and this part is important, so don't skip it!) "Love in," inhaling deeply, and "Anger out," exhaling fully. Repeat the sequence again and again until your 20 minutes is over. Feel the words, visualize health and strength and love flowing into you, tension and hesitation and anger flowing out of you. Let the words and the breath merge and become you.

This meditation is also great for anger management, impatience, and ebbing self-esteem, something men often experience but are far less likely to admit. Whenever you are feeling depressed, unworthy, unable, or insecure, take a few minutes to breathe and say the mantra: *Health in, tension released. Strength in, hesitation released. Love in, anger released.* You can be who you want to be, and you can have a wonderful, satisfying, fulfilling life. Live every moment fully and let the universe inspire you.

Mindful Minute

The Daoists have a good way of thinking about negative energy: They suggest that the negative vibes released are transformed by the Earth, just as the garbage and scraps you put into your backyard compost are transformed.

Relax

Rein in your anger, which some experts define as "depression turned outward." Anger can motivate us to make necessary changes, and it can also destroy us. Find ways to use anger constructively. A professional therapist may help in this healing journey.

For the Whole Family

Meditation doesn't have to be a solitary pursuit. It can also be a family affair! This is great news for parents who rarely have a moment to themselves. Peace and tranquillity with the kids in tow? Could it be possible?

A New Sense of Togetherness

Meditation with kids isn't the same as meditation on your own or even meditation with another adult partner. But it can still be fulfilling and relaxing. It also provides your family with one more activity to do together, and the relaxing and spiritual nature of meditation will help to bond you together. Let meditation serve as a common ground and family priority, and your family will grow stronger.

Setting Kids on the Right Path

Meditation is also a great way to teach children the techniques of stress reduction, contemplation, conflict management, and spiritual reflection. The sooner they learn these skills, the better they'll be able to navigate adult life. Try this meditation with the whole family:

Have everyone sit in a circle, legs crossed, knees touching. For younger kids who can't be expected to sit still (say, under five years), allow them to sit or lie in the middle of the circle. (If they squirm or roll around, that's okay. You're setting an example, and they'll catch on eventually.)

Next, have each person in the circle make the Om mudra (see Chapter 15, "Seated Meditation: Finding Center") with his or her hands. Each person places his or her hands on their knees so that their knuckles or fingers lightly touch the knuckles or fingers of the person on either side. Now, the family is connected in a physical circle and an energy circle.

The Om mudra.

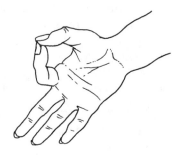

Now, lead your family in the following mantra pattern. Begin by saying each word below, then have each family member repeat it, one at a time, around the circle. When the mantra reaches you again, change to the next word. Go through the cycle three times and have the whole family say the sequence of mantras in unison three more times:

➤ *Love*

➤ *Peace*

➤ *Happiness*

➤ *Serenity*

➤ *Family*

➤ *One*

Bliss Byte

Teaching kids to be mindful will do more than help them in school (though it probably will do just that). It will also teach them to be more attentive people, better listeners, more empathetic, and loving, and more joyful and appreciative of the beautiful and fascinating world around them. Children can also use mindfulness and quiet reflection as tools to help them through difficult times, whether peer rejection, an excruciating test, or even a family tragedy. The best way to teach kids mindfulness is through your own example.

As You Age

As you pass midlife and head into the golden years, meditation can be more than a stress-reduction technique. It can also be a center of peace in your life, a way to manage health problems, a method of health maintenance, and a great way to boost and maintain your self-esteem.

Aging doesn't have to be accompanied by health problems, but it often is. It doesn't have to be accompanied by depression, but it often is. It doesn't have to be accompanied by a loss of joy, ambition, and purpose, but it often is. If you start now to combat all of these negative conditions, you'll enjoy your golden years more. Even if you do have to deal with some of the conditions associated with aging, you'll be better equipped.

As menopause is a major transition for women, retirement is a huge one for men and, increasingly, for women, too. Because men have traditionally been the "breadwinners," however, and have associated their lives so closely with their professions, they may experience feelings of no longer having value or a purpose. Joseph Campbell once said that men and women often change roles as they age: women become stronger, more assertive, and more involved in the outside world. Men become more nurturing, more interested in staying at home, and more interested in pursuits of the home, including gardening and cooking. Campbell also once said that as his own body aged, it was a great reminder to him that it was time to move more into spiritual pursuits. These could be the best years of your life. Make the most of the wisdom, experience, and perspective you've earned and live life for all its worth. Show those young'uns how it's done!

Begin and end each day with meditation, if your schedule allows (or, if it doesn't allow, adjust your schedule). If meditation is difficult at first, don't despair. Practice makes perfect, and the more you meditate, the more you'll anticipate and come to depend on these sessions for mental maintenance and spiritual renewal.

Any of the meditations in this book are appropriate for you, but you can also try this one:

Mindful Minute

Gerontologists from Tufts University put a group of frail nursing-home residents ages 87 to 96 on a weight training program and found that within eight weeks, the residents experienced a 300 percent increase in muscle tone. So seniors, try some gentle movement meditation, walking meditation, or yoga. Keep using that mind-body. Consult your physician before beginning any exercise program.

1. Sit on the floor or in a comfortable chair with your back straight and your eyes closed. Breathe deeply a few times. Scan your body for spots of tension and breathe into them.

2. When you feel fairly relaxed, visualize yourself walking easily down a winding stone path. The sun is warm and mild. On either side of you are beautiful, delicate trees with bright green leaves and pink blossoms. Petals flutter onto the path as a gentle, cool spring breeze rustles the trees. Purple crocus and yellow daffodils are peeking through the grass at the feet of the trees. You feel happy and energetic. You've got a spring in your step and happiness in your heart. Look all around you and notice every detail of this lovely spring day.

3. Soon, the path turns a bend and the trees grow thicker, taller, and more lush. You smell the scent of freshly mown grass and the air is decorated with birdsong. The sun is higher in the sky and warmer, but still comfortable and comforting. The stone path is lined with bright lilies and wild roses, like a garden gone slightly wild. The breeze is warm and smells vaguely of the ocean. You feel calm and content. Look all around you and notice every detail of this languid summer day.

4. Now, the path turns another bend and the trees begin to blush. The breeze is fresh and cool, and it rustles the leaves on the trees as they slowly change into scarlet, bright orange, yellow, and many shades of red. Leaves float down through the cool air and decorate the path with their bright colors. You breathe deeply, and your heart fills with joy. What a beautiful place to be! You notice a wooden bench on the side of the path and decide to sit for a while. You sit, and the bench is surprisingly comfortable. The sun is warm above, and the sky is a brilliant blue. The trees are on fire with color, and the cool air is bracing and energizing. Breathe it in and relish the smell of autumn. You feel such a surge of energy that you rise from the bench and return to the path, walking with a renewed sense of purpose and direction.

5. As you move through the lovely autumn day, gratitude and thanksgiving overflow in your heart, and you find yourself joyfully chanting the words "Love, love, love!" because you know this is your life, and it is the most beautiful phase you've yet experienced. You can hardly wait to see what comes next! Continue to breathe and when you are ready, open your eyes and embrace the day.

Meditation, mindfulness, visualization, and attention to the breath are right for any gender, any age, any inclination. Embrace meditation and make it your own, then watch your life burst into bloom.

The Least You Need to Know

➤ Meditation can help women cope with the discomfort of menstruation, with infertility stress, with pregnancy, breastfeeding, motherhood, and menopause.

➤ Meditation can help men learn to view life in new ways, boost their physical and mental health, and mend self-esteem.

➤ Meditation is a great family activity and can help kids grow into adults who can handle stress and enjoy life.

➤ Meditation can help seniors make the most of the best years of their lives: the golden years!

Rx: Meditation

Meditation itself doesn't exactly heal. Chanting a mantra won't slay bacteria, and mindfulness won't mend a broken bone. In fact, we want to make it clear right from the start that no matter how in tune your mind-body connection is, you should seek medical care when you're sick or injured. Meditation, however, can be a remarkably helpful adjunct: It can remove some of the obstacles that may be keeping your body from healing itself. In this chapter, we'll help you explore the role that meditation can play in your own health and healing.

Ayurveda Equals Homeostasis

Different cultures have all developed their own systems of health and medicine. The history of medicine around the world would make a fascinating and lengthy book. But one of the oldest systems of health, and one of the most holistic (which means it looks at and treats all aspects of the mind-body) is the Indian system of *Ayurveda*.

From A to Om

Ayurveda is the oldest organized system of health care. Literally "science of living" or "art of life," Ayurveda involves a combination of customized diet, yoga exercises, meditation, hygiene rituals, massage, and a regular daily routine into a philosophical system of energy balancing. Ayurveda has recently become popular in the West largely due to the writings and influence of Deepak Chopra, M.D.

From A to Om

Homeostasis is the tendency of a system (such as a body, a group, or an ecosystem) to maintain an equilibrium or balanced state.

Ayurveda has literally been translated as "science of life," and it is just that: an all-encompassing approach to living. According to Ayurveda, humans have the capacity to live far longer life spans than we do. The only reason our lives are cut short is because we don't optimize our mind-body systems. Ayurveda helps keep the body in balance so that it can operate the way it was meant to and remain healthy far into old age.

A Western word for this balance is *homeostasis*. Homeostasis is the tendency of a body (or even an entire ecosystem) to remain in a balanced state. For example, even when it's really hot outside, your body makes adjustments so that its internal temperature remains at approximately 98.6° Fahrenheit. Few bodies operate in true homeostasis in a world full of toxins, addictions, pollutants, stress, and negative habits, but for a truly healthy mind-body, finding and maintaining balance is crucial. Your body is trying continually to find that balance, so help it along. Remove those roadblocks (such as negativity, eating junk food, being sedentary, and letting stress get to you)!

Ayurveda utilizes many methods to maintain mind-body homeostasis, including aromatherapy, massage, a diet tailored to your individual tendencies, herbal medicine, special hygiene practices, and the diagnosis of imbalances through the learned reading of the pulse. One of the most important aspects of Ayurveda is meditation.

Deepak Chopra, M.D., one of the West's most renowned proponents of Ayurveda, says in his book *Perfect Health*, "Physical impurities in cells have their equivalents in the mind: fear, anger, greed, compulsiveness, doubt, and other negative emotions. Operating at the quantum level, they can be as damaging to us as any chemical toxin." In Ayurveda, meditation purifies the mind in the same way other techniques purify the body.

The point of meditation as part of Ayurveda is to cleanse the mind by refining thought to subtler and subtler levels until it finally stills, giving the mind complete peace, rest, and renewal. Now your body can heal itself a little bit more easily.

Using Your Body Knowledge to Heal

You know yourself better than you might think. You know what it means to have a vague sense that something isn't "right," that you're "coming down with something," or that you're "under the weather." You might not be able to produce the technical term for what's wrong, but you know. And your body knows, too.

You can use this body knowledge to your healing advantage, and meditation is the connection, the translator, and the conduit for healing energy your mind sends to your body. Visualizations can help your body to send you a message. And don't forget good old-fashioned intuition. Don't ignore that "sixth sense."

How to Talk to Your Doctor About Holistic Health

Just a few years ago, few medical doctors gave serious credence to natural medicine. Now, however, an increasing number of M.D.s recognize both the popularity and the legitimacy of the holistic health approach, though many are still skeptical of treatments and therapies that haven't been validated by a host of scientific studies. And they've got a point: You should be cautious about who is responsible for your health and what therapy he or she uses to treat you. You don't want to throw your health into the hands of someone who doesn't know what they are doing or who is using substances and techniques that might prove harmful. But many holistic health therapies have been well tested, and if your doctor is doing his or her homework, you should be able to work together to provide a safe, effective, and more natural health plan for you.

Mindful Minute

According to a 1987 study by Dr. David Orme-Johnson at Maharishi International University, meditators between 19 and 39 years old visited their doctors 54.7 percent less often than nonmeditators of the same age, and meditators over age 40 visited their doctors a whopping 73.7 percent less often than their nonmeditating peers. In addition, meditators had 87.3 percent fewer hospital admissions for heart disease and 55.4 percent fewer hospital admissions for tumors of all types.

Mindful Minute

One reason natural medicine is gaining in popularity in the West so quickly is because people are losing faith in conventional health care. Among the top 10 reasons for hospitalization in the United States are adverse reactions and side effects from medications. Over-medication and adverse affects from drug interactions are a common problem, especially in the elderly. Plus, meditation today is cheaper than surgery tomorrow!

Relax

When choosing any health care practitioner, whether of traditional medicine or alternative natural medicine, be sure that he or she is a licensed professional. And make sure that any new treatment regimen you begin is done in coordination with your primary care physician. A coordinated treatment plan, created by a health care team composed of *all* your health care providers, is the best way to ensure your maximum health and well being.

Make an appointment for a check-up with your primary care physician, then explain that you are interested in combining natural medicine with your regular health care routine. Whether you're seeking help for some chronic condition or are hoping to head off disease by practicing preventive medicine, your doctor may be able to tell you which therapies might prove helpful to you. He or she might also be able to warn you away from therapies that might be dangerous, or at best, a waste of money.

Health Is Balance

To *holistic* health practitioners, health means balanced life-force energy. It tends to be much more focused on maintaining health and preventing disease than on treatment.

Conventional Western medicine, also called *allopathic medicine*, works in just the opposite way. It tends to focus on treating diseases once they occur than on helping the body and mind maintain health in the most natural ways possible.

Many holistic healing methods, such as Ayurveda, homeopathy, herbalism, aromatherapy, traditional Chinese medicine, and folk medicine, use the concept of balancing the whole system in one way or another. One way to balance the body is to first balance the mind. A balanced mind encourages a balanced body by making symptoms of imbalance more clear to the mind-body, rather than masking them with emotional or psychological symptoms.

But where do you go for competent and qualified holistic health care, and how do you know which therapy is right for you? Why not start with your own doctor?

Bliss Byte

Depending on where you live and what your health care options are, you may not be able to find a primary care physician who supports or knows a lot about natural medicine. That doesn't mean you can't make some changes in the way you take care of yourself, however. Take a cue from holistic medicine and practice preventive medicine by eating fresh, organic, unprocessed food, exercising regularly, and meditating.

Types of Natural Medicine Popular in the West

Type	Description
Ayurveda	The Indian "science of life"
Homeopathy	A subtle medical therapy based on the idea that "like cures like"—remedies that would cause certain symptoms are given to cure those symptoms
Herbalism	The treatment of disease with herbs
Aromatherapy	The treatment of imbalances through the inhalation or application to the skin of essential oils
Traditional Chinese medicine (TCM)	The ancient Chinese system of acupuncture and herbal medicine
Folk medicine	A return to true traditional healing methods originating in different countries at a very local level, and may include use of herbs and foods in various forms to treat everything from a headache to a sprained ankle to depression

Blending Allopathic and Natural Medicine

First of all, it's extremely important for you to discuss your use of any alternative therapies with your regular doctor. Because allopathic and natural medicine are each suited to different types of problems, they are most effectively used in conjunction with one another. But if the right hand (your doctor) doesn't know what the left hand (your herbalist or your homeopath, for example) is doing, you could be putting your health in jeopardy. Allopathic and natural treatments can work beautifully together, but they can also work at odds if the lines of communication are shut down. So be open and forthright about your health habits and the health care professionals you see, and everyone can work together as your own personal health care team.

From A to Om

Holistic or **natural medicine** involve a whole mind-body approach to health. These methods emphasize preventive medicine and are often effective at relieving chronic conditions like recurrent colds, mild headaches, arthritis, and even cancer. **Allopathic** medicine is the mainstream Western approach to health care, based on treating symptoms and isolating a specific disorder rather than treating the whole person.

Creating a Health Care Team

Assembling your own health care team starts with selecting a primary care doctor who has a similar view about health issues as you do. If you like to get in and out of the doctor's office with as little fuss as possible, like to be told what to do without asking questions, and have no problem putting your whole trust in your doctor, then you'll be happier with a doctor who doesn't dilly-dally, gets down to business, tells you what you need to do without long, detailed explanations, then leaves you alone.

If, on the other hand, you want to know exactly what the doctor is doing at all times, why he or she is prescribing certain medications or treatments, and what you can do in your life to improve your health, you'll want a doctor who is willing to spend time talking with you. You won't want an impatient doctor or a doctor who has no interest whatsoever in alternative treatments. Shop around. These days some insurance plans are making it easier to switch doctors if your doctor isn't living up to your expectations. When choosing your insurance company or HMO (if your employer gives you a choice!), be sure to find out about its policies on choosing and changing health care providers. Of course, doctors aren't miracle workers, but you should feel confident that your doctor makes your health and welfare a priority and is willing to engage in the level of communication you desire and that is reasonable.

Next, you'll want to consider what other health care practitioners you might use. Again, your doctor might be of some help here. Could you benefit from acupuncture? From massage therapy? From a chiropractor? Would any herbal remedies support your efforts toward creating a healthy lifestyle and maintaining internal balance? What about homeopathy? Does your doctor recommend any home remedies for minor conditions like colds and coughs? Choose the other members of your health care team with care. Ask questions, make sure they have proper training and certification, and make sure that you feel comfortable with them. If you and your qualified herbalist click, you'll be more able to put certain aspects of your health care in his or her hands. But if that massage therapist rubs you the wrong way (so to speak), you should keep looking for someone more suitable to your own personal needs and personality—as long as he or she has the proper professional certification.

Relax

Taking responsibility for your life and health is an important step in your own health care. Avoid blaming others, and don't be afraid to ask for help. Ask questions of the professionals on your health care team and request their advice and counsel. Be proactive about your own well-being and participate in the care you receive.

How the Mind Contributes to Healing

The research is still controversial, but the scientific community is becoming increasingly willing to admit that the mind does indeed contribute to healing. Relaxation techniques actually lower levels of stress hormones in the body, slow heart and breathing rates, reduce blood pressure, and lessen the perception of pain in people who suffer from chronic pain. People with positive attitudes tend to live longer, get sick less often, and heal faster. Mind and body are inextricable.

If you're facing surgery, you have a unique opportunity to use the power of your mind through meditation in a way that can dramatically reduce your presurgical anxiety and postsurgical pain. Studies have shown that patients facing surgery fared much better when they:

➤ Are given clear and complete instructions about what to expect

➤ Are given presurgical suggestions about ways to reduce postsurgical pain, such as by consciously relaxing the muscles around the site of an incision

➤ Are confident that the surgery is necessary

➤ Understand what will happen during the surgery

➤ Listen to relaxing music via headphones and a cassette player during surgery

Many of the above conditions are in your hands. Explain to your doctor that you want to know everything possible about what to expect. Ask about ways to reduce postsurgical pain. Get a second opinion about whether your surgery is necessary. Read about the surgery. Make sure your surgeon has performed the particular surgery many times before. And ask about whether you can bring a cassette player and headphones into surgery with you. Even under general anesthesia, evidence suggests you still perceive the music at some level, and so music that invokes a positive response may help your body to deal with the surgery. (Of course, if you choose to play music out loud, make sure the surgeon likes the music, too, so his or her performance can also be enhanced!)

Some institutions are good about handling the patient's anxiety and informing the patient about ways in which he or she can take an active approach to preparation and recovery. Others aren't so good, especially where the staff is trained only in the procedures themselves and not in mollifying the patient. But don't accept the brush-off. You deserve to know everything you can about what will make surgery easier on your mind and body.

Bliss Byte

Many kinds of medical treatments can be enhanced using creative visualization techniques. For example, patients undergoing radiation treatments for cancer can imagine the radioactive particles as a healing army infusing the body with restorative warmth and flushing out the invading cancer cells (or an advancing tide flowing to shore to flush and remove the impurities as it retreats again). Patients who ask their health care providers to explain how a specific treatment works inside their bodies can use this knowledge to develop creative visualization exercises that are based on the treatment process. The experience of the treatment is transformed, through the patient's imagination, into a healing ritual that is specifically nurturing to the mind-body of the person receiving treatment.

Studies show that very specific, one-on-one instruction to a patient about exactly what to expect in recovery significantly decreases recovery time. If you can convince a doctor or nurse to provide you with this information, your anxiety will diminish, and you'll be prepared. Such instruction can be invaluable in influencing the course of your surgery. As the information enters your brain and your consciousness, your body will hear it, too, and respond. Studies conducted by the Department of Anesthesiology at the University of California, Davis, Medical Center and other institutions have shown or suggested that:

➤ Patients may be able to control their level of comfort during surgery (as measured by micromovements in facial muscles) by thorough preparation, presurgical counseling, and listening to relaxing music during surgery.

➤ Patients given specific instruction about how to relax muscles around an incision site resulted in less need for postsurgical pain relief and quicker discharge time.

➤ Patients given specific instructions about how their gastrointestinal systems would begin to recover after abdominal surgery, including suggestions that the gurgling and churning sounds indicative of intestinal functioning would begin soon after surgery, experienced a return of function significantly sooner than patients who didn't receive the suggestions. The instructed patients also left the hospital an average of one and a half days sooner.

➤ Patients can control the amount of blood lost during surgery by being given specific presurgical instructions about directing blood away from the incision site during surgery and back toward it after surgery to encourage healing. The group given these instructions lost significantly less blood during surgery.

Getting such instruction may not be easy, however. In many cases, preparing for surgery is a task you must take on yourself. But who better to prepare your body than you? If you are facing surgery, have a plan. Prepare your mind as you prepare your body, so they can work together with the efforts of the surgeon. Make sure your plan includes the following elements, loosely based on suggestions by Henry L. Bennett, Ph.D., and Elizabeth A. Disbrow, M.A., of the Department of Anesthesiology at the University of California, Davis, Medical Center, for designing your own presurgical program:

➤ **Do your research.** Ask your doctors to explain everything you should expect. Discuss options for medication, anesthesia, and pain control with your doctors. Read up on your surgery, and if your reading brings up new questions, don't hesitate to ask your doctor.

➤ **Have a meditation plan.** Visualization can be an effective technique for surgery. Plan ahead what you will visualize, what mantra you might want to keep in mind, what imagery you'll focus on.

➤ **Turn up the volume.** Some studies show that patients may be affected by what surgeons and other people in the operating room say, even if they don't consciously hear or remember it. To protect yourself from any negative influences on your recovery, bring along a cassette recorder with auto-reverse and listen to relaxing music or taped instructions for relaxation and recovery.

➤ **Instruct your body.** For several days before surgery, repeatedly remind yourself that during surgery, you will direct your blood away from the incision site, and that after surgery, you will consciously keep the muscles around your incision site totally relaxed, allowing for sufficient blood flow to nourish and heal you.

➤ **Be assertive.** Hospital staff are under a lot of stress and they may need to be reminded to give you information, help, or support. If you are feeling in need, ask for help. Of course you can't get in the way of the staff performing their jobs, but often if you just ask for some moral support, a hand to hold, or have a specific question or request, someone will be glad to oblige.

➤ **Know your medication.** Request that the anesthesiologist tell you what he or she is going to do before it is done, rather than after, so you can feel more in control when you begin to feel the effects. Ask what pain control medications will be available after surgery and discuss the effects of the various options. Be ready to adjust your dosage, too. You may not need as much as the patient in the next room.

➤ **Acknowledge your fear.** Few people face surgery without at least a twinge of fear. Of course it's scary. Surgery has risks and involves a distinct and unavoidable loss of control. Be open with yourself about your fears, talk to people, and consider a presurgical counseling session or two so you can handle your fear in a way that works for you.

➤ **The glass is half full!** As in any other type of life crisis, positive thinking can work wonders. Know that you are facing surgery for good and important reasons, that you have done everything you could to prepare, and that you trust your surgeon. Send positive thoughts and prayers to your surgeon to guide her or him in caring for you. Remember to be assertive about asking for what you need—health care providers work for you! And last of all, relax. Let the professionals do their work. Expect the best, and look forward to coming out of surgery and rallying your body's healing power.

Meditations to Heal By

While a book of meditations to fit every illness and injury would be hefty indeed, we'd like to give you a few suggestions for using meditation to heal some common health problems. In each of the following meditations, sit or lie comfortably and remember to breathe deeply, infusing your body with healing oxygen.

For the Heart

If you suffer from cardiovascular disease, you aren't alone. One million people die every year from cardiovascular disease, and it is the number one killer in the United States. One source estimates that 50 million Americans have cardiovascular disease and don't know it.

Perhaps your heart problem isn't so extreme. Whether you suffer from heart palpitations or serious angina (chest pain), heart-centered meditation can be therapeutic and can ease the anxiety that may exacerbate a heart condition.

Begin meditating by following your breath. When you feel relaxed, bring your attention to your Venus or heart chakra, the energy center behind your heart (see page 117). Now, imagine your breath is shifting so that you are breathing from your heart chakra. Feel your breath flowing around and past your heart, flooding it with healing energy. Imagine the arteries around the heart muscle opening and flowing with nutrients. Feel the rhythm of your heart. If you can't actually feel it beating, imagine a slow, strong beat and breath in rhythm with it, five beats per inhalation, 10 beats per exhalation. You can even put your hand over your heart and rub gently. Visualize your heart strong, pulsing with health, exuding compassionate energy. Stay with your heart for 10 or 15 minutes, then let your breathing return to normal.

Whenever you are feeling anxious or have a twinge of chest pain, relive the feeling of this heart meditation, visualizing the arteries opening and the sound of the slow, healthy, strong heartbeat. Dr. Dean Ornish has found a strong connection between the occurrence of heart disease and issues having to do with love, and emphasizes the importance of emotional support and connection with others in healing heart disease. Form a support network to support all aspects of your heart.

Bliss Byte

Lie on your back with your knees bent. Bring your arms out so that they make a T with your body. Let your knees fall to the left, your head to the right. Keep your shoulders against the floor. Relax. Open your heart. Breathe. After a comfortable time, bring your knees to the right, your head to the left. Breathe, relax, open. After a comfortable time, come back to center. Feel better?

For the Lungs

Whether it's asthma, pneumonia, tuberculosis, bronchitis, emphysema, or pleurisy, lung disorders can be scary. Few things induce a feeling of panic like not being able to take a deep breath or to breathe well enough to nourish the body with sufficient oxygen.

Asthma is particularly prevalent in the United States, where approximately 6 percent of children are affected, compared with 1 to 2 percent worldwide, and the incidence of hospitalization due to asthma in children is up 500 percent in the last 30 years! A 1985 study published in the *British Medical Journal* showed that 60 minutes of daily deep breathing, yoga postures, and meditation resulted in fewer asthma attacks, less need for medication, and greater lung capacity for asthma sufferers.

Over two million people contract pneumonia each year in the United States, and between 40,000 and 70,000 die from it. According to the U.S. Lung Association, approximately 14 in 100,000 people are affected by tuberculosis. Lung cancer is the leading fatal cancer in the world. This year, 67,000 women will die from lung cancer, which is more than breast cancer and ovarian cancer deaths combined.

If you have a lung disease or condition, meditation can help to ease anxiety, which in turn can help to ease bronchial constriction. Also, because stress increases your respiration rate, forcing your lungs to work harder, stress management is important for lung problems. Try the following meditation:

Mindful Minute

Researchers estimate that if Americans stopped all smoking today, lung cancer deaths would be dramatically reduced within 20 years. Eighty-five percent of lung cancers can be directly linked to smoking.

Sit comfortably with your back straight to allow your rib cage (and thus your lungs) plenty of room to expand. Now, concentrate all your attention on your breath and attempt to breathe very slowly. Inhaling through your nose, see how high you can count without straining (at the rate of about one count per second). Then, exhaling through your nose or mouth (whichever is more comfortable and feels more natural), see if you can increase the count. Repeat, trying to increase the count each time. No speeding up your rate of counting! And no straining. Imagine prana, or life-force energy, filling your body and revitalizing your lungs with each inhalation.

If you feel your focus wandering away from the breath, gently bring it back. Once you've reached your maximum count, stay with it for a few more breaths, then breathe normally again, close your eyes, and feel the calm. According to Chinese medicine, lung problems may be related to issues of grief and sadness. With each exhalation, imagine releasing your grief, letting it go, and replacing it with life.

For the Digestive System

If the number of commercials on television for antacids and acid controllers is any indication, digestive problems are rampant in the United States. Whether you suffer from simple indigestion or a peptic ulcer, gastroenteritis or constipation, you know that digestive problems can make you miserable. What to do? Calm that pesky digestion with some targeted meditation.

Sit comfortably and place your hands on your stomach, lower abdomen, or wherever the discomfort lies. Breathe deeply for several breaths. Then, as you breathe, imagine you are breathing in the color blue. It is clear, soothing, cool blue energy. Feel it moving into you and imagine it flowing down your esophagus, into your stomach, and into your intestines, coating your entire digestive system in calming blue energy (see Chapter 8, "Energy Central," for information on blue auras). Feel your muscles relax, including the muscles around your digestive system. Keep inhaling the soothing and refreshing blue energy until your stomach feels calm. (If you're experiencing stomach pain or nausea that makes you feel cold and clammy, imagine the color is a warm pink rather than a cool blue.)

Bliss Byte

If your stomach is upset, rub your tummy slowly in a clockwise direction. As you rub, repeat the phrase, "With loving energy my digestion heals." Continue this affirmation as you slowly circle your stomach with healing energy.

For the Liver

Your liver, the second largest organ in your body (your skin is the largest), is actually a gland below your diaphragm in your abdominal cavity. Its function is to process carbohydrates, fats, and proteins, make bile, and filter our toxic products from the blood. Disorders of your liver might include hepatitis, cirrhosis of the liver (which may be caused by hepatitis or long-term, alcohol abuse), and liver cancer. For liver disorders, try the following meditation:

Sit up very straight; slouching cramps your abdominal cavity. Imagine your liver sitting just below your diaphragm. Breathe in very deeply from the abdomen and imagine your bowl-shaped diaphragm compressing your liver as it expands downward to make room for your lungs. Continue to breathe very deeply and visualize that with every inhalation all the toxins and impurities are gently pressed from your liver, and with every exhalation, the impurities flow out of you with your breath, transformed into life-affirming joy. Imagine your liver becoming cleaner, refreshed, and renewed. Continue for about 10 minutes, then sit quietly for a few more minutes and contemplate the feeling of inner purity.

In Chinese medicine, the liver is connected with anger issues. If you have liver problems, make an effort to resolve and heal any anger in your life.

For the Immune System

Lots of things can depress our immune systems, and stress is one of the most obvious. Whether you suffer from allergies, develop frequent colds, or suffer from full-blown immune system disorders like Hodgkin's disease or AIDS, you know how important it is to have a strong immune system. To help strengthen yours, lessen the stress in your life by meditating once or twice every day, come hell or high water. Try this one:

Lie flat on your back on the ground, as in shavasana (see Chapter 18, "Shavasana: It's Not Just Lying Around!"). Close your eyes and breathe deeply several times, relaxing your muscles, feeling all impurities and toxins leaving your system with each exhalation. Now, bring your attention to your Mars chakra (see page 116–117), the seat of action energy behind your navel. Visualize the chakra as a wheel slowly beginning to spin. As it spins, it begins to let out tiny sparks as it generates power. Imagine this spinning, sparking wheel is your immune system, gearing up to protect you. Slowly, the circle begins to expand as it grows in energy. It extends outward and spins until it encompasses your entire body in a transparent spinning shield of protective energy. Now the spinning slows and the shield begins to strengthen. Feel the shield seal itself around you so that no germs, allergens, or impurities can reach you. Slowly open your eyes and attempt to retain this feeling of the spiritual barrier against negative energy you have created. Carry it with you throughout the day.

Bliss Byte

For a quick reduction in stress, increase the length of your exhalation to your inhalation. For example, inhale for four counts, exhale for eight counts.

For Chronic Pain, Especially Back Pain

If you live with chronic pain, you know how it can color every aspect of your life, even your thoughts. You experience stress that is seemingly unending. You may suffer from depression, a feeling of hopelessness, or a constant state of heightened emotion. Whether your pain is a headache, backache, joint pain, or something else, we understand how hard life can be for you. So do others, and pain clinics have sprung up around the country to help people manage chronic pain. One technique used for pain management is mindfulness. Try this:

Lie comfortably on your back as if in shavasana (see Chapter 18) or in another position that minimizes your pain. Close your eyes, take several deep breaths, then breathe normally. Now open your awareness to your body. Rather than ignoring your pain, acknowledge it. Imagine you are an outside observer, and you are watching your pain. Give it a shape. Does the shape move? What color is it? If the pain changes, imagine the shape corresponding to the change. Watch your pain. Now, imagine it floats out of you and hangs in front of you where you can see it more easily. Watch it with interest. Try not to let your mind become engaged with the pain. Don't enter it. Stand back, but continue to watch its every move. Get to know it.

Relax

Don't let chronic pain lead you toward feelings of hopelessness. Consider these beautiful words from Dr. Bernie Siegel: "What keeps me going is the knowledge that the world was created to express love and as an expression of love."

After you've spent several days on this meditation, you can try to consciously change the shape, color, and movement of your visualized pain (see Chapter 8 for more on aura colors). Is it bright red? Imagine painting it blue. Does it have a jerking motion? Imagine setting it on a lake and watching it bob gently on top of the water. Imagine changing its shape to a circle, then watching how it reacts.

Eventually you may be able to gain some degree of control over your pain, but don't rush this step. Just watching it as an observer and without entering it is often enough to make pain manageable. You may even find that you form a relationship with your pain. Why not? If you have to live together, for whatever length of time, it makes sense to get along.

We recognize that we have omitted many illnesses and conditions that could respond well to meditation, and only space alone limits the scope of this chapter, but we hope the meditations provided will give you inspiration to craft your meditation practice to meet your own individual health needs. When part of the mind-body falters, the *whole* you can play a big part in the process of renewal.

The Least You Need to Know

➤ Ayurveda is a whole-life system of health that includes meditation in its efforts to balance the body for greater vitality and longevity.

➤ You can work in conjunction with your primary care doctor to form a health care team that uses both conventional and natural medicine to best care for and maintain your health.

➤ Your mind can be a powerful ally in the healing and recovery process.

➤ Meditation can be a tonic for the heart, lungs, digestive system, liver, immune system, chronic pain (especially back pain), or whatever else may ail you.

Chapter 27

Om Away from Om: Spiritual Travel

In This Chapter

➤ Making a pilgrimage to one or more of the world's most spiritual places

➤ What to bring, how to stay safe, and who to bring along

➤ Meditating in foreign ports and en route

➤ The new you back home again

Maybe you're one of those readers who's been engaging in a daydream ever since we first mentioned the word "pilgrimage" in Chapter 6: You, on the move, witnessing the worldwide evidence of humankind's spiritual quest in person. For those of you who love it, travelling can be an excellent way to broaden your spiritual horizons and expose yourself to new ways of life, explode your own assumptions and prejudices, and learn new ways to meditate, too!

Seeing the World's Most Spiritual Places

Why not do something different for your next vacation? Forget the beach, the big city, the generic tour of Europe. Consider crafting your own spiritual tour, either by paying homage to a single spiritual spot or by stringing together a couple of meaningful places in the same area. Combining your vacation with a pilgrimage could result in the best vacation you ever had!

Making Pilgrimages and Paying Homage

Muslims are expected to make a *pilgrimage* to Mecca at least once in their lives. Perhaps you could make a similar rule for yourself: At least once, visit a place that holds true spiritual meaning for you. Learn about it, anticipate it, prepare for it, travel to it, pay homage to it, show it respect, meditate in it, and experience it. You'll remember it for the rest of your life.

From Dharamsala to Stonehenge: A Sacred Map

For anyone who cares to go exploring (as an arm-chair traveler, virtual traveler on the Internet, or as a real traveler), the world is full of sacred places. We've presented several of the most spectacular in the list below. This list, of course, is not all-inclusive and is meant to be a springboard to get you thinking about the kinds of spiritual places that might intrigue and inspire you. Take a look and start planning—for next week, next year, or 10 years from now. Or just enjoy researching and learning about sites considered greatly profound by different cultures around the globe and throughout history.

Some of the sacred places on our list are located in what you might call the world's "hot spots." These places may be best experienced for now as an arm-chair or virtual traveler—at least until conditions improve for tourists and pilgrims such as ourselves.

If you really want to go there though, do your research carefully—and be sure to contact the U.S. embassy for any country you are considering visiting before planning and attempting your travel. Personally, however, we'd err on the side of caution and forego travel to "hot spots." Better safe than sorry!

➤ **Yangon (Rangoon)** in southern Myanmar (formerly Burma, that country below China and just northwest of Thailand) on the Yangon River is the home of the spectacular gold-plated Shwedagon Paya (pagoda), which stands high above the city on a hill. According to legend, the shrine was built to house eight of the Buddha's hairs. It is a beautiful place surrounded by statues, temples, shrines, images, and pavilions.

➤ **Lhasa** is a city in Tibet (now a Chinese province in western China) to which many have made pilgrimages. Once the seat of the Tibetan government,

Lhasa is still the location of the tombs of the previous Dalai Lamas. Lhasa is now under Chinese rule, however, and the Dalai Lama is noticeably missing from his homeland. (He is in exile in India and still considered a public enemy by the Chinese government.) Visiting Lhasa isn't simply a matter of skipping over the border. The Chinese embassy in Kathmandu will issue group visas but not individual visas, and you'll find it much easier if you arrive in Kathmandu with a Chinese visa already in your passport.

➤ **Dharamsala, India**, is the current home of the exiled Dalai Lama, so if you're looking for him, head to India rather than Tibet.

Dharamsala, though an Indian city, is understandably significantly influenced by Tibetan culture. It has a Tibetan monastery and a school of Tibetan studies. Meditation courses, Buddhism courses, and spiritual retreats are available in Dharamsala.

➤ The **T'aj Mahal** in Agra, India, has been described as the most extravagant monument ever built for love. When people think of India, they often think of the T'aj Mahal, which was built by Emperor Shah Jahan in honor of his second wife, who died in childbirth in 1631. The Emperor was so heartbroken by her death that it is said his hair turned gray overnight. Although not a place of worship (the T'aj Mahal has several false mosques and one true mosque, but it can't be used for worship because it faces the wrong way), its grandeur and spectacular beauty is inspirational.

➤ **Sukhothai-Si Satchanalai** is a magnificent abandoned ancient city in Thailand containing many Buddhist temples. Sukhothai literally means "dawn of happiness."

➤ The **Temple Gardens of Kyoto** in Japan are monuments to the concept of the Japanese garden. The imperial capital between A.D. 794 and 1868 B.C., Kyoto is filled with sacred sites. The Higashiyama district offers the opportunity for quiet walks around its temples. The **Sanjusangen-do Temple** holds 1,001 statues of the Buddhist goddess of mercy. Northwest Kyoto has many beautiful Zen temples, including the **Kinkaku-ji Temple**, which was burned to the ground in 1950, then rebuilt and completely covered in gold foil.

➤ Moving back west, **Jerusalem** is one of the most sacred cities on the planet, and Jews, Muslims, and Christian all consider it holy. Jerusalem contains the tombs of many of the Biblical patriarchs and lies at the foot of **Haram-ash Sharif/Temple Mount**, where Mohammed ascended to heaven and where God instructed Abraham to sacrifice his son. The **Dome of the Rock** mosque, Al-Aqsa Mosque, and Islamic Museum are on the Mount. The **Western Wall**, at the base, is the remains of the Jews' most holy shrine, the First Temple, now an open-air synagogue. Christians may also want to visit the **Church of the Holy Sepulchre**, built

Relax

It is interesting that many holy cities, such as Luxor, are places of great spiritual insight—and also the sites of significant social unrest. This is perhaps an interesting subject for meditation on the powerful nature of spiritual places.

over the site where Jesus was supposedly crucified, buried, and resurrected. This church is the culmination of a walk down the **Via Dolorosa**, the route Jesus walked to crucifixion.

➤ **Luxor** is a city in Egypt built on the site of the ancient city of Thebes. **Luxor Temple**, built by Pharaoh Amenophis III, and the **Temples of Karnak**, are on the site. The latter made up a primary place of worship in Thebian times. You can reach Luxor via Cairo by daily buses or trains. The current danger posed by terrorists in Egypt, however, definitely makes Egypt a candidate for arm-chair travel only! The United States and British authorities are currently warning tourists away from Luxor in particular.

➤ Most people who visit Saudi Arabia are there for one reason: to make a pilgrimage to **Mecca**, the holy city of Islam. All Muslims are supposed to make a pilgrimage to Mecca once during their lifetimes and that makes for a big crowd! Mohammed was born in Mecca in the sixth century. The catch is, you can't visit Mecca unless you are a Muslim. **Taif**, located in the mountains above Mecca, can be visited by anyone.

➤ On to Europe! **Chartres Cathedral** in Paris, France is the home of the Chartres labyrinth (see Chapter 16, "Walking Meditation: Peace Is Every Step") through which seekers can walk, symbolically journeying into their own souls then back out again with new insights.

➤ **Vatican City** has its own head of state (who else but the Pope?), its own postal service, its own money, media, train station, army, and tourist office. **St. Peter's church** is there, as is the site of the original church built in A.D. 326 to honor the site of St. Peter's martyrdom and burial (the church was demolished in the early sixteenth century). The current church took 150 years to build and houses the spectacular Bernini altar and the work of Michaelangelo, Raphael, and Bramante, among others. If your spiritual inspiration is art, don't miss the **Vatican Museums**.

➤ Skipping over the "pond" to the British Isles, don't miss **Stonehenge**! This 5,000-year-old structure consisting of a ring of huge stones in a pattern set into the ground. The mystery of Stonehenge is how the 50-ton stones got to where they are from South Wales. For a less touristy and jam-packed experience, check out the stones at **Avebury**, which are more accessible than Stonehenge and, according to some, even more impressive. Avebury's stones are dated from 2600 B.C., and include a stone dubbed the "Barber Surgeon Stone." Supposedly, a skeleton of a medieval travelling barber was found buried beneath the stone, which probably fell on him. Avebury (also the name of the village) is 30 miles east of Bath and just over eight miles north of Stonehenge.

➤ Moving on to Central America, **Tikal** is a spectacular Mayan ruin in Guatemala, right in the middle of the jungle. The ruins include towering pyramids, plazas, an acropolis, temples, and a museum surrounded by real live rain forest.

➤ **Palenque** is a Mayan ruin in Mexico, and a bus/ferry connection to Tikal link these two sites, practically inviting that you visit them both. Palenque is also surrounded by jungle and only 34 of the 500 Mayan buildings believed to be 1,500 years old have been excavated. All were built without metal tools, pack animals, or the wheel.

➤ **Mexico's Yucatán Peninsula** is considered by many to be the realm of the Maya, who live there today, in the same site as their ancestors. Mayan ruins can be found near Mérida at **Uxmal** and **Chichén Itzá**.

Relax

Military activity is unpredictable around the Mexican/Guatemalan border. Travelers visiting Tikal and Palenque should restrict their itineraries to the main tourist routes, remain highly vigilant about personal security, stay alert, and contact their embassy in Mexico City before traveling to the sometimes violent area.

➤ As long as you're in Mexico, don't neglect the Mayan ruins at Oaxaca, including Albán, Mitla, Yagul, and Cuilapan.

➤ In Lima, Peru (in South America), visit **Machu Picchu**, the "Lost City of the Incas." Although the heavy tourist traffic may not seem conducive to spiritual reflection, Machu Picchu is *the* must-see site on the continent.

➤ For a North American experience, visit Arizona. There you can experience **Chaco Canyon**, an Anasazi (ancient Native American) center of culture between A.D. 900 and 1130 Chaco contains approximately 30 ancient buildings of masonry, each containing hundreds of rooms. **Canyon de Chelly** and **Canyon del Muerto** are two spectacular canyons in the heart of the Navajo nation that have provided shelter for Native Americans for 2,000 years. A trail runs to the bottom of Canyon de Chelly leading to the White House Ruins.

➤ In Colorado, check out **Mesa Verde**, the first cultural park set aside by the United States National Park System in June 1906. You can walk through cliff dwellings and villages on the top of the mesa built by ancestral Pueblo people between A.D. 600 and A.D. 1300. Mesa Verde National Park was also designated as a World Cultural Heritage Site in 1978. Mesa Verde is Spanish for "green table."

Preparing to Travel

Once you've got your destination in mind, you can begin to prepare for your trip. Remember, safe travel only! Set a date or a goal year. Read up on your destination. Plan a rough itinerary, not too packed with activities. A structured but easy schedule allows for spontaneity and for a relaxed ambience. Then, organize your list of necessities.

What You'll Need

International travel requires more preparation than travelling in your own country, but in either case, it pays to be prepared. Because the list of necessities for travel outside your own country is more complete, we'll assume that's where you're going. If not, simply eliminate the items with a *.

Mindful Minute

If you have a true emergency, the Passport Agency can rush your passport application, but they require an additional $30 and proof of your emergency (plane tickets in hand for immediate travel, for example).

➤ **Passport.*** Most countries won't let you in without one. And speaking of spontaneity, if you don't have a passport, you can't just rush to the airport and hop on a plane to Paris or India. Passports can take up to a month or more to process, so it's a good idea to keep a current passport all the time, just in case, or plan well enough ahead that your passport will be ready by the time you are ready to go. A U.S. passport is valid for 10 years (for adults). Apply for your passport at your local post office, courthouse, or passport agency.

➤ **Visa.*** Not the credit card, but official permission to enter a country, which many countries require in addition to a passport. Visa requirements, fees, necessary qualifications, and time required for processing vary depending on the country, why you want to enter the country, and how long you intend to stay. The consulate of the country you would like to enter is the source for visa information.

➤ **Money.** Traveler's checks are safest, but carry a small amount of local currency with you when you first enter a country. Then, exchange larger amounts at a local bank or currency exchange, which will have better exchange rates than hotels or in the United States. Always keep a $50 bill hidden somewhere separate from your other money *for emergencies only*.

Bliss Byte

Always travel with a budget. (Unless you have an unlimited supply of money!) Remember pretrip costs (passport, guidebooks, supplies such as luggage), travel costs (to and from your destination and travel within and around your destination), and daily expenses for food and lodging. A realistic daily expense budget is between $30 and $50 per day, depending on the type of trip you are taking. (In some cases it could be much more—especially if you love shopping and/or luxury accommodations!) A good rule of thumb is to take about 25 percent more money than you think you'll need, just in case.

➤ **International Student Identity Card (ISIC).*** If you're a student, you can save a lot of money with an ISIC card (your own college ID card isn't usually good enough). The ISIC card may get you cheaper airline tickets, cheaper phone calls to home, and other discounts. You'll also receive sickness and accident insurance, $25,000 emergency evacuation coverage, and access to a 24-hour hotline for travelers in need of medical, legal, or financial assistance. Teachers can get similar discounts with the International Teacher Identity Card, and people 25 and under can also get similar benefits with the GO 25: International Youth Travel Card.

➤ **Your own over-the-counter medications:** Aspirin, acetaminophen, antacid, antihistamine, decongestant, anti-diarrheal, etc. Leave all medications in the original bottles. If you're taking prescription drugs, have your doctor write out a written prescription for you to take with you for proof that you really require the medication. It may also be prudent to take a prescription for antibiotics with you; speak to your physician about this before planning any overseas trip. And, as ever, it's better to drink bottled water when traveling abroad.

➤ **Your calling card.** Making long-distance calls home is cheaper and easier with a U.S. calling card. If you don't have one already, get one, preferably with special rates for international calls, before you leave.

➤ **A light suitcase or backpack.** Find luggage that is lightweight and easy to carry. Then, pack it lightly with your essentials, allowing room for souveneirs! This list is adapted from the Lonely Planet web site—which is definitely a must to check out if you're considering overseas travel (www.lonelyplanet.com).

  ➤ One pair of walking shoes
  ➤ One pair of flip-flops or shower shoes

➤ Three to five pairs of socks

➤ Five to seven pairs of underwear

➤ One to two pair of shorts

➤ One to two skirts/pants

➤ Two shirts

➤ One sweater/sweatshirt

➤ One poncho/rain jacket

➤ One light jacket

➤ One bathing suit

➤ One hat

➤ One semi-nice outfit

➤ Prescription medicine and prescriptions

➤ Toothbrush and toothpaste

➤ Soap and shampoo

➤ Comb and/or brush

➤ Sunscreen, moisturizers, cosmetics

➤ Deodorant

➤ First-aid kit

➤ Contraceptives/condoms

➤ Aspirin or other pain reliever

➤ Tissues

➤ Tampons

➤ Razor blades

➤ Eyeglasses, sunglasses, contact lenses, and cleaning solution

➤ Camera and film

➤ Swiss army–style knife

➤ Flashlight

➤ Address book

➤ Travel journal

➤ Pocket calculator

➤ Books, guides, and maps

➤ Day pack

➤ Laundry soap and line

➤ Sewing kit

➤ Stuff bags/plastic storage bags

➤ Sleeping bag

➤ Change purse

➤ Umbrella

➤ Luggage lock and tags

➤ Battery-operated alarm clock

➤ Moist towelettes

➤ Batteries

➤ Adapter and voltage converter

➤ Passport (and visa if required)

➤ Tickets and rail passes

➤ Student ID card

➤ Money belt or neck wallet

➤ Cash, traveler's checks, credit cards, ATM card

➤ Insurance information

Bliss Byte

One of the best things you can do to keep the memory of your trip-of-a-lifetime alive is to keep a travel journal. In it, record where you went and what you did, how you felt, insights gained, or any other musings. Even if it seems tedious at the time, you'll find yourself looking on it later, able to relieve the trip and the feel of the places you visited.

Better Safe Than Sorry!

Foreign travel sounds exciting and exotic. But dangerous? It can be, especially if you aren't prepared. To minimize the chance of accident or misfortune, practice the following safety precautions when traveling abroad (or anywhere, for that matter).

Relax

Not up for booking a passage to India? Worried about traveling off the beaten track? Consider a trip to a spa or resort here in the United States that offers meditation classes as well as facials, massage, yoga, other classes and seminars of interest, and good, healthy meals. Make a pilgrimage to your well-being!

Pre-Trip Precautions:

➤ Know the local customs and the political situation. Contact the U.S. State Department for reliable information. Keep track of anything in the news to do with the country you plan to visit for at least a month or two before your trip, if possible.

➤ If you know anyone or can contact anyone who has lived in the country you plan to visit, ask for any insights.

➤ Make copies of all important documents you will need related to your travel (passports, visas, traveler's check numbers, etc.). Leave one copy at home and be sure at least one person knows where to find it. Keep the other copy with you somewhere separate from the real documents, such as in a hidden pocket of a suitcase or in a neck or waist pack.

➤ Buy a neck wallet, money belt, or waist pack and wear it under your clothes. Keep your money and other valuables in it, including your passport and visas.

During Your Trip:

➤ Never, ever leave valuables unattended, even if the place you are in seems safe. Theft is a very real possibility in many countries (including our own). If you're carrying any kind of purse or pack with you, make sure you are physically attached to it at all times.

➤ Don't break the laws of the country you are visiting. Every year, for example, hundreds of Americans land in foreign jails because they were carrying, using, or were suspected of using illegal drugs. It isn't worth it!

➤ When the sun goes down, travel with a buddy and stay in populated areas. Tourists are often targeted for theft and/or violence. Light or dark, always stay alert and aware of what is going on around you.

➤ Act confident, even if you don't feel confident, so you don't look like an easy target. Always trust your instincts about situations and people.

➤ Avoid public arguments and political demonstrations.

➤ Do everything you can to stay healthy during your trip. Eat well, sleep enough, and get some exercise—and, yes, continue your meditation practice! If you get sick during your trip, get treatment. Contact the U.S. embassy for instruction on where to go for medical care.

➤ Make sure your health and accident insurance will cover you while travelling and that it will cover you for the entire trip. If yours doesn't, purchase a special trip policy that does.

Who to Go with

Should you travel alone? Travelling with a friend is safer, of course. On the other hand, travel on your own can be an amazing experience, teaching you about yourself. Marilyn Vos Savant, listed in the Guinness Book of Records Hall of Fame for having the highest IQ, was once asked in her column how to truly know yourself. She suggested travelling to a foreign land on your own, preferably one in which you don't know the language. Being by yourself and with yourself can be both frightening and enlightening. You'll certainly learn something. And you can rely upon your daily practice of meditation to access an inner core of strength and serenity throughout your trip.

Travelling with family, a friend, or a group definitely has its perks beyond safety, however. When you come upon something beautiful or an insight strikes you, you've got someone to share it with. You've got someone to talk to over dinner and companionship along the way to combat the loneliness and homesickness many encounter when travelling, even if they're having the time of their lives. Ultimately, the decision is up to you and largely depends on what kind of trip you plan to take.

Tips for Meditating Wherever You Are

Travelling has a way of transforming your consciousness so you enter a sort of altered state. Your surroundings are unfamiliar and your routine is nonexistent or replaced by a different one. Everywhere, your senses are filled with new stimulants. How are you supposed to turn all that off and meditate? It's hard enough at home!

Actually, meditating in a foreign place can be just the push you need to climb to a new level in your meditation practice. Precisely because you have broken out of your routine, your mind-body is working in new ways, working harder, and experiencing more. Your thinking becomes sharper, and you become primed for new experiences. You're ready for anything.

One interesting way to incorporate your meditation practice into your travel: Bring along a sketchbook and draw sculptures or artifacts you see that depict meditative poses. From Native American totem poles to Mayan figurines to Greek statues, meditative poses can be seen in all cultures around the globe. Research the history behind each pose and annotate your sketchbook with the information. Adapt the meditative pose and incorporate it into your own daily meditative practice.

Here's an example of what we mean. The fertility statue shown in the following figure was carved by people living on a group of Greek islands in the South Aegean called the Cyclades; the figure dates to between 2600 and 1100 B.C. When standing in this meditative pose, the woman can feel her belly moving in and out with each breath as she holds her womb in her arms—the source of a new life.

Adapting meditative poses, such as the one seen here in this Greek fertility statue, can be a profound way to incorporate your spiritual travels and discoveries into your daily meditation practice.

Mindfulness during travel is essential to get the most out of the experience, and sitting in mindful awareness without thought can be incredibly enriching "on the road." But easier said than done. What can you do to get yourself to sit down and meditate (or walk and meditate, or lie down and meditate)? Read on for some more suggestions.

If You Lived Here, You'd Be Home Now

One way to make your mental journey part of your physical journey is to do a little pretending. As you sit in that quaint, tiny rented room in Paris or Kyoto or Dharamsala, pretend you *are* home. What if you had lived here all your life? Or, what if from now on, this were to be your home? If you lived here, you would continue your meditation practice as always, yet it would be different because you would be different. Try it. Temporarily change your reality and see what it does for your meditation.

From Trains, Planes, and Automobiles

But meditation doesn't have to be limited to your on-location locations. It can also be practiced en route and can be a great way to modify the stress of travel, the delays, the crowds, the cramped quarters, the waiting and waiting and waiting that often accompanies travel. Of course, you don't want to meditate while driving. But when you are stuck in that coach-class airplane seat all the way to Thailand, that long train-ride across Europe, or if you're a passenger on a cross-country car trip from New York to Arizona, you'll find meditation is a great and productive way to pass the time. (As long as you're not the one flying the plane, conducting the train, or driving the car!) A few suggestions:

➤ If you have a window seat on an airplane, bring your attention to the view and watch it with total mindfulness, without judgment or engagement beyond an appreciation of its beauty and variety. See if you can find natural mandalas in the clouds or on the ground below.

➤ If you have a center or aisle seat on an airplane, close your eyes and listen carefully. Try to distinguish all the different sounds you hear: the sound of the engine, the voice over the speaker system, the roll of the drink cart down the aisle, and the conversation. Distinguish the sound of all the individual voices you hear. Notice each pitch, tone, inflection. Focus on one sound at a time, then move on to the next. (But don't eavesdrop; that's not polite!)

➤ Stuck in a train car packed with people? Bring your attention to your breath and follow the sound and feel of it. Alternate this attention to an exercise in which you see how long you can draw out your inhalations and exhalations.

➤ Stuck in a train car by yourself? Sit as comfortably as possible and with your eyes slightly open but unfocused, repeat the mantra, "Wherever I go, I am always here."

➤ Although it isn't quite meditation, keep yourself amused and the driver of the car you are riding in awake by playing a sense-impression game. How many different colors can you see? How many circles can you see? Any natural mandalas? Name every sound you can hear. Name every scent you can smell. Imagine the feel of the different textures you see around you. And taste? Stop for a nice meal at a restaurant you've never tried before (no fast-food chains allowed). Order the local specialty and savor every bite.

But There's Still No Place Like Home

Anyone who travels knows the joy of returning home. Let your trip change you. When you get home, don't fall back into your old routine. Alter some aspect of your regular meditation practice by introducing something from your travel—either a memento or keepsake from your trip that you can use to meditate upon and remember your wonderful trip abroad, a mantra you learned there, or perhaps even your travel journal, which you can also use as a subject for meditation. If you've been an arm-chair or virtual traveler, consider placing a poster of the sacred place in your at-home meditation room for inspiration as a subject of meditation.

Cherish your home, which is your place to be grounded and safe. Welcome the familiar feeling of meditating at home, too.

Compared to your amazing, stimulating, colorful travels (arm-chair, virtual, or real), your old stomping grounds beckon a safe, familiar haven. Auntie Em, there's no place like home!

The Least You Need to Know

➤ Travelling to spiritual places around the world can be a great way to add depth, dimension, and wisdom to your own spiritual journey.

➤ You can travel to sacred places without leaving the comfort of your own home. Arm-chair or virtual travel is a great way to learn about other cultures and their traditions of meditation.

➤ Research your destination well and make sure you take along all essentials, from a first-aid kit to necessary passports and visas.

➤ You can meditate wherever you are, and you can also meditate while on your way there.

➤ When you return from your travels, let your meditation practice reflect your new experiences and new wisdom.

Chapter 28

Gaia Meditation for the Twenty-First Century

In This Chapter

➤ What is Gaia?

➤ Earth consciousness and humankind

➤ How to meditate with a spouse, partner, or friend

➤ Meditation to heal the Earth

You've heard the expression "Mother Earth." You may or may not have heard any of the thousands of other names people throughout history have given to Earth, such as *Gaia*, a name for the Greek Earth goddess. Why have so many cultures across the Earth come up with the same idea, of Earth as some sort of female deity or entity to which we all belong? Because the Earth is our mother, of course. Our *metaphorical* mother, right?

Actually, according to certain theories, the expression goes beyond the metaphorical. What if the Earth actually has a consciousness of some sort? Could it be a living entity? As the twenty-first century approaches, more and more people are asking the question. Scientists and spiritual seekers alike are beginning to explore the extent of our connection with the planet we inhabit. What is the nature of the planet? Who is she? And then, by extension, who are we?

Lovelock's Gaia Theory and the Environment

From A to Om

Gaia is the Greek name for the Earth goddess who produced all of life. In the twentieth century, Gaia is synonymous with biologist James E. Lovelock's theory of the self-regulating nature of the planet Earth, as its internal "homeostasis" responds to changes from internal and external stimuli.

In his books *Gaia: A New Look at Life On Earth* and *Healing Gaia: Practical Medicine for the Planet,* biologist James E. Lovelock proposes that Earth is, indeed, a living entity and that all its parts, from its core of molten lava to its plant and animal life, are something like "body parts," making up the whole. Just as each of us is made of cells, which are made of molecules, which are made of atoms, perhaps we make up a smaller part of the entity Earth. In thinking about the Earth, Lovelock postulates, we need to consider its physiology. The Earth, then, is viewed as a self-regulating organism always striving to maintain a state of balance or homeostasis, the same physiological balance the human body maintains in relation to its ever-changing external environment. Lovelock sees this process as a purely scientific one of checks and balances.

Taking Lovelock's hypothesis one step further, however, perhaps we, humankind, are the equivalent of a nervous system for the planet Earth. Could the evolving consciousness of humankind mean that the planet is slowly developing consciousness as well? Is Earth becoming self-aware?

Bliss Byte

Devote an entire meditation session (or more) to expanding the limits of what you believe to be "you." First, visualize the spinning atoms that make up your body. Breathe as a collection of atoms. Then, slowly expand your consciousness to encompass the molecules, the cells, the organs. Breathe as each of these. Expand into your astral layers and breathe through them. Expand into your family, your community, your country, your continent, and at last, the planet. Breathe as each of these in succession. Breathe through the bliss of your causal body and feel the interpenetration of awareness through each body—physical, astral, and causal—as it achieves oneness with the Earth and the universe. Imagine there is no dividing line separating your atoms from the planet, indeed from the universe as a whole.

One World, One Life

Many ancient theories propose humans as manifestations of universal consciousness. If we are part of the awakening Earth—its brain, perhaps—then we *are* the Earth, just as a wave is the ocean but not the whole ocean, or our brains are us but not the *whole* us. And if we are merely the "organs" of a larger consciousness, does that diminish us in any way? Do we die out the way our own cells die, sloughed off with a brush of the hand? Are we gone as fast as a wave disappears back into the ocean?

Even if the Earth is somehow greater and more conscious than the sum of its parts, we still make up the Earth, and whether we are its heartbeat or its thoughts or its life-blood, Earth wouldn't be the evolved being it is (she is?) without us. Either we are organic matter whose sole purpose is facilitating the evolution of a higher conscious-ness, *or* we are an intricate part of that evolving consciousness and will reap the benefits of its progress.

We lean toward the second interpretation because we've seen a similar phenomena at work in the body on a smaller scale. There is a widely accepted theory that memory, consciousness, and soul permeate all the tissues of the body. Just as a repressed emo-tional trauma can release during a targeted massage, transporting the person who repressed the trauma into the original emotional state (which suggests that the memory of the trauma was repressed into the body's actual tissue), we hold the con-sciousness of the Earth within our bodies. We are all evolving together, Earth and all its parts. And we are all responsible for each other.

Our merging of Lovelock's hypothesis that the Earth has a physiological character consistent with living organisms with the idea that the Earth also possesses its own consciousness mirrors what is emerging in current medical and scientific thought about the human body. The mind-body connection is changing the way traditional Western medicine views the health and well-being of the physical body. We're not just simply body, or simply mind, we are mind-body, interpenetrating and interconnected.

What does meditation have to do with all of this? Plenty. When we meditate, we not only benefit our own mind-bodies, but the Earth's as well. Meditation, after all, is a conscious method of uniting mind, body, Earth, and universe.

Our Earth, Our Responsibility

Seeing yourself as part of a living Earth brings with it certain compelling responsibili-ties. Awesome responsibilities. Suddenly the boundaries of "you" are much, much bigger. Taking care of yourself means more than eating right, exercising, and meditat-ing once a day. It also means taking care of the planet. Consider this quote from Dr. Lovelock's essay, "The Evolution of Gaia," in the collection *Greenhouse Glasnost: The Crisis of Global Warming* (The Ecco Press, 1990):

In Gaia, we are part and partners of a democratic entity. The rules are insistent: Species that harm the environment are voted out through natural selection. If we are truly concerned for mankind, we must respect other organisms. If we think of nothing but selfish human greed and ignore the natural life of the Earth, we have set the scene for our own destruction and that of the comfortable Earth we know. Just now, we seem like the Gaderene swine driving our cars down to a sea rising to meet us.

Relax

Environmental destruction goes beyond a symbolic representation of the destruction of our own bodies. Pollution of the planet actually compromises the health of all those who inhabit it. Air pollution damages our lung tissue. Water pollution poisons our systems. And the sights of degradation and destruction depress us and increase our stress.

Perhaps you eat well and avoid junk food, but occasionally toss that veggie burger wrapper on the ground when you can't find a convenient trash receptacle. Do you shun smoking, but drive your car every day—even when you could easily carpool, bike, or walk? Do you meditate but rarely spend time outside? Recognizing yourself as part of the entity that is the planet Earth means that if you don't put junk food in you, you also don't subject the planet to it. That planet is you and you are that planet.

If you wouldn't pollute your own lungs with cigarette smoke, why would you pollute the air around you? If you work on your own mental health, why would you live in isolation from nature?

And don't we owe our Earth Mother respect and protection? She has taken care of us since the beginning of our habitation on the planet, providing us with food, water, air, and warmth, the means to build shelter, and with unlimited opportunities. We haven't always been grateful children. We've taken and taken and taken. We've depleted her resources and covered her with pollution. Are we finally recognizing our errors? Perhaps slowly we are coming to understand how we should treat our mother. Or, if you see humankind as truly a part of Earth, maybe Earth is at last recognizing, by means of the evolution of human consciousness, how to take care of herself.

Is There a Gaia Mind?

We admit that the idea of a "Gaia mind" is quite a leap from the standard point of view that we are our own beings and Earth is the mass of rock and plant life we inhabit. But others have made the leap before us. Many others, in fact. You don't have to believe it to consider it, so why not ponder the question, "Is there a Gaia mind?"

The Consciousness Research Laboratory (CRL) engages in some interesting research that supports the idea of a conscious Earth. You could interpret their findings in other ways, of course, but what if they do represent some degree of consciousness in the terra firma? According to their report on the research they conduct, environmental factors apparently influence the occurrence of human performance, including *psychic*, or *psi*, performance.

CRL analyzed records of 911 crisis calls, death rates, admission to psychiatric facilities, lottery payouts, Las Vegas casino gaming profits, and sports performance to see how they correlated with a variety of environmental variables. Changes in weather, geomagnetic fluctuations, the lunar cycle, and even tidal effects were shown to correlate significantly with human behavior, including lottery and casino payouts. One of the more prominent influences seems to be the lunar cycle, suggesting that some of the folklore associated with the moon may be based in something quite real.

From A to Om

To be **psychic** means to access the human ability to intuit that which is not readily apparent. Psychic phenomena is also sometimes called **psi** (pronounced *sigh*). Psi is the first letter of the Greek alphabet and the first letter of the Greek word **psyche**, which means, literally, "breath." A **parapsychologist** is someone who studies psychic phenomena.

Why on Earth (pun intended!) would the natural world so affect human performance and consciousness? One simple explanation would be that we are all part of one interpenetrating and interconnected system, one larger, more subtle consciousness. We are tied together by more than proximity. We are a single organism. We are Gaia.

Kant and the Collective Unconscious

Remember Jung's ideas about the collective unconscious? He proposed that there were certain ideas or archetypes common to all of humankind and present in our unconscious minds. But where did these ideas come from, and why do we all have them in common? All people certainly don't have the same experience, nor do we have the same genetics (although you could argue that we all came from a single genetic source). Why, then, do we all have certain ideas in common, produce certain symbols independently in different cultures, and share so many similar beliefs?

Immanuel Kant had his theories, too. Kant believed that each individual, when given the freedom to create his own ethics and rules, would consciously obey the laws of the universe. He believed the world was evolving toward an ideal society ruled by reason, which would "bind every law giver to make his laws in such a way that they could have sprung from the united will of an entire people, and to regard every subject, in so far as he wishes to be a citizen, on the basis of whether he has conformed to that will."

But where does this universal law, this "united will of an entire people" come from? Why does it exist at all? Kant theorized that it did exist, and that this collective unconscious force contained certain true principles. Moral laws were universal, Kant believed, whether or not a Supreme Being existed, and through reason, these laws would become apparent. We didn't make our laws randomly. The principles were out there in the ether somewhere, in the unconscious universal energy field.

Many would, of course, claim that moral principles come from God or some divine force, and that Gaia is really just one interpretation of God. But many others see the Gaia mind as quite separate from God, or complementary to a "higher" power. Gaia mind is the "lower" power. Not the evil power, but the power of the Earth, right here, right now, under us, around us, and, well...us. It doesn't transcend us. It *is* us.

Intuition and Field Consciousness Effects

You've probably experienced a flash of intuition before, and maybe you follow this insight regularly. Intuition doesn't have to be something as obvious as an inner voice commanding you, "DON'T GET ON THAT AIRPLANE!" It can be as subtle as "Call your daughter right now" or "Take that job." But where does intuition come from? Are we all a little bit *psychic*?

Dean Radin, Ph.D., Director of the Consciousness Research Laboratory and one of the world's leading parapsychologists, has uncovered a phenomenon he calls "field consciousness effects." In his book *The Conscious Universe*, Dr. Radin writes:

> *Understanding such experiences requires an expanded view of human consciousness. Is the mind merely a mechanistic, information-processing bundle of neurons? Is it a "computer made of meat" as some cognitive scientists and neuroscientists believe? Or is it something more? The evidence suggests that while many aspects of mental functioning*

are undoubtedly related to brain structure and electrochemical activity, there is also something else happening, something very interesting.

Part of what is going on seems to be that when people all focus their mind power on something far away, that something—whether a sick friend or a random number generator on a computer—seems to be influenced. Studies on this effect have been careful and thorough, following all the rules of science. Something is going on outside of our brains, beyond us, and we can make it happen.

Could it be something akin to the notion of the Gaia mind? Are we all part of a single system, and when we effect change with our minds, is the system "thinking"? Could be...could be. And if that's true, then our individual practice of meditation contributes tangibly to the health, well being, and healing energy of our global Earth consciousness.

According to Dr. Radin, there is a collective, tangible psychic awareness that has demonstrable effects, such as in studies demonstrating the long-distance effect of prayer (see Chapter 6, "Say a Little Prayer"). When CRL studied what they and others call "distant healing," they used studies that employed conventional scientific methods, such as randomized, counterbalanced, *double-blind protocols*. CRL's research involved individuals and groups, separated by distance in some experiments, by time in others. Overall, the research indicated that the human body can be influenced by distant mental influence of others, and that this influence can be shown in the laboratory under controlled conditions.

From A to Om

A **double-blind protocol** is a system of medical study where one team of researchers works with two groups of patients. One group of patients receives a specific treatment while the other group, unknowingly, receives a placebo. A second group of researchers evaluates the results.

Bliss Byte

Are you going to wait for absolute, definitive, 100 percent guaranteed proof that your positive thoughts and prayers can heal the people you love? Or are you going to give it a try just in case? You aren't losing anything by trying, but your loved ones, and even those you don't know, could gain immeasurably.

CRL has also done research to determine if inanimate systems can be influenced by human thought. Their research demonstrated what they call a "field consciousness effect," apparent when groups of people direct their focus onto an object, such as a random number generator. If harnessed, just think what positive meditation power the human race would gain!

Perhaps precisely because the implications are mind-boggling, even the rigorously scientific studies are difficult for many mainstream scientists to accept. Humans influencing matter with their minds? Nature influencing human minds with its cycles? Absurd! That's like saying the Earth is round! Or that humans could invent a machine allowing people to communicate instantly with each other from any point on the globe, or that we could walk on the moon, or clone a sheep!

We're not saying that anyone has proven the existence of a collective unconscious, let alone a Gaia mind. But more and more, scientists are recognizing that things happen that they can't yet explain. Humanity may be on the verge of a new breakthrough that could dramatically alter the course of our evolution. We aren't quite there yet, but there are stirrings. We think the idea is worth consideration, that we are all connected in some larger way. If nothing else, it makes a great subject for meditation.

Bliss Byte

Shakespeare (via Hamlet) once said, "There are more things in heaven and earth than are dreamt of in your philosophy, Horatio!" Get in touch with those phenomena in your own life that science can't yet explain. Make a list of experiences you've had that logic can't explain, hunches that paid off, flashes of intuition, or things you've seen or heard that defy logic. The more you pay attention, the more you'll see.

Do We Think Together?

Have you ever felt so in-synch with someone that you could finish each other's sentences? Have you ever known, on an intuitive level, what someone was thinking?

Bliss Byte

Consider the people in your life. What do they all have in common? What traits draw you to them and connect you to them? Do most of your loved ones share common traits? What does this say about who you are? Make a list of adjectives that describe the qualities you admire most in your family and friends. Take a look at the list. Use each word as a subject for meditation.

If we are part of some greater, more complex, more spectacular whole, even if that whole consciousness—that Earth consciousness—hasn't yet developed its awareness fully, perhaps the potential awareness of that whole is far beyond our individual potentials. Every step we make in our individual spiritual journeys may be combining to move Earth consciousness ever forward to some far greater understanding than we could ever reach on our own. When we tap into our own reservoir of psychic intuition, made stronger through the regular practice of meditation, perhaps we are accessing that great Earth consciousness and putting it to use in a tangible and beneficial way.

Whether you believe that Earth has a consciousness or that humankind has a collective unconscious, you can still progress in your spiritual journey with more than just your self in mind. In Buddhism, a *boddhisattva* is someone who is seeking enlightenment purely for the benefit of others, and that includes humankind as a whole. You can be a boddhisattva by serving your fellow sentient beings in whatever capacity best suits you and by making a connection with your fellow humans. Where would your brain be if your neurons didn't make connections with each other? Those connections are what give you intelligence and awareness. Perhaps all it takes for Gaia to wake up is a little more connection between humankind.

Meditations for Two or More

You needn't always meditate alone. Although meditation seems like a solitary pursuit and is most effective when practiced alone, some of the time meditating with others will help to keep you grounded. It may even fuel the energy of the

From A to Om

A **boddhisattva** is someone who serves not only humankind, but all sentient beings. Helping others is this person's spiritual quest, as he or she is already enlightened and awake. The boddhisattva chooses to remain of this world, delaying nirvana for the purpose of using compassion to ease the pain and suffering of others.

collective unconscious! You can meditate with your partner, your friend, your child, or a group containing a combination of any of the above!

Double the Chakra Power

This chakra meditation is a good one to try with a friend. The idea is to concentrate and energize your chakras with the help of a companion. Consider it the equivalent of a massage for your body. This partner meditation is a physical and mental energizer. (Note: This meditation works best with people of similar height.)

Bliss Byte

One great way to keep a marriage or partnership strong and fueled with love is to remember at least once every day how the two of you are spiritually bonded. Let your mind transcend the mortgage, the kids, the daily routines, and all the other mundane things that bind you together. Get in touch with your deeper spiritual commitment, and you'll be better able to keep life, love, and expectations in perspective.

Before you begin, decide which one of you is partner A and which is partner B. Also, decide if you would both feel more comfortable performing this meditation with your eyes open or closed. (Either way will work, but the exercise is most effective if you are both doing the same thing.) Ask your partner where he or she is storing stress or tension. As you meditate on each chakra, send healing and restorative energy toward your partner with special attention to easing those areas of discomfort.

Now, stand about arm's length from your partner, face to face. Put your arms on each other's shoulders. Proceed as follows:

➤ Partner A inhales deeply as Partner B exhales fully.

➤ Partner A exhales fully while Partner B inhales deeply.

➤ Repeat three times.

➤ Partner A says: *Together, we energize the Saturn chakra.*

➤ Both partners visualize the chakra at the base of the spine spinning and projecting its energy to the Saturn chakra of the other partner.

➤ When partner B feels ready, he/she says: *Together, we energize the Jupiter chakra.*

➤ Both partners visualize the chakra in the lower abdomen spinning and projecting energy to the Jupiter chakra of the other partner.

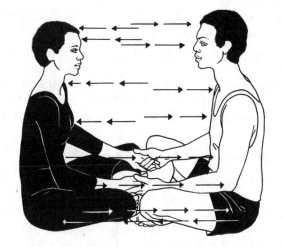

Connecting the chakras through meditation.

➤ When partner A feels ready, he/she says: *Together, we energize the Mars chakra.*

➤ Both partners visualize the chakra behind the naval spinning and projecting energy to the Mars chakra of the other partner.

➤ When partner B feels ready, he/she says: *Together, we energize the Venus chakra.*

➤ Both partners visualize the chakra behind the heart spinning and projecting energy to the Venus chakra of the other partner.

➤ When partner A feels ready, he/she says: *Together, we energize the Mercury chakra.*

➤ Both partners visualize the chakra in the throat spinning and projecting energy to the Mercury chakra of the other partner.

➤ When partner B feels ready, he/she says: *Together, we energize the Sun chakra.*

➤ Both partners visualize the chakra in the forehead (the third eye) spinning and projecting energy to the Sun chakra of the other partner.

➤ When partner A feels ready, he/she says: *Together, we energize the Thousand Petalled Lotus chakra.*

➤ Both partners visualize the chakra at the crown of the head spinning and projecting energy to the Thousand Petalled Lotus chakra of the other partner.

➤ When partner B feels ready, he/she squeezes the shoulders of partner A, then both partners repeat three breath sequences as described at the beginning of this exercise, but this time, partner B inhales first.

➤ Repeat with partner B leading. Or let partner B lead next time.

➤ As the meditation draws to a close, become aware of the energy moving rhythmically between you and your partner upon each inhalation and exhalation. The energy travels much as the tide advances and retreats from the shore. Imagine the energy as the great circle of life that you create with your bodies and breath. Your chakras are open, linked with positive, healing energy. Finally, inhale deeply and exhale together with the sound of the universe. Oooommmmmmmmmmm.

The power of this meditation can be further strengthened if afterward, the partners sit together and discuss their impressions and feelings during the meditation.

Put Your Heads Together

Practice shavasana with a partner (see Chapter 18, "Shavasana: It's Not Just Lying Around!"). Lie head-to-head so that the crowns of your heads (your Thousand Petalled Lotuses) are touching. Don't speak. Simply lie in relaxed awareness for a preagreed period of time. Allow your energy to flow back and forth as it will, and allow yourself to feel the connection with your partner.

This exercise can also be practiced by more than two. Simply lie with heads touching, like spokes on a wheel. The wheel of life, perhaps? Ommmmmmm…

Relax

Never underestimate the power of human touch. Holding hands without talking while walking together through nature is another great way to meditate together.

Bliss Byte

Sit next to your partner. Both of you close your eyes. Whisper into your partner's ear, "Who are you?" Let your partner respond. Continue asking softly these three simple words, "Who are you?" Wait patiently for responses. Continue asking. Continue discovering.

Positive Energy to Transform the World

Another way to expand the power and energy of your meditations beyond yourself is simply to keep humankind, societies across the globe, and the planet itself in mind during your meditation. If Dr. Radin, his colleagues, and the other researchers studying the effects of directed mental effort on the nature of reality are truly on to something, you can actually help to transform the world with the power of your meditation.

Send positive healing energy out into the world so that it showers over humankind like a healing rain. Send loving energy to the international community so that all countries and people may learn to coexist in harmony. Let your love, your optimism, and your positive energy influence the world, because it can. Expand your consciousness beyond the boundaries of yourself, and the evolving world and the evolving you will become one and the same.

Peace on the Journey

What a challenge and what a joy it is to be human and to be alive and conscious on the face of the planet this very moment. As we all journey through the labyrinth that is life on Earth, moving toward and away from and back toward our own inner lights, we wish you a peaceful journey toward your own personal enlightenment. Your mind can change your own reality and quite possibly the reality of those around you. It can heal, it can strengthen, it can energize, it can create, and it calm. Most of all, it can wake up and live.

Bliss Byte

For a truly peaceful meditation, sit alone or with a partner or group and chant the mantra, "Om, shanti, shanti, shanti." **Shanti** means "peace," and **Om** is, of course, that mantra-of-all-mantras meant to reflect the primal sound of the universe. The mantra can be interpreted as, "Universal peace." (You could even say that, instead, if it makes you feel more comfortable.)

We hope you will use meditation for all these reasons, to release the tension and stress of your life and to open the floodgates for the love and joy that the universe has to offer you to come rushing in. Let meditation heal your pain, nurture your joy, and inspire you to serve your fellow human beings and your Mother Earth in the best way you can. Let meditation open that little window into your soul that wouldn't open until your mind grew quiet. Let meditation show you how to live, then do it: Live, live, live! We don't want you to waste one more minute of this precious life on this precious Earth. Wake up with us. Let's change the world together. Meditate.

The Least You Need to Know

➤ Biologist James E. Lovelock and others have proposed that the Earth is actually a living entity and that humans are one component of this entity.

➤ Being a working part of a conscious Earth means we have the responsibility of caring for the Earth as it cares for us.

➤ If the Earth is a living entity, does it have consciousness? Theorists from Immanuel Kant to Dr. Dean Radin have tackled the question from different angles.

➤ Meditating with others could be a way to increase the energy in the collective unconscious.

➤ Your energy in meditation can heal and transform the world.

From A to Om: Glossary

Acupressure   A technique originating in china that involves the stimulation of pressure points by pressing on them with fingers, elbows, palms, etc., for pain relief and healing. It works on the same theory as *acupuncture* but is less invasive.

Acupuncture   A centuries-old technique that originated in China. Hair-thin needles are inserted into pressure points for pain relief and healing. The theory goes that by stimulating pressure points, acupuncture releases blocked areas and equalizes life-force energy, allowing the body to solve its own pain and heal itself.

Adrenal glands   Located at the top of each kidney, these glands produce special hormones in response to stress, such as *adrenaline* (also called epinephrine) and *cortisol* (also called hydrocortisone).

Adrenaline   Also called epinephrine, adrenaline is a hormone released in the body in response to stress that prepares the body to react to a crisis by facilitating quicker response time, among other things.

Affirmation   A verbalized desire stated in positive terms.

Ahimsa   The yoga abstinence of nonviolence.

Ajna chakra   See *urna*.

Allopathic medicine   The conventional, mainstream Western approach to health care, based on treating symptoms and isolating a specific disorder rather than treating the whole person.

Alpha waves   Brain waves that cycle up and down on an EEG about eight to 12 times per second and usually correspond with a drowsy state or, in meditation, a very relaxed yet alert state.

Altar   A natural or constructed platform or table used for sacred purposes, upon which sacred objects can be placed to aid in worship.

Anapanasati Sutta   See *Sutra on the Full Awareness of Breathing*.

Angina   Chest pain or discomfort due to some degree of obstruction in the coronary arteries, sometimes caused by any condition in which the heart has to work harder, such as physical or emotional stress, strain, or exertion.

Aparigraha   The yoga abstinence against greed.

Archetypes   Symbols and concepts common to all human experience that arise separately in different cultures and times. Some common archetypes of human experience are: the Anima and Animus (female and male spirits, respectively), the Wise Old Man, the Earth Mother, Darkness, and the Trickster.

Aromatherapy   The therapeutic use of essential oils, either applied to the skin or inhaled, for healing and mood alteration. Essential oils are aromatic oils distilled from plant sources such as flowers, leaves, and bark. Pure essential oils are produced by steam distillation.

Arteriosclerosis   A condition in which the arteries become hardened and/or lose elasticity, sometimes resulting in small cracks in artery walls.

Artherosclerosis   A condition in which fatty deposits accumulate inside artery walls. These deposits often collect in the cracks caused by arteriosclerosis. When arteries become blocked by deposits or blood clots, heart attacks or strokes may result.

Asanas   The postures or exercises of yoga, designed to help the yogi master control of the body.

Asteya   The yoga abstinence against stealing.

Astral body   The realm of mind and emotions, extending slightly beyond the physical body.

Aum   See *om*.

Aura   The colored halo-like visual result of the vibrations that surround every material object, including people, plants, animals, trees, and inanimate objects.

Auric sight   The ability to see auras.

Autonomic nervous system   The part of the nervous system responsible for bodily functions such as heartbeat, blood pressure, and digestion.

Ayurveda   From the Sanskrit roots *ayus* meaning "life" and *veda* meaning "knowledge" or "science," Ayurveda is an ancient system of health with the purpose of maximizing human potential and defying sickness and aging through specific healing techniques including the prescription of certain foods, herbs, exercises, massages, and meditations.

Bandhas   Literally "to bind" or "to lock," these muscular locks are used during yoga postures and breathing exercises to intensify the energy of *prana* in the body. The three primary bandhas are *mula bandha* (at the perineum), *uddiyani bandha* (at the naval), and *jalandhara bandha* (behind the chin).

Bardo Thödol An instruction manual for death meant to be read to someone as they die and move into the bardo so they know what to do. According to this book, which gives a detailed explanation of what happens after death, the soul moves through several stages in the bardo, then back through the same stages toward rebirth. Also called the *Tibetan Book of the Dead*.

Bardo The intermediate state between death and rebirth into the next life, according to reincarnation philosophy.

Beta waves Brain waves that cycle between 13 and about 30 cycles per second, sometimes associated with deep meditative states.

Bhakti Yoga See *yoga*.

Bija The essence of the mantra that gives the mantra its energy.

Biofeedback A technique through which a person learns to control various internal processes, such as brain waves or blood pressure, by seeing them displayed on a monitor.

Bliss sheath The mind-body layer consisting of divine energy which houses our potential for inner peace and happiness. Part of the *causal body*.

Boddhisattva Someone who is seeking enlightenment purely for the benefit of others. Boddhisattvas devote their lives to the service of humankind, and sometimes even defer their own personal spiritual quest to better serve humankind as a whole.

Botanicals Formulas made from plant sources, which include herbs, herbal combinations, and substances made from various parts of plants.

Brahmacharya The yoga abstinence involving chastity.

Buddha Literally "enlightened one," the term refers to anyone who has achieved enlightenment. However, most people think of a man named *Siddhattha Gotama* who lived in India in the sixth century B.C. Siddhattha Gotama was a prince who renounced his privileged life in search of truth, and attained enlightenment at the age of 35. He spent the next 50 years teaching and travelling throughout India.

Buddhism The religion based on the teachings of Siddhattha Gotama, Buddhism comes in many forms, but *Zen Buddhism* is probably the most well known in the West. Known as *Ch'an Buddhism* in China before reaching Japan in the second century, Zen Buddhism's aim is to achieve enlightenment through meditation, also called zazen (other forms of Buddhism advocate reaching enlightenment in other ways, such as service to mankind or study of sacred texts).

Causal body The realm of the spirit, extending slightly beyond the astral body.

Ch'an Buddhism The Chinese form of Zen Buddhism.

Chakras Psychospiritual energy centers in the body. The seven major chakras are called different things by different people. In this book, we refer to them as the Saturn chakra, the Jupiter chakra, the Mars chakra, the Venus chakra, the Mercury chakra, the Sun chakra, and the Thousand Petalled Lotus chakra.

Chi (also *c'hi* or *Qi*)   The Chinese word for life-force energy.

Chi Kung   See *QiGong*.

Chinese medicine   Also called *traditional Chinese medicine* or *TCM*, Chinese medicine is a complex subject with many aspects including the balance of forces within the body. The branches of Chinese medicine are meditation, astrology and geomancy, martial arts, diet, massage, acupuncture, moxibustion (burning herbs on the surface of the skin to stimulate healing), and herbal medicine.

Clairvoyance   The psychic ability to perceive things that can't be seen physically.

Collective unconscious   A concept developed by Carl Jung, one of Sigmund Freud's earliest colleagues and the founder of the school of analytical psychology. According to Jung, everyone has a personal unconscious containing the results of the individual's life experiences, and also a collective unconscious, which contains experiences of the entire human race. The collective unconscious contains archetypes or basic ideas common to all people throughout time, and these archetypes can affect our behavior as intuition. It can also be viewed as an unconscious connection between all people of all times.

Cortisol   Also called hydrocortisone, this hormone is released in the body in response to stress and prepares the body to react in a crisis by providing improved healing action, among other things.

Creative visualization   A meditative technique in which the meditator imagines that the conditions or things he or she desires are already manifest, helping to bring those conditions into being.

Dalai Lama   Believed by Tibetan Buddhists to be a reincarnation of the Buddha, when a Dalai Lama dies, his soul is thought to enter a new life, who, after being identified by traditional tests, will become the next Dalai Lama.

Delta waves   Brain waves that cycle between $1/2$ to two times per second, and usually correspond with deep sleep.

Descartes, Rene (1596–1650)   A French philosopher and mathematician who is sometimes called the father of modern philosophy. Descartes attempted to apply rational, inductive reasoning to philosophy using principles inherent in science and math.

Devata   The individual aspect of God associated with the mantra.

Dharana   The technique of orienting the mind toward a single point in order to cultivate concentration.

Dharma   A universal force or movement toward the good. It is sometimes translated as "duty" or "ethics," but is a force that exists apart from humans, as opposed to a moral code humans devised.

Dhyana   The Sanskrit word for "meditation," referring to the process of quieting the mind to free it from preconceptions, illusions, and attachments.

Dikenga   A symbol of the Congo religion consisting of a circle with a cross in the middle.

Distance intentionality   A concept that refers to directing an intention toward something at a distance. Prayer is one example.

Eightfold Path   A system of standards and guidelines for living (and eventually, for attaining enlightenment) developed by the Indian sage Patanjali in his written text, the *Yoga Sutras*.

Enlightenment   Also known as *samadhi* in Hinduism and *nirvana* or *satori* in Buddhism, enlightenment is that perfect state of supreme bliss in which the self is completely absorbed into a sense of oneness with the universe.

Feng Shui   The ancient Chinese art of placement. It involves arranging interior spaces and placing houses and buildings within a landscape to best facilitate the flow of energy and ensure health, prosperity, wisdom, and other positive qualities to the inhabitants.

Fight-or-flight reaction   The body's response to extreme stress, allowing it to react more quickly and with greater strength and speed so that it can fight or flee from a perceived threat.

Five sheaths of existence   The sublayers of the subtle body, including the physical sheath, vital sheath, mind sheath, intellect sheath, and bliss sheath.

Flow   A state of total concentration leading to complete absorption in an activity, whether sports, creative pursuits, work, or even working a crossword puzzle.

Folk medicine   A return to true traditional healing methods originating in different countries at a local level including the use of herbs and foods in various forms as medicine.

Freud, Sigmund (1856–1939)   An Austrian physician, neurologist, and the founder of psychoanalysis, a technique of talk therapy for investigating unconscious mental processes and treating psychological disorders and illnesses.

Gaia   The Greek name for the Earth goddess who produced all of life.

Gamma waves   Brain waves that cycle faster than 30 cycles per second and sometimes associated with advanced stages of meditation.

Gassho   A Buddhist hand position in which the hands are held together in front of the chest as if in prayer.

Goddess   The feminine principle in the universe, sometimes referred to as Mother Earth or represented by the great goddesses of mythology such as Athena, Artemis, or Persephone.

Guided imagery   A meditation facilitated by another person (or your own voice on a tape).

Guru   A personal spiritual advisor who assists in the attainment of enlightenment. The Sanskrit word literally means "dispeller of darkness."

Harmonics   Also called *overtones*, harmonics are a phenomenon connected with sound, in which faint higher tones which are mathematical ratios of the base tone can be heard when a tone is sounded.

Hatha Yoga   One form of yoga that emphasizes physical postures or positions, called asanas, for increased health and awareness.

Hemoglobin   A molecule in red blood cells responsible for carrying oxygen from the lungs to the tissues and carbon dioxide from the tissues back to the lungs.

Herbalism   The treatment of disease with herbs.

Herbs   Plants used for medicinal or therapeutic purposes (and also for cooking).

Holistic medicine   Sometimes called alternative medicine or natural medicine, this type of health care involves a whole mind-body approach to health emphasizing preventive medicine and often effective at relieving chronic conditions like recurrent colds, headaches, arthritis, and even cancer.

Holotropic breathwork   A psychospiritual bodywork technique developed by Stanislav Grof, M.D., and his wife, Christina, in 1976. It combines rapid breathing with loud music, meant to invoke an alternate state of consciousness that loosens psychological barriers and frees repressed memories and emotions.

Homeopathy   A subtle medical therapy based on the idea that "like cures like"— remedies that would cause certain symptoms are given to cure those symptoms.

Homeostasis   The tendency of a system (such as a body, a group, or an ecosystem) to maintain an equilibrium or balanced state.

Hyperventilation   "Overbreathing," or breathing too rapidly and shallowly. It is characterized by a feeling of not being able to get enough air, as well as dizziness, racing heart, fainting, and muscle cramps.

Hypnogogic state   The transitional state between waking and sleeping when the mind is particularly open to suggestions or images from the unconscious and the individual may have strange visual, aural, or tactile "experiences" or hallucinations.

Hypnopompic state   The transitional state between sleeping and waking when the mind is particularly open to suggestions or images from the unconscious and the individual may have strange visual, aural, or tactile "experiences" or hallucinations.

Insight meditation   See *Vipassana meditation*.

Intellect sheath   The mind-body layer consisting of higher understanding and unclouded thought, extending slightly beyond the mind sheath. Part of the *causal body*.

Ishvara-pranidhana   The yoga observance of devotion.

Jalandhara bandha   A yogic muscular lock behind the chin, used to intensify the energy of *prana*.

Jnana Yoga   See *yoga*.

Jung, Carl (1875–1961)   A Swiss psychiatrist who founded the analytical school of psychology. Jung coined many common psychological terms used today, such as "complexes" (as in "inferiority complex") and the notion of extroverts and introverts. He believed dreams were attempts to work toward wholeness by integrating the different levels of the unconscious.

Jupiter chakra   Psychospiritual energy center behind the lower abdomen, the source of creative energy.

Kant, Immanuel (1724–1804)   A German philosopher whom many consider the most influential thinker of modern times. Kant believed that reason would always lead the individual to right action, and that every individual should be given freedom of self-government because this freedom would allow individuals to act according to universal laws, which could be realized through reason.

Karma Yoga   See *yoga*.

Karma   A Sanskrit word referring to the law of cause and effect, or universal balance. Everything you do, say, or think has an immediate effect on the universe that will reverberate back to you in some way.

Kensho   Also called insight-wisdom, kensho is a sudden-understanding experience of seeing into the essence of things. It is considered a step toward true enlightenment.

Ki   The Japanese word for life-force energy.

Kilaka   The force required by the yogi to persist in working with the mantra.

Kirlian photography   A type of photography that allows energy fields or auras to be seen on film. During the 1940s, a Russian photographer named Kirlian developed the technique, which proved to many the existence of auras.

Koan   A short question, riddle, or verbal illustration meant to demonstrate a Zen realization. Because words are contrary to Zen realizations, however, koans don't make sense on the surface. The point is to pop your mind into a different, enlightened way of seeing.

Kundalini Yoga   A mystical form of yoga centered around awakening and employing kundalini energy.

Kundalini   Literally meaning "she who is coiled," kundalini refers to an energy force in the body that lies inactive at the base of the spine but can be awakened. Often compared to a sleeping snake, when awakened, it is said to travel up through the chakras to the crown of the head where it can effect spiritual changes such as enlightenment, and even, according to some, physical changes in the body, such as the ability to control previously involuntary bodily functions. It is the energy of self-actualization.

Laughing meditation   A form of meditation in which the meditator laughs. In India, large groups of people gather together in the streets, make funny faces, and laugh together. Some advocate waking up each morning and laughing for five minutes before the day begins. The laughter may be forced at first, but will soon become genuine as you realize how wonderfully funny life can be.

Life-force energy   Energy that animates the body and the universe, and which, when unblocked and properly directed, can help the body to heal itself. Also called *chi*, *ch'i*, *Qi*, *ki*, *prana*, *pneuma*, and *rlun*.

Lucid dreaming   The conscious awareness that you are dreaming.

Maharishi Mahesh Yogi   An Indian swami who came to the United States in 1955 after graduating from Allahabad University with a degree in physics, studying for 13 years with Swami Brahmananda Saraswati (a world-famous teacher) and spending two years in the Himalayas in silence. In the 1960s, the Maharishi had many celebrities as students, including The Beatles and the Beach Boys.

Mala   Beads used to keep track of recited mantras. Malas contain 108 beads, including a larger bead called the *meru*.

Mandala   A beautiful, usually circular geometric design that draws the eye to its center and can be used as a point of focus in meditation.

Mantra   From the root *man* meaning "to think" and *trai* meaning "to protect or free from the bondage of the phenomenal world." It is a sacred sound or combination of sounds chanted during meditation that resonate in the body and is meant to evoke certain energies.

Mars chakra   Psychospiritual energy center behind the navel, the source of action energy.

Meditation   From the Indian Sanskrit word *medha*, which can be translated as "doing the wisdom" and from the Latin root *meditari*, which means to muse or ponder, meditation can refer to many different techniques meant to tone and/or relax the mind.

Mercury chakra   Psychospiritual energy center in the throat, the source of communication energy.

Meru   See *mala*.

Mind sheath   The mind-body layer consisting of emotions and thoughts, extending slightly beyond the vital sheath. Part of the *astral body.*

Mind-body   The whole self. The term carries with it the connotation that mind and body are inextricably linked, and what affects, benefits, changes, or hurts one does the same for the other.

Mindfulness   A form of meditation that was originally developed in the Buddhist traditions of Asia but is practiced today by many, from meditators in monasteries to physicians in stress-reduction clinics. Mindfulness can be defined as awareness of each moment as it occurs and a purposeful attention.

Moxibustion   Burning herbs on the surface of the skin to stimulate healing.

Mudra   A hand position that redirects energy emitted from the fingertips back into the mind-body by connecting the fingers and hands to each other in different ways.

Mula bandha   A yogic muscular lock at the perineum, used to intensify the energy of *prana.*

Mysticism   The belief in direct experience of God, universal consciousness, or intuitive truth.

Nada Yoga   The yoga of sound and sound vibrations.

Nadis   Internal channels or pathways prana uses to flow through the body and through the chakras.

Neurons   Nerve cells.

Neurotransmitters   The chemicals produced in nerve cells that travel from one nerve cell to another, delivering marching orders from the brain to the rest of the body.

Nirvana   The Buddhist term for the state of absolute bliss attained upon recognition that the self is an illusion and nonexistent.

Niyamas   Five yoga observances or personal disciplines: *shauca* means purity, or inner and outer cleanliness; *santosha* means contentment; *tapas* means self-discipline; *svadhyaya* means self-study; and *ishvara-pranidhana* means devotion.

Om   Sometimes spelled *aum*, this Sanskrit word is the sound of the vibration of the universe according to yogic thought, and it is said that the entire world is manifested from this one sound. It is often used in meditation to help center and clear the mind so the mind-body can become more conscious.

Overtones   See *harmonics.*

Paradoxical sleep   See *REM sleep.*

Parapsychologist   Someone who studies psychic phenomena.

Patanjali   Probably born between 200 B.C. and A.D. 400, Patanjali was an Indian sage and the author of the *Yoga Sutras*, a collection of succinct aphorisms in Sanskrit that have largely defined the modern practice of yoga.

Physical body   The gross body we can see and touch.

Physical sheath   The mind-body layer consisting of the physical body.

Pilgrimage   A journey to a holy place.

Placebo effect   The idea that if someone believes something, such as a pill, will work to cure a condition, the condition will seem to be cured even if the "cure" couldn't have had any direct affect.

Pneuma   The ancient Greek word for life-force energy.

Prana   The Sanskrit word for the life-force energy that animates all physical matter, including the human body, and is taken into the body through the breath.

Pranayama   The practice of breathing exercises designed to help master control of the breath and to infuse the body with *prana*.

Pratyahara   The practice of withdrawing the senses and focusing inward.

Pressure points   Points along the energy channels in the body where energy tends to pool or get blocked. Pressing, massaging, or otherwise manipulating these points can help to rejuvenate energy flows through the body, facilitating the body's ability to balance and heal itself.

Psi   Psychic phenomena.

Psychic   To be sensitive to forces beyond the physical world. Psychic phenomena is also sometimes called *psi*.

QiGong   Also called *chi kung*, QiGong means "energy skill" and is sometimes translated as "empowerment." It is a 5,000 year-old system of health and life-force energy maintenance and also a healing art. It is the forerunner of *T'ai Chi* and the other martial arts systems from China. QiGong typically exists in three forms: martial, medical, and spiritual.

Raga   The main melody line of a mantra, which should be imitated exactly to preserve the specific vibration of the mantra.

Raja Yoga   See *yoga*.

Rajasic   A quality characterized by anxiety and agitation, according to yogic thought.

Reiki   A type of bodywork that emphasizes the manipulation of life-force energy through the chakras. The Reiki practitioner places his or her hands on the receiver over the chakras, working along the front and the back of the body.

Reincarnation   The belief that the soul is reborn over and over in different bodies as it struggles to reach enlightenment. Once enlightenment, or true understanding, is achieved, the soul is released from the cycle of rebirth.

REM sleep   Sometimes called *paradoxical sleep*, REM sleep (or rapid eye movement sleep) is the stage of sleep in which dreams occur. During this stage, brain waves resemble waking brain waves, yet muscles are completely relaxed, producing a paralyzing effect (called *atonia*).

Rinzai Zen   A sect of Zen Buddhism which employs the use of the *koan* during *zazen*.

Rishi   The ancient seer to whom the concept of the mantra was originally revealed thousands of years ago.

Rlun   The Tibetan word for life-force energy.

Rosary   A string of beads divided into different groups, with different short prayers, such as the Hail Mary, the Lord's Prayer, and the Fatima prayer, corresponding with each group, in the Catholic faith. Also, the prayers associated with these beads.

Sakti   The dynamic creation energy released in the yogi through repetition of the mantra.

Samadhi   See *enlightenment*.

Santosha   The yoga observance of contentment.

Satori   See *enlightenment*.

Sattvic   A quality characterized by vitality, strength, and peace of mind, according to yogic thought.

Saturn chakra   Psychospiritual energy center at the base of the spine, the source of dormant, potential, or kundalini energy.

Satya   The yoga abstinence involving truthfulness.

Sentient beings   All life forms who share the characteristic of consciousness and the ability to perceive.

Serotonin   A neurotransmitter, a chemical in your brain responsible for transmitting messages, that has a calming, relaxing effect and can cause drowsiness.

Shauca   The yoga observance of purity.

Shavasana   Literally "corpse pose," this yoga pose is the most important of all yoga poses, designed to bring the body into total, conscious relaxation.

Siddhattha Gotama   See *Buddha*.

Smudge stick   A bundle of dried herbs (sage is one of the most common) tied together and burned for the purpose of purification.

Smudging   A burning and purification process of the Native American tradition involving the burning of smudge sticks.

Soto Zen   A sect of Zen Buddhism which employs a "just sitting" method in zazen, based on the idea that sitting like the Buddha when he attained enlightenment will eventually bring about enlightenment.

Stream of consciousness   The unchecked flow of thoughts, either spoken or written, as a literary technique designed to portray the preconscious impressions of the mind before they can be logically arranged. Therefore, stream-of-consciousness expression usually appears nonsensical, lacking cohesiveness and logical sequence.

Subtle body   The whole self including all its various layers and energy fields which extend slightly beyond the physical body.

Sun chakra   Psychospiritual energy center behind the forehead, the source of intuitive energy.

Sun chakra   See *urna*.

Sutra on the Full Awareness of Breathing   An ancient Buddhist text, also called the *Anapanasati Sutta*, considered by many to be among the most important meditation texts in existence. In this sutra, a disciple of the Buddha tells the story of the Buddha instructing his disciples on the importance of breathing in full awareness, which will eventually "lead to the perfect accomplishment of true understanding and complete liberation."

Sutra   A Sanskrit term translated as "simple truth," "thread," or "bare bones." In yoga philosophy, a sutra is a precept or maxim, or a collection of these, such as Patajali's *Yoga Sutras*. Sutras use the fewest words to convey the teaching. In Buddhism, a sutra is a scriptural narrative, usually a discourse of the Buddha, such as in the *Sutra on the Full Awareness of Breathing*, where a disciple recounts a sermon of the Buddha.

Svadhyaya   The yoga observance of self-study.

Swami   A title of respect for a spiritual person who has attained a certain level of understanding and wisdom.

T'ai Chi   Meaning "way of the fist," T'ai Chi is a martial arts system and fitness method developed from *QiGong*. Today, T'ai Chi has evolved from its martial arts origins into a practice of movement meditation for peaceful purposes.

Tamasic   A quality characterized by lethargy and inactivity, according to yogic thought.

Taoism   Both a religion and a philosophy in China which advocates following the Tao, or the way of nature (although the word *Tao* is translated in many different ways, including "Way of the Cosmos," "Way of Heaven," "Way," "One," or "Path"). Simplicity, unity of all things, and becoming one with the Tao are all concepts of Taoism.

Tapas   The yoga observance of self-discipline.

TCM   See *Chinese medicine*.

Ten Fetters   According to Zen Buddhism, 10 fetters exist that keep us from true freedom and enlightenment: the illusion of ego, skepticism, attachment to ritual, the delusion of the senses, ill will, materialism, desire for an immaterial life, arrogance, restlessness, and ignorance of the true nature of reality. To be free of these 10 fetters leads to satori, or enlightenment.

Ten Perfections   According to Zen Buddhism, 10 perfections exist that are qualities of an enlightened person, and also are goals for the enlightened-to-be: generosity, morality, renunciation, wisdom, energy, patience, truthfulness, resolution, loving kindness, and a calm mind.

Tenzin Gyatso   The current and fourteenth Dalai Lama, who was forced into exile in India on March 16, 1959 by the Communist Chinese government occupying Tibet. In 1989 he received the Nobel Peace Price for leading nonviolent opposition to Chinese rule of Tibet.

Teresa of Avila, Saint (1515–1582)   A Carmelite nun and Christian mystic from Spain who founded the religious order of the Discalced (also called Barefoot) Carmelite nuns, who enforced strict observance of the original, severe Carmelite rules at the convent. Teresa's writings, all published posthumously, are still read today. Teresa was canonized in 1622; she was proclaimed a Doctor of the Church (the first woman to receive this honor) in 1970.

Therapeutic Touch (TT)   A controversial technique in which patients are treated by practitioners who never touch them. In TT, the practitioner's hands usually stay about four to six inches above the skin of the receiver, touching and manipulating the energy field, though not the body itself.

Theta waves   Brain waves that cycle between three to seven times per second and usually correspond with light sleep or deep meditation.

Thich Nhat Hahn   An exiled Vietnamese monk and peace activist who is one of the foremost contemporary proponents of mindfulness.

Thousand Petalled Lotus chakra   Psychospiritual energy center at the crown of the head, the source of enlightenment energy.

Tibetan Book of the Dead   See *Bardo Thödol*.

TM   See *Transcendental Meditation*.

Traditional Chinese Medicine   See *Chinese medicine*.

Transcendental Meditation   Also called TM, Transcendental Meditation is a mantra-based form of meditation introduced to the West by the Maharishi Mahesh Yogi. Today, TM is the most studied form of meditation. Over 4,000 pages in over 100 scientific journals have appeared describing scientific studies on the effects of TM.

Trataka   A yogic eye exercise/meditation involving gazing at a candle or flame and designed to strengthen the inner vision.

Tryptophan   An amino acid that comes from protein from the food we eat.

Tyrosine   An amino acid that comes from protein from the food we eat.

Uddiyani bandha   A yogic muscular lock at the navel, used to intensify the energy of *prana*.

Unconscious mind   The thoughts, feelings, desires, and impulses of which the individual is unaware but that influence behavior.

Urna   The *third eye*, or area of the forehead between and about an inch or two above the eyes within your head, thought to be an energy source and the source of un-clouded perception. In Sanskrit, the spot is called the *ajna chakra*. In yoga, it is also sometimes called the *sun chakra*.

Venus chakra   Psychospiritual energy center behind the heart, the source of compassionate energy.

Vinyasa   A steady flow of connected yoga postures linked with breathing exercises in a continuous movement.

Vipassana meditation   Also called *insight meditation*, vipassana means *insight* and the technique is considered a meditation method the Buddha himself taught. It is simple, requiring only mindful awareness and labeling of thoughts, feelings, and emotions as they are observed.

Vital sheath   The mind-body layer consisting of lifeforce energy surrounding and flowing through and from the body. Part of the *astral body*.

Yamas   Five yoga abstinences or forms of discipline that purify the body and mind: *ahimsa* means nonviolence; *satya* means truthfulness; *asteya* means not stealing; *brahmacharya* means chastity or nonlust; and *aparigraha* means nongreed.

Yang   See *Yin/Yang*.

Yantra   A linear symbol similar to a *mandala*, often with a symbol or written words in the center.

Yin   See *Yin/Yang*.

Yin/Yang   Two interconnected forces inherent in all things. Some things are more yin, such as the moon, the body, and the female nature. Some things are more yang, such as the sun, the mind, and the male nature. Yin and yang work together to keep the universe balanced.

Yoga   From the Sanskrit root *yuj*, meaning "to yoke or join together," yoga is a 5,000-year-old method of mind-body health with the goal of enlightenment. It has many "paths" or methods, including *Karma Yoga* which emphasizes action and service to others; *Bhakti Yoga*, which emphasizes love of God; *Jnana Yoga*, which emphasizes intellectual striving; and *Raja Yoga*, sometimes called the "King of Yogas," which emphasizes techniques for controlling both mind and body. These techniques include exercises, breathing and relaxation techniques, and meditation.

Yogi   Someone who practices yoga.

Zabuton   A thick meditation mat or small futon placed under the *zafu*. These items make meditation more comfortable and help to put the body into a three-point or tripod position for greater stability.

Zafu   A small pillow for sitting during *zazen*.

Zazen   The Japanese word for the Zen Buddhist technique of seated meditation.

Zen Buddhism   A form of Buddhism emphasizing meditation as a way to achieve enlightenment.

Zendo   A Zen meditation hall.

In Search of Nirvana: Suggested Reading

Andrews, Ted. *How to Uncover Your Past Lives*. St. Paul, MN: Llewellyn Publications, 1997.

Artress, Lauren. *Walking a Sacred Path: Rediscovering the Labyrinth as a Spiritual Tool*. New York: Riverhead Books, 1995.

Austin James, M.D. *Zen and the Brain*. Cambridge, MA: MIT Press, 1998.

Brauen, Martin. *The Mandala: Sacred Circle in Tibetan Buddhism*. Boston: Shambhala, 1997.

Budilovsky, Joan, and Eve Adamson. *The Complete Idiot's Guide to Massage*. New York: Alpha Books, 1998.

Budilovsky, Joan, and Eve Adamson. *The Complete Idiot's Guide to Yoga*. New York: Alpha Books, 1998.

Cameron, Julia. *The Vein of Gold: A Journey to Your Creative Heart*. New York: Jeremy P. Tarcher/Putnam, 1996.

Cameron, Julia. *The Artist's Way: A Spiritual Path to Higher Creativity*. New York: Jeremy P. Tarcher/Putnam, 1992.

Carradine, David, and David Nakahara. *David Carradine's Intoduction to Chi Kung*. New York: Henry Holt and Company, 1997.

Chearney, Lee Ann. *Visits: Caring for An Aging Parent, Reflections and Advice*. New York: Three Rivers Press, 1998.

Chih-I, Thomas Cleary, tr. *Stopping and Seeing*. Boston: Shambhala, 1997.

Chopra, Deepak, M.D. *Ageless Body Timeless Mind*. New York: Harmony Books, 1993.

Chopra, Deepak, M.D. *Creating Health*. Revised ed. Boston: Houghton Mifflin Co., 1991.

Chopra, Deepak, M.D. *Perfect Health.* New York: Harmony Books, 1991.

Cortis, Bruno, M.D. *Heart & Soul.* New York: Pocket Books, 1995.

Crompton, Paul. *Tai Chi: A Practical Introduction.* Boston: Element Books, 1998.

Csikszentmihalyi, Mihaly. *Flow: The Psychology of Optimal Experience.* New York: HarperCollins, 1990.

Dalai Lama of Tibet. *Awakening the Mind, Lightening the Heart.* San Francisco, CA: HarperSanFrancisco, 1995.

Davich, Victor N. *The Best Guide to Meditation.* Los Angeles: Renaissance Books, 1998.

DeMello, Anthony. *Awakenings: Conversations with the Master.* Chicago: Loyola Press, revised edition, 1998.

DeMello, Anthony. *Taking Flight: A Book of Story Meditations.* New York: Image Books, 1986.

DeMello, Anthony. *Wellspring: A Book of Spiritual Exercises.* New York: Image Books, 1990.

Epstein, Mark, M.D. *Going to Pieces Without Falling Apart: A Buddhist Perspective on Wholeness.* New York: Broadway Books, 1998.

Farhi, Donna. *The Breathing Book.* New York: Henry Holt and Company, 1996.

Franck, Frederick. *Zen Seeing, Zen Drawing.* New York: Bantam Books, 1993.

Goldman, Jonathan. *Healing Sounds: The Power of Harmonics.* Rockport, MA: Element Books Limited, 1997.

Goleman, Daniel. *Emotional Intelligence.* New York: Bantam Books, 1995.

Goleman, Daniel, and Joel Gurin, eds. *Mind Body Medicine.* Yonkers, NY: Consumer Reports Books, 1993.

Gore, Belinda. *Ecstatic Body Postures.* Santa Fe: Bear & Company, 1995.

Greeson, Janet, Ph.D.. *It's Not What You're Eating, It's What's Eating You.* New York: Pocket Books, 1990.

Hanh, Thich Nhat. *Breath! You Are Alive.* Berkeley, CA: Parallax Press, 1996.

Hanh, Thich Nhat. *The Miracle of Mindfulness.* Boston: Beacon Press, 1987.

Hanh, Thich Nhat. *Peace Is Every Step.* New York: Bantam, 1991.

Kabat-Zinn, Jon, Ph.D. *Full Catastrophe Living.* New York: Dell Publishing, 1990.

Langer, Ellen J. *Mind-Fulness.* Reading, MA: Addison-Wesley, 1989.

Levine, Stephen. *Guided Meditations, Explorations and Healings.* New York: Anchor Books, 1991.

Lewis, J.R. *The Dream Enyclopedia.* Washington, D.C.: Visible Ink Press, 1995.

Linn, Denise. *Quest: A Guide for Creating Your Own Vision Quest.* New York: Ballantine Books, 1997.

Linn, Denise. *Sacred Space: Clearing and Enhancing the Energy of Your Home.* New York: Ballantine Books, 1995.

Luk, Charles. *The Secrets of Chinese Meditation.* York Beach, ME: Samuel Weiser, Inc., 1994.

Marharishi Mahesh Yogi. *Science of Being and Art of Living: Trancendental Meditation.* New York: Meridian, 1995.

Moore, Thomas. *Care of the Soul.* New York: HarperCollins, 1992.

Moore-Ede, Martin, and Suzanne LeVert. *The Complete Idiot's Guide to Getting a Good Night's Sleep.* New York: Alpha Books, 1998.

Moyers, Bill. *Healing and the Mind.* New York: Doubleday, 1993.

Osho. *Meditation: The First and Last Freedom.* New York: St. Martin's Griffin, 1996.

Pliskin, Marci, and Shari L. Just. *The Complete Idiot's Guide to Interpreting Your Dreams.* New York: Alpha Books, 1998.

Reid, Daniel. *Traditional Chinese Medicine.* Boston: Shambhala, 1996.

Rinpoche, Sogyal. *The Tibetan Book of Living and Dying.* San Francisco: HarperCollins, 1992.

Roberts, Elizabeth, and Elias Amidon, eds. *Life Prayers.* San Francisco: HarperCollins, 1996.

Robinson, Lynn, and Lavonne Carlson-Finnerty. *The Complete Idiot's Guide to Being Psychic.* New York: Alpha Books, 1998.

Rothfeld, Glenn, M.D., and Suzanne LeVert. *Ginkgo Biloba.* New York: Dell, 1998.

Samuels, Michael and Mary Rockwood Lane. *Creative Healing.* San Francisco: HarperSanFrancisco, 1998.

Schulz, Mona Lisa, M.D., Ph.D. *Awakening Intuition.* New York: Harmony Books, 1998.

Serure, Pamela. *The 3-Day Energy Fast.* New York: HarperCollins, 1997.

Siegel, Bernie, M.D. *Love, Medicine & Miracles.* New York: Harper Perennial Library, 1990.

Siegel, Bernie, M.D. *Prescriptions for Living.* New York: HarperCollins, 1998.

Swami Sivananda Radha. *Mantras: Words of Power.* Spokane, WA: Timeless Books, 1994.

Teresa of Avila. E. Allison Peers, tr. and ed. *Interior Castle.* New York: Image Books, 1972.

Trungpa, Chogyam. *Meditation in Action.* Boston: Shambhala, 1996.

Van de Castle, Robert L., Ph.D. *Our Dreaming Mind.* New York: Ballantine Books, 1994.

Varela, Francisco J., Ph.D., ed. *Sleeping Dreaming, And Dying: An Exploration of Consciousness with The Dalai Lama.* Boston: Wisdom Publications, 1997.

Weil, Andrew, M.D. *Spontaneous Healing.* New York: Ballantine Books, 1995.

Weiss, Brian L., M.D. *Through Time Into Healing.* New York: Simon & Schuster, 1992.

Wise, Anna. *The High-Performance Mind.* New York: Tarcher/Putnam, 1995.

Index

YES, send me my copies of Joan's wonderful tapes and books.

Special Audio Tape Offer

❏ "Total Relaxation…with Shavasana" $7.50

Massage Video

❏ *My Swedish Massage with Joan* $19.50

Massage Audios

❏ "The Art of Massage Made Simple" $10.50
❏ "Foot Massage for Body, Mind, and Sole" $10.00

Yoga Audios

❏ "Yoga with Joan" $10.00
❏ "Breathworks!" $10.00
❏ "Sun-Salutations! with Joan" $10.00
❏ "Yoga at the Beach" $10.00

Yoga Books

❏ *The Little Yogi Water Book* $8.00
❏ *The Little Yogi Energy Book* $8.00
❏ *Fat-Free Yoga* $8.00
❏ *Yo Joan* $10.00

Shipping/handling charges:
Audio/Book   Add $2.50 for 1–2 items; add $.50 for each additional item.   _____
Video   Add $4.50 for first video tape; add $1.00 for each additional video tape.   _____
                                                          Sub-Total   _____
                               Illinois residents add 6.75% sales tax   _____
                                                          TOTAL   _____

Payment to be made in U.S. funds. Prices and availability are subject to change without notice.
❏ Check or money order enclosed.
❏ I would like to charge to: ❏ MasterCard   ❏ Visa
Acct.#: _____
Exp. Date: _____
Signature: _____

Send this order form with your check, money order, or charge information to:
Yoyoga, Inc.
P.O. Box 5013
Oak Brook, IL 60522
Fax (630) 963-4001
Allow 4 to 6 weeks for delivery.

Ship to:

Name: _____
Address: _____
City, State, Zip: _____
Telephone: _____

Don't Let Yourself Feel Overwhelmed, Stressed-Out, and Just Hanging on by a Thread!

Feeling Good Is As Easy As 1 – 2 – 3, with

Holistic experts Joan Budilovsky and Eve Adamson bring you the only three books you'll need to relax, rejuvenate, and restore your aching mind and body. *The Complete Idiot's Guide® to Yoga* is a wonderful introduction to yoga postures and yoga theory that you'll enjoy no matter what your current fitness level—beginning to advanced. In *The Complete Idiot's Guide® to Massage* you'll learn about the many different kinds of massage techniques—from Swedish to Reflexology to Shiatsu and more; you'll also find out how to get (and give!) the best massage you've ever had. Learn to relax and focus on what's really important to you in *The Complete Idiot's Guide® to Meditation.*

Be good to your "self" and get energized with **Yoga**, **Massage**, and **Meditation**. Three times the charm for a happy, healthy you!

All three titles are available at booksellers everywhere, or by calling Macmillan Publishing at (800) 428-5331.